Advanced Praise

"Crisply written, thoroughly researched, and chock-full of relevant anecdotes, Radically Transparent is sure to become the definitive guide for members of any company or group who want to join and shape the often brutally honest conversation across social media about their brands, products, and people."
—TOM GILES, Editor, Technology & Science, BusinessWeek.com

"Radically Transparent is an indispensable guide to managing your reputation online. Beal and Strauss provide a compelling, well-researched, and actionable roadmap to protecting your most competitive asset in this fast-changing networked world. With compelling case studies and tools to use right now, it's a must-read and a surefire wake-up call!"
—DR. LESLIE GAINES-ROSS, Chief Reputation Strategist, Weber Shandwick

"Just a few years ago, it was fairly easy to outrun a disgruntled customer, a misinformed journalist, or some other minor blunder. That time now belongs to another world. Today's hyper-connected socially responsible individual can connect with millions across the globe and inform not only friends but legions of others as an exercise of radical transparency. Are you listening or are their words falling on your deaf corporate ears? Are you joining their conversation or hoping you can drown out their words with yours? What do people know about you from a simple online search? Radically Transparent illuminates a path that leads to an engaging conversation with your customers. Read this book so that you can participate, measure, and influence what others are saying about you."
—BRYAN EISENBERG, *Wall Street Journal* bestselling author of *Waiting for Your Cat to Bark?*

"Branding has evolved from a one-way monologue to a two-way conversation. It's vital you know the strategies needed to join the conversation and build your Radically Transparent *reputation."*
—JOHN BATTELLE, Chairman, CEO, Federated Media and national bestselling author of *The Search*

"One of the best-written books I've seen on a vitally important topic: the underbelly of transparency in the age of Google. How do you control your digital identity when everything is findable online? Read this engaging book for practical, persuasive answers."
—DEBBIE WEIL, corporate blogging and social media consultant and author of *The Corporate Blogging Book*

"Radically Transparent *is a must-read for anyone trying to take their business online. Beal and Strauss have written the first book that gives you the step-by-step advice you need to create, manage, and protect your online reputation—which will be the heart and soul of your brand in the future.*"
> —TIM SANDERS, former Chief Solutions Officer at Yahoo! and bestselling author
> of Love Is the Killer App: How to Win Business and Influence Friends

"*When your customers can become your most powerful marketers, for better or worse, every individual and company with a brand reputation to protect must know how to swim in the 21st-century waters. In* Radically Transparent, *Beal and Strauss apply their expertise in online positioning to the tactics of message control in a world where a single individual can undermine a global corporation. This book is not about fighting back. It is about embracing new values, gaining awareness of a company's total image, and developing a holistic reputation.*"
> —BRAD HILL, Director, Weblogs, Inc., (AOL) and author of Blogging for
> Dummies

"*This book will teach you how to get connected—and stay connected—to your audience in the brave new world of social media.*"
> —JIM LANZONE, former CEO of Ask.com

"*Businesses no longer have the luxury of hiding their flaws behind faceless contact centers and anonymous press releases. Today, their every move is documented, scrutinized, and discussed by an army of constituents, who share their observations and opinions with like-minded people around the world. There's no place to hide any more. The new global conversations will change institutions forever.* Radically Transparent *is a survival guide for the future of business. Expertly researched and skillfully written, it documents momentous change in the business landscape and offers plaintalk advice to executives and marketers who are trying to keep up. Read this book if you want your job and your business to be relevant five years from now.*"
> —PAUL GILLIN, author of The New Influencers, former editor-in-chief,
> TechTarget.com and Computerworld

"*I literally could not put this book down. In fact, I Krazy Glued it to my left hand just to make sure. But my eyes were glued to every page, also.* Radically Transparent *is both simple to understand and profound in its implications. If you think that the Web won't affect your business, that your public relations folks will safeguard your reputation, and that you just need to redouble your efforts at message control, let Andy Beal and Judy Strauss open your eyes. There's still time for you to wake up, but don't let the alarm ring too long—it might be the bell that tolls for you.*"
> —MIKE MORAN, author of Do It Wrong Quickly and coauthor of Search Engine
> Marketing, Inc.

"An important read for graduating students entering the job market. Beal and Strauss provide step-by-step instructions for creating a positive Web presence to draw and impress recruiters."

—MILTON D. GLICK, President, University of Nevada, Reno

"Don't be reputation roadkill. Get Radically Transparent *to protect your business online."*

—CATHERINE SEDA, author of *How to Win Sales & Influence Spiders*

"Radical transparency is the currency of modern marketing and brand management, and we are all brands whether we realize it or not. The river's already flowing, but you really don't want to jump in until you learn how to navigate, and that's what Beal and Strauss offer with this invaluable book. As they show again and again, it's definitely better to swim—in the direction you desire—than to sink into the mudflats of the new Web 2.0 world!"

—DAVE TAYLOR, strategic management, social networking consultant and blogger, Intuitive.com

"In today's modern marketing world, the influence has shifted to participants online. They share their opinion about products, services, and brands and thus impacting the purchasing decision of their network. Your reputation, which is being discussed online, will need to be monitored so you can eventually take part in the conversation. You'll need a book like Radically Transparent *to be part of this conversation."*

—JEREMIAH OWYANG, author of Web Strategy Blog

"If the Internet has enabled one thing it is the ease with which anyone—a person or company—can easily create and manage their own unique brand identity. Radically Transparent *is a must-read because it outlines exactly how you can keep track of your brand identity in a world where the difference between a great reputation and a tarnished one is the click of a mouse."*

—AVINASH KAUSHIK, author of *Web Analytics: An Hour a Day*

"Finding the best marketing techniques to engage with your online audience as they participate in social networks is one of the biggest challenges facing you as a marketer today. Previous books focusing on online PR have been limited to war stories and self-promotion but have been short on practical advice. In Radically Transparent, *all the practical questions are answered in an engaging style: how do I create buzz around my campaign? What type of blog do I need? How do I make it more effective? How do I monitor and manage my reputation in the social networks? Exactly what you expect from two leading web marketers."*

—DAVE CHAFFEY, Director, Marketing Insights Limited and author of *Internet Marketing* and *SEO Best Practice Guide*

Radically Transparent

Monitoring and Managing Reputations Online

Andy Beal

Judy Strauss

Wiley Publishing, Inc.

Acquisitions Editor: WILLEM KNIBBE
Technical Editor: CINDY AKUS
Production Editor: ERIC CHARBONNEAU
Copy Editor: LIZ WELCH
Production Manager: TIM TATE
Vice President and Executive Group Publisher: RICHARD SWADLEY
Vice President and Executive Publisher: JOSEPH B. WIKERT
Vice President and Publisher: NEIL EDDE
Book Designer and Compositor: MAUREEN FORYS, HAPPENSTANCE TYPE-O-RAMA
Proofreader: NANCY HANGER
Indexer: TED LAUX
Cover Designer: RYAN SNEED
Cover Image: © CORBIS

Library of Congress Cataloging-in-Publication Data

Beal, Andy, 1974-
  Radically transparent : monitoring and managing reputations online / Andy Beal, Judy Strauss.
    p. cm.
  ISBN 978-0-470-19082-1 (pbk.)
  1. Corporate image—Computer networks. 2. Corporations—Public relations—Computer networks. I. Strauss, Judy. II. Title.
  HD59.2.B43 2008
  659.20285'4678—dc22

                                    2007051638

Dear Reader

Thank you for choosing *Radically Transparent: Monitoring and Managing Reputations Online*. This book is part of a family of premium quality Sybex books, all written by outstanding authors who combine practical experience with a gift for teaching.

Sybex was founded in 1976. More than thirty years later, we're still committed to producing consistently exceptional books. With each of our titles we're working hard to set a new standard for the industry. From the paper we print on, to the authors we work with, our goal is to bring you the best books available.

I hope you see all that reflected in these pages. I'd be very interested to hear your comments and get your feedback on how we're doing. Feel free to let me know what you think about this or any other Sybex book by sending me an email at nedde@wiley.com, or if you think you've found a technical error in this book, please visit http://sybex.custhelp.com. Customer feedback is critical to our efforts at Sybex.

Best regards,

Neil Edde
Vice President and Publisher
Sybex, an Imprint of Wiley

In memory of my dad, the greatest man I ever knew.
—Andy Beal

For my precious siblings: Jeff, Janet Tracey and Dee
—Judy Strauss

 # Acknowledgments

It is our pleasure to express our appreciation to the many individuals who helped us create this written work. First, we have enormous gratitude for the individuals who generously shared their opinions, experiences, and expertise by allowing us to interview them. Their stories enrich these pages. Next, we thank the hundreds of pioneers who learned the hard way that reputations online are valuable assets easily scarred in the social media. Stories of their struggles and triumphs helped us to create a blueprint for successful reputation management online.

We also gratefully acknowledge the many editors at Wiley who gave us a place for showcasing our ideas. Our sincere thanks to Willem Knibbe (who recognized the need for a book on reputation management and helped us keep our sanity during the writing); Cindy Akus, a phenomenal technical editor who helped us improve the book through her many great suggestions; Pete Gaughan, our hard-working editorial manager; Eric Charbonneau, the production editor who brought it all together; copyeditor Liz Welch; and the other talented members of the Wiley production team.

Finally, we want to thank the friends, family, and colleagues who gave us their support and accommodated us while we burned the midnight oil and put other projects on hold. To them we are indebted beyond words.

Andy Beal

I would like to thank God for the blessings that came with the opportunity to write this book. I'm thankful that many great people motivated me to share my thoughts and provided advice along the way—in particular, Avinash Kaushik, Catherine Seda, and Bryan Eisenberg. And my heartfelt thanks to my wonderful coauthor, for being there to encourage and guide me through each step of my first book.

I'm grateful to the many talented people that I've had the pleasure to work with over the course of my career. The list is long but I'd be remiss if I didn't say thank you to Mike Grehan, Danny Sullivan, and Ben Wills.

When you write a book, you realize just how much you rely on the support of your friends and family. My sincere thanks for the prayers and support from everyone including Ted and Eleanor Franks; my wonderful in-laws, Dickie and Judy Jarrett; and of course my family, especially my parents Trevor and Valerie Beal.

Lastly, I could not have written this book without the support, encouragement, and love of my beautiful wife Sheila. Every day she reminds me to live my life "authentically," and her belief in me is the source of my drive and motivation to be a better person. I love you, sweetheart.

Judy Strauss

My smart and competent daughters, Cyndi and Malia Jakus, gave me excellent counsel and listened to my endless tales while writing this book. I am very grateful for their love and support. I also want to thank my women friends for their encouragement and good ideas—especially Susan Buchanan and Judy Miller.

I dedicate this book to my siblings—Jeff, Janet, and Tracey Snoyer, and Dee Key—because they have put up with me over the years and never wavered in their love and confidence. Janet gave me many great ideas for the book, and she and Tracey were my personal cheering section. Jeff and his wife Lynn have always been there for me, and Dee is my newest best friend. My father left a great legacy with his children, my siblings.

Finally, I want to thank my teachers. Andy Beal taught me many things, not the least of which was the proper expansion of the acronym, SERP (search engine results pages). Dave LaPlante helped get me started on this topic, and our brainstorming sessions were very valuable. I have also learned more from my university students over the years than they realize. I am blessed to work with them.

About the Authors

Andy Beal is a consultant and one of the world's most respected experts in online reputation monitoring and management. He has worked with Motorola, Lowe's, Quicken Loans, NBC, GlaxoSmithKline, and SAS. Founder of the award-winning Marketing Pilgrim blog (marketingpilgrim.com), Beal has been featured in *Dow Jones*, *Washington Post*, and *Business Week*. He is a frequent speaker at such trade shows as Search Engine Strategies and Direct Marketing Association, has published more than three dozen articles, and has been featured in *The Wall Street Journal*, *Washington Post*, and *Business Week*.

Dr. Judy Strauss is a consultant, international speaker, former entrepreneur, and previous marketing director of two companies. She is an award-winning author of 11 books and numerous scholarly articles on internet marketing topics. She coauthored *E-Marketing*, the first textbook on internet marketing. She currently teaches e-marketing, communication, and strategy topics to MBA and undergraduate students at the University of Nevada, Reno. She has won numerous awards for teaching, writing, and entrepreneurial activities.

Foreword

It's not easy being transparent. We're taught not to share intimate private details with others lest that information be used against us. At work we are taught by PR professionals to stay quiet unless approved to speak, and even then, to give only "talking points." In business school we're taught to write official communications like press releases and how to make sure they don't say things that'll get you into trouble.

Let's not even start on your advertising department. If you stand in the middle of Times Square in New York City, you'll see hundreds of advertisements from tons of big companies like Nike, Kodak, and General Motors. Now, based on any of those ads, can you tell me five facts about any product? For instance, what those products do well at and what they don't do well at?

No.

Our entire corporate world is based on keeping secrets, only sharing information that's been decided on by committees, and only letting "media trained" employees speak on behalf of the company. Heck, at some companies like Apple it's even worse. Almost no one is allowed to talk to the press on the record and, then, you better not get quoted saying something that is "off message."

So why would *anyone* want to be transparent in this kind of "command and control" corporate age? One where PR professionals and lawyers look out for risky speech and make sure that the committees stay in control of the message? Why would you want to let your—gasp—lowest employees speak on blogs or on social media sites, or post videos on YouTube?

Here are a few reasons:

1. You'll get better product feedback. The Google Calendar team tells me they watch blog search engines every morning for people who say something about their products and then people on the team answer that blog in its comments. This gets better feedback. Why? Because people stop giving feedback if they don't think they are being listened to. Or, even worse, they might increase the level of critical commentary until they *do* get listened to.

2. Your best customers will become more evangelistic. I once met a guy who had a Plymouth Prowler. He knew the color of the factory floor, among other facts.

Clearly he had been given a tour and had friends who built the cars, and because of this knowledge he was an even more authoritative and interesting evangelist on behalf of the company. You'll need evangelists like this to spread the good news about your products far and wide.

3. Your recruiting will improve. The guy who runs Facebook's application platform told me he left Apple Computer, at least in part, because he wasn't able to blog while working at Apple. It's not the first time I've heard something like this. At Microsoft, the Channel 9 videoblog was mentioned by college students more than any other single thing as a reason why they sent their resume in.

4. You'll have fewer PR crises—and the ones you do have will be over faster and with less brand damage. If your employees can answer the tough questions without worrying about whether they are "approved" to speak on the company's behalf, they'll head off PR troubles earlier.

5. You'll have better Google Rankings. Think about a company the size of General Motors or Microsoft. Tens of thousands of employees blogging or adding info on social networking sites like Facebook. That's bound to have an effect on how corporate pages show up in Google.

At Microsoft we opened up by using blogs and by hosting videos shot with a $250 camera on Channel 9 and saw all these results. Even better, people started praising us for becoming "more human." That was an attribute that couldn't have been gained any other way.

Don't get me wrong. It wasn't all smooth sailing. Here are some downsides:

1. You'll have some rude comments. The Internet doesn't have accountability and even lets people post totally anonymously. Lots of times you'll get comments or replies that'll drive you nuts. I've even seen threatening comments or racially charged ones. You'll need to have a policy about how to deal with these, but on corporate sites I run I institute a "living room rule." If I wouldn't be comfortable with the speech in my own living room (and I'm pretty liberal there), then I just delete the post.

2. You'll need to know your corporate culture well. I got to know Microsoft's lawyers and PR professionals and what they worry about. At Microsoft we had a mailing list for all bloggers to share information and get help. I highly recommend doing that internally in your own company. Being transparent sometimes means knowing just how many clothes you can take off before your coworkers start to get nervous.

3. It takes work. In the old world you might send a press release out or call a few reporters. Shel Israel, a seasoned Silicon Valley PR professional, told me that he used to be able to call a handful of reporters to get buzz for his clients. Now, he told me, he has to deal with dozens of journalists and bloggers to get the same kind of coverage (and he has a blog and other sites as well).

4. It's possible to make mistakes. Are you writing a corporate blog without having a team check over posts (I never had anyone check my posts before publishing). Well, you might make a mistake. You might leak a product detail that you thought was already discussed in public. Or you might discuss something else that strains relationships with customers, suppliers, partners, or coworkers. What do you do if you make a mistake? This book helps you avoid them, but also deal with the aftermath of a firestorm.

Some other things you might not be comfortable with or know how to do. How about building your own personal brand? Yeah, those of us who read Tom Peters might know why this is important and have some sense of how you might go about it, but how about those of you who don't have any clue who Tom Peters is? You'll learn here how to build your own brand and also how to build your own personal network.

Plus, now monitoring your company's reputation online isn't as easy as the old days when you had a press clipping service. This book provides lots of tools and helpful hints to measure how you're doing online and to help you respond to customer concerns.

The latest thing that I'm using to increase my transparency and engagement with my constituencies is live, cell phone–based videos that I can do from anywhere there's a cell phone network: Qik, Mogulus, Seesmic, etc. I even interviewed the founders of YouTube on the floor of the Consumer Electronics Show by using Qik.

Are you trying new approaches to try to be more transparent and available? Some other things I do:

1. Post my phone number on my blog. You wouldn't believe the good things that come my way because of this. One day I got on the BBC because they couldn't get ahold of Microsoft's PR department, for instance.

2. Share my personal photos on Flickr or SmugMug. By doing this people get to see I'm creatively doing photography and they also get to see what kinds of things I enjoy shooting pictures of. Plus they can add their own comments, which makes it more likely we'll have a conversation about something that interests them.

3. I post a new video every day, sometimes to Qik, sometimes to other places. This lets them get to know me and see how I behave. If I have visual things to show off, this lets me share those as well. For instance, want to see my new laptop? It's hard to explain what's cool about it, but in one minute of video you'll see why I like it so much.

4. I participate in microblogging communities like on Twitter, Pownce, or Tumblr. Microblogging tools are often easier to post to and sites like Twitter force posts to be fewer than 140 characters. It's hard to get "wordy" when you have so few characters to work with.

This book will help you do all of this, and more. It'll be interesting to see what you do on your path to lead a radically transparent life. For me, I've found transparent life to be one that's very rewarding and fulfilling. Every time I travel I have someone to go to dinner with because of my personal transparency, and other good things are coming my way, too. John Edwards, for instance, invited me on his plane when he announced he was running for President of the United States. Why? Because he needed someone who was credible and transparently communicating to verify for the world how he was using social media in his campaign.

If presidential candidates are getting it, why not you?

—Robert Scoble, managing director of FastCompany.TV, coauthor of *Naked Conversations*

Contents

Chapter 6   Managing Your Reputation with SEO   109

Chapter 7   Using Multimedia Content to Engage Your Audience   141

Chapter 8   Writing Engaging Text   169

Introduction

You can't buy a good reputation. It is something earned over time, based on your character, words, and actions. You work hard to build and protect a good reputation that earns you, your company, and its brands respect and trust. This turns into sales, better partner and customer relationships, and less trouble when you make that inevitable mistake while in the media spotlight.

Have you checked the internet lately to see whether it is helping or hurting your reputation-building effort? There's a conversation about you online right this minute and you are probably unaware of its contents. Somewhere online, a disgruntled customer might be posting a video of your product malfunctioning (it happened to Kryptonite), talking trash about your product performance (it brought both Dell and Dr. Katrina Tang to their knees), or a stranger may be sending a false company memo to the online news media (it happened to Apple Computer). In the meantime, you are diligently providing exciting new content for your website and crafting digital brand messages that will boost your sales to new heights—unaware of the reputation undermining happening elsewhere online, and unaware of how to use the internet's new frontiers to your reputation's advantage.

The internet is flooded with words, images, and pictures that affect your reputation, both positively and negatively. What does this content reveal about you? This book will help you to monitor, build, manage, and repair your reputation online. It will help you harness this powerful always-on, radically transparent new networked world. A search for "reputation management" in Google in November 2007 yielded 54.8 million links to web pages, with the number increasing daily. This book has fewer pages and will save you time in this valiant effort.

Social Media Changed the Rules

Everyone is a publisher in the social media world of blogs, wikis, photo and video sharing, forums, and networks for meeting like-minded people. Social media are online tools and platforms that allow internet users to collaborate on content, share insights and experiences, and connect for business or pleasure. And we believe what we read from strangers in the social media: some 52% of survey respondents from developed nations said they find "a person like yourself" to provide the most credible information—equal only to the trust in doctors, and much higher than that from your CEO or company spokesperson (according to PR firm Edelman).

Businesses previously needed only to worry about something negative when it appeared in a newspaper or on the evening news. Now there are more than 110 million blogs, with over 1.6 million posts per day, and over 250 million pieces of tagged social media tracked by blog search engine Technorati. Individuals previously lived in relative anonymity, and potential employers knew nothing beyond the contents of a resume or testimony of a given reference. No longer.

The name of the game is egalitarian participation by one and all from the Fortune 100 CEO to your dentist—they are talking about you and they are being talked about by others. These conversations used to be limited to traditional media, e-mail, or the water cooler, but now they appear where millions can see them online. Word-of-mouth was previously spread among friends and families, but now extends across continents to the masses with the click of a mouse. Consider these examples:

- In an article for MSN.com, columnist Scott Burns asked, "Is Home Depot Shafting Shoppers?" His description of personal experiences at the retailer led to a conclusion that home improvement company Home Depot "is a consistent abuser of its customers' time." That same day, the MSN staff received 10,000 e-mails and 4,000 comments in the story's Talk Back section describing all of Home Depot's problems.

- Commercial blender company Blendtec received over 6 million page views in a one-week period for its hilarious "Will It Blend?" series, posted on YouTube and the company's website. In the series, CEO Tom Dickson attempts to blend everything from an iPhone to a garden rake. The videos were created to introduce the new and pricey home food blender and resulted in a 40% increase in blender sales, according to *The Wall Street Journal*.

- Matt Mullenweg, WordPress blog platform creator, is the #1 Matt in the world, according to Google. At his blog you'll see a radically transparent Matt, with writing about his open source software philosophies, and plenty of personal information from his interest in jazz to his next speaking engagement and his last trip with his girlfriend. Matt had a huge reputation blemish when he was exposed for using search engine spamming to reach the #1 spot (a mistake he quickly corrected). He is the comeback kid with a great reputation through lots of positive content (at age 22).

What Is Radically Transparent?

Radically transparent means being open and honest online, admitting mistakes, engaging stakeholders in discussions about you and your brands, and even revealing your internal processes. There is little censorship in the world of online social media—the community values raw truth. The internet community immediately comes down hard on those who employ conversation spin, control, manipulation, or spam. Anonymity is discouraged, and nearly all posts to a conversation include the author's real identity. On this new playing field, you need to be authentic or someone will discover the truth and you'll be exposed to millions. Astute companies, such as *Wired* Magazine and Dell Computer, are taking it a step further and being radically transparent by revealing their internal processes. They engage customers, listen to them, make changes in company procedures and products, and report back in open forums via social media. This book will tell you how to become forward-thinking like these companies.

Why Reputation Management and Monitoring?

Traditional word-of-mouth has long been considered one of the most powerful of market forces, and the social media made it public. "What's new is the extent to which consumer opinion drives reputations," said Andy Sernovitz in *Fast Company*. "A third of the population has reviewed something online, and any one of those reviews can be read by millions of people." Social media are like word-of-mouth on steroids. Consider the following compelling facts:

- Ninety-five percent of chief executives believe that corporate reputation plays an important role in achieving their business objectives, according to a survey by PR firm Burson-Marsteller.

- Sixty-three percent of a company's market value is attributable to reputation, according to PR firm Weber Shandwick.

- The top 10 "World's Most Admired Companies" enjoy a total shareholder return of nearly three times that of the S&P 500 as a whole (18.5% versus 7.1%), says The Hay Group, a global marketing consultancy and *Fortune* magazine partner.

You may already have a reputation management plan in place, or perhaps a plan to repair your reputation during a time of crisis. If so, does it include monitoring the internet for rumors and capitalizing on the social media to build your good name online? The people who trust each other more than they trust you will write about you online the minute you make an error. This book will show you how to detect this conversation or find the images immediately; tell you whether, when, where, and how to respond; and give you step-by-step instructions on engaging with stakeholders online in reputation-building ways.

What Skills Do I Need?

Stellar reputation monitoring and management online takes research, public relations, and search engine optimization skills. Content is king online, so you'll need to write, take photos, and perhaps create online videos and podcasts—or find staff who are good at these skills. We give you very specific guidance in this book, suggesting reputation-enhancing ways to build a buzz online and showing you how to write engaging blog posts, and we even show you how to make the lowly e-mail into a reputation-enhancing tool. You'll learn how to post comments online that emphasize your expertise, and how to move all of this good content to the top of Google's search engine results pages for your keywords. We even help you to reevaluate the "About Us" portion of your web page, your head shot, and every detail in your own web content channels.

How Long Will It Take?

Crafting and executing a reputation management and monitoring plan depends on whether you are a Fortune 100 company, the owner of a small business, or an individual employee who is upwardly mobile. It depends on how much content you currently have online and how much you already know about the social media. You can set up some basic reputation monitors for your company, brands, or personal names with as little as two hours startup time. Or you can spend more time to become the first in your industry to fully embrace the social media and rise to the top quickly. You can outsource some of it, but online reputation management and monitoring needs your personal touch—or that of your staff. Only you can distill that online chatter into actionable items for improving your offerings and reputation.

Who Needs This Book?

Companies, both large and small: A stellar reputation helps your company achieve objectives, retain customers and employees, build partner and supplier relationships, protect them in times of crisis, and ultimately increase shareholder value.

Brands. Product and service brands live and die on their reputations for delivering as promised. The social media provide abundant opportunities for engaging stakeholders in ways that will improve your offerings and make your reputation soar.

Directors and C-level executives: Your CEO's reputation is a very important component of your company's reputation, according to 87% of the respondents in a study by PR firm Hill and Knowlton. Also important are reputations of your CFO (75%), your company chairman (40%), and other nonexecutive directors (23%).

Individuals: Individual reputations are especially important for business owners, managers, CEOs, politicians, professionals, salespeople, graduating students, and just about anyone who has a client-based business. Most of us rush to Google to check out someone we've just met as a prospect, salesperson, or for any type of future collaboration. Do you want to stay marketable in your profession? According to ExecuNet, a leading recruiting firm, 78% of executive recruiters routinely use search engines to learn more about candidates, and 35% have eliminated candidates based on the information they found.

What's Inside

Part 1, "Understanding Your Online Reputation," demonstrates the power of social media online to build or destroy your reputation and how to engage customers on this new playing field.

Chapter 1: Your World Is Now Radically Transparent The switch from traditional media and corporate monologues on websites to social media on the internet makes everyone a journalist. They will judge you, your company, and your brand. Reputation management requires new skills in this radically transparent world.

Chapter 2: You Don't Own Your Company's Reputation Companies can spend millions of dollars each year to promote and manage their brands, yet a single negative blog post can destroy a reputation within days. The power to control a brand is rapidly shifting away from the companies that have the deepest pockets, and instead, it's the companies that best listen to and engage their customers that win the reputation race.

Chapter 3: Developing Your Personal Brand Individual director, CEO, and employee reputations are key components of company and brand reputations. Entrepreneurs and professionals live or die based on their contacts and reputations. The internet adds another layer of complexity to individual reputation building; however, there are first-mover advantages for those individuals who act now, using the internet to increase their connections with relationship-enhancing content.

Chapter 4: Navigating the New Rules of Engagement The shift from traditional to social media requires new skills, tools, and an understanding of social media platforms. Customer engagement means trusting, listening, and learning from your stakeholder communities, and responding to their comments with quality content in an honest, authentic manner. It also means joining and participating in networks they frequent, and having the courage to be radically transparent.

Part 2, "Building Your Radically Transparent Reputation," gives you specific tools and shows you how to use them for building your stellar reputation online.

Chapter 5: The Art of Generating Buzz In your quest to become radically transparent, you'll need to impress those who control the media. While mainstream journalists used to hold the power to influence your customers, that power is now shifting to bloggers and citizen journalists. By understanding how public relations has evolved—and learning the new approaches to sharing your message—you can influence what's said about you.

Chapter 6: Managing Your Reputation with SEO The contents of 10 blue search engine links can decide whether your company wins a new contract or you win that promotion. Although you can't guarantee which web pages will appear in a Google search, search engine optimization (SEO) can help tip the scales in your favor.

Chapter 7: Using Multimedia Content to Engage Your Audience Astute companies use relevant digital images, video, and audio to demonstrate their expertise and gain respect. You can solicit fabulous multimedia content produced by the citizen journalists and also craft your own content for posting on your websites and in the social media.

Chapter 8: Writing Engaging Text Great writing will engage your important stakeholders and enhance your reputation online. Regardless of whether you write white papers, books, blogs, web pages, e-mails, or instant messages, make every word count. You can do this with professional, engaging, and deliberate writing adapted to any situation, as described in this chapter.

Chapter 9: The Power of Blogs Building and launching a blog can add a lot of value to you and your business but is not something that should be done halfheartedly. The software you select, the style of blog you use, and the way you engage your readers all play an important role in determining your success or failure in the blogosphere. Understanding what your stakeholders expect from you and how to reach them with an authentic, radically transparent voice will ensure your blog is a positive reflection on your reputation.

Chapter 10: Social Networking Social networking provides an opportunity for your stakeholders to connect with one another and discuss your reputation. By understanding the different types of social networking platforms—and the best way to engage them—you can lay a foundation that builds a positive reputation for you or your business.

Chapter 11: Your Online Activities: You Are What You Do Your actions have a huge impact on your reputation. Stakeholders review your books at Amazon, your products at Epinions, your online retail store at Shopzilla, and your performance on eBay—the more positive the reviews, the better your reputation. In Second Life and other virtual worlds, you can build a fantastic reputation that will cross over to your first life—it may be time to join the 11 million avatars in that virtual world.

Part 3, "Monitoring, Repairing, and Planning your Online Reputation," gets you started on discovering your current reputation online and turning it into the one of your dreams.

Chapter 12: The Importance of Reputation Monitoring Monitoring the Web will ensure you're alerted the moment your reputation faces critique. To get the most out of your online reputation monitoring, you'll need to know why it is important, what keywords to monitor, where to watch, and when to take action.

Chapter 13: Monitoring Your Online Reputation Many free and inexpensive tools make it possible to set up a monitoring system without breaking your budget. If you prefer to automate your monitoring efforts, there are some solutions that offer to do the heavy lifting for you—while still keeping you in full control. Alternatively, if you'd rather your reputation-monitoring campaign be handled by experts, you can outsource the task to a professional monitoring firm.

Chapter 14: Repairing Your Online Reputation Despite your best efforts to build a positive reputation, there will be occasions when your brand faces an attack from a blog, forum, or social network. How do you identify a reputation attack, when should you engage your attackers, and what steps should you take to repair your damaged reputation?

Chapter 15: Seven-Step Action Plan To craft the kind of reputation online that will open any door, you need a reputation management and monitoring plan. The seven-step plan in this chapter asks you to do some deep introspection about your offline character and goals, then to devise strategies and objectives for reaching your reputation dreams using online media. In the process, you'll set up monitoring tactics and a crisis management plan for long-term sustainability.

Ready to get started? Turn the page and prepare for a stellar reputation online!

Understanding Your Online Reputation

Companies can spend millions of dollars each year to promote and manage their brands, yet a single negative blog post can destroy a reputation within days. The switch from corporate monologues to customer dialogue online means that you have more reputation risk than in the past.

These chapters lay the groundwork for your radically transparent *online reputation. You'll learn about the social media and how the balance of power has moved from companies to internet users. We'll focus on the company and its brands as well as individual reputations on this new playing field. You can use this environment to your advantage if you learn the new rules of engagement.*

I

Your World Is Now Radically Transparent

1

The power is with the people. Companies and CEOs previously controlled their reputations in both business and consumer markets, aided by public relations (PR) firms and crisis-management plans. Individuals monitored their reputations via feedback from clients and people in their personal and professional networks. The switch from traditional media and corporate monologues on websites to social media on the internet makes every internet user a journalist. People will judge you, your company, and your brand. Reputation management requires new skills in this radically transparent world.

Chapter Contents

JetBlue Airways Hits Bumpy Air

JetBlue Airways, the low-fare darling of the airline industry, had a bad day that lasted more than two months. A Valentine's Day ice storm in 2007 left passengers in planes on runways for ten hours and in northeastern U.S. airports for much longer. A total of 1,100 planes were grounded over a six-day period. How could their favorite airline do this to these loyal customers? What started with an understandable act of nature became a crisis due to JetBlue's internal communication system failure. Flight crews and airport personnel could not coordinate well with corporate decision makers to handle the unhappy customers.

JetBlue had over seven years of stellar reputation that became quite tarnished in just a few days. Scrambling to make this right, Founder and then-CEO David Neeleman responded with classic crisis-management savvy:

- On February 19, he accepted responsibility and made a public apology, which received national coverage across traditional media outlets. He also sent e-mail and paper letters to customers expressing his regrets on behalf of the company.

- Also on February 19, he posted a video on YouTube introducing the "Customer Bill of Rights," explaining what the company would do to make sure this never happened again.

- On February 22, JetBlue posted the Bill of Rights on its website.

- On March 19, Neeleman reported back about JetBlue's progress in a company blog entry titled "Talk is Cheap."

All this while the company was dealing with over 5,000 media requests and calls from PR professionals offering their counsel. In the meantime, the internet rapidly filled with public opinion. Customers posted their own YouTube videos on February 19, showing themselves abandoned in airports, eating junk food for 24 hours and hoping to get somewhere. Others commented on Neeleman's apology video: "I'll pass on the Kool-Aid, thanks. This airline is a joke and anyone who buys this B.S. from this moron deserves to be stranded for 10 hours w/ no food, water or toilets! Boycott Jet-Blew!!" Before the Bill of Rights appeared, the following comments were posted on Jet-Blue's website regarding the three-day posting delay: "I love Jet Blue…The message of the video is great, but, why can't I get the Bill of Rights on the Jet Blue website?" And: "I couldn't live without JetBlue! I appreciate your personal message and attention to every new problem. We ALL learn from our mistakes."

By May 7, nearly 300,000 people had viewed Neeleman's video and nearly 500 had commented on it. Like judges, the internet community was still critiquing this incident in May 2007, reviewing the company's reactions to both the crisis and the community conversation, and evaluating Director of Communications Jenny Dervin's every word and move. People also posted comments about new JetBlue incidents and compared them to the Bill of Rights: Were they followed, they asked? JetBlueHostage.com emerged as a blog filled with customer, employee, and public opinion about it all. A six-day incident, handled well by the traditional PR book, did not completely return JetBlue to its previous high-flying status.

Conversation in social media amplified JetBlue's crisis, showing the need for new PR practices. This incident led to the replacement of founder and CEO Neeleman on May 10. The company handled this crisis reasonably well, yet it continues to plague JetBlue—what could they have done differently?

The Reality of a Transparent, Always-On, Wired World

JetBlue's problems started with a genuine crisis, but sometimes this mob mentality begins in a most unexpected way. In an article for MSN.com, columnist Scott Burns asked, "Is Home Depot Shafting Shoppers?" His description of personal experiences at the retailer led to the conclusion that home improvement company Home Depot "is a consistent abuser of its customers' time." That same day, the MSN staff received 10,000 e-mails and 4,000 posts in the story's Talk Back section describing all of Home Depot's problems. How could Home Depot CEO Frank Blake learn about and handle a huge reputation problem like this that blooms to gigantic proportion within hours?

The rise in social media means that anyone can post pictures or write about your company, 24/7 online, and will. Business customers and consumers alike actively judge your company and comment online for their network members' enlightenment. In the business-to-business (B2B) market, word-of-mouth communication influenced 53% of work-related purchases by business decision makers—some of it online, according to research firm Keller Fay Group. In the business-to-consumer (B2C) market, Jupiter Research found that 90% of large companies believe consumer recommendations are important in influencing other consumers' purchase decisions. Astonishingly, despite this awareness only 20% of corporations have a formal process in place for monitoring blog posts written about their company, according to Harris Interactive.

Defining Moment: Citizen Journalists and People Paparazzi

Citizen journalists are internet users who contribute their perspectives by posting writing, images, or videos to online blogs, forums, and websites. People paparazzi are those citizen journalists who take photos or videos and upload without subjects' permission. Citizen journalists can be B2B customers, consumers, prospects, or any other stakeholder. In contrast to media-employed journalists, citizen journalists rarely need editorial approval or fact verification before posting, and they are not held to the same standard of balanced and unbiased reporting. Citizen journalists are the authors of user-generated media (UGM), also called consumer-generated media (CGM) or social media.

Citizen journalists don't limit their reputation-tarnishing conversations to companies—they also threaten the personal reputations of individuals. A total of 23% of Americans search online for the dirt on colleagues, customers, and employees (according to Sean Michael Kerner of ClickZ, a resource for interactive marketing news). Recruiting firm ExecuNet found that 78% of executive recruiters routinely use search engines to learn more about job candidates, and 35% have eliminated candidates based on the information they found. Thanks to the availability of information on the internet, others can quickly learn about your actions, history, and point of view.

At risk are C-level officers, entrepreneurs, professionals, marketing executives, salespeople, job seekers, and others. Citizen journalists and people paparazzi have devices to capture your every move (cameras and video phones), software to create and manipulate content, and a network for distribution to millions of people in e-mail, blogs, or video posting sites (e.g., YouTube). "Nastiness can erupt online and go global overnight," says *BuzzMarketingForTech* blogger Paul Dunay. All this without your knowledge—and potentially discovered first by your important business customers and partners.

Jack Welch, Sir Richard Branson, Dr. Deepak Chopra, and Dale Carnegie translated their outstanding personal reputations into business profits. Celebrities and politicians trade on their reputations, as do all of us. In one unusual example, Janet Schoenberg was evicted from her New York apartment and felt her case was not being properly handled by Judge Jerald R. Klein. Janet could find no way to attract attention to her perceived inequity, so she put the judge up for sale on eBay. She posted a picture and offered free worldwide shipping (according to *The New York Times*, the best offer after four days was $127.50). The judge didn't discover this misuse of his image until a reporter called. Nor would most men think of looking for disgruntled ex-girlfriend postings about them at DontDateHimGirl.com.

Every day, people discuss your personal and corporate reputations on blogs, forums, and niche websites. This kind of transparency requires new reputation-management skills.

People Power

The balance of power moved toward consumers when the television remote control emerged, escalated with the computer mouse and digital video recorders, and is now firmly entrenched thanks to technologies that allow everyone to publish online. "The power of the consumer's voice has never been stronger… It is impacting consumer behavior and how companies operate," according to David Daniels, vice president and research director at market research firm JupiterResearch. This is why *Time* magazine named "you" the person of the year in 2006.

Chris Anderson of *Wired* and author of *The Long Tail* calls this phenomenon a "pyramid inversion." It is an inversion from corporate power (C-level executives and

PR firms) to consumer power, and it is a twenty-first–century reality. "What's new is the extent to which consumer opinion drives reputations. A third of the population has reviewed something online, and any one of those reviews can be read by millions of people," according to interactive marketing veteran Andy Sernovitz in *Fast Company*.

This view was validated by PR mega-firm Edelman in its 2007 Trust Barometer. Some 52% of survey respondents from developed nations said they find "a person like yourself" to provide the most credible information—equal only to the trust in doctors, and higher than any other type of communicator (see Figure 1.1).

Percent responding, "If you heard information from each of these sources, how credible would the information be?"

A person like yourself — 52%
Doctor or health care specialist — 52%
Non-profit organization or NGO representative — 47%
Academic — 44%
Financial industry analyst — 43%
Regular employee of the company — 35%
CEO or leader of your company or employer — 32%
CEO of a company — 26%
Public relations executive — 14%

Figure 1.1 Edelman Trust Barometer 2007

> **Thought Byte: Credible Sources**
>
> You probably use a myriad of trusted sources for your information, including "people like you." What special interest forums, groups, or blogs do you read? Do you trust what you read in them?

Who is a "person like me?" Traditional demographics don't capture it. According to Edelman research, people place the highest trust in those who share similar interests, are in the same profession, and hold similar political beliefs. This follows academic research showing that consumers strongly consider the opinions of like-minded people and thus have an important influence on their purchasing behavior. This partially explains the power of internet special topic forums, blogs, and reviews on industry websites, such as tripadvisor.com

The internet special interest tribes have the power to build or ruin your reputation with their online chatter. This is why a single cyclist was able to bring Kryptonite to its knees in 2004 by posting a video showing him opening the bike lock with a BIC ballpoint pen.

From Minimally Transparent to Radically Transparent

The Web ushered in an era of corporate transparency. It used to be that you had to attend Detroit's North American International Auto Show each fall to see the new models. By the mid-1990s, companies began announcing new products online and communicating with stakeholders via websites. They now had a fine communication outlet for the press releases landing in traditional media wastebaskets. In 1998, the U.S. Securities and Exchange Commission began storing public company financial reports in its Edgar database. What was already public became accessible anytime, anywhere, from any connected computer.

Slowly it escalated. Secret corporate memos and private e-mails started circulating online, and celebrity's private cell phone numbers were published. Comparison-shopping websites, such as bizrate.com and pricegrabber.com, compared online retail pricing for electronics, books, and other items. Amazon and other recommendation sites began publishing consumer reviews. A few people started badmouthing their companies in blogs and were immediately fired. Blogger Heather Armstrong has the distinguished title of being the first to get fired in 2002 for critiquing her colleagues and their work in her blog, Dooce.com. Many others followed. That was the age of minimal transparency, and it is now the "good old days."

Today, it is completely "open kimono." If companies, professionals, or just about anyone doesn't reveal their weaknesses for the world to see online, someone else will—as with JetBlue's critics who still evaluate every flight problem to see if the company follows its Customer Bill of Rights. The internet community demands transparency and honesty and those who don't follow this new creed pay for it with a cyber-tongue lashing or worse (Kryptonite reportedly lost $10 million due to a product recall after the BIC pen video incident).

> ### Thought Byte: Your Online Reputation
>
> You may be wondering what people say about you online. Google yourself, your brands, and the company name. Check yourself out in the blogosphere at Technorati.com or blogsearch.google.com. What surprises you? Things may have changed since the last time you did this experiment.

Examples abound. Wal-Mart and PR firm Edelman got a wake-up call with their flog (fake blog), *Wal-Marting Across America*, that was presented as a couple of customers talking about their experiences in a motor home—but was indeed an orchestrated trip being paid for by Wal-Mart. It not only hurt the retailer and its PR firm, but author and freelance writer Laura St. Claire fell from grace too. Colorado State University professor Jonathan Rees uncovered the deception when he challenged the writers of *Wal-Marting Across America* because their descriptions of Wal-Mart were always glowing and positive. He wrote in his own blog, "They pay an unspecified sum to these people to say how great Wal-Mart is—I think it is deceptive."

In a *Wired* article, "The See-Through CEO," writer Clive Thompson suggests, "Fire the publicist. Go off message. Let all your employees blab and blog. In the new world of radical transparency, the path to business success is clear." Show what you are doing, reveal your processes, acknowledge your mistakes, and participate fully in conversation that concerns you. Be radically transparent or risk your reputation and top line.

How Social Media Change the Playing Field

Businesses previously needed only to worry about something negative when it appeared in a newspaper or on the evening news. Individuals lived in relative anonymity, and potential employers knew nothing beyond the contents of a resume or testimony. The world of information moved at a snail's pace, and public perception of a brand could be managed by those who had either the connections or the money.

Traditional word-of-mouth has long been considered one of the most powerful of market forces, and social computing makes it public. The internet provides a megaphone for the disgruntled—with no entry barrier, little legal accountability, instant commentary, full multimedia communication, and a free distribution channel to millions worldwide. And people like them find these complaints credible.

Positive words exist online, but the negative opinions seem to draw the huge crowds. It is easy to attack someone while in pajamas behind a home computer, and everyone has an opinion. "Online is where reputations are made now," according to Chief Reputation Strategist Dr. Leslie Gaines-Ross at public relations firm Weber Shandwick.

All this is made possible by social media—online tools and platforms that allow internet users to collaborate on content, share insights and experiences, and connect for business or pleasure. It involves multimedia and includes blogs, wikis, photo and video sharing, forums, and networks for meeting like-minded people. Social media are sometimes referred to as social computing or Web 2.0.

Characteristics of Social Media

Everyone is a publisher in the social media world. The name of the game is egalitarian participation by one and all—from the Fortune 100 CEO to your dentist. Company spokespeople and employees sometimes initiate conversations and are active participants via blogs and such, but social media content is still primarily community driven in a bottom-up process. Although hamburger chain Wendy's International, Inc. and other companies have MySpace pages, their kind are in the minority among MySpace page publishers.

Whereas traditional websites and e-mail blasts broadcast the company line, product talk online now gives full attention to the consumer voice. The company line has traditionally been a slick monologue, full of marketing verbiage and unexciting spin. The consumer voice is honest, raw, fast, brutally direct, and humorous. It is no wonder that other consumers prefer to read it.

Sometimes following a mob mentality, citizen journalists are more revealing and critical than traditional journalists. Further, citizen journalists comment on rumors and opinion, and some don't check the facts as diligently because they don't have the same guidelines and editorial review processes as traditional media. Citizen journalists also deconstruct and reveal biases in traditional media reports. Then they challenge one another's views. No rock is left unturned.

This rich tapestry of corporate and consumer voices adds complexity and balance to the online conversations. It is a dialogue, not a monologue. Employees and just about anyone can and do join the fun. It is a rapid-fire conversation across numerous sites: discussion that mushrooms like an atomic bomb within hours and takes a Herculean effort for organizational monitoring and participation. Few have the time and skills for managing this 1:1 dialogue, but without it a long-built reputation can be damaged in hours.

There is broad distribution of consumer generated content over the internet network, as opposed to the communication centralization of traditional mass media and web page content. Marketers employing social media call it a *pull* tactic (with users asking for content of choice) versus the *push* of traditional media (where users passively receive content), as depicted in Figure 1.2 (adapted from Dion Hinchcliffe's *Web 2.0* blog)

Social media require honesty, disclosure, and as we've already said, transparency. There is little censorship in this world—the community values raw truth. The community immediately comes down hard on those who employ conversation spin, control, manipulation, or spam. Anonymity is discouraged, and nearly all posts to a conversation include the author's real e-mail address.

A multiplier effect quickly spreads information over the Web, often unedited and usually commented upon by new authors. Hot headlines show up on Digg.com and receive votes for the best story. Blog site content depends on keeping current with stories in its special interest niche, so bloggers are quick to pick up headlines and link to site originators. The negative news spreads like wildfire, fanned by citizen journalists, and this is why a full-blown reputation crisis can appear within hours. JetBlue experienced this firsthand.

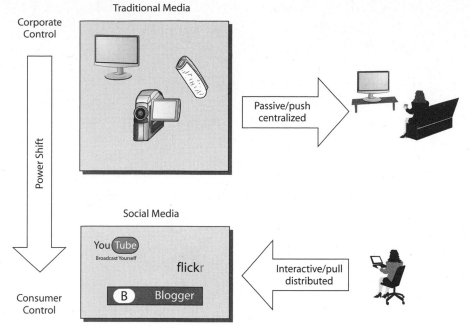

Figure 1.2 From traditional to social media

Thought Byte: Media Importance

Does your reputation rely more on traditional or social media? To answer this, consider the number and positive or negative sentiment of mentions your company, brand, or key personnel receive in each medium. Where do your biggest critics publish?

By now you are getting the point that the internet is abuzz with conversation, and some of it is definitely about you and your company. With the explosion of social networks and consumer-generated media, no organization, brand, or individual escapes online mention by stakeholders, like it or not. The people paparazzi can take your picture without your knowledge and post it online: such was the fate of actor Michael Richards, who was caught by an audience member's cell video phone during a racist tirade to a shocked crowd. That video will be available forever on entertainment blog TMZ.com.

It takes very different skills to build, monitor, manage, and repair a reputation in light of social media.

Social Media Abound

Technorati tracks more than 110 million blogs with 1.6 million daily blog posts (18 updates a second). The blogosphere continues to double approximately every 6 months—adding over 175,000 new blogs each day. Flickr, the photo sharing site owned by Yahoo!, hosts 485 million photos (up from 5.5 million in 2005). These are not all vacation pictures, but many contain reputation-damaging images. Entering **ycantpark** into a Flickr photo search reveals 335 pictures of cars and motorcycles poorly parked—complete with readable license plate numbers. Many of these are employee vehicles at Yahoo Inc.'s Sunnyvale, California, headquarters.

Google indexes more than 20 billion pages of content, and social networks such as MySpace and Friendster continue to grow their user base at a fantastic pace. Google maintains the entire archive of Usenet discussion groups dating back to 1981. As user-generated media such as blogs, forums, and social networks continue to multiply each day and remain archived forever, the power to create or destroy a reputation has moved from mainstream media to the average consumer.

Individuals and corporations now realize that their online reputations are very fragile. Social networks such as Digg, LinkedIn, YouTube, and Facebook continue to add thousands of new users each day, and this environment demands constant reputation monitoring. See Table 1.1 for an overview of social media.

▶ **Table 1.1** Social Media Overview

Social Media	What is it?	Examples
Social networks	Associations of internet users for social connection	MySpace, Facebook, LinkedIn
Search engines	Databases allowing users to search for content	Google, Yahoo!, MSN, America Online, Ask
User review sites and forums	Special interest communities with user product reviews	Tripadvisor, Amazon, CNET
Blogs	Online multimedia journals with frequent updating	Technology: TypePad, Blogger, Wordpress. Site: Marketingpilgrim.com
RSS	Brings content to user desktops	Technology: Bloglines, FeedBurner. Sites: most media and blogs
Tagging	Metadata that helps users find a photo, news story or Web page	Del.icio.us, Flickr, Digg
Wikis	Collaborative publishing on websites	Wikipedia, Wikihow
Podcasts	Digital audio, and sometimes video, for user download to computers, iPods, or other devices	NPR, Comedy Central, National Geographic, ESPN

Reputation 101

Now for a short tutorial on reputation, just to be sure we are on the same page. According to Merriam-Webster (www.m-w.com/) reputation is defined as

> **"** 1) an overall quality or character as seen or judged by people in general, and 2) a place in public esteem or regard: a good name. **"**

Reputation is not what the company or individual thinks about itself, but what others think. It is pure perception that may or may not be based on fact. It is the esteem that an entity has in the eyes of its stakeholders.

Contrast this with a brand or company image—the beliefs and attitudes held by stakeholders based on brand experience and company communication. Image is based on a product's or company's attributes and is much broader than reputation, which is solely based on character judgments. For example, JetBlue's image is based on the brand promise, including its fares and routes, on time record, employee service and friendliness, and so forth. Its reputation is based on the trust to deliver what it promises and the respect for its corporate values and actions.

Character and Reputation

Abraham Lincoln once said that "Character is like a tree and reputation like a shadow. The shadow is what we think of it; the tree is the real thing." Actions depict the character, and opinions in reaction reveal the reputation. Because reputation is based on a character judgment, it begs the question: What is character? In organizations it involves a complex set of features, including both performance and ethical behavior. It is not that different for an individual's character.

Trust is a key component of any reputation. Stakeholders demand authenticity, credibility, and honesty. According to the 2007 Edelman Trust Barometer, "providing quality products or services" and undertaking "socially responsible activities" are the two most important things a company can do to build trust. We'd also include "quality workplace management" and "financial performance" (or at least lack of irregularities) based on commonalities in the work of Harris Interactive, Weber Shandwick, and criteria for *Fortune* magazine's annual America's Most Admired Companies list.

Radically Transparent will not aid you or your company in developing a good character: you already learned that from your parents, school, and religion. Slip and you will fall in the social media. Or, don't slip and you still may fall when the citizen journalists get the rumor mill going. Even the best character can draw online criticism and if you or your firm are not yet being discussed online, you will be soon. Incidentally, if you are not the topic of online conversation this may indicate a bigger problem: you have no reputation at all because no one cares. This book will help you monitor your online reputation and manage stakeholder perceptions of your character. These things were not taught in school.

Reputation Influences

The reputations of an organization, its brands, and its employees operate in a context that is sometimes uncontrollable (Figure 1.3). For example, a country reputation affects brand reputations exported from that country. Further, what people think of Bill Gates affects Microsoft's reputation. When Robert Scoble wrote his famous blog as technical evangelist at Microsoft (Scoblizer.com), his reputation influenced and was affected by those of Bill Gates and Microsoft.

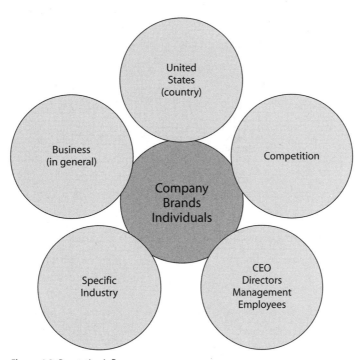

Figure 1.3 Reputation Influences

At the broadest level, a company's or brand's reputation includes that of its country of origin. The current reputation of the United States is quite low in many countries, and this has a real economic impact on U.S. firms selling abroad. For instance, in Edelman's 2007 Trust survey with college-educated, high-income residents, 60% of Americans trust McDonald's, but only 26% of residents in France, Germany, and the United Kingdom trust the company. Edelman concludes that for the third year in a row, American brands operating in Europe have a trust discount—other studies suggest a discount of up to 20% for U.S. brands in foreign markets. *Business Week* suggests that this U.S. trust discount nears the top of "the list of the Biggest Problems No One Cares About."

Do consumers trust business in general? In the United States, 53% did in 2007, up from 44% in 2002 during the Enron and WorldCom ethics scandals (according to Edelman). This is an all-time high for business trust, but it handicaps an individual business in the reputation game.

Industry reputations affect its corporate members. An Ipsos MORI study revealed the proportion of consumers holding positive impressions of various industries: food industry (65%), banking (51%), and tobacco (14%). Companies operating in unpopular industries have an uphill reputation battle.

Similarly, the competition can affect a firm's reputation because buyers make comparisons. When Home Depot is in the spotlight for poor customer service, Lowe's suddenly looks better to consumers.

Now for the company management. The CEO reputation is a very important component of the company reputation, according to 87% of the respondents in a study by PR firm Hill and Knowlton. Also important are reputations of the CFO (75%), the company chairman (40%), and other nonexecutive directors (23%). When the company reputation is damaged, CEOs receive nearly 60% of the blame, according to PR firm Weber Shandwick. This may be why David Neeleman, JetBlue CEO and founder, left his post after the February crisis.

Finally, every employee can affect a company's reputation through interactions with customers, friends, and family. This explains why internal marketing is such an important tactic.

Obviously, some of these contextual influences are more controllable than others. In this book we present strategies and tactics for managing organizational and individual CEO and employee reputations, but it is important to consider that larger influences can derail the best plans.

Reputation Is a Valuable Asset

After removing radio personality Don Imus from his MSNBC program for making racist remarks on air, NBC News President Steve Capus noted that advertisers had begun pulling dollars from the network. Capus said, "I ask you, what price do you put on your reputation? And the reputation of this news division means more to me than advertising dollars. Because if you lose your reputation, you lose everything." Those advertising dollars may well have kept flowing out if NBC hadn't handled this situation so skillfully.

Much research validates the connection between a company's reputation and revenue. For example, a Harris Interactive study found that a sterling reputation increases consumers' "intentions to buy a company's products and services, recommend them to other people, buy a company's stock, and recommend the stock to other investors." In the pharmaceutical industry a PricewaterhouseCoopers study discovered that 78% of consumers consider a firm's reputation when selecting drug treatments.

The Hay Group, a global marketing consultancy and partner with *Fortune* magazine, noted that the top 10 "World's Most Admired Companies" enjoy a total shareholder return of nearly three times that of the Standard & Poor's (S&P) 500 as a whole (18.5% versus 7.1%). People and businesses buy from companies they like and trust. Further, they don't want to be associated with firms that have poor reputations. It pays to monitor your reputation carefully and take action as needed to keep it stellar.

Pay special attention if it is stellar: JetBlue's reputation crash was worse because of its perfect reputation pre-Valentine's day 2007. Other airlines that also grounded planes and passengers did not get the same strong negativity in social media, perhaps because these delays were expected from them.

Thought Byte: Your Reputation Equity

What is the value of your reputation? Your organization's? Think of some worst-case scenarios and how they could hurt your bottom line.

Loose tongues (and typing fingers), e-mail abuse, and internet fraud can kill your reputation in a minute. The Weber Shandwick PR firm estimates that it takes four years to recover from a reputation blemish, and another three to make it sustainable.

This huge asset needs careful guarding.

Now for the Good News

This same social Web we've been describing is full of treasures for astute companies. You can easily find and use them for improving your reputation online. One key is to follow the old adage: if you can't fight 'em, join 'em. The citizen journalists want the object of their stories to join in the conversation.

The internet is a great research tool for hearing what's on your customers' and other stakeholders' minds. Learn from the dialogue. It is a lot cheaper than holding focus groups in multiple cities. Academic research shows that two-thirds of customers never voice complaints to companies. The ease of internet discussion allows them to complain to other like-minded consumers with full transparency to the company. Unilever's Axe personal care brands for men hosts private forums for selected customers and listens to them chat about life, love, Axe products, and more. Dell and Amazon are particularly adroit at listening to customers and designing products and technology to meet their needs. JetBlue created the Bill of Rights as a response to its customer troubles. What could be better than the opportunity to eavesdrop on a million customers as they honestly chat about your products online?

Thought Byte: Online Reputation Research

You probably have many ways of learning about customer perceptions. What systems do you have in place to research your reputation online?

It might seem overwhelming to monitor 110 million blogs, but that is unnecessary. Your stakeholders tend to hang out together online in special interest forums and blogs (remember: "people like me"). Sometimes called "centers of influence," a firm or individual can identify a handful of important websites for monitoring. For instance, a hotel will watch reviews posted on travel agent sites, such as Expedia, Travelocity, and TripAdvisor.

You can also work with individuals to solve product problems. Research shows that a negative comment about a brand is about 10 times stronger than a positive comment in shaping public opinion. It is easy to identify an individual complaining online about a product or service problem and e-mail the consumer directly to make it right. Lenovo, the technology firm that acquired IBM's Personal Computing Division, picks off a few extreme and vocal customer complaints a day and responds to them personally. What a great opportunity to find the dissatisfied and turn them into brand advocates.

As another bonus, you can monitor online conversation automatically. This is one of the great features of internet technology. Reputation watchers use Google and Technorati, Really Simple Syndication (RSS) feeds, and more, to bring relevant conversation right to their desktop computers the minute it happens. We'll show you exactly how to set up your own conversation monitoring in Chapter 13.

Companies such as Dell, Wal-Mart, Microsoft, and Kryptonite have all experienced the power of consumer-generated media. Even the U.S. government's intelligence community has realized the wealth of information that can be gleaned from monitoring blogs. As Open Source Center (OSC) Director Douglas J. Naquin told *The Washington Times*, "A lot of blogs now have become very big on the internet, and we're getting a lot of rich information on blogs that are telling us a lot about social perspectives and everything from what the general feeling is to … people putting information on there that doesn't exist anywhere else."

The social media are not only for reputation monitoring and repair—you can also start the conversations that build your reputation. Honest, open disclosure and genuine interest in feedback will get the ball rolling. We'll explain how to do this in Parts 2 and 3 of this book.

Become Radically Transparent

By now you are getting the picture—the citizen journalists are discussing you, your company, your brands, and more online. Maybe they are chatting about your CEO or brands in blogs, posting images on Flickr and YouTube, and rating your actions on eBay and your reviews on Amazon or ePinion. Or perhaps your own online postings need a checkup to see if they support your desired reputation—for example, what image does your outgoing e-mail, website, and blog portray, and are your bio and contact information on your company's website up-to-date and accurate?

> **Thought Byte: Start with the Low-Hanging Fruit**
>
> Check your bio, head shot, "About Us" and contact information on the company website and update if needed. Then, look for information currency in the signature file appended to your outgoing e-mail and the white papers and press releases referencing you online.

The guidelines in this book will make it easy to present your best self online without fanning the flames or getting into reputation trouble. They are based on best practices among the internet's star brands. We've grounded them in solid marketing and corporate branding principles. You'll find short tutorials in four key skills of online branding in social media: research, public relations, search engine optimization, and online content generation. It is ultimately about the content online, but no one will see it if you don't have these other skills and know how to connect with people online. Research skills help you to find out where you currently stand online and to set up a monitoring system. Search engine optimization (SEO) helps you move closer to becoming the #1 listing on search engine results pages. PR gets the word out and also helps with SEO—these are tried-and-true strategies for creating a buzz about *you*.

PR and SEO are two very different skills because one focuses on building relevant messages for the media while the other concentrates on building relevant content for the search engines. Can't write? We'll help you with that, too. Social media require different writing skills than either traditional or web page writing (it's about the dialogue, remember?).

We wrote this book as a menu of strategies and tactics, knowing that one size does not fit all. You may already be well known online and want to jump to sections on how to repair your image in the face of online criticism, such as what happened to JetBlue. Or, you may be well known only in the real world yet want to become #1 on Google for your personal or corporate name. Finally, if you are new to this, like most of us, we show you how to start at the beginning and build a stellar online reputation. No time? You get to pick how much to do based on your situation.

There's a conversation going on about you right this minute. It's time to learn how to join that discussion and become radically transparent.

You Don't Own Your Company's Reputation

Companies can spend millions of dollars each year to promote and manage their brands, yet a single negative blog post can destroy a reputation within days. Consumers and employees use the Web to discuss businesses, their services, their products, and their executives. They're finding that their voices carry far and loud thanks to social networking sites, blogs, and online message boards. The power to control a brand is rapidly shifting away from the companies that have the deepest pockets—instead, it's the companies that best listen to and engage their stakeholders that win the reputation race.

2

Chapter Contents

Dell's Hell

> **"** I just got a new Dell laptop and paid a fortune for the four-year, in-home service...The machine is a lemon and the service is a lie...DELL SUCKS. DELL LIES. Put that in your Google and smoke it, Dell. **"**
>
> —Jeff Jarvis, BuzzMachine.com, June 21, 2005

During the 1990s and early millennium, Dell Inc. built a solid reputation as a computer manufacturer that produced quality desktop and notebook machines, while providing customers with industry-leading support. A decade of dependable customer service, competitive prices, and built-to-order solutions made Dell the default choice for millions of consumers and earned it a U.S. market share of 28.2% in 2004, according to global market intelligence firm IDC. Dell was seemingly destined to continue expanding its phenomenal success, setting a goal of reaching $80 million in revenue by 2008.

In the early 2000s, as part of a plan to reduce the costs associated with its customer service, Dell made the decision to outsource its technical support to India, a move that had become increasingly commonplace among technology companies seeking to reduce labor costs. The decision appeared to be a wise one, at least superficially, with Dell increasing its U.S. market share to 28.8% the following year. Dell was on a roll and the future looked as rosy as it could possibly be.

Unfortunately for Dell, on June 21, 2005, popular blogger Jeff Jarvis unwittingly opened up a can of worms, with a single post to his blog that would become the catalyst for a two-year period of scrutiny and criticism of the computer company's customer service. For the next two years, Dell would become known, not for its quality products and industry dominance, but instead for its association with two short words—"Dell Hell."

Thought Byte: Evaluate Every Blog Post

There's an important lesson to learn from Dell. Don't ignore a blog post, simply because the author is not relevant to your industry or doesn't appear to have an audience with your customers. If Dell had reacted quickly to Jarvis's first post, they could have saved themselves months of criticism.

Jeff Jarvis is not a computer expert. He doesn't write for *PC World*, CNET, or any other computer-industry publication. He's not the type of person to tweak or fine-tune a computer, nor is he the kind of person who buys a super-sophisticated machine.

In fact, when he bought his Dell notebook, Jarvis opted for the four-year, in-home warranty service, paying extra for the peace of mind that comes from knowing that he'd never once have to troubleshoot the hard drive or replace the microprocessor. He bought a computer from one of the world's largest and most respected manufacturers, and he expected it to work as advertised.

Unfortunately for Jarvis, and ultimately for Dell, the notebook computer in his possession was a "lemon." He had problems with the hardware, couldn't connect to his network, had issues with the central processing unit (CPU), and the machine overheated continually. When he tried to take advantage of his "in-home" service plan, he was told that any technician sent to his home would not have the parts to repair the computer, and that Jarvis would need to send the machine to Dell for repair—leaving him sans computer for up to two weeks. Clearly feeling misled by Dell and extremely frustrated, Jarvis decided to share his chagrin and anger with the readers of his popular media and news blog, BuzzMachine.com.

> " …All I should care about is having a computer that works. How it works and how it's made is their problem if I have a warranty, right?
>
> But that's what bothers me most: I bought that warranty, the top-of-the-line, most expensive warranty that warrants to send someone to my home to repair my machine.
>
> Except that's a big fat Dell lie. The person they would send to my home would not have the parts (or, according to some of my commenters, the expertise, training, and intelligence) to repair that machine.
>
> Smells like fraud to me.
>
> Smells like a class-action suit to some of my commenters and emailers… "

The response from his site's readers, many of whom had their own blogs, led to what can only be described as a snowball of negative sentiment, rolling down a Mount Everest–sized hill of underlying frustration, and gathering momentum and voracity as it went. Jeff Jarvis had become the blogging equivalent of the child who pointed out the emperor's new clothes were actually nonexistent. His criticism of Dell's customer service, or lack thereof, emboldened others to come forward to claim that, they too, had suffered at the hands of Dell's diminishing customer support. Dell faced an angry mob of online detractors replacing handwritten letters with blogs, exchanging mantra-like chants with online comments, and swapping arguments at customer service desks with bitter exchanges at online forums and chat rooms. Dell was truly facing its own reputation "hell," a backlash unlike any it, or any other company at the time, had seen.

Facing a Customer Revolt Online

Over the following three weeks, Jeff Jarvis published a total of 12 blog posts about Dell's poor customer service, each one more damaging than the previous, and each gaining hundreds of thousands of readers who collectively left thousands of comments.

Dell was facing a corporate reputation crisis. No doubt, Dell had previously prepared a "crisis communications plan"—a common practice among the public relations (PR) department of many large companies—but it wasn't prepared for the onslaught to come from the internet. Dell's crisis communications plan didn't include provisions for reacting to a web-based attack, it didn't map out how to engage online critics that numbered in the thousands, and Dell didn't know how to react. So it didn't.

> ### Thought Byte: Are You Prepared for a Crisis?
>
> Does your company have a crisis communication plan that includes responding to online attacks?
>
> If your business were to face an online assault to its reputation, how would you react?

Dell was caught in the crossfire and it was taking enemy fire from all sides. Its once spotless reputation was now being picked apart by a rapidly spreading theme (or "meme" as it is often called on the Web) that found its fuel, not from the likes of CNN or *The Wall Street Journal*, but from citizen journalists and their hordes of followers, often no more recognizable than the nickname or avatar they used to represent themselves online. Not knowing the best way to manage the situation, Dell did what most would— it decided to withdraw. It gave no official response to the social media outcry and instead acted as if, by simply refusing to pander to the complaints of a blogger and his following, the crisis would run out of gas and vanish as quickly as it had started. So sure of its strategy of nonengagement, Dell went as far as closing its Dell Customer Support Forum—a popular online destination for customers wishing to exchange comments and questions about Dell products. It vanished on July 8, 2005—just weeks after Jarvis's initial blog post.

To suggest that a single blogger was solely responsible for the sudden negative consumer sentiment would be an exaggeration of the events. Although Jarvis may have become the unofficial spokesperson for everyone facing Dell Hell, the real reason for such a huge reputation crisis can be traced to many months earlier. Dell's decision to reduce spending on customer service had created an underlying ripple of customer angst—before the situation was mentioned on any blog. Indeed, in 2004, just the year before, complaints to the Better Business Bureau rose 23% and were already up an additional 5% when Jarvis posted his complaint. In addition, a survey conducted by the University of Michigan indicated Dell's customer satisfaction rating fell 6.3% in 2005, bringing the company's ratings in line with those of the industry. Even more enlightening, a 2005 search on Google for the phrase "dell customer service problems" brought back an astonishing 2,950,000 indexed pages (that number has since grown to more than 7,000,000). Jeff Jarvis was not the reason for Dell's declining reputation—he was merely the messenger—but his blog post was the catalyst that brought the topic widespread attention.

Dell's reputation was in a tailspin. It had become the victim, not of an in-depth expose by *60 Minutes* or *Nightline*, but of a single blog post that became the battle cry for a community of Netizens (internet citizens). It would take Dell almost 12 months before it decided that a head-in-the-sand approach to its online reputation was not the best policy. A year after Jeff Jarvis's blog complaint, Dell discovered the only way to repair and build back its reputation would be to become radically transparent.

Dell Finds Its Transparent Voice

On July 10, 2006, Dell launched the first of many radically transparent initiatives, designed to add a human voice to what had become a sea of corporate rhetoric and carefully crafted media statements. Direct2Dell.com was the company's first foray into engaging its critics. Lionel Menchaca was appointed "Digital Media Manager" and become the web community spokesperson for all matters related to Dell's customer service and product initiatives. "Real People Are Here and We're Listening," would serve as the title of one of Dell's first blog posts, signaling the company's desire to listen to its customers and learn from its mistakes.

After months of scouring blog entries and reading forum posts, Dell was ready to open up its kimono and engage in a radically transparent mode of conversation. According to Menchaca, Dell "learned how to talk like a regular individual" and realized why it was important to "show customers that you are closing the loop." It sounded like a simple plan, after all—what most customers wanted was a chance to be heard and have their issues addressed. When they came knocking previously, Dell had closed the door on them, not interested in having any one-on-one conversations. Now, realizing the folly of its ways, Dell was ready to engage, ready to listen, and ready to respond.

Direct2Dell became Dell's first "post-Jarvis" initiative, designed to reverse course its initial decision to ignore social media—but it wouldn't be its last. Dell went on to launch blogs in multiple languages, create Studio Dell for podcasts and videos, increase the number of Dell-supported forums to seven, and even build its own social networking community: IdeaStorm.com. Dell realized that customers were discussing its products and customer service, whether it joined the conversation or not, and it finally realized that ignorance was not, in fact, bliss.

Listening to Customers

"We know our customers are having conversations about Dell, twenty-four-seven, around the world, in all languages," says Bob Pearson, vice president of corporate group communications for Dell. "We want to be a relevant part of those conversations." In fact, you'd be hard pressed to find a better example of a company that has learned the errors of its ways. Dell is one of the few to embrace not only social media as a communications channel—with blogs, forums, and podcasting—but to entwine itself so finely in the conversations of its customers that few business decisions inside the company are made without first listening to customers requests. "Something we say inside Dell [is that] we want the customer walking the hallways," enthuses Pearson. "You can't be in a meeting without saying, 'this is what the community wants.'" And this newly found desire to listen to customers is not simply a PR initiative designed to pay lip service, but a company acting on the feedback received. "This is not a communication exercise, this is not a feel-good thing, this is part of the DNA of Dell," explains Pearson.

While Dell's new practice of monitoring its detractors and listening to its customers has gone a long way to help rebuild its tattered reputation, the company has gone beyond simply listening and responding to criticism. Dell's not looking to simply fake its interest in what its clients have to say—the company is one of the few that actively engages its web following and seeks their suggestions on everything from new products to company initiatives. If you ask Pearson what Dell receives in return for actively participating in online conversations, he's quick to tell you: "We're benefiting from it so much."

While Dell may have started out its path to radical transparency with the launch of its first customer-centric blog, it is its social networking platform, IdeaStorm, that actually feeds the company with valuable customer insight. Designed to mirror the functionality of social tagging used on sites such as Digg.com or Reddit.com, Dell's IdeaStorm was created to function as a giant online suggestion box. Here's Dell's own description of IdeaStorm's purpose, taken from the site:

> **" ...** The name is a take-off on the word "brainstorm" and it is our way of building an online community that brings all of us closer to the creative side of technology by allowing you to share ideas and interact with other customers and Dell experts. You can suggest new products or services you'd like to see Dell develop or tell the world how you feel about major trends in technology and society. We hope this site fosters a candid and robust conversation about your ideas.
>
> Our commitment is to listen to your input and ideas to improve our products and services, and the way we do business. We will do our best to keep you posted on how Dell brings customer ideas to life. **"**

Dell Engages with Customers

Can listening to its customers' ideas and suggestions really help Dell grow its business and impact the direction it takes with new products and services? "We already have 20 business changes within the company," reports Pearson, within just a few months of launch. In fact, after barely three months of existence, the IdeaStorm website proudly reports the submission of more than 5,000 ideas, over 20,000 comments, and north of 350,000 idea endorsements. The site is such an overwhelming success for Dell that a staggering 100,000 people responded within days when the company took the bold step of announcing new machines running the open source operating system Linux (instead of Microsoft's Windows). Dell had gone from ignoring the voice of the individual customer to embracing it, nourishing it, and eventually hanging on its every word (see Figure 2.1).

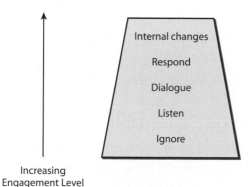

Increasing
Engagement Level

Figure 2.1 Levels of customer engagement

So how did Dell benefit from its decision to become radically transparent? It's still early, but the company is showing signs that its social media initiatives are paying off. Since the launch of the Direct2Dell blog, the company's stock price has risen from a July 2006 low of around $19 a share to a consistently held share price of $25. In

August 2006, when faced with a crisis involving the recall of millions of laptop batteries, Dell displayed its new transparency by reaching out to customers to answer their questions, setting up the DellBatteryProgram.com website to assist identifying faulty batteries, and posting nine blog entries to the Direct2Dell site.

There are other signs that Dell's reputation is benefiting from its radical transparency. According to Google's own search trends, the number of queries for "dell customer service" has declined since the middle of 2005 (Figure 2.2) and by mid-2006, Better Business Bureau complaints were down 40% to just 3 customers for every 10,000. By most metrics, Dell's initiative to engage its customers is a roaring success.

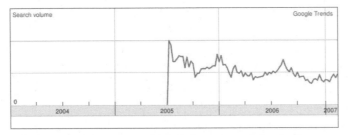

Figure 2.2 Chart showing search trends for "dell customer service" on Google

Brand Control Is Shifting to Citizen Journalists

So why are companies, like Dell and JetBlue, finding themselves subject to the scrutiny of their customers? What's causing customers—both external (consumers and investors) and internal (employees and directors)—to suddenly step up on to their virtual soapbox, voice their concerns, ask their questions, and criticize businesses? Why is it that customers are no longer content to listen to carefully crafted press statements, put up with the poor service received by businesses, or blindly accept what they're told on their television or radio? Just as the Web leveled the playing field of business—with smaller businesses empowered to compete with the Fortune 500s of the world—it also enabled the voice of the minority. Whether you're a mega-company, such as Dell, or a small, local business, what's said about your company online can affect your reputation, your future customer's decision making, and, ultimately, your bottom line. What starts as a ripple of discontent on the Web can quickly turn into a huge wave of negative media sentiment, as Dell discovered. To understand why your company should become radically transparent, we need to first look at why the old ways of communication are no longer working, how the internet is empowering customers to speak up, and what you stand to gain by engaging the online chatter.

You Don't Control Your Reputation

Companies collectively spend billions of dollars each year in advertising and PR campaigns. With various media channels at their disposal—television, radio, print, and internet—corporations of all sizes throw dollar after dollar into campaigns designed to carefully craft perceptions of them. These efforts are all designed to shape feelings about a company, responses to their products, interaction with their employees, and the associations made when thinking of them.

Likewise, businesses implement similar efforts with their own employees and internal stakeholders. The company mission statement, the corporate handbook, the annual meeting, and the CEO's newsletter all contribute to the internal perception of who the company is and what it stands for. Whether externally or internally, companies work hard to build and maintain their brand. Take a look at *Fortune* magazine's list of the most admired companies in 2007 and you'll see many examples of brands that have been built to conjure up a positive feeling, emotion, or perception.

America's Most Admired Companies (Source: *Fortune* 2007):

1.	General Electric	11.	Goldman Sachs Group
2.	Starbucks	12.	Microsoft
3.	Toyota Motor	13.	Target
4.	Berkshire Hathaway	14.	3M
5.	Southwest Airlines	15.	Nordstrom
6.	FedEx	16.	United Parcel Service
7.	Apple	17.	American Express
8.	Google	18.	Costco Wholesale
9.	Johnson & Johnson	19.	PepsiCo*
10.	Procter & Gamble	19.	Wal-Mart Stores*

* tied

Think of Starbucks and you'll likely think of baristas serving up fresh-brewed coffee. Hear the name Target and images of the bright red bull's-eye and large, clean stores come to mind. Seeing Google mentioned brings to mind fast, reliable search results with an uncanny knack of knowing exactly what you need. Yet, even these highly respected companies have faced their own online reputation crises. Starbucks CEO James Donald once told *The Seattle Times* that he would know if he had been successful if his employees attended his funeral—yet within hours employees had posted comments such as "I'd love to attend his firing" on Starbucksgossip.com. When Target decided to stop Salvation Army collections outside its stores during the holiday season, it found itself facing a backlash from the blogosphere. And, even Google, a company that is often rated as the most trusted brand in the world, is facing criticism from the digerati concerned about its liberal privacy policy.

Your Marketing Is Boring Your Customers

Although Dell may be the poster child for how easily even the most respected brand can find itself at the mercy of citizen journalists, its story, and those of Starbucks, Target, and Google, are not isolated incidents. Customers—both external and internal—are pushing back at corporate-speak, canned communication, and polished advertisements. They've found that their own voices carry far and wide when echoed by their peers. Online, one vote counts. The internet is empowering and engaging, and its audience is practically crying out to hear what the average Joe has to say. They've found new knowledge in listening to one another's opinions and they've decided to reevaluate everything they know about your brand by simply listening to the experiences of others. They trust one another more than they trust you.

In his book *Purple Cow*, author and marketer Seth Godin explains why customers are ignoring traditional messaging and looking for something more authentic. "I believe we've now reached the point where we can no longer market directly to the masses," says Godin. He explains that customers have grown deadened to traditional marketing and advertising; they've moved on and are seeking something extraordinary, something radically different. Godin believes that customers, like motorists who've grown bored of seeing nothing but black-and-white cows lining the fields of a country road, have desensitized themselves to the constant bombardment of advertising designed to influence their perception of a company's brand. "The traditional approaches are now obsolete," says Godin. Customers are looking for something different, something they can find passion in, something they can get excited about. As Godin suggests, customers are looking for a Purple Cow on the road to recapture their attention. For businesses, the Purple Cow happens to be the voices of its employees, customers, and other stakeholders—all spotlighted online.

Dell may have found itself at the mercy of a popular blogger's rant, but most companies won't find such a loud, singular voice crafting the online perception of its brand. In fact, if it were as simple as identifying just a handful of influential internet advocates and critics, you would be able to put this book down right now, take a quick review of the Web, and make direct contact with those who hold the power to influence how others perceive your business. But it's not that simple, unfortunately. The power to influence the perception of your company's brand doesn't rest with one or two popular blogs, forums, or message boards. Godin's Purple Cow manifested itself as a huge, thundering herd of citizen journalists. Millions of voices are on the Web every day, discussing your and your competitors' business and deciding whether or not you are living up to the brand perception you've so carefully crafted with all of your advertising and PR dollars. "One hundred years of marketing thought are gone," suggests Godin. It's time to find your radically transparent voice. It's time to first listen to, and then join, the conversations that are going on every day about your company, your products, your services, your executives, and your employees.

It is now a dialogue—the company monologue won't cut it anymore.

Your Marketing Is Boring Your Employees

The people you need to listen and respond to are not just a select list of influential consumers. Sure, you'll always find what Malcolm Gladwell calls the "mavens" in his book *The Tipping Point*: consumers who "have the knowledge and the social skills to start word-of-mouth epidemics," but the people who discuss your business aren't always easy to spot and they're not always the usual suspects. In fact, just as important, if not more so, than your company's external customers are your internal ones, such as employees, business partners, and investors. The people inside your company are often just as likely to discuss your brand outside of your company.

The very people you rely on each day to build products, service clients, and help your company live up to its publicly built perception are often the ones who hold your brand to the highest standards of corporate governance. They're matching your internal messages to the ones you convey outside the company. They're comparing the taglines you use in your million-dollar advertising campaigns with the internal memos that get sent over the corporate intranet. Most of your internal stakeholders will likely be your strongest allies; they'll fight for you, defend your reputation, and bring their own trusted voice to the many public conversations. Yet they have the potential to be your harshest critics, most outspoken attackers, and determined detractors.

Companies that become radically transparent don't just pay attention to the sentiment and feedback of their external customer base; they realize that, in order to have any chance of success, they'll need the assistance of those internal advocates who share their same passion and belief. You'll need to show a unified front, and demonstrate that the money spent in advertising to craft and shape your brand is substantiated by your employees who live and breathe your business every day.

Thought Byte: Get Feedback from Your Employees

What do your employees think about your brand? Consider conducting a simple survey to see how your employees describe your brand. Do they understand what you're trying to build? Do their perceptions correspond with your intent?

Becoming "radically transparent" starts with your own internal audience. You must learn how to reach them with honest, plainspoken messaging. You need to let them know that you value their opinion, respect their input, and fully trust them to help you in your efforts to engage with your customers. By doing so, not only will you gain tremendous insight into the inner workings of your business, but you'll also build an army of company evangelists who will keep their ear to the ground, monitor your reputation for you, and be there to champion your cause. And you'll need their help.

Internet Conversations Have Replaced Coffee Shop Chatter

In a coffee shop, within minutes of where you're reading this book, two or more people have gathered together and are discussing the poor workmanship of a product they just purchased from a well-known company. Others are on the phone, sharing recommendations for a business where they've personally received great service. And, somewhere, right this minute, employees are gathered in a break room, discussing how unfairly they've been treated by their boss. These conversations have always existed and will continue to exist so long as there are companies to buy products from, businesses providing services, and executives managing employees.

Thanks to the power of that modern innovation, the World Wide Web, these conversations now go on every minute of every day, in stores, homes, and offices—but what was once a few friends within earshot are now a few hundred thousand strong. Although the pre-internet age meant that these conversations were mostly untraceable, unknown, discreet, hidden, and somewhat secretive, these discussions are now happening in plain view, if you know where to look and care to listen.

> **Thought Byte: Take a Look in the Mirror**
>
> What would customers say about your company? Take a moment for some honest reflection. What might customers be saying about your brands and CEO? Make a mental note of the topics now—both positive and negative—and you'll be in a better position to understand the threats and opportunities to your company's brand.

The Cluetrain Manifesto, written by web luminaries Rick Levine, Christopher Locke, Doc Searls, and David Weinberger, was largely regarded as the first awakening to the notion that "markets are conversations" yielding a wealth of information to those willing to explore them. As Locke explains, "The Internet became a place where people could talk to other people without constraint. Without filters or censorship or official sanction—and perhaps most significantly, without advertising." Conversations that had previously taken place in locations that not even the best Cold War–era spy could have uncovered, are now being broadcast to millions of internet users, eager to share their voice and listen to the voice of others. "The Net connects people to each other, and impassions and empowers through those connections," suggests Locke.

In fact, a strange thing happened when people started to integrate the internet with their daily lives. Once quiet, reserved individuals suddenly found the confidence to speak up and make their opinion count. They found the internet to be a way to break down corporate spin, carefully crafted marketing messages, and slick advertising. The Web gave customers the power to reshape your brand, to peek behind the Wizard of Oz curtain, and to share with others exactly what they've learned about your company. As Doc Searls so succinctly describes:

> **"** …finding themselves connected to one another in the market doesn't enable customers just to learn the truth behind product claims. The very sound of the Web conversation throws into stark relief the monotonous, lifeless, self-centered drone emanating from Marketing departments around the world. Word of Web offers people the pure sound of the human voice, not the elevated, empty speech of the corporate hierarchy. Further, these voices are telling one another the truth based on their real experiences, unlike the corporate messages that aim at presenting what we can generously call a best-case scenario. Not only can the market discover the truth in the time it takes to do a search at a discussion archive, but the tinny, self-absorbed voices of business-as-usual sound especially empty in contrast to the rich conversations emanating from the Web. **"**

Forget the Needle; First You Need to Find the Haystack

So, if the conversations have moved from coffee shops and break rooms, where exactly did they go? You may already be convinced that your company is being discussed on the internet, but where exactly? The internet has hundreds of billions of pages, with authors scattered across the entire world. If Google can discover only a fraction of the content that resides on the Web, how is any business supposed to know where to start locating and joining these conversations? "Technology is making these conversational needles lots easier to find in the Internet haystack," suggests *The Cluetrain Manifesto*'s Rick Levine, and just as most offline conversations have their typical locations (coffee shop, break room, and so forth), online conversations have their normal cyber hangouts.

In Part 2 of this book we'll walk you through these different cyber hangouts and describe the voices you'll need to use for customer engagement and for becoming radically transparent. However, now is a good juncture to introduce you to the key types of social media, and their *mode d'emploi*, so that you can get a better understanding of where you'll need to hang out in order to listen, monitor, and engage.

In Chapter 1, we gave an overview of the social media channels being used by your company's customers. Most of these should be familiar to you, but others may be new to you, or perhaps unclear as to what exactly they mean. The internet is very much a living organism, diverse in its use, broad in its taxonomy, and somewhat subjective in its classifications. Indeed, you could break the internet up into a handful of broadly defined channels, or you could use a labeling system so complex that it would make the classification of species—domain, kingdom, class, and so forth—look elementary. We're not going to dig deeply into all the different uses of the internet—there are customers waiting to hear from you—so instead we'll focus on demystifying the most commonly encountered platforms utilized by customers when it's time for them to dissect your brand.

Blogs Are the New Soapbox

What is a web log, or blog? Ask that question of a dozen people, and you'll likely get a dozen different answers in return. According to a definition found on the information site Answers.com, a blog is defined as:

> 66 (We**BLOG**) A Web site that contains dated text entries in reverse chronological order (most recent first) about a particular topic. Blogs serve many purposes from online newsletters to personal journals to "ranting and raving." They can be written by one person or a group of contributors. Entries contain commentary and links to other Web sites, and images as well as a search facility may be included. Blogs may also contain video. 99

It's interesting that the text includes "ranting and raving" as part of the description. Blogs were by no means created so that the average Jill could spend her day thinking up things to gripe about or topics to evangelize. In fact, early blogs were the work of geeky tech types—those early adopters—or teenagers discussing the activities of their pet dog. Even today, of the 110+ million blogs that blanket the internet, many are dominated by these two subsets of users—the technology savvy and generation Y—but as blogs have grown in ease of use and popularity, so too have the types of people who have a blog and the ways they are put to use.

With publishing platforms such as Blogger.com, MoveableType.com, and Word-press.com, making it easy for everyone to set up their own web logs within minutes and start publishing their inner monologue to the masses, it's no surprise that the practical uses of blogs have spread to just about any topic you can imagine. It's this easy access to virtually idiot-proof web publishing that has empowered many consumers to speak up and share their opinions on just about every topic imaginable. No wonder, then, that blogs are often one of the most critical channels of communication for corporations to monitor. In addition, many companies realize the benefits of implementing a corporate blog as part of their efforts to be radically transparent.

In Chapter 9, we'll explain how you can wield the power of a blog to help you become radically transparent and, in Chapters 12 and 13, we'll also show you how to track and listen to blogs that might have an impact on your brand. For now, the importance of blogging to your company's online reputation can be summed up like this: Jeff Jarvis published his Dell Hell rant on a blog. Enough said.

Search Engines Became Reputation Engines

With billions of pages of content floating around the Web, users have come to rely on Google to help them discover the hidden nuggets of information, to help them separate the digital wheat from the cyber chaff. The technology Google uses to complete this task is what enabled it to become so successful and dominate other, once-popular search engines such as Yahoo!, Microsoft, and AOL. While Google's algorithm uses a secret list of more than two hundred variables, its success is a result of its proprietary PageRank scoring system for links. Effectively, Google analyzes the number and quality of links that point to any given web page, compares them to other web pages on the same topic, and decides, within a split second, the order in which web pages should be displayed for any given search term.

Google is more than just a search engine—it's a reputation engine. Each link a web page receives is like a virtual vote being cast by other web pages. The more quality links from web pages that reside in a similar theme neighborhood (see the sidebar "Theme Neighborhoods"), the greater the chance a web page has to show up in the first 10 or 20 listings for a particular search query. And, as search engine users, we tend to place our trust in the results we receive from Google—which is partly the reason for its huge success—believing that whichever pages happen to show up at the top of the list must be the most relevant, most popular ones for the entered search query.

In his book *The Wisdom of Crowds*, author James Surowiecki explains our trust in Google, suggesting the "idea of 'social proof,' which is the tendency to assume that if lots of people are doing something or believe something, there must be a good reason why."

Defining Moment: Theme Neighborhoods

What do we mean by *theme neighborhoods*? If your business is selling blue widgets, Google needs to determine that your website deserves to be on the first page for a user's search for "blue widgets." One of the ways it does this is to look at the other web pages that have linked to you. Links to your site from other widget sites helps assure Google that your business is about widgets. If those other sites also use "blue widget" in the text they use to link to you, and the link comes from their "blue widget" page, your chances of ranking well in Google just went up further. Jeff Jarvis's blog shows up so prominently on Google for the phrase "dell hell" because many other sites discussed the topic and linked back to Jarvis's blog.

It's this blind trust in Google's ability to find the most relevant search results that allows us to often find contentment in the first page of suggested links presented. For this same reason, when we enter a company brand, product model, executive's name, or even just the name of our next date, we tend to base our opinions around what we discover. If what we observe in the first one or two pages of search results is all positive, chances are that will influence us enough to form an equally positive opinion of that company or person. At the same time, if these search results happen to include negative sentiment—say, a blogger's rant about a faulty computer—any positive perception will be severely diminished. In Chapter 6 we'll further explore how perception of any brand—whether corporate or personal—can be influenced by what shows up in search engine results, and we'll demonstrate tactics you can use to exert some influence over what is displayed.

A New Forum for Online Discussions

Perhaps the most mature online medium for exchanging opinions is the humble forum. A forum, also called a message board, describes a place where two or more people gather to exchange opinions, news, and comments in a threaded conversation about a topic of interest. Unlike blogs, where one voice (the blogger's) tends to have a monopoly over others' (those who leave comments), forum users share an almost equal voice with one another, starting many threads (topical conversations) that can lead to dozens and dozens of replies.

There are millions of forums on the Web, some of them dating back to 1981, and others with tens of thousands of members among their ranks. With forums often arranged around a niche topic (a certain stock, software development, the pharmaceutical industry, iPods, *Star Wars*, frequent fliers, and so on), forums grow thanks to the passion of their users and are only sometimes policed by moderators, who are often the forum's owners or those that have been members for a long time. Consequently, a popular forum can have dozens of active threads on any given day, with little restriction on the creation of new threads by its members.

With so many conversations, often happening in almost real time, forums can be both an engaging place for a company's customers to exchange opinions or ask questions *and* a nightmare to monitor and keep track of each individual conversation. On any given day, a forum could have dozens of topic threads, each with more than 100 points of view, added to the mix.

> ### Thought Byte: Find Your Customers' Favorite Forums
>
> Do you know the popular forums for your industry? Now is a good time to start thinking about which forums might be popular among your customers. If you don't already know which forums are important to your business, head to your favorite search engine and search for generic words for your industry, followed by the words "forum" or "message board"—for example, "widget forum."

Forums are both a blessing and a curse to any company looking to monitor, manage, and engage its customers. Packed with a wealth of useful information that a company could use to gather essential feedback, forums are also hangouts for consumers, customers, and even your competitors looking to attack, critique, and spread rumors about your business. Throw into the mix the difficulty in monitoring forum threads and the ability of users to hide their real identity behind that of a made-up persona or avatar, and you'll understand why forums are an important yet difficult medium for any business to engage.

Social Networks Connect Your Customers

Poll anyone between the ages of 13 and 30, and chances are the majority of the respondents will have at least one membership or profile on a social network site. Whether it's a MySpace.com account—where teens and twenty-somethings create their own personal web experience, enabling them to share their thoughts, photos, and videos with a network of friends—or a profile on YouTube—so people can upload their favorite video content (which often includes copyrighted works), share videos with others, and view videos uploaded by other members—chances are high that at least half the people you speak to are involved in some kind of online social networking experience.

Don't assume, though, that those over the age of 30 are not involved in some kind of online networking either. Sharing book reviews on Amazon.com, posting photos of grandchildren to Flickr.com, business networking on LinkedIn.com, or leaving feedback about a product purchase at Epinions.com are activities that spread across every age group. In fact, from sharing a favorite news story on Digg.com, to answering the question posed by a user on Yahoo!'s Answers service, to travelers leaving a review of a hotel on TripAdvisor, no other medium for sharing views, opinion, feedback, praise, or criticism is as pervasive as that of social networks. In Chapter 10, we'll further explore the importance of social networks and explore how you can leverage them as part of being radically transparent.

Growing Your Business the Radically Transparent Way

As you can see from the sample of online channels we just discussed, managing your corporate brand is no longer a simple act of employing talented public relations professionals to carefully craft sound bites for your next press release. Nor is it sufficient to merely train your employees and executives on the best way to conduct themselves should they happen to speak to a journalist from the local newspaper or find a CNN video camera squarely in their face. Useful feedback about your products or attacks on your company's credibility can come from a multitude of different internet channels. In addition, the voices behind those "rants and raves" can originate from more than just a handful of internet-savvy consumers who just love to be the center of attention.

Becoming radically transparent is no simple task. It involves shedding your corporate sound bites and learning to speak with honesty. It requires a desire to listen to customers and act on both their praise and their criticism. Most of all, being radically transparent takes sincerity. Is it hard work? It doesn't have to be. Many companies have successfully become radically transparent, while others have struggled. Yet those that have realized the potential that comes from a new way of communicating with customers have discovered hidden strengths and a wealth of market research that was previously untapped. They've discovered that listening to their customers, learning from their conversations, and acting on their feedback is about more than just fighting reputation fires. Sure, you can do a lot to protect your business, but there are fantastic opportunities you'll discover with your new approach to customer engagement.

As Dell ultimately learned, by listening to your customers, clients, employees, and stakeholders, your business will ultimately become stronger. You'll tap into a wealth of information that was previously hidden from you—whether it's discovering your recent press conference was particularly well received by investors, or your new product launch appears to be going well but consumers would really prefer to have feature X or option Y, or perhaps learning that your competitor's clients are really unhappy with the new price hikes and are looking around for an alternative vendor... By listening to and engaging in online conversations, your business can benefit incredibly. As Levine so succinctly describes in *The Cluetrain Manifesto*, these conversations are going on, with or without you:

> **❝ Online markets will talk about companies whether companies like it or not. People will say whatever they like, without caring whether they're overheard or quoted—in fact, having one's views passed along is usually the whole point. Companies can't stop customers from speaking up, and can't stop employees from talking to customers. ❞**

It's time to grab that empty glass, place the open end to the wall of cyberspace, and put your corporate ear to the other. There's a lot to be learned from those who care enough to talk about your brand. They're having their conversations, assuming that no one is listening, expecting to only hear from a company via a corporate spokesperson or some template email announcement. They're not expecting you to be listening, and they certainly don't expect you to join in with their conversation. Yet they're crying out to be acknowledged and they're desperate to hear from someone that speaks their language. Listen to them, learn from them, talk to them, and then show them that you care about their feedback. In return, they'll become your biggest asset, they'll be more trusting toward you, and they'll be less inclined to go on the attack. Your business will grow, your customers will be happy, and you may just avoid your own Dell Hell.

Developing Your Personal Brand

Individual director, CEO, and employee reputations are key components of company and brand reputations. The careers of entrepreneurs and professionals live or die based on their contacts and reputations. On a personal level, individuals barter their reputations when in the job market or when trying to achieve personal goals. The internet adds another layer of complexity to individual reputation-building, especially because it is difficult to know how much of your personal life to reveal online. However, there are first-mover advantages for those individuals who act now, using the internet to increase their connections with relationship-enhancing content.

3

Chapter Contents

From Geek to Web Super Star

His business card reads, "1. Go to Google. 2. Type 'Matt.' 3. Click 'I feel lucky.'" Matt Mullenweg, WordPress blog platform creator, is the #1 Matt in the world, according to Google. Follow the card's instructions and you'll learn everything about Matt, from his next speaking engagement to his last trip with his girlfriend. You'll find his philosophy on open source software, his interest in jazz, nearly 15,000 photos, and his tangle with the citizen journalists when he was exposed for using search engine spamming to reach the #1 spot (a mistake he quickly corrected). According to Matt, "the more you put out there about yourself, the more you're controlling your online persona, rather than letting other people control it." Matt is a well-respected, well-known online star through his own device—all at the ripe old age of 22 (see Figure 3.1).

Figure 3.1 #1 Matt in the world

Your Personal Reputation

Matt Mullenweg, Charles Schwab, and Michael Dell are brand names, carefully crafting offline and online reputations to achieve their career goals. Personal branding is a skill long-used successfully by CEOs (Richard Branson and Donald Trump), professionals (Kenneth Starr and Dr. Deepak Chopra), authors (Tom Peters), athletes (David Beckham and Tiger Woods), celebrities (Oprah Winfrey and Sean (Diddy) Combs), religious leaders (Rick Warren and T.D. Jakes), and others. These people know how to use public relations to gain media coverage and create a buzz, and how to respond to negative publicity. They know that their images and reputations come from personal communications and activities, interactions with other individuals, and conversations among the public—much as do company and product brand reputations.

These celebrity people brands continually shape their public personae to desired ends and become more famous, powerful, and profitable in the process. However, internet chatter added another layer of complexity, making celebrity reputations a lot harder to manage. The traditional media sometimes pick up citizen journalist ramblings and photos, causing celebrity online reputations to bleed into their offline reputations. According to Jeff Chester, executive director of the Center for Digital Democracy, "…a new digital puritanism is arising… even a relatively innocent remark or situation online can backfire and ruin someone's entire career."

The internet also leveled the playing field, creating exciting opportunities for the relatively unknown. Thanks to skillful use of the internet for reputation building, regular people like Matt Mullenweg can become well-known people brands without a crew of PR and other consultants.

Believe it or not, you already have a brand reputation in your personal and professional networks. Just ask a friend or colleague if you are trustworthy and have the integrity to follow through on your promises. Ask them to identify your distinctive competencies at work or in your personal activities. Just as brands attempt to meet customer needs, individuals meet relational needs—for example, we count on the salesperson to be honest and ensure that our order is delivered as promised. We want our advisors, medical professionals, and others to solve our problems honestly and competently. However, in relationships the heart rules, not the mind. Given equal competencies and price, we go for the person we like.

The internet's social media provide a perfect stage for connections and trust—key ingredients of an individual's reputation. If you learn how to play on this stage, you can be rewarded with more money, power, fame, or connections. Professionals just like you gain new jobs from their LinkedIn contacts (professional online network), increase client numbers, receive collaboration offers from unexpected places, and become well-known experts—getting them speaking and writing invitations. This chapter will help you to understand how to create your personal brand as a springboard for building it into a stellar reputation online.

We Are Talking About You

Reputation management is not just for the rich and the famous. Your personal image is a part of the company's overall reputation if you are an owner, director, CEO, or any customer-facing employee. To test this idea, just think of the last time you thought about closing your account because of how the customer service rep on the phone treated or misled you. As you hung up, you might have thought that a company allowing its reps to give you bad information is not trustworthy. Or suppose there is a restaurant you always frequent because you trust and like your favorite waiter. This restaurant has a great reputation in your mind, and you tell your friends and associates about it. "Reputation influences all the goals a company can set—obtaining a higher stock multiple, generating higher profit margins, attracting and retaining the best employees, finding strong business partners, and capturing both the attention and loyalty of customers," according to the folks at PR firm Fleishman-Hillard. Employee communications and subsequent reputations are a part of this overall picture.

Your individual reputation is also critical if you are upwardly mobile or looking for a new job. It affects just about any goal you desire. Just ask the 2007 Miss U.S.A. contestant, Katie Rees, about her dethronement after racy photos of her were found online. Whether you're a college student yet to make your way in the corporate world or a high-flying executive of a Fortune 500 company, what you say and how you act online affects your personal reputation in career-enhancing or -detracting ways. Next we'll highlight just a few of the individual roles strongly affected by their online reputations.

The CEO

Consider the fine reputations of Michael Dell and Richard Branson and their impact on their companies' reputations. When Doug Parker, CEO of US Airways, was arrested for drunk driving in January 2007, he responded in a written statement: "In this instance, my actions have not reflected well on US Airways and for that, I apologize." Parker was concerned about how his mistake might affect the company's reputation—especially in an industry where drinking and driving airplanes is a bad thing. The story was picked up by bloggers and the online reputation-damaging chatter commenced. His Wikipedia entry mentions his other DUI offenses and Topix.net critics were brutal: "He lied to police: 'I only had three beers...' What do you think he does to his employees?"

Research shows that CEO and corporate reputations are closely linked. This is partly because of the CEO's high profile and role as company spokesperson. A survey by PR firm Burson-Marsteller found that when CEO reputations are favorable, over 90% of decision makers are more likely to purchase the company's stock, believe the company when under media attack, and recommend the company as a good business partner. The decision makers in this study included other CEOs, senior business executives, financial analysts and investors, government officials, and business media stakeholders. Interestingly, the same research found that nearly 80% of CEOs pay a good deal of attention to their reputations. We wonder how much of this attention is paid to the online environment.

What builds CEO reputation? Credibility, a code of ethics, appropriate communication, motivating employees, and attracting a management team, according to Leslie Gaines-Ross's book, *CEO Capital*. These are CEO "characteristics," critical to a good reputation, but remember that reputation is based on perceptions. CEOs and their PR people must now focus on the social media conversations that can make or break their reputations and affect the company as well.

> **Thought Byte: Admirable Online Reputations**
>
> Think about your CEO, colleagues, and competitors. When you check out their online pages, bios, and other material, does it generate trust and respect? Which among them do you admire most, and is this reflected on the internet?

The Politician

People love to discuss politicians at all levels of government, and the internet is a perfect venue for it, underlining the need for political candidates and incumbents to manage their reputations online. California's Governor Arnold Schwarzenegger and former Vice President Al Gore successfully positioned themselves as champions for environmental issues, and the citizen journalists are yakking about it. Bloggers discuss the governor's record and compare it to his words, and while most are positive about the "Jolly Green Governor," at least one blogger calls him "the Fake Environmental Hero."

Online sentiment about political candidates can affect election results—remember Senator John McCain's legendary temper in the 2000 presidential campaign? We can still read about it online. Moving forward to the 2008 presidential campaign, a Marketing Pilgrim study conducted in June 2007 showed that 15 of the 18 declared 2008 presidential candidates had negative search engine result listings associated with their names. The study examined the first 20 search results for each candidate's name to determine the number of pages with positive, negative, or neutral sentiment. Interestingly, only Barack Obama achieved zero negative sentiment results, and Republican Ron Paul had a 70% positive sentiment score. We'll show you how to do this kind of analysis for your personal reputation in Chapter 13.

Understanding the internet's power to reach voters, both Senators Hillary Clinton and Barack Obama posted online videos announcing their exploratory committees for the 2008 U.S. presidential elections. Unlike Clinton's video, however, Obama's included the technology to allow posting on blogs and other sites, thus encouraging more viral viewing and capitalizing on social media.

Now hip to the role of social media, all major candidates have posted numerous videos on YouTube. We wonder how they are managing their reputations in light of the thousands of unfavorable video reviews, however, with people critiquing everything from their platforms to their records and hairstyles. In addition, the candidates must monitor user video postings. How can Rudy Giuliani respond in a reputation-building way to his YouTube video showing him dressed in drag and being kissed by Donald Trump? And what about the two-minute video of John Edwards fixing his hair, critiqued by nearly 750,000 viewers, many of whom mention his $400 haircuts? Cleverly, Edwards responded with another YouTube video that demonstrated the relative importance of haircuts versus the war in Iraq.

The Professional

The careers of health workers, attorneys, architects, and other professionals live and die on their reputations. Local search sites and specific rating sites, such as RateMDs.com, allow customers to evaluate local professionals, and ZoomInfo builds profiles based on what their automated search robots find online, leaving it to the profile owner to later submit any updates or corrections.

Dr. Katrina Tang, a homeopathic practitioner, had a patient complaint in 2000 that resulted in many negative document postings and online discussion from the complainer over a several-year period. She had to close her practice due to client loss and continual harassment—much of it online—before the medical malpractice hearing even took place to establish her innocence or guilt. Dr. Tang's ZoomInfo profile currently includes 14 listings, some of which include the full text of the old Board of Homeopathic Medical Examiners hearings about the complaint. Dr. Tang had plenty of time to present her side of the story and build a positive reputation online that might have saved her business. However, medical practitioners do not normally have access to these skills. This is a sad story because the suit against Dr. Tang was eventually dismissed due to unsubstantiated claims.

Students are brutally honest at RateMyProfessors.com: "This guy is a jerk. He is arrogant and condescending," according to one of several anonymous student posts regarding one university professor. A search for author and speaker Tom Peters at

ZoomInfo revealed 772 different online website sources to generate his automated profile. He may not appreciate the first sentence on the first listing being a quote from an old 2003 article: "On the 20th anniversary of *In Search of Excellence,* Peters admits, 'I had no idea what I was doing when I wrote *Search.*'" Conversely, his honest and radically transparent comment fits well in social media environment

At ZoomInfo.com, you can create your own web profile to control your identity—probably worth a few minutes of time. We'll show you how to manage all your network profiles in Chapter 10.

Savvy professionals realize that a lack of an online presence is a great opportunity to set the tone for a stellar online reputation. Brett Trout, an Iowa patent attorney, is a good example. He started Iowa's First Law Blog in 2003 (*blawg IT* at blog.bretttrout.com/), which was a finalist in the 2006 Weblog Awards. Trout also maintains his firm's website (BrettTrout.com). He has a LinkedIn profile, is a member of the investment community's Go BIG Network, and has articles, a podcast interview, blog posts, and references to his speeches and book—lots of reputation-building content scattered around the internet. He is no slouch at search engine optimization: when searching for him on Google, links to his work completely fill the first two pages of results. All this has brought him many new clients outside of his local area.

> **Thought Byte: Your Professional Online Reputation**
>
> Check yourself out on Google and ZoomInfo. Do you find anything troubling? If you do, skip to chapters 10 (social networks), 13 (reputation monitoring) and 14 (reputation repair) and learn how to make changes.

The Salesperson

Think about the last interaction you had with a sales rep—did it leave a favorable or unfavorable impression about the salesperson and the firm? Studies show that 85% of a company's brand image is driven by sales interactions, not marketing campaigns, according to Jeff Summers, former General Manager of the Siebel Sales Product Group, a customer relationship management (CRM) software company. This is certainly true in the business-to-business (B2B) market. Salespeople rely on connections and contacts, so what better place than the internet's social networking sites to build these?

Sales professionals have always known that trust is a key component in long-term customer relationships. For example, one of the Avon Products, Inc. Las Vegas reps, Birdie Jaworski, wrote a blog titled *Beauty Dish* that included trashing Avon products she doesn't like: "I don't know how I'm going to get through a two-week trial [of an anti-aging cream]! This stuff is giving me whopper zits!!!!!" See an example of her honest product ratings from her blog in Figure 3.2. Birdie scores high on the trust scale. This authenticity got her coverage in the *The Wall Street Journal*, *Time* magazine, and *The New York Times*.

In Jaworski's online letter explaining her June 2007 decision to move from Avon to bigger and better things, she writes: "I liked being a lone beacon, someone who blogged the sorry damn truth about every product—the great ones, the ones that should have never seen the light of day." She estimates that her blog brought 600 new sales reps to Avon, and she has the e-mails and "downstream earnings" to prove it. One of her reasons for quitting was that she was never recognized by Avon for the publicity and her estimated million-dollar contribution to the company via her blog.

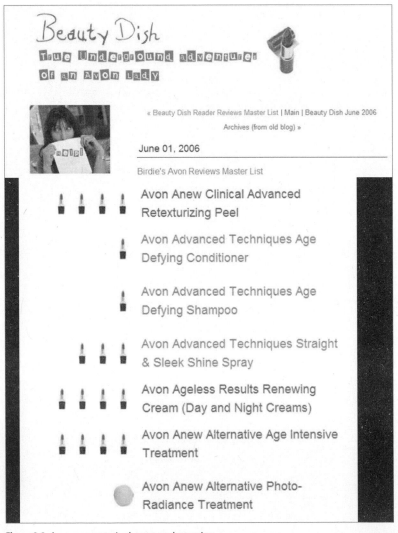

Figure 3.2 Avon representative honest product review

The Upwardly Mobile and Recent Graduate

Looking for a job? Your online reputation matters. Recruiters didn't hire between 35% and 51% of job candidates they checked out online, according to studies done by executive recruiting network ExecuNet Inc. and online job site CareerBuilder. Stories abound about MySpace and FaceBook pages that took candidates out of the job pool. But it gets much deeper than that. Tien Nguyen, a UCLA senior, wasn't getting many interviews until he removed a satirical essay he'd posted online, "Lying Your Way to the Top." He immediately got several job offers, according to *The New York Times*.

Stacy Snyder was close to graduating from Millersville University when administrators found a photo of her with drink in hand on her MySpace page. The photo was titled "drunken pirate," and even though she was above age, they accused her of promoting underage drinking and barred her from receiving her education degree (giving her an English degree instead).

Beyond removing negative impressions, recent graduates and professionals alike now see that they can present themselves online in an attractive way for recruiters. The internet is an exciting online resume for these candidates—one that can differentiate their brand from competitors. James Wieland, a thirty-something meteorologist, posted a short video on YouTube showing him giving a weather report. He added music and the comment, "Looking for Personality?" and sent the link to news directors. He currently works as a meteorologist at West Palm Beach, Florida's WPTV NewsChannel 5. In another success story, Catherine Germann was contacted in 2005 by a job recruiter after he saw her personal website and noted a mutual friend. Her personal website was squeaky clean and ready for job recruiters.

Recruiters evaluate job pool candidates online for good communication skills, a professional image, whether they seem to be a good fit for the company culture, and to validate their resume claims. Did you ever stop to think that a recruiter might be able to verify your role on a particular project by searching your current company website? And don't forget—everything is cached on Google forever.

You

Don't identify with the previous roles? Your online reputation is still important because it can affect your personal and professional goals. Anyone can be built up or destroyed in social media. Some NASCAR drivers use BuzzManager to follow user-generated content on message boards, sports blogs, YouTube, podcasts, and elsewhere. This firm compiles a Buzz Rating score, from 1 to 10, to let the drivers and other sports figure clients know how well they are connecting with fans on a daily basis.

Now for the absurd, but potentially important: if you are single, you can count on your new date checking you out at Google, Facebook, and other social media sites. What they find may reveal common interests that spark the union, even though they can't reveal in person that they snooped and know all this about you. Like job recruiters, singles also sometimes find fetishes that turn them off. Any socially rude behavior might appear pictured online. RudePeople.com, Flickr, and YouTube often contain documented complaints by citizen journalists and the people paparazzi. There are many other places that catalog perceived offenses:

- Bad driving? Look for your license plate on PlateWire.com or BadDriving.com.

- Poor parking job? Watch Caughtya.org, or look for Flickr photos with tags such as "ycantpark."

- Don't pick up your dog droppings? You can find videos of this offense at YouTube and photos of the crime scene at Flickr.

- Littering? Check out LitterButt.com. This site doesn't post photos, but will send complaint letters to the government of the state where the offense occurred.

Don't forget about your activities at eBay or reviews on Epinions.com and Amazon.com. These sites allow user ratings of sellers and reviewers. Prolific and influential book reviewer Harriet Klausner has posted over 14,000 book reviews at Amazon.com. This feat generated very positive articles about her in *Time* magazine, *Wired*, and OpinionJournal.com. We'll discuss how your online activities can influence your online reputation in Chapter 11.

The point is, your online reputation is vital to your success, regardless of your profession.

Online Content Is King and Contacts Are Queen

Americans search online for information about colleagues, customers, and employees. Hiring managers investigate potential employees online. We frequently check someone out online after a meeting, and we bet you do too. You've probably done an "ego search" at Google and smiled at your fame, but did you dig deeply to see if the information buried in those links was accurate, up-to-date, or consistent with the image you want to present?

Defining Moment: Ego Search

An ego search is the practice of searching for one's own name, nickname, or screen name, using any search engine, to see what articles or images appear online. Ego searching is also called ego surfing, vanity surfing, or simply Googling yourself, and is what is quickly turning Google from search engine into a "reputation engine."

We all want to do business with companies and people that we trust. While content is all important online, relationship trust depends on connection with others. Paralleling offline networks, we build trust online through the associations with others in our social media networks, and the conversations and content we share with those connections. It is a dialogue, not a monologue, as we've said before. This is a common theme for online reputation management—refer to the social media discussions in Chapters 1 and 2.

Individuals use different tools online than offline for building individual reputations—everything from the way you write e-mail to the white papers you author on your company site. Even your choice of communication method makes a difference. Do you use text messaging for immediate communication from a cell phone, instant messaging to call a meeting, or e-mail from a cutting-edge PDA? Or do you take a couple of days to respond to your e-mails and prefer the telephone for communication? We'll discuss these choices in Chapter 8 and how they affect your reputation.

Thought Byte: Your Contacts

Your Rolodex or PDA contact lists contain relationships critical to your professional success. They also contain contact information for your friends and family. How could you replicate these networks and continue to build them online?

Define or Be Defined

Do you want to present your best self online, or do you want the social computing community to do it for you? Beyond the big three search engines (Google, Yahoo!, and MSN), you need to know where to look for content about you, and what to do with it when you find it—before your important stakeholders form an image of you that may not be career enhancing. If there is a blank slate, people will write on it, and you want to be the one who tells the story of who you are. "You're going to define yourself or your audience will define you," according to Rob Key, CEO of Converseon, an internet marketing communications agency.

When Matt Mullenweg's search spam story broke, he was vacationing in Venice, Italy. His sister read him the story via telephone and he walked around the city for 30 minutes trying to find a Wi-Fi connection. Eventually he had to take a boat to the airport to connect and respond with his perspective on the situation before the chatter got out of hand. Matt recognized that maintaining his good reputation is worth a lot of effort. We are all invisible due to the internet, and need to be constantly vigilant to maintain our online reputations. "You cannot communicate your way out of reality," according to Leslie Gaines-Ross, chief reputation strategist at PR firm Weber Shandwick. But you can certainly provide your perspective on the situation.

Of course, for the relatively unknown, this is a terrific opportunity. If you are starting from scratch, you can present yourself as you wish, before someone else depicts their version of you. If Matt can become an online brand star at 22, you can definitely do it too. Start now before the inevitable happens, and the citizen journalists build it for you. If you've been transparent online for some time, you have the opportunity to create the reputation you want right now by repairing or burying the negative and crafting your appearance on page one of Google, and elsewhere.

> **Thought Byte: What's Your Online Reputation Status?**
>
> **A.** I'm a blank slate online.
>
> **B.** There are a few things online about me, mostly informational.
>
> **C.** There are some positive and negative things online about me.
>
> **D.** There is so much online about me that I don't know how to get a handle on it.
>
> If your answer is A or B: you can still define yourself online. C and D: you are already defined online.

Online Reputation Management Is a Core Life Skill

Companies know about the convergence of online and offline communications platforms. They present their brands in both traditional and new media, using many techniques for managing their reputations. The same prescription applies for individual reputation management. For example, the Forbes Magazine Celebrity 100 list uses both the Web and traditional media to rank contenders (along with income).

This social media world is a bit different and more complex, however, and begs new techniques, as we've already mentioned. "Managing your personal online reputation will be a core life skill," according to Spannerworks blogger Antony Mayfield. One mistake can keep you from your goals; for instance, Mike Klander, former V.P. of Canada's Liberal Party, had to resign after posting photos of Toronto New Democratic Party candidate Olivia Chow and comparing her to a Chow Chow dog with the caption "Separated at Birth." The moral to this story: watch what you say about others, as well.

As Matt Mullenweg discovered, the worst thing in his life happened on his first-ever vacation, when he was away from the internet. We live in an always-on world that requires constant monitoring to control our online reputations. Matt already had a strong and positive online reputation, and that helped him weather this storm. He also had a system in place to monitor the internet while away—his family. In Part 2 of this book, we'll help you build these new life skills to become a stellar personal brand online.

Individual Branding Basics

Famous individuals use the same basic branding principles applied by Coca-Cola, Google, and other well-known corporate brands: namely, identifying your competitive strengths and communicating them to desired audiences. This involves a lot of research, planning, communication tactics, feedback metrics, and continual revision. It is a systematic process, and thus, the techniques we describe in this book apply equally to companies and individuals seeking star reputation status online.

Every individual already has a brand reputation, but most have neither managed it nor built it using branding principles. Well-known individual brands sometimes find fame by chance, but they soon learn that brand reputation sustainability takes the same kind of effort used by product brand managers. Just ask any sports figure or celebrity, such as Britney Spears, or political candidate, such as Rudy Giuliani. Famous individual brands retain a stable of consultants to help with both their personal appearance and press coverage: press agents, speechwriters, event managers, handlers, PR firms, coaches, fashion consultants, nutritionists, lifestyle designers. Conversely, you probably only rely on yourself—fortunately the internet provides easy and automated opportunities for managing and monitoring your reputation.

Before starting, however, you need to know who you are as a brand. Which stakeholders matter to you, what benefits do you deliver to them, and what are you trying to accomplish with your personal brand? Many books will help you to build a unique brand position offline, so we just touch on the key points here.

Thought Byte: Your Personal Brand

What problems does your brand solve for the people with whom you interact? When people want advice about something, which questions drive them to seek yours? Maybe you are the one who solves computer issues for colleagues, or maybe you recommend great suppliers. Perhaps you are a leading attorney, marketing innovator or financial analyst.

Stakeholders

Who are the stakeholders you want to influence? An individual's stakeholders are people who share their values in their personal lives, or who depend on the quality of their work in their professional lives. You'll have groups that you influence and other groups that affect your career and quality of life. One place to start is listing all the roles you play, both personal (e.g., mother, friend, president of the PTA) and professional (author, consultant, customer, employer, marketing director). Then think of the audiences for each role. It is important to include both professional and personal stakeholders because online the two blend in ways that can increase your authenticity. That is, if you can reveal some of your personal interests online, it will build relationships among professional stakeholders. This is a well-known truth among professional salespeople offline. Conversely, if you don't reveal some of this yourself, the citizen journalists might do it for you. For instance, one of our colleagues was recently listed online as a dance instructor at a nudist gathering.

CEO Capital presented a CEO stakeholder chart, which we adapted and extended to personal stakeholders in Figure 3.3. The goals with this stakeholder identification exercise are to know in which groups your reputation matters, and then to start thinking of all your audiences in a 360-degree view. You are doing it now in an informal way by watching how much you reveal at work and being careful not to talk about work all the time among your family. Make this formal before considering your online reputation.

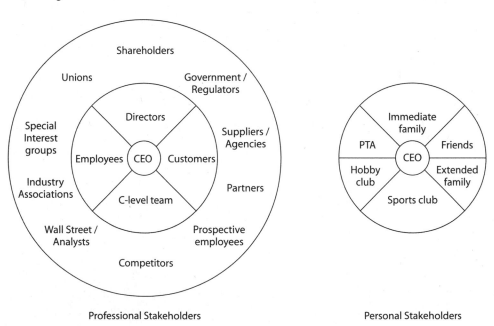

Figure 3.3 CEO stakeholders

Who Do You Think You Are?

The Forbes Celebrity 100 pegs individuals according to a survey of 46 different personality characteristics: Donald Trump, at position 12, is perceived as aggressive and confident, while author Dan Brown (ranked 10th) is intelligent and talented. Who are you and how do you want to be perceived among your stakeholders? Some things to consider:

Values What are your enduring values? Consider traits such as being honest, authentic, achievement oriented, religious, financially conservative, adventurous, or creative. See David McNally and Karl Speak's book, *Be Your Own Brand*, for an individual brand values inventory questionnaire.

Personality Are you laid back, aggressive, energetic, collaborative, analytical, generous, inquisitive, critical, or passive? Inventories such as the Myers-Briggs Type Indicator (MBTI) can help (e.g., it measures introversion and extroversion).

Competencies Are you a great writer, speaker, leader, or salesperson?

Knowledge niche Where does your expertise lie: fast-food industry operations management, patent law (e.g., previously mentioned professional Brett Trout), or politics?

Activities and interests Do you adore golf or other sports? Do you travel, cook, garden, blog, or paint?

The point of all this introspection is to 1) discover personal interests that you can share online, 2) find a professional knowledge niche, and 3) use these to define a personal brand position that will set you apart from competition in the reputation game.

Steve Jobs, co-founder and CEO of Apple Computer, is described on Wikipedia as a "quirky, individualistic Silicon Valley entrepreneur." He is also "a persuasive and charismatic evangelist for Apple, [with] some of his employees…[describing] him as an erratic and tempestuous manager." We know him as the "comeback kid," returning to Apple after being ousted from his own company at age 30. Wikipedia discusses his personal life as well: his hefty $1.00 a year salary at Apple, his trek around India, his fights with Michael Dell and Bill Gates, his bout with cancer, and his liking both the Beatles and Bach. This honest disclosure endears us to the comeback kid, and above all, we respect his amazing creativity. Without this level of personal disclosure, Jobs's "character flaws" might take center stage and his stakeholders might not be so charmed. Business 2.0 identified his distinct position among individual brands as follows: "Jobs's genius as a designer, product manager, and pitchman is that he's never comfortable unless he's pushing the envelope." Steve's distinctive reputation mark is all over the Apple website and its products.

What is your distinctive position? Get it down to a paragraph and you can use it as a guide to building a stellar online (and offline) reputation. For example, Ben Cohen, co-founder of Ben & Jerry's Ice Cream, is well known for his commitment to socially responsible activities. All his activities, speeches, and work revolve around this clear niche.

Who Are You?

One quick way that marketers learn about brand images is through projective techniques. We ask consumers questions such as the following: If Google were an automobile, which brand and make would it be? Is your attorney like a Porsche? How about your personal brand? Are you the BMW while your nearest competitor is the Volkswagen? Further, if you were a movie star, who would you be? A superhero? These exercises help to define your position among competitors.

Beyond this basic position check, create a personal inventory of your values, personality, professional competencies, knowledge niche, and activities and interests. Build these lists into key components of how you'd like to be perceived. If you keep this in front of you while creating online content, it will guide your reputation building.

What Are Your Goals?

What are your short-, intermediate-, and long-term career goals? If you are running an organization, doing business development, or looking for business partners, online branding is a critical skill that can be used to differentiate yourself from competitors. If your intermediate-term goals include shifting energy toward philanthropy (e.g., Bill Gates) or into a different industry, you can start repositioning your brand online now. Matt Mullenweg told us that he has political aspirations and thinks a lot about how the online rambling about him today might affect him in 20 years. That's something we should all think about—where do we want to be in 20 years, and does our online persona help or hurt us? Virginia Senator George Allen had a lapse when he was caught on camera insulting a young man from the Democratic competitor's campaign and calling him "macaca" (a racial insult against African immigrants). This incident appeared immediately on Wikipedia and elsewhere online for perpetuity, and Allen's subsequent apology does not always accompany it.

Thought Byte: Your Goals

What are your short-, intermediate-, and long-term career goals? Did the information you found on Google and ZoomInfo support them?

Align Your and the Company's Reputations

You are not in this alone, unless you are a one-person company. Corporate, product brand, and employee reputations are interrelated, yet, every employee is likely to have an online presence unmonitored by the corporate communications staff. This communications decentralization began with desktop computing over 25 years ago and is now firmly entrenched with the internet's social media. As mentioned in Chapter 1, some early bloggers were fired for what they wrote about colleagues or products, but now the trend is to create policies that guide employee blogging and to give the employees free expression (see the sidebar "Guidelines for IBM Bloggers: Executive Summary" for IBM's policies).

Guidelines for IBM Bloggers: Executive Summary

- Know and follow IBM's Business Conduct Guidelines.

- Blogs, wikis and other forms of online discourse are individual interactions, not corporate communications. IBMers are personally responsible for their posts. Be mindful that what you write will be public for a long time—protect your privacy.

- Identify yourself—name and, when relevant, role at IBM—when you blog about IBM or IBM-related matters. And write in the first person. You must make it clear that you are speaking for yourself and not on behalf of IBM.

- If you publish a blog or post to a blog and it has something to do with work you do or subjects associated with IBM, use a disclaimer such as this:"The postings on this site are my own and don't necessarily represent IBM's positions, strategies or opinions."

- Respect copyright, fair use and financial disclosure laws.

- Don't provide IBM's or another's confidential or other proprietary information.

- Don't cite or reference clients, partners or suppliers without their approval.

- Respect your audience. Don't use ethnic slurs, personal insults, obscenity, etc., and show proper consideration for others' privacy and for topics that may be considered objectionable or inflammatory—such as politics and religion.

- Find out who else is blogging on the topic, and cite them.

- Don't pick fights, be the first to correct your own mistakes, and don't alter previous posts without indicating that you have done so.

- Try to add value. Provide worthwhile information and perspective.

Note: The full policy is available at:

www-128.ibm.com/developerworks/blogs/dw_blog_comments.jspa?blog= 351&entry=81328

Microsoft was a pioneer by allowing its employees to write blogs with honest information and critiques of company products, yet it was always clear that company secrets were closely guarded. Robert Scoble's *Scobleizer* blog gained a large following, enhanced Microsoft's reputation, and carried the following disclaimer: "Robert Scoble works at Microsoft (title: technical evangelist). Everything here, though, is his personal opinion and is not read or approved before it is posted. No warranties or other guarantees will be offered as to the quality of the opinions or anything else offered here."

Now, back to you. Follow the company's guidelines for all communication online, and don't badmouth the hand that feeds you—unless they invite honest product evaluations. Beyond that, keep your distinctive personal position in mind, and communicate in a way that will help you achieve your goals with all stakeholders. We'll show you how in later chapters.

How Much to Reveal Online?

Trust is a slippery idea, and one way to create it is through authenticity online. "Trust is built faster and maintained longer when people believe you are being real, not putting on a false front to cover up what's really going on inside of you. Authenticity doesn't come easily, however... courage is not in abundant supply in our world," according to McNally and Speak in *Be Your Own Brand*.

Reveal yourself as a real person online. Beyond that, you'll have to make a decision about how much of your personal life to show online: to be minimally or radically transparent (Figure 3.4). It all depends on your current position, future goals, comfort level, and more. We encourage you to push the envelope, however, and go for a level of disclosure that builds relationships and opens doors. Ricky Gervais, English comedy writer and co-creator of *The Office* TV series, did just this when he gathered a couple of friends and created 12 weekly 30-minute podcasts in November 2005. Gervais announced, "I want to do a radio show where I can say what I want, when I want and that's free for anybody who can be bothered to listen." Within two months there were 12 million downloads. Shortly afterward, he created a new series and sold the podcasts online for $1 each. Do and say what you want online and make money in the process.

Matt Mullenweg shares his personal photos and love of jazz online and these things make him more personable and authentic to potential business associates. Robert Scoble is known to drop personal comments such as, "I didn't get to the Under the Wire conference. Sigh. I slept in and missed my plane." This type of self-revealing endears authors to their audience, but where to draw the line? You don't want to reveal so much that your credibility is damaged, you risk losing your job or that your identity is up for grabs. Nonetheless, we live in a transparent world and your personal side will appear online, like it or not, so it might as well come from you.

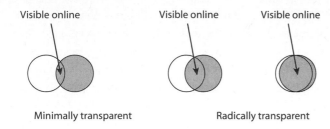

Professional persona

Personal persona

Figure 3.4 Three levels of online transparency

Thought Byte: Personal Transparency Online

How much of your personal life are you comfortable revealing online? Pictures of your children or last vacation? Your personal interests? What else?

The Flip Side

We're sure that about now you are thinking of roadblocks and questions about all this. "Do I really want to spend all this time creating content online and in the meantime expose myself to cyber crooks?" There is definitely risk and potential downside, but we've seen enough success stories, including ours, to believe it is worth your time. See the sidebar "FAQs About Online Reputation Management for Individuals" for frequently asked questions.

FAQs About Online Reputation Management for Individuals

Q. I don't have enough time for this.

A. None of us do, but what is the risk to your career if you don't find the time? Like Matt, someone might spin negative about you and you won't catch it before extensive damage is done. It is also important to realize that you can decide how much to do based on your time, position, career goals, and more. For instance, you can start with simple weekly incoming e-mail Google alerts on your name and adapting your e-mail signature file to reflect your distinctive position. Or you can start a blog, contribute to the company blog, and use search engine optimization tactics that could eventually move you to the #1 position on Google, just like Matt. This book is a cafeteria of tactics, and you can choose more or less based on your individual situation, time allotment, and ambitions.

Continues

FAQs About Online Reputation Management for Individuals *(continued)*

Q. I can't write.

A. We can all learn to write well, but if this doesn't sound like fun, you can still create a desirable online reputation. You can start by researching where you currently stand online, and then use PR tactics to build your image. You can get others to write about you and link to your website, you can post pictures, you can create biographical profiles via cut and paste from your resume, and more. Regardless, we recommend that you work on your writing and use spell and grammar checks if you send e-mail, because this is part of your online image. Not writing well is not a good reason to ignore your online image.

Q. Will I get sued for disclosing things about my friends or talking about other people online?

A. Slander, libel, and other legal considerations apply equally online and offline. Because you are probably not a journalist well versed in copyright or other law, you will have to follow a few simple guidelines and be careful. You can find this information in your legal department or an many online sites, but for now just use the values you grew up with—for example, treat others as you want to be treated and don't swear in a public forum or use disrespectful/derogatory language.

Q. Can I get fired for what I say in my blog or other online places?

A. Yes. Sometimes when people get behind a computer they somehow feel protected and write things that they might not say in-person. To protect yourself, always review your company's blog policy and if your company doesn't have one strongly suggest that they create one. Start small with your online participation, and build more as you feel comfortable, all the while being clear about your employer's guidelines.

Q. If I reveal too much online, I may have my identity stolen or be open to other crimes.

A. Remember the days when nearly everyone said they wouldn't purchase anything online because they were afraid of credit card fraud? We discovered that this crime is more likely offline than online, and the same is true for most other technology crimes. Your open access mailbox outside your home or office is more at risk for identity theft than is your online persona, and anyone can currently spend $9.95 to do a people search and get all kinds of personal information about you—including your maiden name, your children's names and addresses, and the last 20 years of your contact information. We think it is better to be proactive, see what is out there, and manage it yourself—all while being careful. We'll tell you how.

Q. Will I lose my privacy if I do this?

A. You've already lost your privacy due to online people searches, phone books, and last year's office party pictures on Flickr. Or, your name may appear in a lawsuit, a response to your book review on Amazon, or an angry e-mail that got circulated. But don't fret because there are so many pictures and words online that targeting you is like picking you out of a Super Bowl crowd or phone book—highly unlikely. We think it is better to take control by researching what is out there already and shaping it into the image you desire. Besides, if you don't find that unflattering picture online you won't invoke the site's privacy features or ask the author to remove it.

Q. I'll lose control and others will misquote me.

A. If you put a lot of text and images online, you are likely to be quoted out of context, but it will be worse if you don't monitor your online image. This is because the citizen journalists and people paparazzi are always awaiting your next move and will put it online anyway. Matt Mullenweg had more control during his search spam incident because he was monitoring and could post his own perspective on what happened to clear things up. Define or be defined.

Q. There is a big price to pay for being highly visible online—I can't even handle my current e-mail load. How can I do more?

A. Yes, this is a problem. Most of us are overwhelmed with e-mail we get from the company website and more. Matt told us that he gets 5–10 phone calls or e-mails a week from strangers wanting him to help manage their reputations. One woman was crying hysterically because when Googling her name, porn sites came up. Because he authored the WordPress software people think he can control the internet. So, yes, you'll get a lot of contact and you'll have to respond with automated responses or ignore them, but in there will be some gems too—such as the career headhunters, your next big client, or your future spouse.

Q. Are you asking me to market myself like a box of cereal?

A. Yes, we are, but not in a used car salesperson kind of way. As we said before, you are a brand, selling yourself to prospects, recruiters, and more. If celebrities, athletes, and others can do it, you can too. Besides, you market yourself when you make the sales brochure called a resume, and when you sell yourself in a job interview or sell your projects to management. So you might as well admit it and learn some principles that will help you do it simply, effectively, and ethically online.

Become a Radically Transparent Individual

By now you may be thinking that little is known about you online, so why worry about all this? If so, congratulations, because you have the chance to create the online reputation you desire. If you use the techniques in this book, you'll have an online brand reputation that will bring you the right contacts and opportunities to get where you are going, and build your company reputation in the meantime. They will come to you because you will be the first real estate salesperson, attorney, MBA graduate, or entrepreneur in your field in your market area to do this. You will stand apart from the competition with your distinctive positioning online and this can bring you more business, greater income, a better job, power, and fame. "When a person succeeds in sculpting a distinctive brand, that person is well known to the target audience, has long-term staying power in the marketplace, is clearly and meaningfully differentiated from competition, and enjoys a corresponding pay premium for his or her well known-ness," according to Irving Rein, Philip Kotler, Michael Hamlin, and Martin Stoller in *High Visibility*, their book about using marketing and PR to raise professionals to celebrity status.

If Lonelygirl15 can do it, so can you. Known as Bree, the self-described 16-year-old American posted videos of her private thoughts on YouTube and attracted millions of fans. She became a YouTube star and was named number 1 on the Forbes.com Web Celeb 25 list (see sidebar for criteria). However, Bree violated a primary rule of radical transparency: be honest (or be found out). In August 2006, she was exposed as 19-year-old actress Jessica Rose, using scripts for the videos. Interestingly, when the wizard came out from behind the screen, her great acting skills landed her movie deals and a commercial for the United Nations. Because acting was the nature of her game, it added to her commercial value. Not everyone has this luck.

Forbes.com Web Celeb 25 Criteria

The Forbes.com Web Celeb 25 list members receive a score based on Google references, Alexa home page ranking, Technorati ranking, and traditional media mentions, as compiled by Factiva. They got bonus points for publishing video or podcasts online.

Be your authentic self online, and be true to your values and personality. Identify your knowledge competencies and communicate them relentlessly to important stakeholders online. Show you can be trusted by being true to your word. Finally, become radically transparent by revealing your personal side and interests in your online content. If you do this, you will reap great rewards.

Before we show you how to build that reputation online, there is one more important piece in this foundation: stakeholder engagement. When using the social media for reputation-building, it is important to recall that they are full of dialogue, not monologue. Turn the page to learn about the new rules of engagement.

Navigating the New Rules of Engagement

The shift from traditional to social media requires new skills, tools, and an understanding of social media platforms. The purpose for tackling this new challenge is to engage customers and prospects, and to drive the conversation in reputation-enhancing directions. Customer engagement means trusting, listening, and learning from your stakeholder communities, and responding to their comments with quality content in an honest, authentic manner. It also means joining and participating in networks they frequent and having the courage to be radically transparent.

4

Chapter Contents

Pontiac Gets Hip with Social Media
Engaging Customers, One at a Time
Rules of Engagement
Tools for Engagement

Pontiac Gets Hip with Social Media

In early 2006, Pontiac ran a TV spot for its G6 model that demonstrated the brand's many features. At the end, the voice-over in the ad suggested, "Don't take our word for it, Google 'Pontiac' to find out!" A screen shot of Google with "Pontiac" in the search box appeared next. This association with Google announced to the world that Pontiac believed in the power of community: that consumers could research and form their own opinions. Several bloggers did Google "Pontiac" and wrote about the ad and what they found, and Pontiac posted the actual TV commercial on YouTube, allowing it to be published elsewhere.

The General Motors Pontiac brand is all over the internet. In addition to company-sponsored websites, it has a strong following of enthusiasts who post photos and videos on various sites, and take part in conversations on online forums. Google Groups hosts the alt.autos.pontiac forum, and Yahoo! maintains hundreds of Pontiac discussion groups. For the GTO model alone, there are a number of specialty groups such as GTOGeezers (for the "over 30 age group"), GTO ClassicCarClub, GTORestorations, GTOGoldenGateGoats, and by model year: 2004pontiacGTO.

In early 2007, Pontiac got the smart idea of bringing its passionate customers and enthusiasts together into one community destination site: Pontiac Underground (www.pontiacunderground.com). The site's content and tag line, "Where Passion for Pontiac Is Driven by You," exhibit the brand's commitment to citizen-generated, social media. Partnering with Yahoo!, the new site's home page includes lots of social media content (see Figure 4.1):

- Videos and photos posted by Pontiac owners, using Flickr and Yahoo! Video databases.

- Knowledge sharing through the information on Yahoo! Answers and user postings.

- Offline and online connection through aggregation of Pontiac clubs, events, and the hundreds of forums hosted on Yahoo! Groups.

- An official Pontiac blog, "Inside Track," along with accompanying comments from users. The Underground also presents relevant Pontiac links from deli.cio.us.com, the social bookmarking site.

Not stopping there, Pontiac became a full participant in Second Life—the 3D virtual world completely built by its nearly 11 million residents. Humans, posing as avatars, interact and chat at Pontiac's Second Life property, Motorati Life. An accompanying Pontiac-created website announces Second Life events, such the Patriotic Car Show and Contest and an invitation for race car driving avatars to compete in the new Solstice GXP racer—all entrants receive a free virtual GXP auto. In mid-June 2007, Pontiac was the third most visited Second Life property (with over 5,000 visits a week), and a third-party survey sample of Second Life residents showed 44% awareness of the brand's presence in the city.

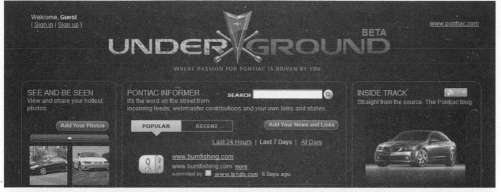

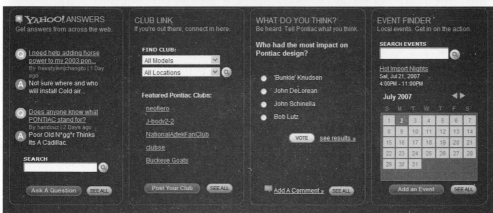

Pontiac Underground, with user-generated videos and forums, along with brand-generated blog and answer database Pontiac's Motorati Life, in Second Life

Pontiac's Motorati Life, in Second Life

Figure 4.1 Pontiac's Social Media Presence

The Pontiac G5 brand allocated all of its budget to online marketing. Its MySpace page, Friends With Benefits, asks G5 owners to register, and promises everyone a $100 Visa gift card once the community reaches 100 people (and $1,000 when it reaches 1,000 registrants). The site had 15,026 linking "friends" in mid-2007.

Pontiac's full immersion in social media serves car buyers well, 94% of whom believe that consumer-generated content helps them decide among vehicles when purchasing a car (according to a J.D. Power and Associates study). Pontiac uses its various web properties to cross-promote, build community, and engage consumers with its brands. It also helps build favorable online reputations for the brands.

Engaging Customers, One at a Time

A couple becomes engaged when their relationship is strong, they trust each other, and they are ready for a long-term commitment. All five senses are affected, they know the strengths and weaknesses of their object of love, and they are fully involved emotionally and cognitively. Every marketer wants her brand to be the love object in this scenario, and customer engagement is one path toward this goal.

Pontiac hooks up its chatty automobile enthusiasts on brand-enhancing web locations and then gets out of the way, providing the context for the brand love magic to happen. Its shift from traditional advertising to social media participation demonstrates many cultural and technological changes we've discussed in previous chapters. Notably, consumers want to hear from other people like them before making buying decisions, and most have access to internet technologies—making information sharing possible on a huge, global scale. Changing media habits, personal digital recorders (such as TiVo), and a trend toward self-initiated product research makes it difficult to hold consumers captive for mass media communication. In this attention economy, the companies that engage stakeholders do well.

There is much debate in the advertising community about this latest buzzword, "engagement." What is it exactly, how do you do it, and importantly, how can you measure its effectiveness? The Advertising Research Foundation (ARF) stepped up to the challenge and held a conference on engagement that resulted in a 22-page document of definitions—as presented by CEOs, advertisers, marketers, consultants, and others.

The ARF concluded with a working definition for both online and offline advertising: "Engagement is turning on a prospect to a brand idea enhanced by the surrounding context." Turning a prospect on includes activating cognitive and emotional associations that create personal relevance and an enduring positive response to the brand. Advertisers stage this engagement within an appealing media context. Reviewing the ARF Engagement Model (see the sidebar, "Defining Moment: ARF Engagement Model") shows the importance of trust in the company, brand, or individual message creator in order for brand impact to occur. Trust will only exist with a positive reputation.

The ARF believes that engagement is beginning to replace the impression advertising model measuring brand awareness and audience numbers. Internet research and audience measurement firm, Nielsen/NetRatings, agrees—it is no longer using page views (number of pages a user views on a website) in favor of the more appropriate measure of time spent on a web page. Length of time is an audience measure that more accurately reflects user time watching videos or contributing material to a website—engagement.

Defining Moment: ARF Engagement Model

The Advertising Research Foundation (ARF) defines engagement as "turning on a prospect to a brand idea enhanced by the surrounding context." As shown here, engagement occurs as the result of an idea and message communicated through the media, such as a website. If the audience trusts the message author, there will be an impact on the brand.

Engagement is related to another marketing concept—experience marketing. Marketers, such as Disney and Pontiac, understand that positive brand experiences will result in positive brand impressions, especially if they engage all five senses: sight, hearing, touch, taste, and smell. Obviously, the online environment can only evoke sight and hearing at the moment, but it is well established that users are more fully attentive when engaged online versus offline (except in controlled offline environments, such as Build-A-Bear). It is also important to note that both environments work in an integrated way to create meaningful brand experiences and subsequent purchases.

The continuing movement of marketing dollars from traditional media to the online environment shows a shift in practice from mass marketing to one-to-one marketing (1:1). Websites full of company-controlled communication enticed more users to the internet, and now the online communities have control and make it their own with the growth of social media. When combined with company-driven customer relationship management practices, this opens a huge opportunity for customer engagement online, as seen with the Pontiac example. Prior to taking the plunge, however, marketers need to understand the rules for customer engagement.

Rules of Engagement

Before reading the ten rules of customer engagement, keep in mind that it is not profitable to attempt engaging every online user, nor is it reasonable to react to every citizen journalist posting in the social media. Richard Sedley, Customer Engagement Director of digital agency cScape, agrees:

> **❝** Customer engagement involves] repeated interactions that strengthen the emotional, psychological or physical investment a customer has in a brand. The key word here is investment. How do we persuade our customers that we are worth their time, effort, money and commitment? We won't be able to engage everyone, and we must accept that those who do engage with us will do so to different degrees and in different ways.
>
> We predict that the process of customer engagement will become one of, if not the, central focus of your digital activities in the coming years. **❞**

Obviously, you'll want to identify key stakeholders for your company or personal reputation management, and determine what proportion of them are active online. Forrester Research suggests six levels of online content engagement from its Social Technographics® research. Forrester proposes that businesses survey their customers to determine the proportion in each segment, thus, learning the best social media for engaging customers and prospects. Following are Forrester's engagement segments, based on extensive survey research and client work:

Creators are the most highly engaged group, representing 13% of online users. Within a month prior to the survey, they had "posted to a blog, updated a web page or uploaded a video that they themselves may have created." Creators are younger and equally divided by male and female users.

Critics are active participants, representing 19% of users. Within a month prior to the survey, they had posted ratings or reviews or commented on blogs. They tend to be older than creators, with 40% also belonging to the creator segment.

Collectors, representing 15% of online users, save things from the Web or create metadata for sharing with their communities. They contribute URLs to social-bookmarking sites, or use RSS feeds. They are more likely to be males.

Joiners represent 19% of users, using social-networking sites or reading blogs. Nearly a third publish their own blogs. This segment includes the youngest users.

Spectators are blog, video, and podcast audience members—the consumers of social media. They represent 33% of all users. More women are in this group, and they tend to have the lowest income levels of all segments.

Inactives are the remaining 52% of online adults who do not participate in social media activities. This segment skews female and their average age is 50.

After understanding your audience, you'll design different levels of engagement depending on your communication goals—such as building or repairing your reputation, or repositioning your image. As well, different situations may require more attention than others. For example, Dell paid much attention to the social media chatter that threatened its customer service reputation (Chapter 2). Conversely, some things become a full-fledged fire when the company puts a magnifying glass on it, and are better ignored. We'll discuss how to tell the difference between these two situations for determining engagement level in Part 3 of the book.

Now, for the basic rules of online engagement with stakeholders of choice in social media. For another perspective, we present the Digital Influence Group's top ten rules in the "Top Ten Tips for Using Social Media" sidebar.

Top Ten Tips for Using Social Media (according to the Digital Influence Group)

1. Educate your organization about what social media is, what the benefits are to the organization, and provide best practices. Don't go it alone.

2. Establish social media marketing governance so that individuals engaging in social media activities clearly understand their roles and responsibilities and the rules of the road.

3. Set clear goals for what the organization wants to achieve using social media.

4. Establish clear metrics to measure the effectiveness of social media in achieving marketing and business goals.

5. When participating in the blogosphere, social networks and online communities, be transparent about who you are, who you represent, and what you are doing.

6. Use plain language, be sincere and candid. Tailor communications according to the interests of the audience. Don't send out generic marketing messages.

7. Provide value-added content and information. Engage and educate. Don't use the hard sell.

8. Welcome feedback, both positive and negative, and respond quickly to it.

9. Participate in other communities as well as build your own. Read and comment on other bloggers' posts and join in the dialogue in the communities.

10. Use rich media (animation, video, audio) and humor to engage audiences.

Source: Digital Influence Group, a social media marketing services company (www.digitalinfluencegroup.com)

1. Trust the Community

Word-of-mouth communication is a critical purchasing decision input for both business-to-business (B2B) and business-to-consumer (B2C) markets. Recall the Edelman Trust Barometer findings—that individuals trust "people like yourself" for credible information—more than they trust businesses or anyone else for that matter, except for doctors. Forrester Research's finding that 90% of consumers trust recommendations from others, while fewer than 10% trust ads, validated this idea.

Companies have asked customers to trust them for decades, and now the tables are turned and companies must show that they trust their stakeholders. If customers and prospects trust each other, then you should trust them too. They are regular people, just like you, with opinions and judgments, sometimes brilliantly insightful and sometimes founded on incomplete information. Whether you do trust them or not, they will continue to talk about you in reputation-enhancing or reputation-detracting ways, so we suggest that you get in the game. Besides, listening with respect will give you interesting and actionable insights about your online reputation.

Wikipedia built its online encyclopedia entirely on user trust. A survey by British science journal *Nature* found that 42 science entries in Wikipedia are "not markedly less accurate" than those in the *Encyclopedia Britannica*. Although errors do occur, the community quickly jumps in to correct them. According to Collin Douma, Group Creative Director at marketing firm MacLaren MRM and author of the *Radical Trust* blog:

> **❝ It has been proven that radically trusting the consumer to operate within fair guidelines produces a better, more informed and loyal customer. Entire codes of conduct, even societal laws are created in these communities (as in any other community) that are not governed by the site administration, but by the people who use it. ❞**

Upside: Many voices add complexity and richness to the company perspective that can result in discovering actionable strategies. Customers want to help themselves to information, saving costs for companies providing it online.

Risks: Rumors can spread like wildfire online. Shared governance with consumers makes it harder to control brand, company, and individual reputations.

2. Join the Networks

In Chapter 3 we noted the importance of professional and personal networks for achieving goals. Business increases when relationships are built on trust and integrity.

We build trust online through the associations with others in our social media networks, and the conversations and content we share with those contacts. This means you need to identify and join networks that include your stakeholders, that are important for your industry, and that align with your goals. Then, of course, you need to participate in these networks if you want the benefits. Pontiac participates in Second Life, MySpace, and the Yahoo! Groups—all centers of influence for its enthusiasts. We'll discuss social networking in more detail in Chapter 10.

A word about the company you keep: your associations are part of your overall reputation. Hang out with the bad kids and it will reflect poorly on you. For instance, when Unilever purchased Ben and Jerry's Homemade Ice Cream, this socially responsible ice cream company came into question by hooking up with a parent company involved in "the largest whale slaughter on the planet," and the bloggers have been quite vocal about it. Also, when Second Life got a reputation hit for an investigation into child abuse images traded by its citizens, it affected all Second Life citizens. Conversely, General Motors claims that "We're touting Google, frankly, because it stands for credibility and consumer empowerment, and we like the association" (according to marketing chief Mark LaNeve).

> **Upside:** Network membership increases potential for business partnerships, referrals, and sales. Connecting with reputable companies can elevate your reputation and brand awareness.

> **Risks:** Network participation can consume much time. Legalized business associations can result in reputation problems if one partner stumbles.

3. Frequent Stakeholder Cyber Hangouts

The "people like me" have regular meeting places online. Pontiac enthusiasts had already formed hundreds of special interest groups at Yahoo!, and all the brand marketers had to do was gather them on a web destination site. Learn where your important stakeholders gather to discuss your industry and products. As mentioned in Chapter 2, this might be special interest forums (e.g., Pontiac), particular blogs, or industry-related social networks, such as an alumni or PR network. Sometimes called "centers of influence," locating these cyber hangouts will help you to observe the discussion and multimedia postings that affect your reputation.

> **Upside:** Cut your reputation management time by finding centers of influence. Identify new target markets.

> **Risks:** Time to find the appropriate properties. The popularity of cyber hangouts can change quickly as new properties are created, so it's important to reassess frequently.

4. Listen and Learn

Marketers have listened to customers via surveys and focus groups for decades, the whole time wondering about the reliability of responses due to a myriad of measurement and sampling errors. Now marketers can listen to the raw and authentic rambling of customers and prospects online, unobserved—not just give lip service to listening, but truly listen and consider the value of these comments. We are not suggesting that you do whatever the citizen journalists say, but that you incorporate the goal-enhancing ideas and respond in a way that shows appreciation and authenticity. Remember, this is a business/customer relationship of trust and loyalty that requires a dialogue, not a monologue.

Pontiac is a good example of how to engage customers within the context of company-driven messaging. PR firm Edelman has called this the social media "sweet spot": the intersection of top-down vertical conversation with customer-driven horizontal conversation. At the sweet spot, companies listen, learn, and use this information to change processes, products, or brand communication. Through this process, the needs and interests of customers and companies become more closely aligned, thus changing the activities of both parties. It is a relationship, after all. Dell experienced this after listening to customers complain about service, making appropriate changes, and communicating them to customers.

> **Upside:** You will learn more about your customers' needs and wants than you imagined possible. You can tackle individual customer problems in real time. You can tap into a huge marketing research resource without spending thousands of dollars to do so.

> **Risks:** You might put too much focus on comments that are not representative of the stakeholder group. It will take time to build a structure for handling so much data.

5. Create Quality Content

Participants need something to say in this social media dialogue online. "Every company needs to think of itself as a media owner or publisher in order to engage with its audience effectively," according to Dave Chaffey, author of nearly 15 books—including the popular *Total E-mail Marketing*. Reputation-enhancing content is relevant and timely, and adds value to the conversation. This content is believable and helpful when it comes from a recognized expert in the field, and in turn it helps the expert build a specialty reputation. Finally, multimedia content that engages the emotions or intellect will more likely attract and keep user attention (sight and sound engages).

Social media content is immediate, requiring instant conversation anytime, anywhere, or from any connected device—as discovered by Matt Mullenweg when he had to respond quickly to allegations of search engine spamming (Chapter 3). Social media contributors deepen the story as new developments occur, constantly building the conversation with frequent updates as needed.

Quality social media content is usually informal because it happens so quickly. The rules of grammar hold to a point, but the goal is to get an informed opinion into the mix while the conversation is hot. Still, informality can go too far—we'll discuss this further in Chapter 8.

> **Upside:** Your reputation as a subject expert will spread and you'll get more business. If your reputation faces a crisis, you'll be given more benefit of the doubt if you've established yourself as a reliable authority.

> **Risks:** Time to generate content or cajole others into it. It is a huge commitment and you must be available 24/7. You must be willing to provide nonbiased contributions to the conversation—otherwise, you run the risk of being labeled as a company flak.

6. Watch Your Voice

Build your reputation by communicating online and offline in one voice—a tried-and-true integrated marketing communication principle. This rule applies to both verbal and visual identities from packaging and logos through brochures and websites. Consistency at all customer touch points means that each blogging employee supports the desired brand and company reputation—even when being critical. In Chapter 3 we presented the story of Birdie Jaworski, the Avon representative who provided brutally honest product reviews. This supported Avon's reputation by showing that customers can trust their reps to sell the best products for their needs. It further helped Avon by showing them which products might be ready for pruning.

In addition, watch your tone of voice. Stay professional, don't overreact, and keep a reputation-enhancing attitude. There is no room for arrogant corporate attitudes or overly defensive responses in the social media, but only honest apologies or presentations of your point of view. When involved in social media conversations, use easily understood language and don't paste company boilerplate into the text. Conversation spin, corporate control, manipulation, and spam are dealt with immediately by the community. Finally, personalize online communications to individuals.

> **Upside:** Your marketing communication will become more effective and efficient. The lack of corporate spin in your messages will keep your stakeholders coming back for more.

Risks: This takes time. If you don't handle customer responses carefully, it will affect your reputation negatively. Push back as much as possible any intervention by your legal or communications department. Remember your internal communication can leak externally, so keep your message consistent to both internal and external audiences.

> ### Thought Byte: Evaluate Your E-Mail
>
> Take a look at a few of your last e-mails to customers. What tone did you use? Were you customer oriented (the "you" viewpoint)? Was there too much corporate spin or was it personalized to the customer and situation? If you were irritated by the original note, was there any arrogant or confrontational attitude in your response?

7. Be Authentic

Truth, honesty, and authenticity are required if you want to have a good reputation online. Authenticity means first, understanding who you are—your values, mission, or character—and second, speaking from these truths. The citizen journalists also require integrity—staying true to your word and keeping promises. JetBlue was criticized online for failing to adhere to every point of its Customer Bill of Rights on every subsequent flight for months. Recall from Chapter 1 that you have to have a trustworthy character first, and hiding your flaws online will only make it worse when the citizen journalists discuss your cover-up all over the Web. When Matt Mullenweg was attacked online for his search engine spamming, he had to jump in quickly to apologize and correct what he called "a mistake."

The Word of Mouth Marketing Association (WOMMA) created an ethics code addressing this, as shown in the sidebar "WOMMA Ethics Code." Also remember that reputation is created within a larger context, and that like reality, you can't communicate a negative reputation association away (i.e., reputations of your country, industry, competitors, and so forth).

Upside: Customers who trust you will be more loyal to your brands than to those of companies that silence customer voices.

Risks: Exposing your flaws opens you to more attacks. Be authentic, but don't try too hard to be a crowd pleaser—you can't please everyone. It's better not to make a promise than to make one and break it.

> **WOMMA Ethics Code**
>
> The Essence of the WOMMA Ethics Code is based on consumer respect and fundamental ethical principles.
>
> The WOMMA **Honesty ROI**:
>
> Honesty of **Relationship:** You say who you're speaking for
>
> Honesty of **Opinion:** You say what you believe
>
> Honesty of **Identity:** You never obscure your identity
>
> Read the entire ethics code at www.womma.org/ethics/

8. Give It Legs

Create content that can easily become viral, thus engaging your stakeholders. This involves creativity, currency, relevance, and technology. Bloggers quickly pick up hot topics, posting their perspectives, and linking back to the source. Consumers quickly pass along interesting content via e-mail. Content designed to travel will have more inbound links, thus increasing relevance and subsequent ranking on search engines (such as Google and Technorati), and will be more highly visible in the social media.

Marketers often create content and hope that it will become viral, but technology can help. Simple social tagging and bookmarking tactics such as adding buttons for "del.icio.us" social bookmarking or "Digg this" for sending a favorite story to Digg.com can help. YouTube offers code that allows users to embed videos in other sites, helping spread the content and YouTube reputation. Finally, Really Simple Syndication (RSS) technology helps others bring your content into their websites or desktops. We mentioned in Chapter 3 that Senator Obama's videos included the technology to allow posting on blogs and other sites, while Senator Clinton's did not. Obama's video had legs and could travel, thus increasing his exposure.

> **Upside:** Your message will spread to the far corners of the internet and build your reputation and business as a result.
>
> **Risks:** It is difficult to stay current with technologies and find content worthy of spreading. Don't be tempted to create content that's highly viral but doesn't relate to your business or brand.

> ## Defining Moment: Viral Marketing
>
> *Viral marketing* is a technique that facilitates and encourages people to pass marketing messages along to others. Clever, entertaining, and interesting videos, photos, text messages, and other communication that gets rapid pass-along online can result in a huge brand impact. Viral marketing is similar to buzz marketing (see Chapter 5).

9. Monitor and Manage Your Reputation Online

Your reputation online needs continual monitoring if you want to keep it in line with your goals. Google and Technorati are your new best friends. As we mentioned in Chapter 2, Google is now a reputation engine, useful for monitoring community perceptions of you, your company, and its brands. It takes a lot more, such as knowing which blogs and forums to watch because search engine content does not include all web content—especially omitting the most current postings.

Once you discover online conversation about you, then what? The art of responding and repairing reputations involves sensitivity to the citizen journalists. You can engage them in reputation-enhancing ways, even when responding to criticism. We'll discuss many simple techniques for monitoring, measuring, and managing customer engagement in Chapters 13 and 14.

Upside: You'll find out what people are saying about you online in time to present your perspectives. You'll have a better grasp of what's being said about your business.

Risks: Time, if you decide to monitor it yourself; or money, if you outsource.

10. Become Radically Transparent

Being radically transparent generates huge respect and improves your reputation. Of course, there are boundaries, but where are they, exactly? For starters, internet communities don't appreciate anonymity in posting. Identify your authorship and tell your honest story. Disclose as much as feels comfortable because showing the personal side builds relationships in business, as well as in personal networks. It is important to have company policies on what employees can share online, but it is obvious that the company's secret formulas need protection (see the IBM policies in Chapter 3). Or, follow the lead of toy manufacturer Lego, who describes the entire product development process in its Lego Mindstorms NXT Step blog (thenxtstep.com).

Denise Stinardo, New Media Manager for the Eastman Kodak Company, runs the *A Thousand Words* blog, authored by employees worldwide. Individuals submit word documents and digital photos describing their work and personal lives. Stinardo's staff assists in resizing the images for the blog but believes that unedited, honest conversation is best:

> " We do not filter our blog comments. Once an individual submits a comment, it appears on our blog immediately. Each comment is reviewed to ensure that it does not contain inappropriate language—this is not acceptable and only then will that comment be removed. "

Also, note that your online activities are like mouse tracks for all to view. The way you conduct sales on eBay comes with feedback ratings, as do your recommendations and reviews on many other sites. That lawsuit involving you, the pictures of your poor parking and party antics, and many other seemingly private experiences can be found in online databases. It is time to find these postings and present your side of the story before the citizen journalists blow it up. You are already radically transparent—now, acknowledge it and respond with honest disclosure to build a favorable reputation online.

Chris Anderson, author of *The Long Tail* and editor-in-chief for *Wired* magazine, wrote about what radical transparency could mean for *Wired*. He discussed showing who the staff behind the magazine are by editing their own "about" pages, blogging, and by providing an unusually in-depth organization chart. He further proposed leveling the field by giving audience comments the same visual power as magazine author material, and by allowing the audience to vote on popular stories. Finally, he proposed showing their online communities what they were working on by opening internal project-related wikis for public viewing and commenting online, and by considering "process as content." This would mean uploading text of interviews and other draft information for users to read and comment upon as the writers develop the story. Anderson, in truly radically transparent fashion, publicly laid out the pros and cons of this proposed shift for *Wired* (see the sidebar "Upsides and Risks for *Wired* Magazine Becoming Radically Transparent").

> **Upside:** Create a killer reputation. Build relationships with business prospects and customers because they respect and like you. Few companies and individuals have reached radical transparency, so you'll stand out from the crowd.
>
> **Risks:** Your competitors will also learn valuable information about you. Once you become radically transparent, any attempt to revert back to a guarded state may be met with suspicion.

Upsides and Risks for *Wired* Magazine Becoming Radically Transparent

Chris Anderson, editor-in-chief for *Wired* magazine, discussed six tactics for transparent media in his blog, *The Long Tail* (www.longtail.com). This is a condensed version from his December 12, 2006 blog post.

Upsides: [Regarding user participation in stories] tap the wisdom of crowds. Open participation can make stories better—better researched, better thought through and deeper. It also can crowdsource some of the work of the copy desk and editors. And once the story is done and published, the participants have a sense of collective ownership that encourages them to spread the word. Maximizes participation. A front page that reflects reader interest better. Stories live and grow, remaining relevant long after their original publication (at no cost to us!) Readers know who to contact. [Regarding showing staff authored bios and organization chart] the organization is revealed as a collection of diverse individuals, not just a brand, an editor and some writers.

Risks: [Regarding user participation in stories] a more predictable and lowbrow front page. If we don't deploy voting tools or (sigh) a login system, trolls may rule. Tip off competitors (although I'd argue that this would just as likely freeze them; after all the prior art would be obvious to all); Risk "scooping ourselves," robbing the final product of freshness. Curating the process can quickly hit diminishing returns. Writers end up feeling like a cruise director, constantly trying to get people to participate. Stories get progressively less coherent as many cooks mess with them. Whatever brand authority the Wired name brings is diminished over time as the stories become less and less our own work. [Regarding showing staff authored bios and organization chart] competitors know who to poach; PR people spam us even more than usual.

Tools for Engagement

Enough talking. Get ready to roll up your sleeves and start building, monitoring, and managing your online reputation in a radically transparent way. Throughout Part 2 of this book, we will walk the fine line taken by all brands, companies, and individual brands—allowing users to generate honest, transparent content about you, yet guiding it toward desired ends. This involves knowledge of specific skills, tools, and online media.

Skills and Tools for Radically Transparent Reputations

Some say that reputation management lies at the intersection of public relations (PR) and search engine optimization (SEO). PR online involves identifying influential bloggers, journalists, and other authors, and impressing them with your knowledge, expertise, and savvy. Good PR generates buzz that enhances your reputation. You'll use an effective online pressroom, engaging website, and press releases that dazzle the less-than-easily impressed. SEO is a skill that helps you manage what appears on page one of a Google, Yahoo!, or other search engine results page. Page one should include all your reputation-enhancing content, and not the negative things others write about you. SEO includes natural search—getting your website or blog to the top of the search engine results page through a number of free tactics, and paid search—buying key words and other ads on search engines.

Great PR and multimedia web content involve other skills, such as writing reputation-building text for maximum impact. You also need to be armed with a digital camera for capturing your star performance at the podium and other reputation-enhancing shots. Then you'll need information about posting these images online. What about adding a video, podcast, or other sound bites to your web or social media content? We'll discuss techniques for writing, speaking, and producing images that engage your stakeholders and build your reputation.

Next is research. In order to monitor your online reputation, you'll need to know where to look and how to do it efficiently. We'll show you how to create online reputation metrics and set up a system for automated reputation monitoring.

Finally, an important part of any project involves good planning. You'll leave this book with an action plan for your personal, company, or brand reputation management. You'll also need to know about how and when to repair your online reputation should the citizen journalists throw some bad words or images in your path.

> ### Thought Byte: How Good Are Your Reputation Management Skills?
>
> It is time to take stock of your skills in PR, SEO, writing, digital imaging, podcast creation, online research, and planning. Which of these do you accomplish yourself or in-house? Which do you outsource? Knowing your strengths is a start.

Online Media for Radically Transparent Reputations

The social media include a diverse set of platforms for posting your multimedia content. Blogging is an excellent way to spread your expertise online, but how to do it in an effective way when you are already too busy to answer your e-mail? We'll show you how to build a personal or corporate blog that engages customers, and how to respond to comments posted by citizen journalists. There are many fine points to blogging, such as which platform to use, how to enhance the blog with RSS feeds, and more.

Social networking sites abound, but which to join? We'll discuss the pros, cons, and characteristics of all the biggest social networks so that you can decide where to jump in. You'll also learn how to optimize your profiles in the networks for full advantage.

Don't overlook the traditional internet platforms, such as the website and lowly e-mail and text message. There are simple things you can do to be sure your outgoing mail enhances your reputation, and to pick among various communication platforms for various purposes. We'll also talk about how and when to use e-mail newsletters and blasts that build your reputation.

Finally, you are what you do online, so if you get involved in eBay, Second Life, Amazon reviews or other recommendation sites, or sell merchandise online, you should watch what mouse tracks you leave behind. Your online activities suggest a lot about who you are.

Building Your Radically Transparent Reputation

II

Building a radically transparent reputation requires the understanding and use of various internet tools at your disposal. Blogs, search engines, video, e-mail, and social networks, all play an important part in how you present your brand to your stakeholders.

These chapters explain which online tools are vital to building a positive online reputation.

The Art of
Generating Buzz

In your quest to become radically transparent, you'll need to impress those who control the media. While mainstream journalists used to hold the power to influence your customers, that power is now shifting to bloggers and citizen journalists. Your corporate and personal identities are in the hands of the public, but that doesn't mean you don't have a say in how they're perceived. By understanding how public relations (PR) has evolved—and learning the new approaches to sharing your message—you can easily influence what's said about you.

5

Chapter Contents

Public Relations Is Moving Online

As the internet grows, it continues to suck in various forms of traditional media. Like a tornado making its way across the landscape of traditional communication, the Web has the uncanny ability to strip away the inadequacies of offline media and expose needs that can only be met on the internet. While we continue to see video, audio, and photos find a better home on the World Wide Web, it's the shift of traditional print distribution to an online audience that has been the most dramatic. When you consider that only 25% of 30-year-olds read newspapers daily (according to the National Opinion Research Center's General Social Survey archive), you'll realize that as younger generations grow up consuming news online, there will be a greater need to ensure that information is readily available on the Web. And if you think that it will be many years before you see the internet overtake print as the most popular form of news consumption, think again! The top 50 newspapers in the United States have a combined daily circulation of around 21 million readers. An impressive number, yet Yahoo! News alone has more than 37 million unique users, according to data collected by PR giant Edelman. In addition, comScore Media Metrix reports that AOL News and Google News add roughly another 29 million combined unique visitors on top of Yahoo!'s circulation—giving the top three online news sources almost three times the daily audience of the top 50 print publications. Even Forbes.com is reported to have more readers than its printed edition.

Few other marketing and communications channels are as affected by the rise of social media than PR. The art of corporate communications is undergoing a dramatic change now that the conversation is moving away from traditional forms of media, such as television, print, and radio, and instead finding a new home on the internet. The shift has taken many companies by surprise as they adapt to a world where canned messages and corporate spin are met with an audience that prefers honesty and transparency. Likewise, PR professionals find themselves learning how to get their clients' messages across to the media, without filtering to the point that they live up to the "flack" stereotype. Richard Edelman, president and CEO of Edelman, defines PR's new challenge:

> **"** There is a role for PR to act as advocates on the basis of total transparency, in fact authentic PR. There can be no effective PR without clear identification of the client, the client's interest, and funding of spokespeople or institutions. The best PR is straightforward, accurate and respectful. We are paid advocates, whose primary task is to promote the virtues of a product or company. **"**

The rise of citizen journalism, social networks, blogs, online press releases, and search engine marketing have given PR many new wrinkles. Although some companies have failed to adapt to the new rules of media engagement, those rising to the challenge have discovered their message moving faster, and more ears listening, when the news is shared with a radically transparent voice.

Using PR to Manage Your Brand

Now that you know the importance of bringing online elements into your corporate communications efforts, what items should be in your radically transparent PR toolkit? Whether you decide to outsource all of your company's PR efforts, you have your own team of media experts, or you are a professional trying to share your story with the media, it's vital that you give thought to the tactics you use to spread your message. If you're thinking ahead, a strategic online PR plan can help you to seed your campaign message and add to it with the use of varying forms of online media. Taking the time to lay a solid foundation for your brand—be it corporate or personal—will make it easy to get your message across and provide the perfect platform of trust and transparency, should you ever find yourself in a crisis.

If you're reading this chapter with the hope of learning how to fix the reputation mess you're in, don't panic. While facing a reputation crisis certainly brings a sense of urgency to any PR effort, you can quickly apply the core concepts of an online PR initiative to even the most urgent of needs. With our help, you'll learn the fundamental approaches to an effective online PR campaign. And while it would take many more books to fully train you in all aspects of public relations—or perhaps even a degree or two—there are some strategies you can learn right away that will make a huge difference. Adding these to your marketing and PR efforts will help you better convey your message, lay a foundation for a solid brand, and provide handy tools should you ever face a reputation crisis.

Further Reading on Public Relations

Radically Transparent will teach you how to leverage online PR to build a stellar reputation. If you want a wider view of PR's best practices, we suggest you read *Full Frontal PR* by Richard Laermer or *The New Rules of Marketing and PR* by David Meerman Scott.

Your Online Pressroom

Okay, we know you're anxious to get out there and start chatting with bloggers or feeding your news to Google, but before you play in the new media playground you've got some chores to handle. If you hope to have any success with your online PR campaign, you should know that your own home—in this case your website—needs to have a place to showcase all your efforts and be a welcome mat to any journalist who happens to visit. Being radically transparent with your corporate communications is not simply the act of cutting corporate rhetoric from your next press release. As with anything you do in life, a solid foundation is vital if you want to fully reap the benefits of your hard work. That's exactly why we don't recommend sending a single press release, nor do we recommend that you start contacting your favorite bloggers, until you've taken the time to put together a smorgasbord of high-quality, exciting information for them to digest.

Meet the Press 24/7

Your own website pressroom is one of the most overlooked details in an online PR campaign. Whether you prefer to call it a press center, media room, or newsroom, the key thing is that you need one. Not only do you need a pressroom, but it must be engaging and social media ready if you want to enable your message to reach the masses. A pressroom tells the world—but more importantly, members of both mainstream and social media—*who* you are, *what* you do, *how* to reach you, and *why* anyone should care. It's the place where members of the press, bloggers, and researchers can go to find your latest news, your corporate stock of photos, and bios of your key executives.

Press Kits Move Online

The online pressroom is very similar to the traditional press kit a company puts together for the media. Glossy folders and neatly printed fact sheets still have their place in public relations, but hosting an online version allows you to share more information and reach a larger audience—plus it helps save a few trees!

As well as offering information about your company, products, and management, your pressroom is unique in that it's one of the few sources of online information about your company that you fully control. You'll discover that having full control of your message is a rare thing when it comes to online PR. As you start sharing your story, sending it out over the many internet channels, you'll realize how your carefully crafted message is sliced, diced, and disseminated by the social media masses. As that information starts circulating the Web, the message is no longer yours. The moment you release it, it becomes the property of customers, stakeholders, business partners, and journalists. That's why you need a repository of information that will act as a clearinghouse for what's fact and what's fiction, as it pertains to your brand. As Richard Edelman explains, in a "multiple stakeholder world" it's important that you "tell your story as opposed to letting others tell your story."

So what information should you include in your company pressroom? Before we describe the components of a social media–enabled press center, let's take a look at an example of a great online pressroom (see Figure 5.1).

Figure 5.1 Google's Press Center

If there's a better example of a social media ready pressroom than Google's, we couldn't find one. Any company looking for a template that shows which items should be included in a radically transparent press center could learn a lot from a company that built its brand and market share by word of mouth and reputation. Now we'll tell you why we think Google's pressroom is so powerful. As we do, keep in mind that great online pressrooms cater to the needs of busy journalists with pressing deadlines, just as great marketing focuses on customers.

Easy to Navigate

One of the biggest mistakes many companies make is that their pressroom is more of a press "maze." We've seen many sites where vital company information is either nonexistent or scattered among their many hundreds of web pages. With any pressroom, your goal is to provide a concise summary of information on one page. Certainly don't feel the need to cram all of your corporate information into one page—we just want the stuff journalists and bloggers will be interested in—and don't make the mistake of having one long page that scrolls to near infinity. Google's Press Center is an example of a good pressroom as they display the most vital information on one page and use clear navigation to direct you to other related content.

Your Latest News

If your company hasn't yet started a blog, the chances are you're still sharing your news via press releases or media advisories (if you are blog-less, don't panic because we'll get you started in Chapter 9). Many companies make the mistake of simply issuing a press release and then relying on their newswire of choice and syndication partners to archive it. Although technically this ensures that you can point a blogger or journalist to all of your press releases, it doesn't exactly make it easy for discovery. An even bigger problem is that all of that great content isn't archived on your own site. By not posting your press releases to your own pressroom, you're wasting the opportunity to tell your own story or direct members of the press or investors back to your own site, and you're losing out on potential visitors from the search engines. Oh, and don't forget to follow Google's lead and add an RSS feed for your press releases—RSS feeds aren't just for blogs.

Defining Moment: RSS Feed

RSS stands for "Really Simple Syndication" and is typically used for sharing frequently updated information such as blog posts, news headlines, or podcasts. RSS feeds allow people to keep track of website content in an automated manner without having to visit the site and check for updates manually. We'll explain how you can monitor RSS feeds in Chapter 13.

Recent Blog Posts

If you have a corporate blog, your pressroom is the ideal place to highlight your most recent posts. It's highly likely that any journalist or blogger visiting your pressroom will be interested in knowing that you have a blog providing updates in a more conversational style than your press releases. Likewise, other stakeholders might not yet be aware that you provide updates via a company blog. This is a great opportunity to share your more recent posts and give visitors the option of reading your reputation-enhancing perspectives or even subscribing to the blog's RSS feed.

Testimonials

As we've already mentioned, stakeholders find tremendous value in what others have to say about your business. For each industry there are dozens of online channels for both evangelists and detractors to share their thoughts on your business. Your own website is the one place you can have full control to display reputation-enhancing endorsements. Like Google, you can use your pressroom—as well as other pages on your site—to show off positive customer testimonials. Sure, visitors will be a little more guarded when reading endorsements that show up on your own site—they'll know you're not likely to show anything negative—but it's still very much worth the time and effort to show the world that your customers love you. Not only will testimonials give you the opportunity to win new customers, but when a journalist or blogger comes looking for background on your company, they're more likely to leave with the impression that you have happy clients.

Rich Media Files

Remember, in the world of social media, relying on plain text is not going to cut it. We live in an ultra-sensory world and visitors to your pressroom will expect to be fed information in a variety of formats. Adding images such as logos, product photos, or management headshots is the bare minimum. Journalists and bloggers often look for images to accompany their articles, and if they can't find those stock images on your own site, you run the risk that they'll look elsewhere and potentially use something less than flattering.

Adding video and audio to your pressroom helps take you into the realm of social media. As we discussed in Chapter 4, full engagement online requires emotion-triggering sight and sound. We're not just talking about B-Roll footage—bland video of your CEO smiling as he walks around the office—nor are we referring to audio of your most recent investor conference call. While these should be in your pressroom, you should also include any media that shows your company in a radically transparent light. Do you have video of your CEO running a marathon for charity? Put it on the site. Did a blogger interview your president for a popular podcast? Let visitors stream the video or download to their MP3 players. Google's pressroom includes a link to a dedicated "Multimedia Pressroom." You don't have to go to this extreme, but you should make it easy for your pressroom visitors to browse your multimedia files. In Chapter 7, we'll explore further the benefits of video and audio content.

Management and Corporate Bios

Even the most basic of pressrooms should include a brief summary of your business and its executives. Just like its offline cousin, the media kit, an online pressroom will contain a description of your business, the services you offer, and the products you make. In addition, this is a great place to include headshots of your executive management, their resumes, and brief details about their expertise. In an online world, it's easy for your corporate background to get wrapped up into an online version of "Telephone." The last thing you want is for a journalist or blogger to collect background information based on what she's read elsewhere on the internet. If you've made it easy for visitors to find your official company bio, they're more likely to use it instead of what they read at Hoover's or ZoomInfo. Google has so many executives it keeps management bios on a separate page. If you place your executive bios on a different page, be sure to include a prominent link to it—Google's "Executive Bios" link is somewhat hard to spot.

Community Relations Efforts

There are few things that can help present a brand in a more positive light than charitable service or projects that help the environment. You don't have to make it onto Forbes's list of *America's Most Generous Companies* in order to start bragging about the work you do for nonprofit organizations. While companies such as Caterpillar, Microsoft, and Best Buy donate millions of dollars each year to charitable causes, your business can gain valuable brand equity by demonstrating that you care. Find an organization that your company is interested in helping and that enhances the reputation of your industry, and donate money, products, or time to help their efforts. This is a a great way to install pride in your employees and also provides a huge benefit to the perception of your brand. You can also showcase the nonprofit work employees do on their own time. Google misses out on the opportunity to showcase their Google Foundation—their pressroom is missing a link to their philanthropic arm, Google.org.

RSS Feeds

As we've already suggested, your pressroom is a great place to share RSS feeds for any items you release to the media. Feeds are not only for blog posts, but they can be used to update customers and the media on your press releases, new videos, or latest product releases. Make sure your RSS feeds are easy to find and subscribe to. Let both traditional and social media know that your pressroom is RSS-enabled the next time you issue a press release or send an e-mail. With this in place, you can keep members of the press updated and coming back to your site more often.

RSS via E-mail

Even though RSS feeds make it easier for anyone to keep up to date with your company's news, not all are taking advantage of this technology. Services such as FeedBlitz.com offer solutions to convert RSS feeds into e-mail subscriptions. This allows you to provide customers and the media with a choice of how they receive your news updates.

Concise Contact Information

The final item on your pressroom checklist is the contact information. Although we've left it for last, it's probably the most vital piece of information you'll add to your press page. Your goal is to make it extremely easy for any member of the media to contact your company. We'll say that again: extremely easy. At a bare minimum, you should list an e-mail address for all media inquiries. Even better, provide options for contacting your company via telephone—using a number that can be forwarded to a cell phone—because if a journalist is about to write a negative story about your company, you don't want to rely on how often you check your e-mail. We can't stress this enough: make it easy for the busy journalist or blogger to contact you.

Your Website Should Be Engaging

While an online pressroom is the core component of any online public relations effort, you shouldn't overlook the many different media you can use to share information and engage visitors on your website. Throughout the remaining chapters of Part 2 of *Radically Transparent*, we're going to help you with the implementation and use of online media such as blogs, e-mail, chat rooms, forums, and much more. Although these tools are not necessarily tied to your company's website, keep in mind that they can all be applied to your corporate communications. You goal is not to overload visitors with too much information, but to provide them with enough easy-to-find options so they can learn about your brand in any format they prefer.

Your ultimate aim is to ensure that your website is ready for your online PR campaign. The moment you start sending social media press releases or start reaching out to bloggers, you've taken a step into a world of radical transparency. We won't say there's no going back, but we will remind you of the adage "You only get one chance to make a great first impression." Your new audience consists of bloggers, citizen journalists, and even search engines. They're going to evaluate your newsworthiness based on how you contact them and what information you're prepared to share. A website that is organized, social media ready, and highly transparent will impress them and, like a secret handshake, will let them know that you "get it." OK, take a deep breath— your PR outreach is about to get a makeover.

The Press Release Gets an Extreme Makeover

The humble press release is one of the most reliable tools for any PR professional. Since the beginning of the twentieth century, press releases have been PR practitioners' biggest asset in their attempt to reach journalists and provide them with a carefully crafted story. In 1906, the Pennsylvania Railroad fell victim to a tragic accident. PR professional Ivy Lee convinced them to issue an announcement to the media—he wanted to shape the story before journalists heard it elsewhere—and since then press releases have been used to spread a company's news. Using carefully crafted messaging, corporate spin, and a predictable format of who, what, where, when, and how, press releases changed little for almost one hundred years.

As the internet enabled communications to morph from telephone, postal mail, and faxes to websites, e-mail, and RSS feeds, the press release changed along with it. Today, thousands of press releases are issued daily, thanks to newswire distribution services such as Business Wire, PR Newswire, and PRWeb. With technology reducing the cost of sending a press release to just pennies per thousand, a press release can be sent for less than $80 (via PRWeb) to reach hundreds of thousands of readers. This ease of distribution creates a lot of noise and clutter. With the increase of daily press releases waiting for them, journalists are overloaded and unable to read and investigate every news announcement that crosses a newswire. At the same time, dozens of online news aggregators have emerged, collecting every single news item and trying desperately to categorize and file each new release. While technology has made it easier and cheaper to issue a press release, that same blessing is also a curse because so much information makes it difficult to sort the wheat from the chaff.

Defining Moment: Newswire

Newswires refer to the service that transmits up-to-the-minute news (such as press releases), usually electronically, to the media and members of the public.

"Water, water everywhere and not a drop to drink." This may be the rime of an ancient mariner, but it also perfectly describes the challenge facing both senders and receivers of press releases at the beginning of the twenty-first century. With so many press releases issued and new technology, such as RSS feeds, making the syndication possibilities virtually endless, finding high-quality news among the junk is almost impossible. Fortunately, before the entire press release distribution system collapses under its own weight, technology is presenting a solution. Instead of press releases relying on journalists as the sole audience, social media and search engines make it possible for anyone with an internet connection to read the latest news announcements. Sites such as Google News, Yahoo! News, and Topix.net have emerged to collect, categorize, and disseminate every press release—slicing and dicing each announcement so that everyone from journalists to hobbyists can zone in on the topics that interest them. Likewise, social news sites such as Digg.com, reddit.com, and Propeller.com allow users to vote on which news was the most important, adding a human filter to the many news stories that surface each day. Finally, social bookmarking sites such as del.icio.us, StumbleUpon.com, and Spurl.net make it easier for average web users to tag their favorite news items and share them with others.

As technology adapts to ensure press releases can be shared with all internet users—including citizen journalists, mainstream consumers, casual bloggers, and mainstream reporters—savvy PR professionals are realizing they no longer have to write structured announcements and PR spin. Instead, PR experts are discovering that multiple audiences mean an entirely new way of disseminating news.

The Rise of the Social Media Release

Whether you're looking to shape the perception of your brand, or simply trying to put out the fires of a PR nightmare, it is vital to ensure that your press release doesn't just rot away in a journalist's e-mail inbox. To do this, it first has to follow a format that encourages others to read, share, and discuss its contents. If you're hoping that you can achieve radical transparency by issuing a bland statement full of PR flack and corporate spin, you'll face ridicule or, worse, obscurity. Instead, follow the advice of those PR practitioners that have embraced new methods of writing a press release. As Lee Odden, president and founder of TopRank Online Marketing, explains, "RSS and blogs for example, provide excellent channels as well as the social bookmarking of concentrated clusters of information. The social media news release attempts to achieve this effect."

The social media press release is still very much in its infancy. In May 2006, PR agency SHIFT Communications released the first ever template that tried to provide an outline for a social media ready press release (see www.shiftcomm.com/downloads/smprtemplate.pdf). Todd S. Defren, principal of SHIFT, explains the need for a social media press release: "The ubiquity of broadband Web use, combined with ever-easier-to-use online tools and relevant, user-generated content is creating a unique opportunity for the PR profession to re-think what we do and how we do it." Shortly after SHIFT's debut of its social media press release template, other PR firms followed suit, including Edelman's debut of its StoryCrafter tool for the creation and deploy of social media news releases.

The social media press release is a radical departure from the traditional press release format, used for almost a century. Here are the core elements of a traditional press release, according to Wikipedia.org:

Headline Grabs the attention of journalists and briefly summarizes the news.

Dateline Contains the release date and usually the originating city of the press release.

Introduction First paragraph in a press release; generally gives basic answers to the questions of who, what, when, where, and why.

Body Further explanation, statistics, background, or other details relevant to the news.

Boilerplate Generally a short "about" section, providing independent background on the issuing company, organization, or individual.

Close In North America, traditionally the symbol "-30-" appears after the boilerplate or body and before the media contact information, indicating to media that the release is ending. A more modern equivalent has been the "###" symbol. In other countries, other means of indicating the end of the release may be used, such as the text "ends."

Media Contact Information Name, phone number, e-mail address, mailing address, or other contact information for the PR or other media relations contact person.

Now contrast the traditional press release with the core elements of SHIFT's social media press release template (facing page).

Contact Information

Unlike a traditional release, contact information is displayed first. This makes it easy for anyone reading the release to quickly identify who to contact for additional information. Notice that the template suggests three alternative points of contact and shares the e-mail and instant messenger address in addition to telephone number and website URL.

Headline

Even with a social media release, the headline and subhead are two of the most important elements. The key difference is that your headline should be written to attract the attention not only of journalists but also customers and search engines. For example, a traditional headline might read, "Dell Announces the Launch of Its Vostro Small Business Brand." When Dell actually made their announcement, they were careful to include popular words for the search engines and engaging words for customers. Contrast the traditional headline with the one Dell actually used: "Dell Introduces New Vostro Brand of Notebooks and Desktops Designed Exclusively to Meet Small Business Needs."

SHIFT communications

SOCIAL MEDIA PRESS RELEASE
TEMPLATE, VERSION 1.0

CONTACT INFORMATION:	Client contact	Spokesperson	Agency contact
	Phone #/skype	Phone #/skype	Phone #/skype
	Email	Email	Email
	IM address	IM address	IM address
	Web site	Blog/relevant post	Web site

NEWS RELEASE HEADLINE
Subhead

CORE NEWS FACTS
■ Bullet-points preferable

LINK & RSS FEED TO PURPOSE-BUILT DEL.ICIO.US PAGE
The purpose-built del.icio.us page offers hyperlinks (and PR annotation in "notes" fields) to relevant historical, trend, market, product & competitive content sources, providing context as-needed, and on-going updates.

PHOTO	**MP3 FILE OR PODCAST LINK**	**GRAPHIC**	**VIDEO**
e.g., product picture, exec headshot.	e.g., sound bytes by various stakeholders	e.g., product schematic; market size graphs; logos	e.g., brief product demo by in-house expert

MORE MULTIMEDIA AVAILABLE BY REQUEST
e.g., "download white paper"

PRE-APPROVED QUOTES FROM CORPORATE EXECUTIVES, ANALYSTS, CUSTOMERS AND/OR PARTNERS
Recommendation: no more that 2 quotes per contact. The PR agency should have additional quotes at-the-ready, "upon request," for journalists who desire exclusive content. This provides opportunity for Agency to add further value to interested media.

LINKS TO RELEVANT COVERAGE TO-DATE (OPTIONAL)
This empowers journalist to "take a different angle," etc.
These links would also be cross-posted to the custom del.icio.us site.

BOILERPLATE STATEMENTS

RSS FEED TO CLIENT'S NEWS RELEASES

"ADD TO DEL.ICIO.US"
Allows readers to use the release as a standalone portal to this news

TECHNORATI TAGS/"DIGG THIS"

Core News Facts

This replaces both the traditional introduction and body elements. Unlike traditional releases that separate information into structured paragraphs, the social media release is written with the web audience in mind. Web users typically browse content more than actually reading, therefore bullet points facilitate in quickly sharing the key points of the release.

Links and RSS Feed to a Purpose-Built Page

With the help of RSS feeds and social bookmarking sites, the social media release allows you to share many more resources than would fit in the actual body of the press release. The SHIFT template suggests building a social bookmarking page that can be kept updated with related news, trends, and market analysis.

Multimedia

There's no need for the reader to hunt around the company's website looking for images or video. With a social media release, you provide embedded links to photos, podcasts, graphics, and video content (as shown by the four labeled boxes). Links to additional multimedia could take the reader to more items located in your pressroom.

Quotes

The traditional release includes quotes from company executives and clients sprinkled throughout the press release content. The social media version clumps them together, making it easier to identify and extract sound bites. By making it easier for members of the media to extract your quotes, you increase the chances they will be used. Ensuring your quotes are used in news articles and blog posts will help you better control your reputation.

Links to Other Coverage

This is the section that allows you to cut down the clutter of the release and instead use hyperlinks to point to related content. You might use this section to convince a reader that your news release is part of a growing trend. Or perhaps you want to direct the reader to research that supports your claims.

Boilerplate

Not much has changed here; many companies will still wish to provide a summary of the company and any financial disclaimers.

RSS Feeds, Social Bookmarks

The last three elements of the social media press release are all designed to encourage the sharing of this news announcement, giving it legs. Providing preformatted links to feeds and popular bookmarking sites might help spread your news faster.

The goal of the social media press release is to be a modular layout, with elements that can be swapped in and out as relevant to the content of the release. You don't need to follow the format exactly as suggested—you might blend the traditional template and the social media one. That's absolutely fine. Odden acknowledges that the social media template "has yet to be accepted as a standard format." Until such time as the social media press release becomes the standard, you'll need to cater to both traditional and new media journalists. Sending two press releases is not the answer, so keep in mind whether your announcement will appeal more to traditional media or social media and customize accordingly. The goal is to look at your future press releases and identify ways to include elements that facilitate the syndication of your news while creating a message that is less self-serving and more transparent.

The key to a successful social media press release is to provide as much useful information as possible in an easy-to-use format. You can't control what is written about your company, but by providing a wealth of information about your business, you reduce the need for the recipient to seek out third-party information about your brand. The more authentic and transparent you appear to be, the less likely someone will feel the need to dig around and see if you have any skeletons lurking in your reputation closet. For these reasons, we believe that the social media press release is more likely to enhance your reputation than the traditional release.

Now you have a blueprint for your next press release. You understand the need for a more informal, less-hype announcement. Your confidence is high that you can put together a press release that will appeal to all audiences—from journalists, to bloggers, to your customers. Before you rush off and hit "send" on your newswire account, there's one vital press release audience we've not yet considered. This audience has the power to share your news with tens of millions of readers, all potentially interested in your company. It has the ability to place your business ahead of all your competitors, raise awareness of your brand, and dramatically increase your online reputation. You might think that with this much clout, we're talking about an audience with the Queen of England, but even she doesn't come close to being as powerful as this audience. This powerful recipient of your press release is a search engine.

Google Reads Your Press Release Too

Ever since the search engines started indexing and distributing news stories, the audience for each press release has grown from thousands to millions. With Yahoo!, Google, and AOL each offering a news-only version of their regular search engine and the addition of news tracking sites such as Topix and Technorati, your press releases now reach far beyond the desks of mainstream journalists. With thousands of press releases issued on any given day, making sure your voice is heard above those of your competitors is vital if you want to ensure your hard work doesn't fall on deaf ears.

Fortunately, the same tactics helping web pages rise to the top of regular search engine results—known as search engine optimization (SEO)—can also be applied to the press releases you send out over the wire. In fact, with careful attention to the wording used in your next press release, you can not only reach the readers of news specific search engines, but the chances are high that your press release will also appear in the web search engine results of Google and Yahoo!, among others. For professionals or businesses looking to ensure their messages reach the largest possible audience—which is especially important in a crisis—optimizing a press release for the search engines is the online equivalent of super-charging a car. While your factory-standard press release is enough to get your message from A to B, fine-tuning the keywords used, and their placement, will help your message reach a much broader audience.

Greg Jarboe, president and co-founder of the online PR firm SEO-PR, cautions that "press releases should be written primarily for humans, with news search engines as a secondary consideration." Nonetheless, Jarboe is among a growing niche of PR professionals who advise their clients on the value of tailoring their press releases to search engine algorithms. The benefits of this tactic are often long lasting, especially when you consider that long after your news is swept off a journalist's desk, it will likely remain available in Google. As TopRank's Lee Odden explains, "We've found that it's fairly common that readers go to Google and search the topic of [our client's] article whereupon our clients have prominent visibility in the search results."

For the radically transparent, a medium that allows you to share your message via the media and the search engines is one you should utilize. While Chapter 6 will provide a full rundown of how to implement SEO tactics to ensure your brand is positively portrayed in the search engine results, there are some specific techniques tailored to press releases.

Search Engine–Friendly Press Releases

As you'll learn with any SEO initiative, your goal when optimizing your press release is to look for opportunities to include words that are highly likely to be used by journalists, bloggers, and customers. These keywords are important because they represent the likely terms used to find information specifically on your business or industry in general. Most press releases are written using dynamic marketing language, designed to capture the interest of the receiving journalist. While it's still important to ensure the headline and body of your release appeal to the human eye, you should also look for opportunities to make the release appealing to search engine spiders and news aggregators. When a search engine "reads" your press release, it's making note of the most frequently used words to determine the theme of the release. The release is then archived until the day one of its users searches for that exact same phrase. As if writing a press release to appeal to journalists and making sure it's social media ready isn't enough, you also need to consider whether you've tailored the release to match the search keywords a Google user may search for in the future. Although this may seem like a daunting task, it's really quite straightforward, if you keep the following tips in mind.

Choose Your Words Wisely

If you want your press release to reach the masses, you have to write for the masses. This doesn't mean you have to provide a watered-down version of your marketing copy, but it does mean avoiding the use of industry jargon and company terminology. In practice it means understanding what someone might search for when looking for your company or your products. For example, a drugstore may well want to tell the media about their new "onsite photo processing" capabilities—a term that they know industry journalists will understand—but it's far more likely that a consumer will search Google for "one hour photo." While the first phrase is technically the best terminology, it's the second string of words that will most likely ensure the press release reaches a wider audience. In Chapter 6, we'll share how you can research the most commonly searched keywords.

Branding Your Way to Number One

It's not just generic keywords that should make their way into your next press release. If your goal is to utilize your PR efforts to better control your online brand, your press releases can be an excellent tool. Many companies make the mistake of not using their company, product, and executive names often enough in their press releases. One mention of the company name and then a slew of pronouns such as "it," "we," and "their" typically ensue. If you hope to have your press releases penetrate the first ten results on Google when someone searches for your company name, you're not going to get far with only a single occurrence of your brand name. Increasing the use of your corporate and executive names will improve the chances of your release appearing on the first page of the search engine results.

Don't Forget Your Stock Ticker Symbol

If your company is publicly traded on one of the many stock exchanges around the world, you should make sure that your message also reaches investors. Being radically transparent also extends to Wall Street—and that means including your ticker symbol in your press releases and crafting your reputation to impress stock analysts.

Consulting firm Communications Consulting Worldwide (CCW) estimated the impact on market valuations of publicly traded companies by improving their reputations.

If...	...had the reputation of...	...its stock would rise...	...boosting market value by
Coca-Cola	Pepsi	3.3%	$4 billion
Wal-Mart	Target	4.9%	$9.7 billion
Colgate	P&G	6.2%	$2 billion
CVS	Walgreens	6.9%	$3.9 billion
Wachovia	Wells Fargo	3.5%	$3.5 billion

Source: CCW & BusinessWeek

Titles That Impress

The news is all about the headline. With technology increasing the volume of press releases sent each day, often it's your headline that's going to determine whether or not a blogger or journalist reads your news. The same holds true when it comes to garnering the attention of the niche news engines and general search engines. Not only does your headline need to be an attention grabber, but when a blogger searches Google News or a customer queries Ask.com, chances are your headline will determine whether they find your release and then read it.

The first goal—making sure your headline is found—can be achieved by ensuring those all important keywords are included in your press release's headline. If a journalist searches for the latest news on consumer electronics, make sure your headline includes the words she's most likely to use. Likewise, many bloggers set up automated searches to notify them if a news item matches a certain word or phrase. You want to make sure your headline includes words likely to trigger that notification. Your secondary goal is to consider where your press release will appear once it makes its way to the main search engine indexes. Popular, relevant keywords in your headlines will improve the chances your press release will make the first search results page and will also play a strong role in whether the searcher clicks through to view your release.

Show Off Your Links

While optimizing your press release will reap huge rewards in your efforts to make your news more visible, there's another important benefit. As you'll learn in Chapter 6, you can greatly increase the chances that your web page, blog, or profile will appear in the first few results of a search engine by increasing the number of external links pointing to it. A press release is a great opportunity to add a link back to the destination of your choice and improve that page's chances of ranking well in the search engine results. For example, add a hyperlink to a product name in your press release and point it back to appropriate page on your website. With press releases often republished at hundreds of different news aggregation sites, adding a link to the content is a great opportunity to get these sites to link back to you. And although many syndication sites will strip out any such links, enough will keep them in the press release content to benefit your efforts.

Enhancing Press Release Distribution

It's a thing of beauty! You've perfectly crafted your press release to be free of spin, ready for social media, and optimized for search engines. Now all that's left is to make sure you use the perfect platform for its distribution. Fortunately, as PR experts started using techniques to ensure their releases were friendly to bloggers, social media, and search engines, they also lobbied the various newswires for better distribution options and tracking. After much kicking and screaming by the major newswire services, they've finally awakened to the huge demand—and greater revenue for them—for options to better disseminate press releases. Led by PRWeb, one of the first services that catered to those wishing to optimize their releases, pretty much all of the major newswires offer some form of enhanced distribution.

Here are just a few of the options that PRWeb offers as part of its "Social Media Visibility" and "SEO Visibility" distribution options:

- A custom RSS feed for your press releases
- Distribution to Yahoo! News, Google News, and Topix
- The option to target multiple industries
- The ability to optimize your release with the "SEO Wizard" tool
- The option to add keyword-rich links to your release
- The ability to add images, video, and files
- The option to add buttons to share your release with social bookmarking sites

Not only can you take advantage of all of these features—as well as the normal distribution—for around two hundred dollars, but many of the newswires are taking advantage of better tracking technology to bring a level of accountability and reporting not previously available. SEO-PR's Greg Jarboe says, "Tracking a press release campaign is as easy as tracking an email marketing campaign. We can tell clients how many page views each press release has received, as well as how many press mentions, how many blog mentions, how much web traffic, how many leads or online sales the campaign has generated." Figure 5.2 shows an example tracking report from PRWeb's service that includes search engine statistics.

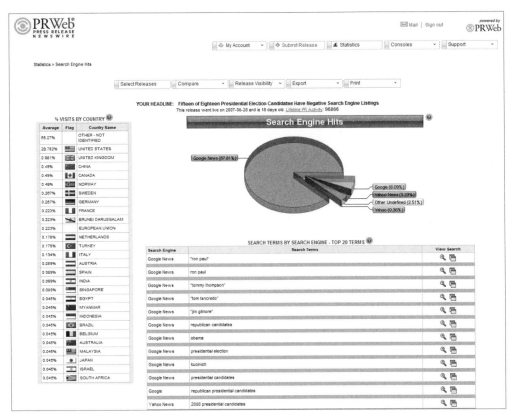

Figure 5.2 PRWeb's search engine report

A Foot in the Conversational Door

Press releases have certainly come a long way in the past few years. A carefully crafted press release can help you share your message with millions of internet users, facilitate their ability to pass it on to others, and still have enough left over to sit at the top of the search engine results pages. With great content and a clear message, your online PR efforts are greatly enhanced by the use of an optimized press release. Yet while it's important to understand how to get the most out of your next press release, you won't fully benefit from your PR efforts unless you learn how to follow up on your release and engage the media.

A press release is not a fire-and-forget tool. You can't simply issue a press release and expect a conversation to start or a crisis to disappear. Indeed, consider your press release more of a foot in the door of the online conversation. Use it as a means of introduction, but if you really want to influence the discussion, you're going to have to introduce yourself to those who have the soapbox. It's time to meet the bloggers!

Welcome to the Blogosphere

For the radically transparent, blogs are an important ally in your quest to shape your online identity and control the spread of potentially damaging information. With Technorati reporting 120,000 new blogs created worldwide each day and the Pew Internet & American Life Project revealing 57 million American adults read blogs, there's no doubting the importance of the blogosphere. Blogging technology has enabled millions of citizen journalists to put fingers to keyboards and share everything from their daily routine to their thoughts on political candidates. Blogging will become a vital part of your marketing and communication efforts, and in Chapter 9, we'll walk you through the many benefits that come from starting a blog. If you're not ready to own your own blog, you shouldn't dismiss the notion of blogs entirely. Your PR plan will be severely diminished without a strategy to identify the bloggers who are influential in your particular area of business. "Some of these bloggers rival the mainstream media in popularity and influence," says SEO-PR's Greg Jarboe. "The key is identifying the bloggers that have the most influence in specific conversations."

Even if you doubt the concept that bloggers rival mainstream media in influence, you should understand that even the most seemingly insignificant blogger can start a chain reaction of publicity—as we've described in previous chapters. While it's true that some bloggers, such as those on Technorati's Top 100 most popular list, have considerably more influence than your 14-year-old niece (who writes about her cat), Jeff Jarvis's Dell Hell blog rant demonstrates that a single blog post can have a huge effect on your brand. Add to this the Euro RSCG/Columbia University study that reveals 51% of journalists regularly read blogs, with 53% of them looking for story ideas, it becomes very clear how important blogger outreach is to your online PR efforts. And, in case you needed further convincing, the lines are blurring with many mainstream journalists also blogging—often for newspaper- or TV-affiliated blogs.

It's no wonder that the savviest of PR practitioners are including blogger outreach as part of their campaign. "We treat bloggers with the same respect as journalists and members of an influential media population," says Kathleen Bagley Formidoni, principal for PR firm blast! PR. Treating a blogger with the same respect as other journalists is a great start, but there are some nuances that go along with any blogger outreach efforts. Bloggers have their own ideas when it comes to journalism, and you'd be wise to learn the rules of the game.

Finding the Influential Bloggers

Including bloggers in your media outreach efforts doesn't mean simply sending out a press release and hoping that a few of the 110 million bloggers will decide to give you a glowing write-up—trust us, it's not that easy. While it's true that every blogger has the potential to put your company in the spotlight—either positively or negatively—at this stage you should be most interested in those who have the wherewithal to help you create a buzz. Just as with journalist contacts, it pays to focus on bloggers who are the most influential in your industry. So how do you determine which bloggers to contact?

The Ones You Already Know

You probably already have an idea of the specific bloggers who should be on your outreach list. Perhaps you're already aware of a blogger who's influenced events in your industry previously, or you've seen your competitors reviewed by a particular citizen journalist. If nothing else, you may simply have your list of favorite industry-related blogs that you read each day. Go with your gut and put them on your list.

Technorati

Technorati is a wonderful tool for discovering all kinds of information about a blog. Technorati keeps track of the Top 100 most popular bloggers—based on link citations—and in addition offers a variety of ways to discover popular blogs. The best way of discovering blogs that are influential in your industry is to search for a generic word that describes your business. A search for blogs about "gadgets" reveals more than 6,000 blogs on that topic. If you then click on one of the blogs listed—or enter an alternative blog by its URL—you learn more about that blog, including information on the author, most recent posts, a screenshot, and the number of other blogs that have linked to it. Figure 5.3 shows the Technorati profile for the popular blog CrunchGear.com.

Alexa and Compete

Both Alexa.com and Compete.com provide traffic estimates for many popular sites. Collecting information through the use of toolbars that web users can install on their browsers, both sites offer services that will first help you discover industry-related sites, and then help you determine which are the most popular. Alexa additionally offers basic demographic information on a blog's audience, while Compete will provide details on how "engaged" a blog's audience is via metrics, such as pages per visit.

Figure 5.3 Technorati profile for CrunchGear.com

Search Engines

All of the top search engines will provide valuable clues as to which bloggers are the most popular. If you enter a generic industry search term at Google.com, then append it with the word "blog," you quickly find popular blogs that are more likely to appear at the top of Google's search results for other industry terms. For example, a search for "car blog" or "computer blog," will return results that are more likely to include blogs related to cars and computers. If you want to be more specific, head to Google Blog

Search and enter an industry term—you'll find only results that come from what Google categorizes as blogs. Be sure to sort your results by "relevance" to have a better chance of viewing the most influential blogs first.

Media Mentions

Determining which blogs are likely to get quoted in mainstream media is a difficult task. Any blog has the capacity to break a story that consequently gets picked up by *The New York Times* or the *CBS Evening News*. That said, once you've compiled your shortlist of potential bloggers to contact, there are a few searches you can make to see if they're newsworthy or not:

- Search for the blogger's personal name at Google News or Yahoo! News. Both these sites tend to focus on mainstream news sites. If your blogger has been quoted in a news story, it will likely show up here.
- Head to your search engine of choice and search for "<blogger's name> of <name of blog>" (the common format for citation of media quotes) to discover if they've been quoted in any significant publication.
- Once you find potential bloggers, identify which blogs they link to in order to help you identify other potential contacts.

Reading the Blogs Before Making Contact

Now that you've drawn up your shortlist of bloggers to add to your PR outreach, don't be tempted to dive in and give them a call or shoot them an e-mail. Your chances of making a connection with a blogger, and having her write a post about you or your business, are greatly increased if you take the time to learn more about her, so you can customize your approach. Just as you respond more positively to a sales call from someone who's researched your company, bloggers are more approachable if you personalize your message. As TopRank's Lee Odden warns, "Pitching is customized and personal by default, not as an exception." This means that each blogger has his own unique preference on how he wishes to be approached by companies and PR firms. Although some may be happy to receive your press release by e-mail, others may suggest that you give them a call. Because each blogger is different, there's not a "one size fits all" recommendation we can make that will cover every blogger you'll encounter. Instead, we'll share with you some tactics that will help you avoid the embarrassment of being the latest entry on The Bad Pitch Blog.

Read Their Posts

Please don't expect a blogger to mention your business or review your products if you don't have the time to first learn about their blog. We can tell you from our own blogging experience that it's easy to spot the e-mails from companies that haven't read a single one of our blog posts. Don't be that guy. By taking the time to read the posts of the bloggers on your list, you'll learn more about their style, their interests, and their peeves, and in addition you'll also likely find some common ground to reference when the time comes to make the actual pitch. Bloggers are overwhelmed with requests, and as with any sales pitch, they attend to the people who've done their homework and present benefits that match their own interests. And besides, you don't want to insult a blogger and end up reading bad things about yourself the next day.

Participate with Comments

Want to improve the chances your pitch will be well received by a blogger? Interact with them first, without any obvious agenda or attempt to sell. Cindy Akus has these words of wisdom for the clients she assists at Crossroads PR: "I tell my clients, you need to engage the blogosphere and care about what other bloggers have to say, before they'll care about what you have to say." That means leaving comments on one of their blog posts—comments that actually enhance the blogger's conversation, not highlight your agenda—and it also means sending the blogger a news tip or sharing your thoughts on industry trends. The key point is to not let your initial contact be a press pitch. Building relationships with just a handful of bloggers on your list will reap huge rewards when the time comes to make your pitch.

Watch Trends

Understanding the news and trends in your industry will go a long way in your attempt connect with a blogger. A cold call to pitch your company's latest product launch will more than likely end in disaster. A better approach is to look for a trend or *meme* that you know is of interest to a blogger on your list. "The Internet enables us to constantly monitor stories posted to the online news outlets and blogs so we know who is writing about what, and from there, determine who will want to hear about our clients' news," says blast! PR's Formidoni. Remember, your press release is your shotgun blast out to the media while your blogger pitch needs to be tailored to what the blogger is interested in and writing about. "We don't send out impersonal form letter pitches, we make sure every pitch or story idea is relevant to a particular blogger's particular interests," advises Formidoni.

> ### Defining Moment: Meme
>
> An internet meme is a theme or idea that spreads rapidly and widely throughout the internet. It can be a piece of news, a video, blog post, or other social media. The key component is that it spreads virally.

The Transparent, Personal Pitch

Want to know the surest way to kill any chance that a blogger will discuss your company? It's easy: simply approach her with a hidden agenda and some carefully worded PR spin. While it might sound obvious that you should be completely honest in your contact with a blogger—or any member of the media for that fact—it's amazing how many times companies are caught trying to push a hidden agenda. Perhaps the most important lesson to learn about bloggers is that the majority hold themselves to a level of honesty and transparency that even journalistic ethics can't match. True, there are many bloggers who will happily sell their voice to the highest bidder—check out PayPerPost.com for an example of a service that lets you buy reviews from bloggers—but the majority of citizen journalists hold themselves to high levels of integrity.

Bloggers Self-Police Their Ethics

When Microsoft sent bloggers high-end laptops in order to test out Windows Vista—with the hope they'd blog about the new operating system—the bloggers themselves came forward and publicly questioned the generosity of the gift. Many worried the free laptops were being used to influence any review they did of Vista. Seeing the reaction, Microsoft later asked the bloggers to return or donate the laptops.

While transparency is a key component to any blogger contact, if you really want to increase your chances that bloggers will listen to your story, providing them with access to your company's top executives will send a message that they're very important to your business. Crossroads PR's Cindy Akus explains, "It's more powerful for my clients to reach out to a blogger than it is for me as a PR person on their behalf. That person to person outreach really gives credibility to the situation." Although this might be impossible for large corporations, nothing gets the attention of a blogger faster than a personal e-mail or phone call from the CEO of a company.

Method of Contact

So how do you actually make contact with an influential blogger? You might think that high-tech journalists would prefer that you send them e-mails—who knows if they even own a phone? Then again, perhaps a phone call would show that you've taken the time to reach them on a more personal level. Unfortunately, unless the blogger in question is smart enough—or inundated with enough pitches—to set up a protocol explaining how she wishes to receive a media pitch, you'll have to go with your gut. If in doubt, Lee Odden suggests that "there is no substitute for human contact whether it's in person or via phone."

Track the Conversation

Now that you've successfully shared your news with your targeted blogger, your work is by no means over. Remember that blogs are conversations and the blog owner is merely the person who starts the discussion on his blog. If you've done your research, you've likely reached a blogger who has many readers, leaves many comments, and may share your news with others—either via his own blog or some other form of social media.

In Chapters 12 and 13, you'll learn how to monitor social media and keep updated on conversations that involve your company or your personal identity. In the meantime, keep a close eye on any conversation that you've played a role in starting. Pay particular attention to the comments left on any blog post that involves your company. Not only will you likely learn from what others have to say, but there's a great opportunity for you to join the conversation, regardless of whether you already have your own blog. As Akus suggests, "Don't walk from the conversation. Keep your eye on it to see if anyone else jumps in or if anyone else tries to engage you."

Laying the Foundation for Reputation Management

Your online pressroom allows you to share your important company information and craft the perception of your brand, and ensures stakeholders can access your own generated media 24/7. New social media press releases empower others to share your message and make your news more appealing to new media. Finally, blogs have the power to share your message with thousands of readers, connect you to other bloggers who may be interested in your company, and even demonstrate to mainstream journalists that your business has a story worth telling the world.

Creating positive buzz is a vital component in the management of any brand, and will help you in your efforts to influence customer sentiment, but nothing is more powerful in the world of conversational marketing than having others champion your reputation. If you're willing to leave the PR filtered messages behind and understand the new ways of spreading your news around the Web, the chances are high that your efforts will pay off with more media mentions and you'll be rewarded with an increase in the positive perception of your reputation.

Managing Your
Reputation with SEO

The search engines hold the power to boost your reputation or crush it. The contents of ten blue search engine links can decide whether your company wins a new contract or you win that promotion. Google has become the new reputation engine, and your stakeholders use it every day when making decisions about which products to buy or which employees to hire. Although you can't guarantee which web pages will appear in a Google search, search engine optimization (SEO) can help shift the power in your favor. Making your web content more relevant and easier to find will help you manage your Google reputation.

6

Chapter Contents

Google Is the Reputation Engine

There's a good reason why Pontiac suggests television viewers don't just take their word for how great their cars are but instead wants them to Google "Pontiac." Likewise, it's no wonder Matt Mullenweg's business card suggests recipients should search for "Matt" at Google.com. With more than 1.26 billion search engine queries carried out globally each day—according to Piper Jaffray & Co.—it's difficult to find any internet user who doesn't rely on a search engine to sift through the Web and locate the most relevant information. And, with Google dominating 52.7% of all U.S. searches—according to Nielsen//NetRatings—both the car manufacturer and the popular blogger understand the tremendous reputation boost their brands receive from being listed in the first spot on the world's most popular search engine.

Search Engine Market Share in the United States

Google has been the search engine of choice for many years, with more than twice the audience of the second most popular search engine, Yahoo!. Nielsen//NetRatings keeps track of the total number of searches conducted at each search engine. Here's the list of the top five most popular U.S. search engines for June 2007.

SEARCH ENGINE	NUMBER OF SEARCHES (000)	SHARE OF SEARCHES
GOOGLE SEARCH	3,906,877	52.7%
YAHOO! SEARCH	1,496,137	20.2%
MSN/WINDOWS LIVE SEARCH	985,706	13.3%
AOL SEARCH	404,036	5.5%
ASK.COM SEARCH	152,268	2.1%

With such reliance on Google—and the supporting cast of other search engines—we blindly trust in the organic results returned for each entered query (see defining moment). Whether you're researching a new car purchase or simply looking up the background on an individual you've recently met, the information you discover on Google will influence whether you judge their reputation to be positive or negative. And regardless of how many search results returned—38 million in the case of a search for "Pontiac"—62% of search engine users will likely find what they're looking for on the first page of search results, according to search marketing firm iProspect. With Google's dominance assured for the foreseeable future and search engine users relying on the first page of search results, your personal and company reputation is shaped by ten blue links on a simple white background. Google is more than a dominant search engine; it's the world's most trusted reputation engine. The results Google displays for a search on your business brand or personal name can determine whether a customer buys your products or an employer offers you a job.

> ### Defining Moment: Organic Search Engine Results
>
> You might think that "organic" search engine results means they're created without chemicals or additives. You'd actually be close to what the term means. Organic search engine results refer to those search engine listings that are part of Google's normal search engine index. They're the result of Google spidering the Web and using its algorithm to determine which results are the most relevant to the search. In other words, organic results refer to those that weren't paid for by advertisers.

In your quest to become radically transparent, Google can be your biggest ally and your worst enemy. As a business, your goal is to ensure that each of the first ten results is a positive reflection on your company, products, and employees. Without doubt, your company website should be listed number one for any search related to your brand—36% of search engine users expect the most relevant company to be listed here, according to iProspect—but it's also vital to ensure that the remaining nine results have a positive influence on your reputation. A single negative search result among the first ten listed at Google could be enough to deter an investor, cause a customer to shop elsewhere, or result in a blogger deciding to write a less-than-flattering post about your business.

For individuals, the search results for your own name can either do wonders to advance your career or wreck your chances of getting that new job. The comments you left on your friend's MySpace page—relating to an all-night drinking party—may have seemed harmless at the time. However, if they appear on the first page of a Google query for your name, they could result in a negative perception of you. And it's not just your family that will discover your cyber-skeletons. More and more employers are using Google as an additional layer of candidate screening. According to executive search firm ExecuNet, 77% of recruiters said they use search engines to check out job candidates before making a hiring decision. And don't assume potential employers will give you the benefit of the doubt, should they find something incriminating. Search results influence 59% of hiring decisions, and 25% of recruiters polled by business social network Viadeo report they've rejected candidates based on personal information they discovered online.

If it seems unfair that just one negative search result could ruin your business or stifle your career advancement, understand you don't have to sit back and accept the verdict cast on page one by Google's algorithm. Although your efforts to become transparent will help you achieve more positive listings on Google, simply being more open and accountable doesn't automatically result in brownie points with the search engines. And while your optimized press releases and blogger outreach will help craft a positive reputation—as will the use of other social media we describe throughout Part 2—you can't assume that this positive sentiment will make its way to the first page of Google.

Simply supplying Google with content that shares your message in a positive light is not enough. If you want your hard work to filter through to what's shown on the first page of Google's search results, you're going to have to ensure that it's packaged in a way that appeals to the search engine's complex algorithm. There's no sleight of hand or black magic involved. You can't fool Google and you can't force it to show only the pages you think should make up the first ten listings that relate to your company name. However, if you understand that Google is looking for the most relevant, most popular, and most appealing content about your business, you can start to feed it what it craves. This is where search engine optimization plays a part in your radically transparent plans.

SEO for Reputation Management

You're likely already familiar with search engine optimization (SEO) and its sibling, pay-per-click (PPC). SEO is often compared to online public relations (PR)—with your goal to influence Google into believing your web content is algorithmically the best match for any related search query. Meanwhile, PPC is strictly an advertising platform—you decide how much you wish to pay to have your web content listed as sponsored links alongside the corresponding organic search results. If you've dabbled in PPC campaigns of your own, or applied any SEO tactics to your web content, you've taken part in the industry known collectively as search engine marketing (SEM). SEM is extremely important to your online marketing campaign, and its use will help your company better reach the hundreds of millions of daily search engine users. However, SEO is the most useful in your efforts to expand your brand reach and connect your message with your stakeholders.

Why SEO Is Better Than PPC for Branding

Just as we don't recommend advertising to achieve radical transparency, we don't recommend using PPC either. Search engine users are very much aware that those links appearing under headings such as "Sponsored Links" have been paid for by the company listed. Andrew Goodman, CEO of search marketing firm Page Zero Media, doesn't recommend PPC for reputation building. "By and large I'd be using paid search just to conduct business as usual," explains Goodman.

Your stakeholders have a greater level of trust in the organic search results and know that you can't simply buy your way in. Fortunately, they're also mostly unaware that those results can be influenced by SEO. If you can push positive web pages onto the first page of any search engine results page, you'll greatly increase the positive perception of your brand.

SEO is extremely complex to implement. Your goal is to define which search terms match your company's products, tweak your web page's code and visible content to better match those terms, and then get the vote of other web pages in the form of links to your site. Dozens of books have been written on the topic, hundreds of blogs discuss the best strategies, and thousands of articles offer thoughts on various SEO tactics. It can take months to learn the basics of SEO and many more years to master them. If you're already considering skipping this chapter, we have some good news for you. Although SEO can be a complex series of web page enhancements, using it to build and manage your brand—either business or personal—is a lot easier than SEO for e-commerce. You don't have to compete for competitive search terms such as "desktop computers" or "home loans." Your goal is to ensure that a search on Google for your personal name or company returns information that you control and endorse, and that portrays you in a positive way. You still need to know some core SEO tactics to achieve this goal, and you can learn them in the next 20 minutes of reading.

Five Steps to Being Radically Relevant for Google

You've carefully crafted your website, blog, or resume to let stakeholders learn about and discuss your brand. Now you want to make sure that it's *your* message that appears at the top of Google's first page of results. This will create a positive reflection of your brand and therefore influence the conversations that take place. Without an attempt to control the web content displayed for a Google search on your brand, the resulting void can be filled by a web page that may be less than flattering or completely unrelated to your company.

Google's search engine algorithm reportedly uses more than two hundred different factors in determining the order of results for any entered search query. These factors are a closely guarded secret—just like the recipe for Coca-Cola's Coke brand. Fortunately, Google wants website owners to have a better understanding of the more important factors, while at the same time pointing out those tactics that aren't such a good idea. If you simply follow the advice given at Google's online *Webmaster Help Center* (www.google.com/support/webmasters), your web content might achieve higher placement in Google's search results. However, the advice is somewhat brief and it doesn't readily apply to your efforts to make your radically transparent content easier to discover in Google. We've blended Google's guidelines with more than a decade's worth of SEO best practices to come up with our "Five Steps to Being Radically Relevant for Google."

Step 1: Identify Your Brands

Google says, "Think about the words users would type to find your pages, and make sure that your site actually includes those words within it."

The Radically Relevant Way

Before you begin any SEO campaign, it's vital to make sure your efforts are focused on the most relevant search terms, known as *keywords*. In a typical SEO campaign, you would brainstorm and research the keywords that best match the content of your web page and that are searched for frequently. In Dell's case they would target words such as "desktop computers" or "notebooks" as part of their SEO campaign to attract qualified shoppers to their website. Fortunately, when using SEO to build your reputation your keyword selection process is a lot easier. Your goal is not to compete for popular industry-related keywords, but to instead ensure that your web pages appear highly positioned on Google for any of your brand names.

For companies, this means making a note of your company name, any product or service names, your trademarks, and your senior executives. Effectively, any keyword that a stakeholder may enter at Google in an attempt to locate information on your company should be on the list of keywords you target. As Jennifer Grappone and

Gradiva Couzin suggest in their book *Search Engine Optimization: An Hour a Day*, "Take a few minutes to put yourself in the mind of each target audience. Imagine that you are this person, sitting in front of a search engine." Even better—conduct a quick poll among target members to find out what keywords they actually use. For individuals, the keyword selection process is even easier—you simply focus on your own name.

If you've identified multiple keywords—which is likely if you're a large business—keep in mind that you won't be able to target a single page on your site for all of these brands. Although it's likely that your website's home page can rank well on Google for your company name, it's a tall order to also ask it to rank high for product names and key executives. Our advice is to not even try. Instead, find the most relevant pages within your website and focus on getting each page to rank well on Google for the best and most relevant keywords. Some pages will focus on product keywords, while others will focus on your brand names.

Don't Forget Alternative Keyword Spellings

When considering which keywords to focus on, keep in mind variations on the spelling of your brands. If you know your company name is often misspelled—for example, "jetBlue" as two words, not one, or Procter & Gamble and the incorrect Proctor & Gambel—then keep this in mind when selecting keywords. Likewise with personal names—do you always use "James T. Smith" or are you sometimes "Jim Smith?"

Step 2: Make Your Website "Spider Friendly"

Google says, "Make a site with a clear hierarchy and text links… Check for broken links and correct HTML… If fancy features such as JavaScript, cookies, session IDs, frames, DHTML, or Flash keep you from seeing all of your site in a text browser, then search engine spiders may have trouble crawling your site."

The Radically Relevant Way

Sometimes all it takes to ensure your web content appears on the first page of Google's results is to make sure the search engine's spider can understand the page in the first place. Many websites look great to the human eye, but when viewed by a lowly search engine spider, they hardly make any sense. Figure 6.1 shows how pontiac.com looks to most visitors and Figure 6.2 shows how it looks to a search engine spider. As you can see, search engine spiders ignore images and page styles.

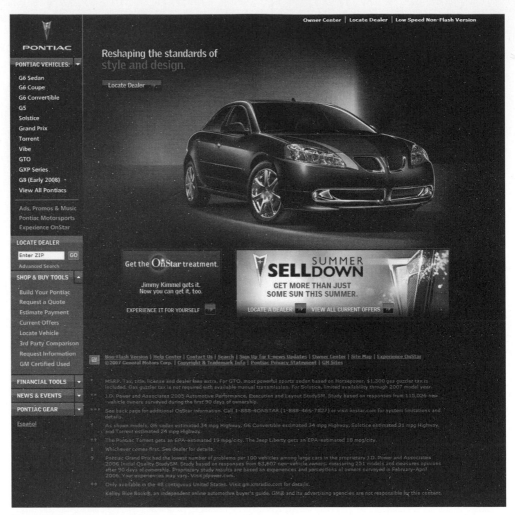

Figure 6.1 Pontiac.com viewed from a web browser

Every page of your site should be clearly named and easy to navigate. A page using the file name *company.com/page_id=256/* is not descriptive enough for Google's spider. Instead, using a more descriptive page name—one that uses one of your identified keywords—will increase the chances the page will rank on Google's first page of results for that keyword. For example, *company.com/john-smith/* is a much better choice, if the page happens to be a bio for John Smith, your company CEO.

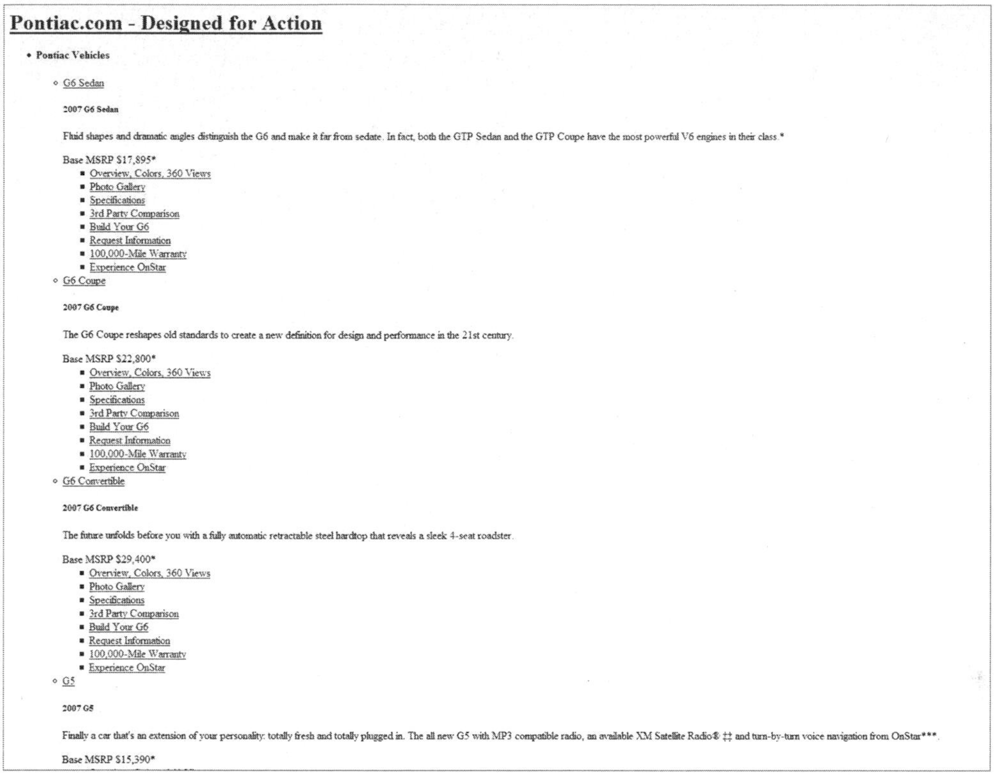

Figure 6.2 Pontiac.com viewed by a search engine spider

In addition to ensuring your web pages are clearly named, it's also important to make sure they're easy to navigate. A search engine spider will attempt to index every page on your website by moving from one page to another. A page that is not easily accessible—because no other page links to it or you're using navigation the spiders have difficulty with, such as Flash, may not make it into Google's index. If Google can't find and index a page that discusses your brand, it won't be there when a journalist researches your company or an employer checks your background.

Defining Moment: Search Engine Spider

A search engine spider is known by many names. *Robot*, *bot*, and *web crawler* are all common names for the small, automated programs the search engines send out to discover web content. Once a page is *spidered*, it is often added to the search engine's existing index of web pages (typically within 2 to 14 days).

Using simple text link navigation will make it easier for the search engines to move to and from one page to another. In addition, whenever linking to another page, be sure to use descriptive text in the link. Using "click here" doesn't tell Google (or your visitor) much about the destination page, whereas "About David Neeleman" informs Google that the destination page is highly relevant to JetBlue's founder.

Step 3: Title Tags

Google says, "Make sure that your TITLE tags...are descriptive and accurate."

The Radically Relevant Way

The TITLE tag is arguably one of the most important factors Google considers when spidering the pages of your website. If your web page were a book in the world's largest library, the TITLE tag would be the book's title running down the spine. Before you even picked the book off the self, you'd have a good idea about its contents. For SEO, the TITLE tag is your chance to tell Google the most dominant keywords for any particular web page. Jill Whalen, CEO of search marketing firm High Rankings, says that out of the two hundred factors that make up Google's algorithm, the TITLE tag is "one of the most important factors in determining rankings."

Many websites have poorly crafted TITLE tags—you've probably seen many that simply say "Home Page" or worse, "Untitled." Not only does a well-written TITLE tag inform the search engine spiders of the main theme for your web page, but it's also the first snippet of information shown to a search engine user. Figure 6.3 highlights how a TITLE tag is displayed in Google's search results.

Figure 6.3 TITLE tag displayed by Google

Most of your web pages will use TITLE tags designed to highlight your products or services. Those pages that contain your radically transparent content—your press-room, for example—should include not only your brand keywords but also a positive statement.

Here's an example of how a typical TITLE tag would look in a web page's code.

`<TITLE>About Us</TITLE>`

Now let's look at a TITLE tag that could help Dell land on the first page of Google's results for the search query "About Dell" and create a positive first impression:

`<TITLE>About Dell: Listening to Customers, Innovating Computer Systems</TITLE>`

As you can see, the suggested TITLE tag would not only increase the chances Google users see the web page—because we used the phrase "About Dell"—but it also sends a positive message before they even click on the result. If you were a journalist conducting research on Dell, you wouldn't even need to view this page to know it contained a positive message.

Every page that discusses your brand should have a uniquely crafted TITLE tag that includes the most relevant keywords for that page. If you can also include a positive statement, it will go a long way in influencing the visitor's perception of your brand.

What Is the Best Length for a TITLE Tag?

While you can use a TITLE tag of any length, Google's algorithm focuses on the first few words. Brian Gilley of consulting firm SEOPosition.com suggests, "Keep your TITLE tag to less than 66 characters as Google's search results will cut off TITLE tags that are any longer."

Step 4: Page Content

Google says, "Create a useful, information-rich site, and write pages that clearly and accurately describe your content."

The Radically Relevant Way

"The search engines love, love, love content. Because they can't understand images, they rely on content to determine what a web page is about," explains Catherine Seda, in her book *How to Win Sales & Influence Spiders*. For this reason, it's important to ensure that each page of your website is focused around a theme of keywords. For a normal SEO campaign, this would involve keeping your optimization efforts for the keyword "notebooks" confined to one or two highly relevant pages—increasing the chances that your web page will rank highly for that keyword in Google's search results. As part of your radically relevant SEO campaign, your goal is to ensure that your web pages are favorably positioned for keyword searches that relate to the name of your company or your own personal name.

To achieve this goal, make sure that you practically spell out the main focus of each web page to Google. If you have a page that contains the career bio of your founder, mention her name a few times on the page. Likewise, if you want a press release for a new product launch to show well in Google, increase the number of times you mention the product name in the release (refer to Chapter 5 for more advice on press release optimization). Increasing the keyword density—the number of times a keyword appears on a page, compared to all other words—is something that search engine optimizers have practiced for many years.

There's no magic number of keyword occurrences that will ensure a web page jumps to number one on Google. While you should increase the keyword density of the page, it's also important to not overdo it. As SEO consultant Jordan McCollum explains, "You don't need your keywords in the text as often as you can possibly mention them; search engines may even frown on that." In fact, getting the right keyword density is often a moving target and you won't necessarily know if you have enough keyword occurrences or too many until Google has indexed the page. In the meantime, the best rule of thumb is to "try to mention your keywords as often as would be natural in a conversation," suggests McCollum.

While you do want to optimize your web pages so that they'll more likely appear on the first page of search results, it's important to not do so at the expense of your radically transparent voice. Remember, you're not only hoping your content is found on the first page of Google, but you want to it represent you well. Catherine Seda reminds us, "Keep in mind that the search engines aren't ultimately your most important audience—your prospects and the press are." If you simply stuff your press releases or resume with keywords you may end up pushing your page to the top of the search engines, but you'll sacrifice your message to get it there. Go ahead and make sure you're using words that match what a blogger may enter at Google when looking for information on you, but heed the advice of Jordan McCollum: "You need to optimize your page's content most importantly to make them appeal to people who visit your site."

Step 5: Incoming Links

Google says, "Make sure all the sites that should know about your pages are aware your site is online… Submit your site to relevant directories such as the Open Directory Project and Yahoo!, as well as to other industry-specific expert sites… Don't participate in link schemes designed to increase your site's ranking or PageRank."

One of the reasons that Google became so popular, so quickly, was its PageRank algorithm. Using a complex mathematical formula, Google is able to quickly understand the most relevant result for a search query by analyzing the linking structure of the neighborhood of pages for that keyword. Mike Grehan, SEO veteran and author of the e-book *Search Engine Marketing*, explains, "They 'know' what specific pages are about and they assume that pages that link together are somehow related. They are essentially sharing their reputation with each other. The more pages that point to a specific page, the more importance or influence that page has in their calculations."

If you want your web content to appear at the top of Google, you'll have to convince the search engine that your page is more relevant and popular than any other. Tweaking keywords and TITLE tags are a good start, but Google won't be convinced until it sees that other web pages are vouching for you. At its core, Google's algorithm considers each incoming link as a vote for your web page. Much like the real world, the web page with the most votes often wins the popularity contest. However, Google understands that not all links are created equal and is looking for links from high-quality third-party pages that are relevant to your page's topic. If you're selling flowers online, a link from the American Horticultural Society website or FTD.com will do more to help your Google ranking than a link from a newly created blog about women's fashions. Jim Boykin, CEO of Internet marketing firm We Build Pages, says, "He with the right 10 links can beat the guy with 1000 of the wrong links." Boykin explains. "I truly believe that the engines are trying to find the neighborhood."

Building links to a web page can be done in a number of ways. Here are the most common methods to get you pointed in the right direction.

- Write high-quality content that web visitors will want to bookmark, share with their friends, and, most importantly, link to from their own website.

- Find relevant websites that might agree to add a link to your web page. If you find a website that focuses on your industry, send them an e-mail and ask that they consider adding a link to your website. Search for sites that rank highly in Google—a good sign that Google considers them trustworthy—and try to get a link from the most relevant page on their website to the one you're trying to optimize.

- You can also buy links from web directories, such as the Yahoo! Directory, and other websites relevant to yours. Sites such as TextLinkAds.com and SponsoredReviews.com make it easy for you to buy links from relevant websites and blogs. However, be warned! Google's policy on buying links is not particularly clear, so we recommend seeking the assistance of an SEO company or consultant should you decide to purchase incoming links to your web pages.

- *Linkbaiting* is a relatively new method of building links to web pages. It takes its name from the practice of creating "buzz-worthy" content that "hooks" a lot of links in a very short period of time. By creating something unique, jaw-dropping, or controversial, your goal is to attract the attention of the blogosphere and social bookmarking sites.

- Look for linking opportunities from your own websites. Google analyzes all links to a web page, so make sure you don't leave a web page isolated without a link from another page on your own site. In addition, if you have more than one website, it can be useful to interlink them. We're not suggesting linking every page of one of your websites to every page of another. But, if you have a page on your corporate website that does well on Google for your company name, a link from this page could help your blog rank well too.

> **Thought Byte: Existing Business Partners Are Great Linking Opportunities**
>
> Before you start building new links to your web pages, take some time to consider your existing opportunities. Do you have any existing business partners that could link to your web page? Approach them and ask them to link to your web pages using the keywords that match your brand names. You'll find this a lot easier than obtaining links from new websites.

As we've already explained, the topic of search engine optimization has filled many books and is the topic of hundreds of websites and blogs. While we've covered the basics, those of you looking for in-depth SEO advice should consider the following resources. The remainder of this chapter is dedicated to helping you proactively manage your search engine reputation and to getting your radically transparent content to the top of Google.

Books

How to Win Sales & Influence Spiders by Catherine Seda (New Riders, 2007)

Search Engine Marketing by Mike Grehan (online at www.search-engine-book.co.uk)

Search Engine Optimization: An Hour a Day by Jennifer Grappone and Gradiva Couzin (Sybex, 2006)

SEO Book by Aaron Wall (online at www.seobook.com)

Websites

www.SearchEngineGuide.com

www.SearchEngineJournal.com

www.SearchEngineLand.com

www.SearchEngineWatch.com

www.SERoundtable.com

www.SEOmoz.org

www.WebmasterWorld.com

Proactive Management of Your Search Engine Reputation

When applied to your radically transparent conversations, SEO has the potential to ensure that your content dominates the first page of results for any search query that pertains to your brand. With most searchers focusing their attention on the first ten results they find at Google, it's important that these results convey a positive sentiment about you as a person or your business. In Part 3, we'll show you how to monitor your search engine reputation and provide steps you can take should a negative listing make its way onto the first page of Google. While there are some tactics you can use to clean up your search engine reputation, it's by far easier to make the investment now, while there's no crisis to worry about. As Nan Dawkins, founder of interactive marketing firm RedBoots, explains, "The more content you have—especially positive content generated by consumers, constituents, and supporters—the easier it is to minimize the impact of a negative ranking."

Laying a foundation in Google means ensuring the first ten listings for any of your identified keywords reflect positively on you or your business. If you can optimize ten different web pages for your company name—and they fill up the first ten results in Google—it's going to be a lot tougher for a detractor's web page to show up at a later date. Using your own website, and the creation of new social media content, it's possible to exert your influence over Google's first page of results. Some social media content works better for businesses reputations (such as MySpace), while others are better suited to personal identities (such as Facebook).

With this in mind, we've outlined ten examples of web content that are best suited to manage the search engine reputation of businesses and another ten for personal identities. Of course, there's a little overlap—a blog can be used by individuals as well as companies—but you'll discover that some social media sites are better suited to one over the other. Get ready to learn how to create a foundation of positive search engine results for your brands. Instead of simply handing you our "Five Steps to Being Radically Relevant for Google" and then leaving you to figure out which web content works best, we're removing the guesswork for you.

124

Google Content for Companies

If you search Google for the keyword "KFC" you'll likely discover that the fast-food company Kentucky Fried Chicken is listed number one and number two on the first page of results. While perusing that same results page, you'll also quickly discover the websites KentuckyFriedCruelty.com and KFCCruelty.com, as well as an urban legends page that answers the question of whether KFC actually uses chickens or "meat from genetically engineered animals"—for the record, they do use chickens. Despite Yum! Brands, Inc.–owned KFC making *BusinessWeek*'s 2007 list of *Top 100 Global Brands*, the company's reputation is subjected to some degree of negative portrayal every time it is researched using Google. And while the company has created a website for *Colonel's Scholars*—their degree scholarship program—and has country-specific websites around the world, KFC hasn't taken control of its Google reputation. In fact, you're more likely to find a video of rats in one of their New York restaurants than a corporate blog post explaining their commitment to customer health.

Unfortunately, this negativity happens to many well-known brands—consumers love to pick on the big guy. Until recently, a search for "Dell" would have revealed a similar story. Jeff Jarvis's blog post and IHateDell.com would be typical of the web content that defined Dell's search engine reputation. Fortunately, Dell realized the power in being radically transparent and at the same time created multiple channels of web content—all designed to influence their stakeholders and, of course, Google. Nowadays, a Google search for the computer manufacturer will likely display their blog, their support forum, and their site dedicated to Linux. Dell's search engine reputation is better protected from the next blog attack, because not only is the company engaging customers, but it's also making sure its online voice uses many Google-friendly outlets.

Most Google users view only the first ten results in Google, with the majority influenced by what they discover. If you want to have the best chance that your voice is what they discover when researching your business, we suggest focusing on the following ten sources of web content.

1. Your Company Website

There's absolutely no reason that your company website shouldn't occupy the number one spot on Google's search results. Unless your business is very new, or you've chosen a company name that is very generic—such as Mortgages, Inc.—Google should have no problem in agreeing that your website is the most relevant there is for any search that matches your company name. Google's algorithm allows its results to show two pages from any single website for the entered search query. While this limitation means you can't expect to see every page of your website listed, you at least should see two pages occupy that all-important first page of results.

You'll likely find your home page takes the number one spot. It's important to not let Google decide which page is the second most relevant page to show in relation to your company brand. Instead, focus your optimization efforts on the pages that include your radically transparent content and portray your business in the most positive way. For example, if your investor relations page doesn't exactly show a positive stock price trend over the past year, turn your attention to your "about us" page or pressroom instead.

2. Corporate Subdomains

Take a tip from Dell, Microsoft, and JetBlue. Each of these companies understands that creating a subdomain is a great way to create a website that piggybacks off the main corporate brand. Not only do support.dell.com, support.microsoft.com, and help.jetblue.com provide targeted web destinations to reach out to customers, but Google treats each favorably too.

Adding a subdomain to your website allows you to take advantage of a weakness in Google's algorithm. Google appears to pass on some of the reputation from the parent domain name, while treating the subdomain as a completely separate web entity—a great way to get around its restriction of only two web pages per site, per search query. Now, before you jump for joy and instruct your webmaster to build dozens of subdomains, there's the caveat. Google will look closely at two things when analyzing a subdomain. First, is there substantial content, such as multiple pages, on the subdomain? Second, does the content differ from the main corporate website? Usually your customer support or career information will meet these criteria. Likewise, a very distinct product line merits its own subdomain, such as Microsoft's office.microsoft.com for its *Microsoft Office* brand (see Figure 6.4).

Another thing to remember with a subdomain—and any website you build— you'll still need to make sure there are relevant links to pointing to it.

Figure 6.4 The office.microsoft.com site

3. Additional Corporate Websites

If you want to book a flight with JetBlue, they'll direct you to jetblueairways.com, not jetblue.com. Have an idea to share with Dell? Visit dellideastorm.com, not dell.com. In fact, take a look at just about any large corporation and you'll discover that one website is often not enough for all of its web content. Even subdomains aren't the best solution for a website that expands beyond the company's normal business activities.

As with subdomains, Google will look closely to ensure that the content is completely different from your main corporate site. However, as you're only interested in the site ranking for your brand, you don't need a lot of effort to convince Google the site should grace the first page of its results. If you're struggling for ideas as to what to create on your new site, here are some suggestions:

- Create a website for your community relations and charitable efforts.
- Build a forum for your customers to interact and share ideas.

- Separate your corporate information from the actual purchasing. The Coca Cola Company has both coca-cola.com and thecoca-colacompany.com.

- Extend your main brand to other sub-brands. Visit virgin.com and you'll see how CEO Richard Branson has extended the Virgin name to more than 30 different companies.

4. Create a Corporate Blog

Your official company blog doesn't have to reside within a directory of your main corporate website. If you decide to set it free, it can happily occupy a unique domain name on its own. While this doesn't give you the benefit of blog readers directly visiting your main website, it does allow you to potentially take up another one of Google's search listings for your brand. Take a look at Dell's direct2dell.com blog to see how they've successfully launched a corporate blog on a separate website.

In Chapter 9, you'll learn more about starting your own blog, and we'll explore the advantages and disadvantages of keeping your blog separated from your corporate website.

5. Create a Social Network Profile

MySpace.com is one of the largest and most popular social networks on the internet, with more than 67 million monthly unique visitors, according to web research firm Compete. While most of the profiles that are registered relate to individuals—making it useful for managing your individual reputation—it's MySpace's willingness to accept business profiles that makes it valuable in your search engine reputation management efforts. Unlike many social networks, MySpace is a great place for a business to create an alternative web presence. A MySpace profile will help you extend the conversation to wide-ranging demographics—more than half of all users are over 35—and the profiles tend to rank well in search engine results.

The key to making a MySpace profile work for your search engine efforts is to pay attention to the name you use for the profile. Not only should you use your company name for the display name—as opposed to the normal use of your personal name—but MySpace also allows you to specify the page name for your profile. When you first sign up, MySpace will allocate your profile a very nondescript URL, such as *myspace.com/12345678*. However, each profile gets one opportunity to change their URL to something more descriptive. We recommend changing the URL to match the keyword that you're targeting for your SEO campaign, such as *myspace.com/ companyname*. Take a look at Figure 6.5 for a screenshot of Starbuck's myspace.com/ starbucks profile.

Figure 6.5 Starbucks MySpace profile page

Once you've set up your profile so that your display name and URL match your brand, you can then decide how much extra effort you'd like to put into your profile. In Chapter 10, we'll talk more about using social networks to help with your marketing conversations.

6. Create Your Own Social Network

Creating a social network profile is quick and easy, but you can take it one step further by creating your own social network. Ning.com is a company that helps individuals and companies create their own social networking sites. Whether you wish to build your own version of Flickr's photo-sharing site, a video-sharing service similar to YouTube, or perhaps a network of friends comparable to MySpace, Ning is a great solution.

The brand value that comes from hosting your own social network is enormous. With some effort, you can create a community for stakeholders and passionate advocates of your brand. For your Google reputation management efforts, Ning allows you to create a site that will quickly fill up with user-generated content—something the search engines can't get enough of—and you can also name the network to match your brand. And while Ning will let you create a social network for free, it also offers a number of white-label options for businesses. For example, for less than $5 a month, you can assign any available domain name you wish to your social network. Setting up a video hosting site and using *companynamevideos.com* can be done quickly, cheaply, and without any headaches. Best of all, you've created another web property to take up one of the top ten results on Google.

7. Create a Wiki

Thanks to astounding success of the online encyclopedia Wikipedia.org, internet users are quite familiar with the concept of wikis. If your company is established and enjoys a high profile, the chances are good that there's already a Wikipedia page that discusses your business, or there's enough justification for the creation of one. Unfortunately, if your business is young or hasn't yet established a well-known brand, you'll find it difficult to achieve an entry at Wikipedia—companies that are not well known tend to get rejected by Wikipedia's editors. If you're lucky enough to have a Wikipedia page about your brand it will likely rank well for related Google search queries.

The good news is that you don't have to rely on a Wikipedia page in order to take up a top ten spot on Google. There are many other wikis your company can use (such as AboutUs.org), and you can even create your own wiki, thanks to services such as Wetpaint.com. Not only does Wetpaint allow you to create a wiki on any topic you wish, but they'll even give you a Wetpaint subdomain such as *companyname.wetpaint.com*.

Set up a Wetpaint wiki for your company and you can create lots of optimized content while also encouraging your stakeholders to contribute their thoughts. If you'd rather just use Wetpaint as a placeholder in Google's search results for your business, you can restrict user contributions to only those you select.

8. Create Your Own Company News Portal

Now that your company news is social media optimized, how about a place to let your stakeholders keep track of your news while also tracking weather, stocks, and movies? Customized start pages such as Newsvine.com and Netvibes.com allow web users to create a home page that includes instant access to their favorite news, blogs, and other social media.

Thanks to Netvibes Universe, companies can create branded start pages and share them with customers, employees, and Google. Newsvine lets you create a customized news portal, and allocates a subdomain to you. Once again, you can create *companyname.newsvine.com* and benefit from an additional page in Google's results, while piggybacking with the credible Newsvine.

9. Build a Page with Google Page Creator

How could you pass up an opportunity to create a web page that's hosted on one of Google's own domain names? Imagine the instant credibility with Google's spider.

That's exactly what's available if you sign up for Google Page Creator (pages.google.com, Figure 6.6). Google provides you with all the tools to create and host a basic website and they'll also let you pick a subdomain such as *yourcompany.googlepages.com.*

While Google doesn't promise any preferential treatment in its search results, it does promise "the pages you create can be crawled by Google within a few hours of publication." Your keyword-rich website can be about anything your wish—perhaps you'll discuss your upcoming investor conference call—and could quickly occupy one of the ten listings on a Google search for your brand.

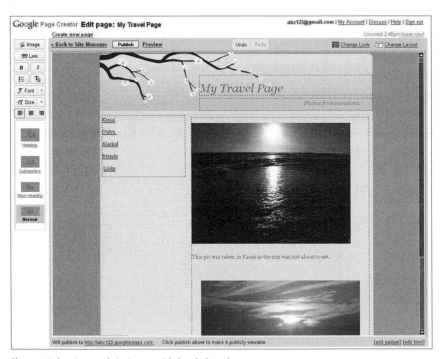

Figure 6.6 Creating a website is easy with Google Page Creator.

10. Create a Co-Branded Page

Not all web content you create needs to be on a domain name that your company owns. Co-branding is often used to help two individual brands join forces and benefit from each other's reputation strengths. The same applies to your Google reputation.

A quick look through the search results page for the query "Dell" reveals a co-branded page for Google and Dell—google.com/ig/dell. This page highlights the business relationship between the two companies—Google is installed on all Dell computers and Dell manufactures Google's Search Appliance hardware—but also demonstrates the power of building a co-branding web page.

Your business partners might not be as auspicious as Google or Dell, but you should evaluate those who might help you with your Google reputation. Take a look at the websites of your key business partners and see how well ranked they are on Google. If you find one or two partners with websites that appear to be trusted by the search engine, approach them and ask if they'd consider a page on their site that discusses your business relationship. If they agree to a page that is named using your brand, and they allow you to provide input on the content used, the page could be another opportunity to positively influence Google's users.

Google Content for Individuals

Despite starring in dozens of blockbuster movies, an Academy Award for "best actor," and topping the "world's most powerful celebrity" list by *Forbes* in 2004, Google's search results won't let Mel Gibson forget a dark chapter in his career. On July 28, 2006, Gibson was arrested on suspicion of driving under the influence and later pleaded "no contest," resulting in a sentence of three years probation and mandatory Alcoholics Anonymous meetings. The resulting media frenzy was fueled by reports that Gibson had made anti-Semitic remarks during his arrest. More than a year later, a Google search for his name reveals a Wikipedia page fully documenting the events, an allegation by TMZ.com that the police tried to cover up Gibson's arrest, and Gibson's mug shot on thesmokinggun.com. Despite many apologies and honest interviews with the media, Gibson's reputation was damaged by that single incident.

Almost one year after Gibson's own DUI incident, celebrity Paris Hilton served 22 days for violating the terms of her parole from a previous alcohol-related reckless driving charge. Yet despite hundreds of mainstream and social media publications covering the incident, there's no apparent mention of it on the first page of a Google search. Instead, you'll find Hilton's MySpace profile, her official website, and an official Paris Hilton YouTube video channel. Paris Hilton's Google reputation is strong enough to withstand even a criminal record.

Much like businesses, Google can portray individuals in a positive or negative light. Employers, customers, journalists, and even your own family will use a search engine to learn about your reputation. If you're unlucky, there may be plenty of other people who share your name—meaning the first page of Google won't be solely about you—but at some point a searcher will find information that is specific to you. Taking the time to create positive content will help ensure those searching find only the information you want them to find.

1. Create a Website

If you're one of the lucky ones, either you already own yourname.com or it's still available via one of the many domain name registrars. If you don't yet own a domain that matches your name, go ahead and grab it now. If your name happens to be Jane Smith or one of the many millions of common name combinations, the chances are someone else has already registered the domain. Don't panic; you can still register a domain name that includes your name—you'll just have to be a little more creative.

Here are some ways to find a domain name that includes your name:

- Include your middle name as part of your domain name.

- Add the name of your city or zip code to the end of the domain name; for example, *johnsmithchicago.com.*

- Add your profession to the domain name; for example, janesmithphotographer.com.

There are many options for registering a domain name that matches your name, but be sure to register the name you most commonly use. You wouldn't want to register jamessmith.com if everyone knows you as "Jim."

Once you have your domain name registered, it's time to add a website. While it can be expensive to set up a website and pay for its hosting, it doesn't have to be. One of the most popular domain registrars, GoDaddy.com, offers a free five-page website and free hosting with each domain name registered. Take advantage of this and create a simple site that explains who you are, your hobbies, and maybe even your uploaded resume.

2. Create a Free Blog

You've already learned that a subdomain is treated as a separate website, while at the same time benefiting from the credibility of the parent domain name. As an individual, you can use this to your advantage and create a free blog in the process.

Both Wordpress.com and Google's Blogger.com offer free blogs that can be set up in a matter of minutes. The best part is that you can select a personalized subdomain and benefit from their credibility. Setting up *yourname.wordpress.com* or *yourname.blogspot.com* (Blogspot.com is Blogger's hosting service) will give you another website to occupy a Google search for your name and give you a blog to share your radically transparent musings with the Web. Check Chapter 9 for an in-depth look at setting up and managing your blog.

3. Join a Social Network

Social networks are a great way to connect with family, friends and co-workers. They're also the place to connect with customers, employers, investors, and the media. While many individuals set up a social networking profile using a nickname or alias—which is fine for the things you do wish to keep private—this doesn't really help you influence your stakeholders or Google's search results. Instead, if you really want to put your social networking profile to work, use your real name when setting it up. As Todd Malicoat of SEO consulting firm Stuntdubl tells us, "I don't think anonymous alias use is of much good for personal branding. Branding your real name keeps you responsible for what you say."

There are a host of social networks that would love to have you join their ranks—we'll explore social networks in more detail in Chapter 10. While setting up a MySpace profile might appear to be the obvious choice, we've found that Facebook.com better serves your two goals: building your personal brand and occupying a Google results page for a search on your name. Setting up a Facebook profile is easy and while you won't be able to manually select the URL for your profile, it will automatically include your first and last name. With one or two links pointing to it, you should find that your Facebook profile moves up Google's results pretty easily.

How Many Social Networks Should You Join?

If you had to pick just one social network to join, we'd recommend Facebook. However, social networks are like shifting sands and therefore it would be prudent to set up profiles at multiple locations. This practice will allow you to test which ones do well in Google and which don't. As Todd Malicoat explains, "Domains and algorithms will come and go, but if you sign up enough times with your name, you will find some sites that will establish trust and rank."

4. Create a Business Profile

While Facebook tends to focus on the "social" in social networking, many networks cater to business professionals. Both ZoomInfo.com and LinkedIn.com allow you to create and edit your business profile, but it's LinkedIn that gets our vote when it comes to managing your personal reputation.

Not only does LinkedIn include some great business networking tools, but it also gives you great customization of the information pertaining to your career. One of the options we particularly like about LinkedIn is the ability to select a more personalized URL for your profile. Instead of letting a series of anonymous numbers represent your profile, you can tell LinkedIn to use your full name. Remember, Google is looking for the pages that best match a search for your name. Any time you can create a profile that also includes your name in the profile URL, you'll increase your chances that Google will include that page on the first page of its results. Figure 6.7 shows the LinkedIn profile for Matt Mullenweg.

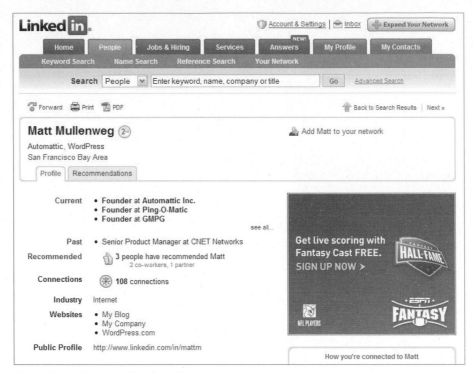

Figure 6.7 Matt Mullenweg's LinkedIn profile

5. Share Your Photos with the World

As you'll learn in Chapter 7, what you say and write is very much complemented by the sensory media you share with your stakeholders. Not only is sharing your photos and images with the world a sign that you're radically transparent, but it's also another great way to influence Google.

Yahoo!-owned Flickr.com is one of the most popular image-sharing sites on the internet. The site boasts more than 7 million registered users and hosts more than 400 million images. Flickr also happens to be a great way to boost your Google reputation. You can use your personal or company names for the profile and customize the page URL allocated to your profile. Another great benefit of using Flickr is that it gives Google a place to discover flattering photos of you. With the search engine selectively showing images as part of its normal search results, Flickr presents an opportunity to show off that corporate headshot when an investor or journalist comes looking. Label your photos with your own name and you'll increase your chances Google will rank the page.

6. Answer Others' Questions

Another profile that can rank well on Google is courtesy of Yahoo! Answers. The service is designed to help users ask questions and receive answers from the community. We like Yahoo! Answers for Google reputation management because you're able to take advantage of a profile that's a subdomain of Yahoo.com. While you can't customize the profile URL to include your name, you can choose whichever profile name you wish and also include your name again in the "About Me" section. Rand Fishkin, co-founder of SEOmoz.org, suggests another way to use Yahoo! Answers to influence your Google reputation: "You can use your company name or personal name in the title of a question. It's another great way to fill up search engine results."

In Chapter 10 we'll explain how you can use Yahoo! Answers to build your reputation and expertise in your chosen field of work.

7. Create a Social Bookmarking Profile

Social bookmarking sites such as Digg.com, del.icio.us, and StumbleUpon.com are very popular components of social media. The profiles that you create on these sites also happen to be very search engine friendly.

StumbleUpon is particularly Google friendly because it allows you to use your real name in the profile and provides you with a subdomain such as *janesmith .stumbleupon.com*. We'll explore social bookmarking sites in more detail in Chapter 10.

8. Using Shopping and Review Sites

Consumer-generated media involves more than writing blogs and uploading videos. The concept of "social shopping" means that more of us are relying on the wisdom of others to help us make our online buying decisions. Amazon.com does a great job of matching consumer reviews with the products they sell, and that's good news for those managing their Google reputation.

You don't have to buy a single product on Amazon.com in order to set up a free profile with them. You can't customize the profile URL, but the page's TITLE tag will include your full name and these profiles tend to rank well on Google. Of course, Google loves content, so be sure to put content in your user profile—Amazon allows up to 4,000 words—and set up your own shopping lists and product reviews.

9. Start Editing Wikipedia

Wikipedia.org is the world's largest online encyclopedia. It also happens to rely on the contributions of volunteer editors. There are few rewards for helping Wikipedia keep track of its more than 7 million articles, but there is one that can help your Google reputation immensely.

As a volunteer editor you can sign up for a profile and share information about who you are, while keeping track of all the edits you've made to the site. With Google favoring Wikipedia's pages, your profile can make its way onto the first page of results for your name. However, there is a small caveat. In order for your Wikipedia profile to jump to the first page of Google, you'll need to be active in your editing. Rand Fishkin gives this advice for boosting your Wikipedia profile: "Instead of making a few big edits to articles you really care about, make tons and tons of little edits, to all sorts of articles on your field." Although that might sound like a lot of work, Fishkin says the payoff can be huge: "Your profile page can rank very, very nicely."

10. Bringing Your Profiles Together

Naymz.com describes itself as a "reputation network that lets you establish and promote your good name online." We like to think of it as a centralized location for sharing links to all of your social networking profiles. With Naymz you can add your profile and talk about your successes. In addition, they're generous enough to let you link to your blog, website, and other social media profiles. Profiles on Naymz tend to rank well in Google's organic search results, and the site offers services to include your profile in Google's sponsored listings as well.

Leveraging Third-Party Content

Do you really have to do all of the hard work yourself? What if you run out of your own content or the time to supply Google—what happens then? The good news is that you don't have to rely solely on the content you create and optimize for the search engines.

With your radically transparent efforts, you're already reaching the press, customers, employees, and investors. Although you can't directly control what they say about you—or dictate their SEO efforts—you can utilize third-party content as part of your Google reputation management. Nothing will be as powerful as the content you create and control directly, but you can still find ways to exert a positive influence over the content that makes its way into Google's search results.

With the right approach, you can use the efforts of other web content creators to serve your own radically transparent needs—while at the same time flooding Google's search results with content that portrays your reputation in a positive light.

Seminars and Conferences

Whether you're a business or an individual, participation in a conference is a great way to build your reputation. If you find yourself invited to speak, you can use this to build your resume and impress future clients or employers. If your business is exhibiting or sponsoring an event, use your involvement to impress customers, investors, and the media. The news gets better when you learn that your involvement in seminars and conferences can help with your Google reputation.

Most events will provide sponsors a profile page that describes your business and the products or services you offer. They'll likely ask you for this description, so make sure you optimize any content to include the keywords you want to rank well in Google. Likewise, as a speaker you'll often get asked to provide a speaker's profile, so that the event can display your experience and expertise. Even though you won't have the same control over the optimization of these pages, you should ask if the page can be named using your chosen keywords—and you can definitely point a link or two to the page. Both strategies will increase the chances of the page displaying at the top of Google's search results.

Associations and Professional Memberships

Joining a professional association for your industry is another great way to show off your credentials while also creating content for the search engines. For companies, ask about a profile page whenever you join any association. Most city chambers of commerce and industry associations will provide you with a place to share details of your business, but you may have to ask for it. For individuals, opportunities could arise from your involvement with the local civic group, your personal membership of industry associations, or even your university alumni association.

Most associations tend to have well-established websites that are trusted by the search engines. Any newly created page will quickly inherit that same level of trust and could penetrate the top ten of Google faster than any social networking profile.

Write Articles or White Papers

If the thought of starting your own blog purely to help with your Google reputation makes you break out in a cold sweat, why not consider writing for someone else instead? There are many great online newsletters, blogs, and article sites that would love to receive an article or white paper from you. It helps them out, because they get someone else to do all of the hard work while providing valuable advice for their audience. It helps you out because it brands you as an expert in your field, and your article may appear in Google.

Look for sites that already rank well in Google and appear to have built up their audience levels. If you can, get them to agree on an author's profile page as this will allow you to include liberal use of your own name and the name of your company. Failing that, ask for your name to appear at the top of the article and a small paragraph about you at the bottom of the piece. If your contribution resonates with the website's readers, it might attract a number of links, which will help get the page to the top of the search engines.

Defining Moment: White Paper

This is the widely used informal name for a fairly lengthy authoritative report, written by an expert, and published either online or offline. Often used for marketing purposes, such as to generate sales leads, white papers are meant to educate and inform readers and not serve as marketing product brochures.

Offer Yourself for an Interview

Of course, you'd love to have *The Wall Street Journal* or CBS call and ask to interview you, but don't overlook the potential of an interview by a blogger or smaller news site.

Many blogs would love to speak to you, and if you approach them and offer an interview, you'll often find them more receptive than mainstream media. Telephone interviews are good, but it doesn't hurt to suggest an interview over e-mail. While this takes a little more effort on your part, you'll find that you'll have greater control over what you say and how you say it. You'll also find that interviewers will be much less inclined to edit your interview if it's already laid out for them in writing. While you don't want to sound like a giant advertisement for your business, certainly go ahead and reference your brand names—which will help you get the interview page on Google's radar.

Once the interview is published, all it takes is a few links from other bloggers and the page will likely move up the search engine results. Add a link from your own pressroom and you'll help that process while also pointing stakeholders to your carefully chosen words.

Give a Helping Hand to Others' Content

One of the biggest reasons a negative page will rank well at Google is because it creates a buzz and other web pages decide to link to it. It's highly unlikely that the Jeff Jarvises of the world spend hours optimizing a negative post—they have better things to do.

With this in mind, you can turn this into a positive strategy for your brand. Any time that your name is mentioned in a positive article or blog post, look for ways to help that page increase its placement in Google's search results. You could link to it from your pressroom, mention it in a press release, or announce it on your blog. Your ultimate goal is to spread the word and build some links to the page. The page is already discussing your brand and including appropriate keywords, so a few extra links might help its search engine ranking.

Buy a Little Blog Buzz

We've already mentioned that you can help your SEO efforts by paying for incoming links from bloggers, but you can also focus purely on the buzz. Companies such as PayPerPost.com, ReviewMe.com, and SponsoredReviews.com are primarily used by search engine marketers to build links to a particular website. That's a short-sighted approach because you can also use these services to create some positive buzz about your brand.

Using these services, you can pay for a blogger to review any website for as little as $40. With a budget of just a few hundred dollars, you can recruit multiple bloggers to flood the search engines with blog posts that discuss your business and its brand. The amount of control you have over what the blogger says is limited and you can't even guarantee the post will be a positive reflection on your company—although it's an unwritten rule that since you're paying the blogger, you're expecting the resulting post to be positive.

Is it effective? Rand Fishkin claims it's "an incredible way to fill up the search results. You can take over your company name, or personal name, with that type of material." Just keep in mind that buying blog posts in this way may be perceived as not being authentic. You should carefully consider the benefits of having positive content in Google with the potential negatives of being associated with paid content.

Keep Looking for New Google Opportunities

Our lists of recommendations for companies and individuals are by no means exhaustive. Many options are available to positively influence what Google's search results say about your brand. As you experiment with different web content, you'll learn that some social networks continue to grow in their Google stature, while others start off strong—quickly landing on the first page of results—then seem to fade for no apparent reason. As Todd Malicoat recommends, "The best thing to do is constantly test new sites" in order to keep a fresh supply of content coming Google's way.

Test, test, and test again. Search engine optimization isn't a onetime event. You can't simply optimize ten pages and expect them to immediately and forever occupy the first page of Google's search results page. Continue to fine-tune your web pages, keep an eye out for new social networks, and identify new opportunities to discuss your brand. Keep our "Five Steps to Being Radically Relevant for Google" at the top of your mind and you'll look at each new web page as an opportunity to influence Google's reputation engine.

The next two chapters show how to create reputation-building content for the hungry search engines and your target stakeholders.

Using Multimedia Content to Engage Your Audience

Are you ready to paint your desired reputation online using a multimedia palette? Astute companies use relevant digital images, video, and audio to demonstrate their expertise and gain respect. You can solicit fabulous multimedia content produced by the citizen journalists and also craft your own content for posting on your sites and in the social media. Everything about you and your brands online paints a picture of who you really are, from your head shot to that podcast interview and the video of your last conference keynote. Craft them carefully and you, too, can be a well-recognized thought leader experiencing business or career growth because you are radically transparent online.

7

Chapter Contents

A Thousand Words

Your Thought Leadership Niche

Introducing the Multimedia Content Palette

SEO for Images, Videos, and Podcasts

Other Multimedia Content

A Thousand Words

The Eastman Kodak Company, a Fortune 500 imaging company, knows the value of photos to enrich a written story. In September 2006 it launched *A Thousand Words,* a blog written by employees worldwide and targeted to consumers. Four months later Kodak introduced a second employee-authored blog to discuss its technology innovations. *A Thousand Nerds* targets students, professional photographers, "other scientists, technologists, early adopters, and key technology influencers/thought leaders," according to Denise A. Stinardo, Manager, New Media, Eastman Kodak Company.

Kodak adapted a lot from its humble beginnings to survive 119 years, and the new blogs help move the company into the 21st century. Stinardo describes Kodak's reputation goal driving these blogs:

> 66 Our goal is to burnish Kodak's technology reputation by presenting the company as digital, innovative and relevant in this digital communication medium, but our approach was different. Instead of having executives' blog, we opened it up to every day employees who had an interest and ability to tell their stories with gripping prose and powerful imagery. Employees from around the world, from New York to California, from Australia and China to Italy and Paris, post content daily during the week. 99

A Thousand Words receives between 15,000 and 20,000 visitors a month. It engages and energizes employees, thus boosting morale and bringing everyone onto the same page for the company's reputation goals. The blog guidelines include adhering to a specific code of ethics; using at least one photo in the post; responding quickly to audience comments; reaching out to friends, colleagues, and family to increase the blog's viral marketing impact; and being "transparent, provocative, fun, insightful, and conversational."

In one particularly fun and engaging post, Jenny Cisney, Information Designer for Kodak.com, decided to experiment with one of the company's products. She wondered: What does the world look like from a dog's perspective? Cisney attached her digital camera and Kodak's flexible-legged Gorillapod tripod to her dog Oscar's collar. She got a lot of blurry pictures, the family cat, and more. Cisney posted the results of her experiment on the company blog and got 25 comments —not bad for one simple employee post about her personal life (Figure 7.1).

A Thousand Words: A Kodak blog about photography - Windows Internet Explorer

http://1000words.kodak.com/

1000 words

A Thousand Words: A Kodak blog about photography

A Thousand Words   **Kodak**

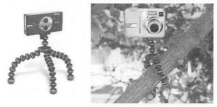

What's a picture worth?

November 29, 2006

Dog Photography: Not of dogs but taken by a dog

We recently started carrying these funky camera tripods in the Kodak Store called Gorillapods. You can bend the legs of this tripod to wrap around all sorts of things to get a good shot.

My mind started churning.

I knew what I wanted to stick the Gorillapod on.... my dog, Oscar. Just like it's interesting to get pictures taken from a child's point of view I wanted pictures from a dog's point of view. But they don't have thumbs. Thus, the Gorillapod.

Granted, the majority of the pictures Oscar took were like this... blurriffic. But we persevered.

Figure 7.1 "Dog Photography: Not of dogs but taken by a dog" (source: 1000words.kodak.com/)

In addition to professionals, consumers, and employees, the Kodak blogs reach journalists through press release RSS feeds and cross-linking between blog postings and online releases on the Kodak.com corporate site. The company press releases sometimes include a reference on the bottom indicating more information is available via the link to one of the blogs.

Kodak also produces two audio or video podcasts a month, thus completing a powerful multimedia approach for engaging important stakeholders. "Kodak Close-Up" podcasts feature company technology and strategy insights, as well as interviews with creative professionals and photographers. Podcasts are available on the Kodak.com website and the iTunes store. Stinardo notes that many professionals enjoy the podcasts on their daily commutes into New York City.

Your Thought Leadership Niche

The Eastman Kodak Company understands everything about traditional and digital imaging. It uses blogs, a website, white papers, an online pressroom with RSS feeds, videos, and podcasts to discuss its knowledge and product applications and learn from various stakeholders in the process. It follows the rules of engagement from Chapter 4, and comes across as innovative, tech savvy, and radically transparent.

What is your knowledge niche? Is it patent law, e-mail marketing, graphic design, life coaching, health care management, or what? It is time to put your stake in the ground and use online multimedia content to assure your desired reputation. As a result, you can become a thought leader in your area of expertise and experience business or career growth. Elise Bauer, partner in the Pacifica Group consultancy, offers the following advice to small companies that compete with little marketing money in crowded fields:

> **" Trust is built on reputation and reputation is generally NOT built on advertising. It is built on what others say about you. Become a thought leader in your field and it won't matter as much how big you are. Companies will look to you for insight and vision. Journalists will quote you, analysts will call you, and websites will link to you. "**

Produce engaging content around your expertise that adds value and differentiates yourself in a way that builds reputation. Place this content all over the Web, as discussed in Chapter 6 (e.g., editing Wikipedia pages in your field). Don't forget that your online and offline thought leadership activities merge to move you toward your goals (see the sidebar "Online and Offline Integration"). As a whole, this communication will have value, meaning, and relevance to your stakeholders.

Introducing the Multimedia Content Palette

Text, images, audio and video: these four items comprise your content multimedia palette for creating a thought leadership and consistent reputation online. Chapter 8 focuses on the words you write for your website, blog, e-mail, and more. The palette tools in this chapter include the photos, videos, demonstrations, podcasts, and other multimedia content on your own or other people's sites. You probably already have experience with these tools on your own web properties and e-mail, but are you using them to paint your reputation portrait on the social media playing field? Kodak does a great job with words and photos, touches on video blog posts, and is just beginning to explore photographer interviews in podcasts. Kodak uses the full multimedia palette to create its digital imaging and feel-good reputation.

The social media present a powerful and often inexpensive showcase for your quality multimedia content. Online PR agency immediate future believes that share of online voice is an overlooked, yet relevant, metric for brand perception research. Its July 2007 social media snapshot of the Interbrand Top 100 global brands showed how these top brands are perceived online. The study calculated share of voice in the blogosphere, online video (YouTube), social networking (MySpace and Bebo), photography sites (Photobucket and Flickr), and social bookmarking, and other content sites (Digg, Ma.gnolia, and Del.icio.us).

Figure 7.2 demonstrates the role of words, images, and video in raising the share of voice for the top 25 brands using social media. It is interesting to note the differing levels of each of tool for each company, and to speculate about whether the company or the citizen journalists initiated the exposure. It is also informative to review the Fortune's *America's Most Admired Companies* (Chapter 2), and see that four of them have an outstanding share of voice in the social media: Apple, Google (both understandable because of their technology products), Toyota, and Starbucks (perhaps because they have passionate customers). This vacuum provides a great opportunity for the other admired companies.

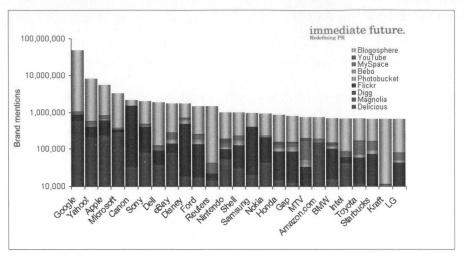

Figure 7.2 Share of social media voice (available at www.immediatefuture.co.uk/)

Every word, picture, video, or sound bite you post, and those that others post about you, reveals who you are and can enhance your reputation as a thought leader, as we've said in previous chapters. Use these tools skillfully and you could be the first in your industry to have a huge social media share of voice and a high Google ranking. The rest of this chapter will talk about how to use digital images, video, and podcasts to engage your chosen stakeholders. Note that there are many books and online articles providing advice about the technology and techniques for using these tools, so we limit the following discussion to their applications for enhancing your reputation online (see the sidebar "Recommended Reading for Online Multimedia Production" for reading recommendations).

Recommended Reading for Online Multimedia Production

Digital Images

- *The Digital Photography Book* by Scott Kelby (Peachpit Press, 2006)

- *Photoshop for Right-Brainers: The Art of Photo Manipulation* by Al Ward (Sybex, 2004)

Digital Video

- *Digital Video Hacks: Tips & Tools for Shooting, Editing, and Sharin*g by Joshua Paul (O'Reilly Media, 2005)

Podcasts

- *Podcasting for Dummies* by Tee Morris and Evo Terra (For Dummies, 2005)

- *Promoting Your Podcast* by Jason Van Orden (Larstan Publishing, 2006)

Great Digital Images Show Who You Are

Is there anyone who doesn't recall the picture of Yahoo! co-founder David Filo, cozy with blanket and pillow, sleeping under his desk (after pulling an all-nighter during the company's early days)? This image did a lot for his reputation as a hard-working entrepreneur who was passionate about categorizing the Web for the world. Everyone respects and likes a person who will reveal himself in this vulnerable, casual, and radically transparent way.

Do the images you display on the Web and in e-mails represent the reputation you want to have? Maybe you don't want to be seen sleeping at your desk, but how transparent do you want to be in your professional and personal lives? If you've been paying attention in previous pages, you'll know what we recommend—profit by showing the real you and the real company.

Images can be used in many ways to build your online reputation. Follow this section's advice and build your radically transparent reputation in the social media.

Don't Leave Home Without It

Like most people, you probably check for these three things when you leave home: wallet, keys, and cell phone. If your phone doesn't have a camera function, add digital camera to the list. We'd guess that the Kodak and Yahoo! employees carry them, and that's how they get such great spontaneous shots that end up on corporate and personal websites and blogs (including poor parking jobs in the Yahoo! parking lot). Employees armed with digital cameras keep the company website images from being stale, boring, and outdated. Maybe your company is different in its ability to keep web images fresh, but they could use a few extra hands, so take your camera along to corporate and professional events. Not yet convinced? Check out the Kodak blogs and see how you feel about the company after viewing the employee images (1000words.kodak.com and 1000nerds.kodak.com).

Your Online Photo Library

If you are like most of us, you have too many digital pictures trapped on computer hard drives, and in digital camera and cell phone memory cards. It is always hard to edit your own body of work, but it will not serve your reputation goals to simply post of all your cool photos online. Instead, build an online photo library that tells the right story. You do this for your product photos in advertising, so follow the same principles for your personal and corporate images.

For example, how do you portray your offices on the company website? Is it a traditional building shot void of life, or is it filled with your enthusiastic employees? Think about real estate photos for a minute. They are usually a straight shot of the house or building for sale, shown with good lighting. Sometimes they depict a cold winter scene (not so good unless it is a mountain cabin), and sometimes a green, lush, scene in spring. However, none except the most forward-thinking homebuilders show people. What if the real estate industry started showing a happy couple sitting in Adirondack chairs in front of the house, a child on a tree swing, or a corporate handshake in front of an office building for sale? This might evoke positive emotion along with the product picture.

Consider the reputation impression you want, remembering how photos can make people laugh, cry, or feel warm and fuzzy about you and your products. Also think about which personal photos you want to share online because personal transparency builds trust.

There are many available resources about taking good pictures and preparing them for the Web. To show how a simple image can convey a person's personality and values, we'll spotlight the commonly used head shot.

Making Your Head Shot Count

Even the seemingly simple head shot with your bio can reveal a lot about you. Some head shots make a person look cool and hip, while some are traditional and serious. What kind of picture would you expect to see for your accountant, ad agency creative director, CEO, or doctor? Figure 7.3 shows head shots for the three different types of firms, as portrayed online: online photo manager Flickr, instant messaging site Meebo, and investment firm Aurora Funds. Each employee got a few pixels of fame and how each used it informs us about her personality and interests. As a whole, these head shots show a range from creative and wacky to very formal. Most of us gravitate to the formal, so you may want to reconsider whether or not this is appropriate for your desired reputation.

Check out the online pictures chosen by 2008 political candidates on the first page of each website to represent their desired personae and personal positioning (Figure 7.4). Some have a context that tells about the person and others do not—one is a family man and one has rural roots in America's heartland. Some are stronger looking, some serious, and some more friendly and smiley. Other nonverbal communication speaks volumes about these people. Some use hand gestures well known as winning (thumbs up), caring (touching others), or strong (finger pointing). Note that John Edwards's family portrait shows him as egalitarian, not patriarch, because of how he is positioned within the family—versus sitting in the center with all hands on him.

Creative: Flickr.com team

Casual: Meebo.com team
(source: www.flickr.com)

Formal: Aurora Funds
investment team
(source: www.aurorafunds.com)

Figure 7.3 Head shots: creative, casual, and formal

We could continue this analysis, but you probably get the point: stage your head shot to convey your desired image and reputation. The Flickr team and political candidates alike are transparent online—albeit in different ways. Both pay a lot of attention to their online images and reputations—do you?

Rudy Giuliani
(www.joinrudy2008.com)

Hillary Clinton
(www.hillaryclinton.com)

John Edwards
(johnedwards.com)

Barack Obama
(www.barackobama.com)

Ron Paul
(www.ronpaul2008.com)

John McCain
(www.johnmccain.com)

Figure 7.4 Political candidate head shots

Images and the Social Media

Once you have your edited photo library and great head shot, you can post photos as needed on the company website, in online pressrooms, in your blogs, in e-mails, in online newsletters, and more. Or you can use a social media website to hold and manage your image reputation portfolio, such as offered by Photobucket (see the sidebar "Online Photo Management Sites"). Photos don't have to exist there in isolation—you can link to them from your own website or outgoing e-mail. For instance, Meebo, the instant messaging website, has a full portfolio of company pictures on Flickr, and brings them into its "About" page via a Flickr badge (multiple pictures rotated in a small rectangle, served from a Flickr image set). Many bloggers feed individual pictures into their sites as well. And don't forget the SEO benefits of your Flickr page, as mentioned in Chapter 6.

If you are new at posting digital photos to an online photo management site, you might try Google's free Picasa software to view and manage the photos on your computer, then send with e-mail or publish to a blog with a simple click (the software automatically resizes the files for quick transmission). Of course, you can also upload images from your mobile device.

Online Photo Management Sites

These are the leading sites, along with descriptions from their pages. We list them in order of page view share, from most to least popular, according to web information company Alexa.com in August 2007.

Photobucket (photobucket.com) is "the web's most popular creative hub, linking billions of personal photos, graphics, slideshows and videos daily to hundreds of thousands of web sites, including: MySpace, Facebook, Bebo, Friendster, eBay, Craigslist, Blogger and Xanga. In addition to linking, Photobucket users share their personal digital media by email, instant messaging, and mobile devices."

Yahoo! Flickr (www.flickr.com) claims to be "almost certainly the best online photo management and sharing application in the world." At Flickr, you can organize and post photos for public or private viewing. You can upload "from the web, from mobile devices, from the users' home computers and from whatever software they are using to manage their photos. And we want to be able to push them out in as many ways as possible: on the Flickr website, in RSS feeds, by email, by posting to outside blogs..."

Kodak EasyShare Gallery (www.kodakgallery.com) claims to be "the leading online digital photo developing service." The "site provides consumers with a secure and easy way to view, store and share their photos with friends and family and get real Kodak prints of their pictures. The site also provides free editing and creative tools and specialty photo products."

Shutterfly (www.shutterfly.com) claims it was "Voted #1 online photo service." It offers photo posting, organizing into photo collages, editing, and printing. Customers can pick up printed pictures at partner Target stores.

Snapfish (www.snapfish.com) "is a leading online photo service" and the only one we examined that has third party reviews: "Best Overall Photo Service: Snapfish delivered the best image quality plus the lowest price (PC World, June 2005)," "Best Quality Photo Books (Good Housekeeping, June 2005)," and "Overall, Snapfish sent the best images. Its' prints all had good exposure, contrast, and detail" (*MacWorld*, July 2005).

Now, let's talk about how to benefit from photos taken by the citizen photojournalists. Forward-thinking companies are beginning to solicit these exciting images, freely offered by internet users. For example, the world of photojournalism changed in July 2005 when cell phone users caught in the London bombings sent eyewitness pictures and videos to the news media. London's *Guardian* newspaper called it the "true birth of the citizen reporter." Reuters' and Yahoo! capitalized on this trend by setting up *You Witness News* to solicit internet user photos for breaking news stories (news.yahoo.com/you-witness-news in beta testing during July 2007). Photo submitters are not paid unless Reuters distributes them to clients, but that doesn't stop the citizen journalists from submitting pictures—it is in their genes.

Figure 7.5 Consumer photo graces Kodak.com

Companies can capitalize on this trend, too. For instance, Kodak.com usually displays a personal photo on its home page—contributed by a site user. Figure 7.5 shows Oksana Pashko's diving picture: "Two-thirds of the world is her aquarium." Lego, the toy company, provides space on its website for photos of cool Lego structures made by customers (and learns from customers about possible new Lego product kits, made from these designs). The Pontiac Underground site, mentioned in Chapter 4, gives one-fourth of its home page for user photos of their cars: "See and Be Seen." Finally, TripAdvisor.com holds traveler photos for most of its customer-reviewed hotels. It doesn't matter that they are not professional quality because, remember, people trust other people like them more than they trust you. If it is too slick, users put it in the corporate spin or advertising category.

> **Thought Byte: Using Customer Photos**
>
> How can you use customer photos to enhance your web properties? Enliven your web pages with images of customers using your products—a great accompaniment to testimonials. Add to your *About Us* pages with informal employee pictures. Of course, you'll want to approve the image posting if it is your company website, but on a blog or community site, anything goes.

Moving Pictures Are Worth Ten Thousand Words

Videos, demonstrations, virtual tours, and other sound-filled moving pictures have the ability to engage viewers because they deliver a full sensory experience. According to speaker, author, and Kellogg Graduate School of Management Professor Philip Kotler, "It is not enough to present a product or service visually... The combination of visual and audio stimuli delivers a 2 + 2 = 5 impact." If a picture is worth a thousand words, a video is worth ten thousand words because it can tell an entire story, appealing to both the emotions and intellect. Television commercials have capitalized on this benefit, and now the bar is raised for online video producers because the online community also wants to see great video online.

High user broadband connectivity was the tipping point for massive online video distribution. Music and news videos led the pack, but the YouTube phenomenon enticed forward-thinking companies to incorporate video into their online content—both on their web properties and at social media sites. Video viewing is a growing trend, with 57% of internet users currently watching videos online (according to Pew Internet and the American Life research).

Video consumers tend to be younger—76% of 18-29 year olds watch online video, as compared with 57% of 30-49 year olds and 46% of 50-64 year olds, according to Pew. Online videos will only help build your reputation if your intended audiences watch them, but please continue reading if your market doesn't skew young because there are many ways to provide value and engage anyone with video, animations, and other sound-filled moving pictures.

Using Videos on Your Web Properties

Pew's video research reveals many opportunities for individual or company reputation-building videos (Figure 7.6). Assuming you are not in the news media or entertainment business, you can still produce a funny or educational video, or post your TV commercials online and draw viewers.

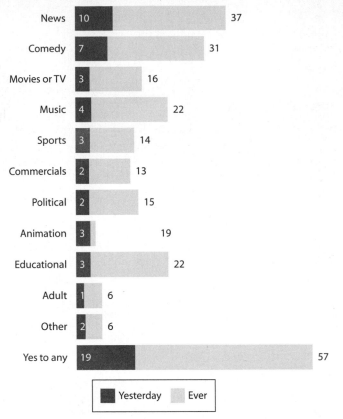

News 10 37
Comedy 7 31
Movies or TV 3 16
Music 4 22
Sports 3 14
Commercials 2 13
Political 2 15
Animation 3 19
Educational 3 22
Adult 1 6
Other 2 6
Yes to any 19 57

■ Yesterday ■ Ever

Figure 7.6 Percent watching video types online. Source: Pew Internet and the American Life research (www.pewinternet.org).

Demonstrations and How-To Videos

Educational videos include demonstrations or how-to videos that instruct your target market about your products and offer technical support. CNET includes video reviews of products on its website, alongside its text article reviews, showing CNET as a cutting edge company (see Figure 7.7 for video examples). Apple Computer and other companies tell consumers that they care by demonstrating how to use products in a step-by-step video—such as the iPhone keyboard demonstration in Figure 7.7.

Commercial blender company Blendtec added comedy to its demonstrations and got over 6 million page views in a one-week period. The hilarious "Will It Blend?" series shows CEO Tom Dickson dressed as a scientist and attempting to blend everything from a cell phone to a garden rake, golf balls, and glow sticks. Blendtec posted the videos on YouTube and Revver, eventually creating a willitblend.com company site to hold the increasing video inventory. The videos were created to introduce the new and pricey home blender and resulted in a 40% increase in blender sales, according to *The Wall Street Journal*. Beyond sales, we think Blendtec created a wonderful, irreverent, high-tech, and well-trusted reputation in the process.

CNET 2-minute video product review
(reviews.cnet.com)

iPhone keyboard demonstration
(www.apple.com/iphone)

Goldstein of The Head, Neck, and
Spine Center of San Diego
(www.lajolladc.com)

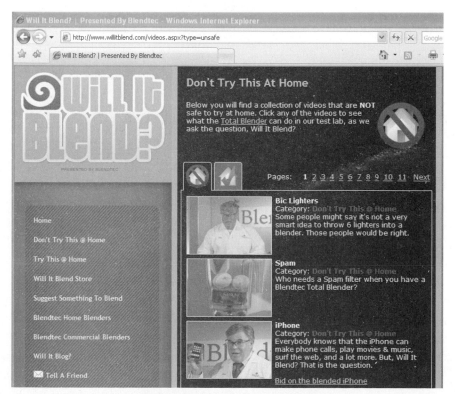

Blendtec's Will it Blend? (www.willitblend.com)

Figure 7.7 How-to and demonstration videos

Online video is a great opportunity for local businesses, too. Dr. Brandon Goldstein of The Head, Neck and Spine Center of San Diego created a one-minute demonstration video explaining the company's services and showing a brief chiropractic exam. The business name and phone number appears continuously as a watermark under the video. Goldstein had the video posted on 35 websites and reported 200 viewings in a short time frame. The Center's web page links to this video on YouTube. This is a great result for a local company.

Virtual Tours

The Scott Fence Company, a Southern California fence builder, hosts a video showing viewers around the plant, demonstrating fence materials and projects in progress. According to Pew, 72 million U.S. internet users (51%) have taken virtual tours online. What better way to create your radically transparent reputation than to show stakeholders the authentic guts of your operation? Most online virtual tours are still more corporate or government spin than transparent process, but Scott Fence is an exception.

Other uses of virtual tours include vacation destinations (e.g., see arounder.com) and real estate tours. Museums and universities also show potential customers, students, or donors the goods. Not all of these have sound, but the interactive click-and-drag panoramas with text or audio are a big step above snapshot images.

The Talking Head Is Boring

Most people will passively watch a news anchor on television, but active internet users do not want to watch a spokesperson jabber about products unless it includes interesting demonstrations or other diversions. Jakob Nielsen, principal of the Nielsen Norman Group, conducted research tracking a subject's eyes as he looked at a 24-second news video online. As shown in Figure 7.8, the eyes moved around to look at several areas other than the spokesperson's head (the amorphous shapes over the screen shows where the eyes rested). This work led Nielsen to conclude that a talking head is boring: "On the web, 24 seconds is a long time—too long for users to keep their attention on something monotonous."

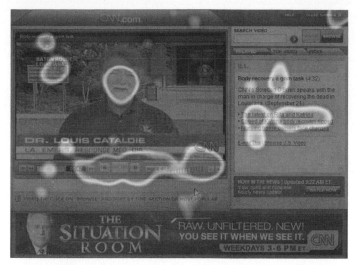

Figure 7.8 Where user eyes rest during talking head video

There are exceptions. Internet users hang on every word in keynote speeches delivered by Steve Jobs, Richard Edelman, Warren Buffet, or other well-known thought leaders. Perhaps when your reputation online reaches that stature, you can get away with a talking head video longer than one minute. A talking head video will also work when the CEO wants to deliver an important and short message. For example, in January 2007 Michael Dell announced his return as CEO in a 16-second video on the direct2dell.com blog. In this instance, Dell's nonverbal communication displays the truth of his words: "I'm very excited to be CEO again; I feel the same kind of energy and drive that I did when we started the company in 1984…"

Be careful how you use talking head type videos. You don't want to bore the people you want to impress.

Video and the Social Media

Video is good for spreading your reputation via word-of-mouth because 32% of all internet users share video content with others, according to Pew Internet and the American Life studies. Users send and receive links to videos from others and watch cool videos with their friends. This explains the rapid spread of the "Will It Blend?" videos. It can also backfire, however. Chevy Tahoe created an ad contest, inviting consumers to use company-issued visual and audio elements to create ads for the automobile. All consumers had to do was create their own superimposed text and arrange the video elements into a 30-second commercial. According to General Motors spokeswoman Melisa Tezanos, nearly 20% of the 21,000 submitted ads depicted the Tahoe unfavorably—with text over the company's visuals such as "creates global warming" and "gas guzzler." Links to YouTube posted negative ads flew around the internet, resulting in hundreds of thousands of video views and reflecting poorly on the brand. Of course, the end result of GM's social media campaign had benefits—2.4 million page views to the ad site (Chevyapprentice.com) and over 16,000 consumer-created positive ads.

> ## Thought Byte: Taking Criticism from Citizen Journalists
>
> Did the Chevy Tahoe online video campaign help or hurt the brand reputation and parent General Motors? On the one hand, they got lots of negative reactions, but on the other hand, 80% of the videos they received were positive and web traffic increased. Also, they got respect from the online community because they reacted well to the negative videos, neither pulling them nor becoming defensive. Many products draw criticism from consumers, so a social media campaign will bring out the negative as well as the positive. Think about your brands, company, and individual reputation—will they benefit from social media participation or do you need to clean up some things first?

Table 7.1 shows all of the ways that internet users engage with online video, from sending links to posting video online.

▶ **Table 7.1** How Internet Users Engage With Online Video

Social Media Activity	Percent of all Online Video Viewers Doing Each Activity (Note: 57% of internet users view online video)					
	Total	Men	Women	18–29	30–49	50–64
Receive video links	75	75	75	76	77	71
Send video links to others	57	59	54	67	55	45
Watch video with others	57	58	57	73	58	34
Rate video	13	15	10	23	11	4
Post comments about video	13	15	10	25	9	5
Upload video	13	16	9	20	12	5
Post video links online	10	12	9	22	7	2

Source: Pew Internet & American Life Project survey, February–March 2007. See www.pewinternet.org for methodology and more information.

Although only 13% of video viewers upload videos (7.4% of all internet users), several companies have been able to entice consumers to create content for their sites—among them, Converse and Frito Lay's Doritos brand. Converse invited consumers to create 24-second ads embodying "the values and spirit of Converse" and to post video submissions at the ConverseGallery—receiving 3 million visitors within months. Converse showed a few of the ads on television.

Doritos's "Crash the Super Bowl" invited consumers to produce and submit 30-second video commercials in a contest that offered winners $10,000 and a free trip to the 2007 Super Bowl game. Doritos enticed citizen journalists with the following instructions: "Maybe it's a story about eating your first Doritos chips or what life is like for the spices on the surface of the chip. Anything. Make the video you'd be excited to see if you were watching TV. Make it yours." Doritos received over 1,000 ad submissions and over 125,000 people viewed the ads in just a two-week period. By most accounts, this was a brilliant use of the brand's Super Bowl advertising budget and a very successful way to engage consumers.

Online news channel CNN.com also encourages its audience to upload photos, audio files, and videos to its I-Report section of CNN.com. These companies understand the social media and rules of engagement.

Another way to engage internet users is to post company created video on social media sites. Political candidates, companies, and professionals post videos online along with the citizen journalists. Most of the videos are on YouTube—according to web measurement company Hitwise, YouTube has a 60% share of the video site market, followed by MySpace Videos (16%), Google Video (8%), and Yahoo! Video (3%). Here are some exemplary corporate YouTube videos:

- David Neeleman, JetBlue founder, posted a video on YouTube introducing the "Customer Bill of Rights," after the 2007 ice storm that crippled operations.
- The "Will It Blend?" phenomenon began with a YouTube post.
- Dove posted its Evolution 2006 Super Bowl commercial on YouTube and within 18 months had 4.2 million page views (versus 500 million impressions for the $2.5 million Super Bowl TV spot). This ad was part of Dove's Campaign for Real Beauty, showing the transformation of a regular-looking woman into a model through make-up, hair, and computer reshaping of her features.

YouTube also allows video viewers to post comments and rate videos, thus increasing user engagement (see Table 7.1—13% of viewers post and rate). Sometimes a video debate occurs in YouTube. Viewers posted videos making fun of Senator John Edwards's expensive $400 haircuts, to which Edwards responded with a video showing haircuts of President Bush and others, then morphing to images from the Iraqi war and Hurricane Katrina. The video ends with the words: "What really matters? You choose."

Have faith that your good customers will show your products in a positive light and ask them to create and upload videos showing them using your products. Plan for a few negative comments, because that is part of being radically transparent and will help you listen and learn how to improve. Consider running a promotion to motivate customers to create video ads, such as the Doritos contest. Or, create your own interesting video and post it on YouTube and your own website. Regardless of how you get involved, do it now—the social media feed on great video and there is still plenty of room to get in on this booming trend.

Tips for Engaging Viewers With Video

"There's something immediate, authentic and engaging about a video that even a well-written blog post can't emulate," according to Debbie Weil, author of *The Corporate Blogging Book*. Internet user–generated video content is often engaging in itself because, as we've said before, people trust others like them. For company-produced video, be sure it contains humorous, interesting, or current content. Also, video production quality is important. According to Pew's research, 62% of video viewers say that professionally produced videos are their favorites (although there certainly are user-generated video exceptions). Beyond that, include the following interactive features to encourage viewers to engage and spread your positive reputation to others:

- Provide buttons for video pause, rewind, and replay. Display video length and elapsed time.

- Jakob Nielsen recommends keeping online video under one minute long and using video for movement or things that cannot be portrayed in still images.

- Since videos may only be watched partway through, put the important messages and key points in the beginning.

- Follow YouTube's example by including interactive items such as "save to favorites," "share" video link via e-mail, "subscribe" to this producer's videos, or "post video to your blog." You can also invite a video response or text comment, or allow viewers to rate the video.

- Encourage interaction with your company by asking if viewers want to subscribe to an e-mail list, visit other of your web properties (via links), or download wallpaper and games.

Finally, think about the context for your video. Refer to Nielsen's eye tracking study and recall that viewers won't keep focused for long—even less so if there is distracting content in and around the video. Use videos on pages that complement the content, such as a quick CEO announcement on the pressroom page.

Social Media Sound Bites

Music and sound effects can create a mood and personality to support your reputation goals. They are appropriate for web properties authored by musicians, museums, symphonies, online gaming, online radio stations, or other people and organizations that rely on sound for their businesses. Otherwise, these audio effects on blogs and websites can be distracting and appear amateurish. The spoken word in a speech or sound bite can be used effectively online, but most users prefer visuals with their sound—so go with the video instead if you can. One big exception to this rule is that sound files are more portable than video for users and don't eat up battery life on iPods and other mobile devices. Users can download and listen on MP3 players during daily commutes, when exercising, and so forth. If your stakeholders want to listen on the fly, by all means give them what they want—Kodak did exactly that with its podcast interviews with professional photographers for commuters.

Thanks in part to the hugely popular iTunes distribution channel, 12% of all internet users have downloaded a podcast (according Pew Internet & American Life research), and nearly 18% of companies offer them (according to digital agency cScape's customer engagement research). While growing, podcast use is nowhere near online video use, so think carefully about whether or not podcasts will build your reputation with intended audiences. If you decide to try podcasts, there are many books and articles about how to find great content, speak into a microphone like a pro, use the right technologies, and promote your podcasts for drawing listeners. For now, we'll just give you a couple of outstanding examples of firms using podcasts for spreading their thought leadership reputation.

Defining Moment: Podcast

"A podcast is a digital media file, or a series of such files, that is distributed over the Internet using syndication (Web feed(s)) for playback on portable media players and personal computers," according to Wikipedia. Podcasts began with purely audio files for the iPod, but now users can download video podcasts ("vidcasts" or "videocasts") for use on many types of receiving appliances. The line between video podcasts and other online video is quite fuzzy at this time, so we recommend learning about making great video when considering a videocast.

Diggnation heads the pack of popular technology podcasts. Hosted by Alex Albrecht and Digg founder Kevin Rose, the show covers the most popular stories on Digg.com (as rated by internet users), focusing on technology and web culture. It has 250,000 listeners, and does a great deal to create a fun, irreverent, and hip reputation for these two hosts.

The *GE on Demand* podcast also targets business customers. General Electric uses scientists to tell the story to stakeholders. GE is a complex company that operates in seven major industries. The podcasts and videos help communicate these complex ideas in a digestible and understandable way, and demonstrate that 130-year-old GE is modern and "imagination at work," according to Deirdre Latour, GE's director of public relations. Like Kodak, GE is trying to dispel the old ideas of who they are and using new media to build modern, cutting-edge reputations.

The 2007 People's Choice Podcast Awards lists *Manager Tools* as a high-traffic podcast winner in the business category. It is a weekly podcast to help listeners become more effective managers and leaders and has been called "one of the most consistently practical, useful and impactful podcasts in the 'sphere today." *Manager Tools* has leveraged this success into conferences, paid content access on the website, and speaking engagements—all of which build the brand reputation.

You don't have to create your own podcast to participate in this game, because it is easy to participate in podcasts produced by others in similar industries or topic areas. If you are a panel member or expert interview subject, it will enhance your thought leadership reputation. For instance, Michael Auzenne of *Manager Tools* was interviewed on the *Bradcast* podcast, and enjoyed positive comments written on the podcast web page as well.

If you use podcasts, be sure you know your audience and whether they want to download this type of media. As well, be sure that the podcast material adds to the body of online multimedia content shouting to the world, "This is exactly who we are."

SEO for Images, Videos, and Podcasts

It is hard to find photos, videos, and podcasts online because they don't have searchable text, as do articles. Many companies are working hard to make video content searchable, such as automating the translation of audio and video speech into searchable text or asking users to label videos and then using the most popular terms for indexing them (watch EveryZing, Google, and Blinkx for future developments). Until these methods become mainstream, you can help the search engines find your multimedia content by creating relevant filenames, engaging titles, appropriate tags, and by placing them in a rich textual context that supports their meaning (on a blog or website). Making your multimedia search engine friendly is especially important because according to Hitwise, search engines send 20% of the traffic to video sites.

Good multimedia filenames and titles are descriptive, including relevant keywords important to viewers. For instance, a real estate property manager might simply title her photo head shot with a name—Jane Smith. To capture more searchers and potential clients, however, she might title the image "Los Angeles Property Manager Jane Smith." This will also help build her reputation as property manager. If Jane is in a video that shows her touring a particular property, she might title it "Jane Smith Offers Space in Bradbury Building, Los Angeles." A good rule of thumb, then, is to include some of the following in your filenames and titles: your name, brand name, company, location (for a local business) and then something succinct about the content (podcast or video) or situation (photo). It is also important to omit unnecessary words such as "wow," "cool," or other things users do not put in search terms (refer to Chapter 6 for more on targeting search terms). For more ideas, simply look at the titles you see on podcast, photo, or video sites.

Defining Moment: Tagging

Tagging is the process of creating labels for online content such as videos, photos, podcasts, or text articles. Tags help organize data online by providing terms for search engine categorization, and by helping to link similar content (such as blog memes or photos of computer desktops). Content creators often tag their work, and content consumers can tag the same work with their own labels. According to David Weinberger, co-author of internet marketing book *The Cluetrain Manifesto*, "You might want to tag… a Stephen King story as 'horror,' but maybe to me it's 'ghost story' and to a literature professor it is 'pop culture.'" Tagging is in the eye of the beholder.

Tags are labels for online content. Del.icio.us may have started this phenomenon by allowing users to write a few words that describe a web site or blog when bookmarking the site. Capitalizing on social tagging, you can review all the bookmarked websites at Del.icio.us that are tagged with particular words, such as "reputation" or "SEO." Flickr was also early in the tagging game, allowing users to tag photos (as well as title them), and to tag portions of the photos with keywords (by drawing a box around a photo object and applying a tag word or phrase). Tags help users find multimedia based on their own personal labels, and also allow them to share this content with others—such as when a Flickr user searches for "cats" and gets all photos tagged with that word. Tagging connects users by their interests—communities form around tagged photos or videos. Viewers can comment on pictures, inviting the photographer to post them on other blogs or websites on the topic. Typical of the Web, tagging is a user-driven attempt at categorizing the vast amount of online multimedia content, and it seems to be working quite well.

Tagging is especially important for the Technorati search engine because it searches tags and even provides widgets for display on your blog or website that show the tags you use most often in your own web pages. See the sidebar "Tag Tips for Terrific Technorati Traffic" for author Jason Van Orden's ten tips for tagging podcasts and generating Technorati traffic—we think it applies well to all multimedia tagging.

Tag Tips for Terrific Technorati Traffic

From *Promoting Your Podcast* by Jason Van Orden:

- Choose relevant tags that describe your content well. Run a search at Technorati for these tags and see if your content fits in that list.

- Mostly use tags that have two or more words (and phrases) because searchers that know what they are seeking tend to use more keywords in their queries.

- Don't break new ground because tagging is based on the wisdom of the social media and new, clever phrases won't likely be used by searchers.

- Use synonyms where appropriate to capture all the possible search terms.

- Use Technorati's "related tags" function to find other tags that might be appropriate for your content.

- Look at Technorati's most popular tags for topics that might match your content.

- Anticipate and follow current events and media stories and include content on these, along with popular tags.

- Use tags that are highly ranked in Google. Search for the tags you are considering in Google and see if they bring up Technorati pages (a good sign).

- Choose tags used by popular podcasts and blogs in your thought leadership niche—this puts you in the social media conversation.

- Use abbreviations where appropriate because users often adopt them (e.g., "nyc" and "N.Y.C." for New York City).

Note that you can also tag videos and images with GPS (Global Positioning System) tags. This will enable viewers to use Google Earth to pinpoint the exact location of the photo or video—helpful if you are selling real estate or want people to see your office building. You can do this by putting the latitude and longitude as a tag, and perhaps adding "Google Earth" or "GPS" to the tag.

According to Pew research, 28% of internet users tag online content. Join them by tagging your own creative multimedia content after posting it on social media sites. This will help others find appropriate tags (because many sites offer suggested tags) and also help the search engines find your content. Most importantly, if you include keywords around your desired reputation or thought leadership area, you'll be building a cohesive body of work pointing to you, the well-reputed expert.

Other Multimedia Content

You probably have a few white papers and other files on your computer that would enhance your reputation as a thought leader if put on your web properties. How about the PowerPoint slides from that last speaking engagement? Just the fact that you are an invited speaker will help your reputation, but sharing some of your information will endear you to social media writers. Dick Hardt, founder of identity and access management firm Sxip, became well known for his unusual presentation style in his 2005 speech about online identity and security (www.sxip.com). It is linked on the Sxip site as "The Infamous Identity 2.0 Presentation." This presentation depicts Hardt as an innovator, not afraid to break out of the bullet point routine.

Webinars are another way to give potential customers in diverse locations a sampling of your knowledge or a demonstration of your products. WebEx and others can assist you with the technology, but be sure to include interactive features to engage your attendees—things such as online polling with immediate reporting, automated e-mail follow-up, and question and answer panels will keep attendees interested and online.

Second Life, the 3D virtual world completely built by its nearly 11 million residents, is a full multimedia playground. Pontiac (Chapter 4) and other companies maintain property there and use it to engage consumers and clients.

Finally, "anything goes" online and creativity is rewarded. For example, Burger King's Subservient Chicken still follows user commands after nearly three years of operation. Neither a video nor animation, but a man in a chicken suit, the bird responds to over 300 typed-in text commands—in often very humorous ways. The site had over 14 million unique visitors within a year. The reason we bring up this classic example is that Burger King's goal of promoting chicken sandwiches translated into a relevant and novel online site that engaged viewers without shouting "Burger King," and which was well integrated to offline marketing efforts.

A Word About Micromedia Content

A growing number of websites offer posting and consuming of small data chunks, known as micromedia. Micromessaging sites such as tumblr.com, twitter.com, eyejot.com and jaiku.com, allow authors to create a 30-second video, audio, or text message on a cell phone or computer and upload immediately for all to view. Authors often use this micromedia content to complement longer text, videos, or podcasts, or just to let readers know what they've discovered online or in a face-to-face conversation.

> ### Defining Moment: Micromedia
> Short text, video, or audio messages published on a designated social media website. Micromedia can be created and viewed by cell phones and computers.

Prominent blogger and author Robert Scoble used micromedia when he created a 30-second interview podcast on his cell phone while at a TechCrunch 9 party. Scoble published it on Twitter and his own *Scobleizer* blog using Twittergram—an online tool for posting a short MP3 file and accompanying 75-characters-or less file title. See Figure 7.9 for micromedia content examples.

Micromedia content is a great idea when you are on the run and want to share an insight that will enhance your thought leadership reputation. If you use it, follow the same rules outlined in this chapter for quality content, and be sure you make it easy to find for your important stakeholders. It is easy to plop stuff all over the Web when you are in a hurry, and we encourage you to make micromedia just part of the whole package that is you.

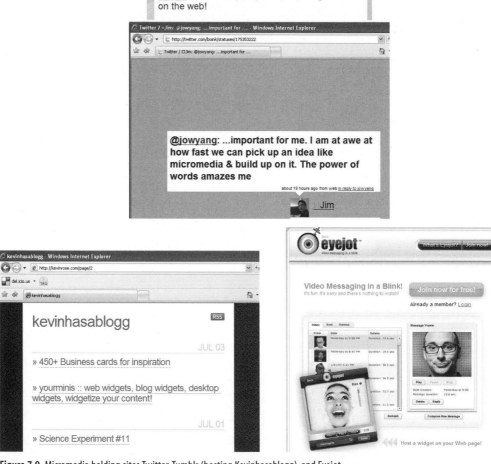

Figure 7.9 Micromedia holding sites Twitter, Tumblr (hosting Kevinhasablogg), and Eyejot

How Your Audience Consumes Multimedia Content

We conclude this chapter with the story of an international treasure hunt through the Web that integrates online and offline multimedia. This is the tale of IT professional Marco Roethling, a 27-year-old German citizen living in Japan. He is the consumer nearly every company wants, purely because of his age demographic. For most brands, if they can't attract young consumers they eventually become history.

The story starts with one of the authors of this book seeing Diggnation's Alex Albrecht and Kevin Rose create their podcast live in the United States and telling friends about the fascinating video podcast (Figure 7.10). One of these friends, Marco Roethling, is intrigued with the author's recommendation and begins listening to the podcast.

1. Roethling (living in Japan) becomes a dedicated Diggnation listener (on his iPod), eventually visiting Kevin Rose's blog on Tumblr, *kevinhasablogg*. Roethling is captivated by a video posted on the blog and sends the link to all of his friends. The video is titled "Lip Dub: Flagpole Sitta by Harvey Danger."

2. Roethling's friends in Germany follow the Google mouse tracks to find out who created this cool video and where these people really work.

3. They follow the video link to Vimeo, an online video-posting site that predates YouTube. The text under the video says, "We did this video one night after work. We are a company called Connected Ventures, a group of friends who work for: Vimeo, CollegeHumor, Busted Tees, and Defunker...and, we're hiring: connectedventures.com/jobs.shtml."

4. Media coverage and great viral marketing got Connected Ventures several hundred resumes: as a result, "Currently, there are no jobs available."

5. Roethling tells Malia Jakus about this video and she uses it in her high school video production classes to demonstrate how to make a high quality and hip video.

6. The authors write about this in the book you are holding.

Four million people viewed the Lip Dub video within two months, 1 million of whom saw it on the Vimeo site. According to Ricky Van Veen, co-founder of Connected Ventures, "We saw a couple of hundred résumés just blindly. People said, 'I don't know what you do but I just want to work at your company.'" Not bad for a video produced at an office party in one take!

This story shows how internet users follow your tracks through the Web in unexpected ways. The video gave Connected Ventures exposure and a positive reputation such that lots of people want to work there. Note that the video received more views on other people's sites than on its own home—this is because it had legs, and was picked up and posted all over the internet. It was the great video, the company's good SEO, and the words of others that created the buzz. A happy ending for any company.

Diggnation podcast starts the story

1 "Lip Dub: Flagpole Sitta" on kevinhasablogg.com

2 Searching for the video creators

3 Video on Vimeo with link to Connected Ventures

4 Connected Ventures: "Currently, there are no jobs available."

Figure 7.10 User trail through multimedia

In the next chapter you'll get the final piece: writing radically transparent content for the Web and e-mail. When you combine images, video, and audio, you will have the full multimedia palette to create the reputation you desire online.

Writing Engaging Text

Great writing will engage your important stake-holders and enhance your reputation online. Regardless of whether you write white papers, books, blogs, web pages, e-mail, or instant messages, make every word count. When writing for the internet, you will walk a tightrope between the quick, short, informal post and the longer, deliberate article, and between the reputation-building brand talk and the social media reader perspective. You can do this with professional, engaging, and deliberate writing adapted to any situation, as described in this chapter.

Chapter Contents

Craft Reputation-Building Text

Words are the foundation of your reputation online. The more positive, radically transparent, and carefully crafted text you create, the better. A well-written article, giving your perspective, will help to build your thought leadership reputation. Some of your words will be short, timely posts, and some will be longer thought pieces, but they all create stakeholder perceptions. When combined with rave reviews posted by your customers, consumers, and other stakeholders, your reputation-building words will hit page one on Google, and any negative comments soon get deeply buried. This is WordPress founder Matt Mullenweg's strategy:

> " In general my strategy has been to err on the side of having too much on line. It would be bad if you Googled your name and there was just that one unsavory thing there, versus a thousand hits. Also the more you put out there about yourself, the more you're controlling your online persona, rather than letting other people control it. There have been some awful, awful things written about me on various blogs and across the Internet. But I know it's not going to be the first thing you come across when you Google my name. "

How do you create reputation-building text for the Web, e-mail, and other text communication for internet delivery? In case you hadn't noticed, most writing is different online than offline. Writers for the print media use a linear structure because it helps move the readers along a logical path from the introduction to the desired conclusion—to prove a thesis, line up all the facts, or develop a story. Whether it is a short article or a book, print writing depends on linear development. The news media usually adhere to this format in their online stories, and you'll also see it in traditional press releases online (recall how the social media release is different). In contrast, most other online writing uses linked chunks of information that depend more heavily on organization than development. Authors organize each written piece in the most effective way for online audiences, whether it is a few words in a hyperlink or a well-developed paragraph of text. Knowing how to write for online audiences will communicate your expertise, show that you understand their needs, and help your reputation online.

Web usability expert Jakob Nielsen reports that "79 percent of our test users always scanned any new page they came across; only 16 percent read word-by-word." We suspect that the every-word occasions occur at magazine and news websites—and probably not on your company site or blog. Nielsen's work also shows that people read the text on a web page in an "F" pattern, scanning the headline first and then jumping around to look at other headlines, bullet points, links, and highlighted words (see www.useit.com for more of Nielsen's 12 years of usability research). This is why a well-organized web page or blog, full of micro content, suits online audiences well.

This chapter touches on the key writing issues affecting your reputation. There are several good books with more complete instruction on grammar, syntax, how to organize information online, and so forth. We recommend *E-Writing* (Dianna Booher) and *Writing for New Media* (Andrew Bonime and Ken Pohlmann). And don't forget about your college English composition textbook and your favorite style manual, such as the Associate Press (AP) Style Book.

Write White Papers and Online Books

Thought leadership is difficult to accomplish with only the short, chunked text found on blogs, e-mail, and web pages. This is why white papers were invented. Place your lengthy research findings, recommendations, and anything that requires a linear argument into a white paper. Write it as you would for print publication, and put it on your website as an HTML file (for search engines to find and index) and a PDF file for user printing You can post these high-quality articles on your blog or website, or send them to others for posting (as mentioned in Chapter 6).

High-quality white papers can promote your thought leadership reputation very quickly. If you are not currently well known in your area of expertise, it can take a longer time to create your niche and become well respected in your field with a blog alone. Authors Robert Scoble and Dave Winer are exceptions with their successful blogs, but a more surefire route is to use both white papers and blogs. Like many thought leaders, online marketing blog Marketing Pilgrim uses a mixture of both formats—maintaining a 65% short, quickly written blog posts and 35% longer article balance. Nielsen recommends, "To demonstrate world-class expertise, avoid quickly written, shallow postings. Instead, invest your time in thorough, value-added content that attracts paying customers." We think you need both the long, thoughtful white papers and the short, timely posts.

If you are really into writing, you could also create an entire book to display your expertise. You can even self-publish at Lulu.com or on your own website and still enhance your reputation. For instance, Dr. Dale Rogers and Dr. Ron Tibben-Lembke wrote a groundbreaking book titled *Going Backwards: Reverse Logistics Trends and Practices*, and published it with free access on their website. The e-book has been downloaded about 50,000 times since 1999 and opened new opportunities for the authors. According to Rogers, "It certainly helped the project sponsor as well. They have grown from $45 million in revenue to over $700 million since we did the book."

White papers and books are important for building your thought leadership reputation. Include them in your content cache. Now, let's move on to writing for web pages and e-mail—short, quick, informal, engaging, and radically transparent words. The next sections cover some of the mechanics for writing online.

Write for Clarity

Communication fails if the reader doesn't get the writer's point. This is not good if your intent is to convey expertise and build trust. Communication clarity comes primarily from word selection, sentence length, and content organization.

Consider the following company description excerpts for word selection and sentence length, taken from two websites:

1. "Leveraging world class infrastructure strengths, mature quality processes and industry benchmarked people management practices, Infinite commits to bring operational excellence to reengineer enterprise business processes." (www.infinite.com)

2. "Dell is the world's leading computer systems company." (www.dell.com)

The first example reads like it was written by someone wanting to pack every keyword about the company into a one-sentence description (or it was written by a committee). The result is fog, a lack of clarity in what it is Infinite actually does as a business. In contrast, the second description is succinct and understandable. If your company can't clearly explain what it does, it will affect stakeholder perceptions. Reach for strong, clear words with unambiguous meaning.

Short sentences are easy to understand. Jakob Nielsen notes that people read 25% more slowly online—a good reason to be more concise on websites, blogs, and in e-mail. Take the advice of novelist Elmore Leonard: "I try to leave out the parts that people skip."

We've already mentioned the importance of organization and content chunking online. Communication clarity also requires attention to sentence placement within paragraphs. Remember what you learned in English classes about topic sentences and powerful concluding sentences? These rules apply online as well.

Write for Professionalism

Now, for the grammar question. Does it really matter online? The answer is yes, if you want to appear professional. The rules of grammar, spelling, punctuation, sentence structure, and such apply online if you want clear communication that positions you in a positive way. The trade-off here is getting the piece posted in a timely manner versus polishing and editing until you miss the window for making an impact with your views. An occasional spelling or grammatical error is usually overlooked, but too many can hurt your professional reputation. "Poor writing is equivalent to someone speaking with spinach stuck between their teeth. Listeners and readers concentrate on the spinach; not what is being said," according to Judith Kallos, author of several e-mail etiquette books.

We've said that informal, quick writing is the order of the day for social media. When writing is informal it is done in a conversational style, similar to what you would use in a face-to-face discussion. Sentence fragments and colloquialisms are how online authors do this. For example, it is more acceptable online than in formal writing to use phrases such as "he did the heavy lifting," or "she quit cold turkey," and "it's a no-brainer." But you will appear less than professional with sentences such as "It ain't never gonna happen" (unless it is clearly done tongue-in-cheek).

Conversational writing can turn into long monologues, so take care to be concise when writing for business purposes. Note that there are gender differences in this regard among the readers you want to impress. For example, research has shown that female bloggers use more words to say the same thing as male bloggers. Our observation is that female writers tend to use more relationship-enhancing words in their writing as well, taking the time to wish people well in e-mails, and such. Many men find this wordiness annoying, while some women find the male two-word e-mail responses annoying. If you are female, trying to impress male clients, try getting more concise in all of your internet writing. If you are a male writing to female audiences, try adding relationship-building words and overlooking the wordy responses from your female senders.

Thought Byte: Text and Your Global Reputation

Does your reputation spread to international markets? If so, you'll have to attend to cultural and language differences in your internet communication—the same cultural nuances you have with other marketing communications. While this is a very complex issue, there is low-hanging fruit, such as being careful not to use English idioms not widely known (e.g., "he kicked the bucket"). Also use the date protocol, "October 1, 2008" instead of the abbreviated "10/1/08" because many countries use day/month/year (obviously, you will use "1 October" if your site has dedicated European market pages). The metric system, 24-hour time, and more can make your life harder when your reputation matters abroad. Is your website up to par for your selected country markets?

Most writers know that good writing happens during the editing process, and not in the first draft. We urge you to take those extra few minutes to reread or ask someone else to review your article, comment, or other post at least once for clarity and grammar—or at the very least run it through a Microsoft Word grammar and spell check. Be especially vigilant when using track changes because Word will not underline any existing errors after you accept changes. Your professional reputation depends on taking these steps.

Write for Engagement

"Whether your content is in the form of a white paper or a blog, for your words to be an effective marketing tool they have to be concise, engaging and offer value to the reader," says copywriter and freelance writer Matt Ambrose. How do words engage a reader and entice him to comment, link, or contribute other content? Foremost is relevant content—the connection with your intended stakeholders. You'll find several other important grammatical and writing style considerations in the remainder of this chapter. For now, we suggest the following guidelines:

It's about the reader, not you. This is a time-honored marketing perspective—customer "needs and wants" rule. Offer value to your followers by writing at the intersection of your expertise and their interests. According to author Seth Godin, "the things that fascinate you about your life are almost always banal to strangers. Strangers want to read about their lives, not yours." Also, write to one person, not the entire audience that reads your content: "Hello, you wonderful blog reader…" versus "Hello to all my blog readers…"

Offer something new. A lot of the blogosphere chatter is a regurgitation of what others say and links to what everyone else is linking to. Bloggers call this an "echo chamber," with links bouncing back and forth to the same basic content and with no new insights. Boing Boing, "weblog of cultural curiosities and interesting technologies" (www.boingboing.net), is usually in the top few most popular blogs, according to Technorati. Even when it refers to current discussion of a popular movie or technology story from *The New York Times*, Boing Boing offers enticing new information and perspective. Because of its fresh content, Boing Boing had 207,390 links to the blog from other blogs in July 2007. Be the trendsetter, with fresh insight, and you will gather comments and links on your writing from engaged readers.

Express a passionate perspective. Clearly state your opinion in your area of expertise, and do it with gusto. Follow the lead of your favorite hotel, movie, or restaurant reviewers—the ones who tell it as they see it without the sugar coating. Fence sitters are uninteresting to social media readers. Likewise, company boilerplate and marketing spin doesn't generate positive engagement, as mentioned in Chapter 4.

Show your personality. A radically transparent writer reveals his nature when writing. If you are the contrarian, comedian, or analyst, show it consistently when you write. People will love you for being authentic (as long as you don't insult your readers in the process). This is why we liked Jenny Cisney's amusing post about her dog's photos on *A Thousand Words* (Chapter 7).

Ask for the order. Invite participation. Write in a way that encourages further discussion and tell your readers how to engage—post a comment, video, photo, link to this blog, Digg this, Reddit it, bookmark it, and so forth. (See Figure 8.1 for an exemplary order-asking blog footer from Web AddiCT.)

Readers love lists.

Figure 8.1 Give your content legs with links to other sites.

Finally, encourage and leverage testimonials. You have surely sought positive testimonials from customers and used them in marketing materials, and now you can extend this practice to the social media online. Because most people trust information from "people like them" more than they trust your self-promotional material, testimonials will go a long way online. This is one reason that viral marketing is so strong online—a link recommendation in a friend's e-mail has a lot of power as an unsolicited testimonial. Powerful content that engages readers often becomes viral content, with an engagement multiplier effect as it appears all over the blogosphere and e-mail inboxes. Also, when people send positive e-mail comments your way, ask them to post on your blog or other social media site or as a recommendation on Amazon (if it is about your book), TripAdvisor (if it is about your hotel), or LinkedIn (as a professional recommendation), and so forth.

Combating Participation Inequality Online

Usability guru Jakob Nielsen notes that a small fraction of internet users contribute online. For example, by his estimate, only 0.2% of Wikipedia's unique visitors in the United States are active contributors to the site, and less than 1% of Amazon's users write reviews—with 167,113 reviews coming from just the top 100 reviewers. Forrester research (Chapter 4) indicates higher participation online, but its definition is broader, including updating web pages and using RSS feeds. Nielsen suggests the following ways to engage your online audience:

Make it easier to contribute. Netflix asks customers to rate by clicking a one to five star rating, making it easier than writing a review in words.

Make participation a side effect of user activity. Amazon makes book recommendations based on purchase and clicking behavior "people who bought this book bought these other books," and "you looked at…you might also consider."

Edit, don't create. Second Life lets users create avatars by applying standard components, rather than creating them from scratch.

Reward, but don't over-reward, participants. eBay uses a shooting red star, earned by the highest reputed sellers as rated by buyers. Don't over-reward because it will encourage a few people to dominate.

Promote quality contributions. Amazon's top 100 reviewers get this special designation, highlighting their reviews as special.

Write Snappy, Engaging Headlines

Headlines make that important first impression, and good ones will draw readers into your content. Great headlines are important for getting attention on Google results pages and when your story shows up at Digg, Del.icio.us, or other social bookmarking sites. Credible headlines that engage your stakeholders will help build your reputation.

What makes a great headline? It should be as descriptive and interesting as possible, making an intriguing promise to intended audiences. Which of the following headlines would entice you to read more about the virtual world, Second Life (all taken from real online headlines)?

1. "Second Life" (video headline)
2. "Someone Comes to Second Life—and brings his book with him!" (newsletter headline)
3. "Second Life Needs One" (blog headline)
4. "Accelerating Universe Talk in Second Life [Galactic Interactions]" (blog headline)
5. "How Madison Avenue Is Wasting Millions on a Deserted Second Life" (story headline)

Unless you have a special interest in one of these topics, we'd bet that headline 5 is the winner. It is worth taking an extra moment to write a good headline or link text. Follow the example set by CNN, Wired, and other news media websites. If you really want to write great, engaging headlines, however, get a book on advertising headlines and learn the fine points about why various words work well for enticing readers to want more.

Use a Deliberate Voice

Voice has three meanings for authors. The first refers to the writer's style. It is your personality and the tone you use. An informal, honest, open-minded, inquisitive tone will garner much more respect in the social media than will a defensive, arrogant attitude—as we've already suggested more than once in this book. Some tones, such as irreverent humor, can endear or repel, depending on your audience. In this way, the social media are the same as face-to-face conversations, so ask yourself before you hit "submit": would I talk this way to my best friend, media reporter, or business associate?

Thought Byte: What Personality Do You Portray Online?

If you were to analyze a sample of your informal writing from e-mails, blogs, forum comments, and elsewhere online, what would it reveal about you? As we discussed in Chapter 3, your values, personality, and expertise are important parts of your reputation. Does your writing reflect the reputation you want to portray? If not, try keeping an index card near your computer that lists the characteristics you want to display through your writing and refer to it until it becomes habit.

The second voice consideration was learned in English classes: active versus passive voice. An active voice means the subject performs the action indicated by the verb: "Mel tested the new iPhone today." A passive voice makes the subject a recipient of the action, versus the source: "The iPhone was tested by Mel today." Most writers struggle to stay in the active voice because it is stronger, more engaging, and more direct—but it is a fight not easily won. Still, we try.

Finally, you can write from the first-, second-, or third-person voice. If you write in the first person, it will sound like you are more important than the reader: "I came…I saw…I conquered," or "my Flickr photos…my day…my new PDA." Seth Godin would not approve (see previous quote). The third-person voice sounds formal and impersonal and does not engage readers as much as the second-person voice does. The second person is the most interactive voice because it puts the reader into the content or story. You'll notice that "you" are featured in this book: your readers will like and trust you more if you use the second-person voice more than the first or third. Of course, *we* have to slip in a "we" and "us" into this book occasionally…oops, *you'll* catch a "we" and "us" occasionally.

Consider the following, taken from three different blog posts in a two-day period on popular Engadget (www.engadget.com). Which is most likely to engage you, based on voice and other engagement techniques you've just read?

1. "While we've already seen what tricks cameras can play right before our very eyes, kameraflage is a slightly different flavor of optical illusion."

2. "As if you weren't already inundated with digital picture frames on this beautiful Friday, here's yet another to chew on."

3. "While a standalone digital photo frame is certainly a novel item to have around the crib, integrating it into a pocket cam for easy portability just sounds so much more useful."

We leave this section on writing with a reminder from author Nathaniel Hawthorne: "Words—so innocent and powerless as they are, as standing in a dictionary, how potent for good and evil they become in the hands of one who knows how to combine them."

Use the Art of Storytelling

Everyone loves a good story. Storytelling is an excellent way to appeal to your stakeholders' emotions. "Compelling stories engage an audience for a long period of time, typically longer than the internet industry can keep visitors on a web site," according to author and ClickZ contributor Cliff Allen. For these reasons, marketers often use stories to showcase the benefits of their products. Kodak's *A Thousand Words* relies on employee words, images, and video to engage customers with personal stories (that feature digital imaging products, of course).

A marketing story usually puts the customer in the role of hero who encounters a problem that the product will solve. This is the storyline for online case studies used by many software firms, such as Adobe—its website displays hundreds of in-depth success stories of customers using various products.

Companies can also be the story heroes. According to marketing professor Grahame Dowling in his *California Management Review* article "Communicating Corporate Reputation through Stories":

> **"** Stories often speak about values and morality, which sits at the heart of the reputation of individuals and companies, they are a natural medium to convey a company's good deeds and aspirations. In a corporate context, they are more believable, more memorable, and they generate more enthusiasm than the various sanitized statements (e.g., values, vision, codes of conduct, corporate plan, and annual report) that companies routinely produce. **"**

A great story has a hero with a fine life until he faces some huge crisis or problem. He looks for solutions, battles the problem, and comes out a winner. To be reputation enhancing, the hero should rely on his good character to make decisions. When a company is the hero, the crisis can be a competitor, a regulator, new technology, or some disaster in the economy. The company battles the problem relying heavily on its mission, values, and behaviors: past, present, and predicted future.

Journalist Subrata N. Chakravarty coordinated analytical coverage of many large corporations as assistant managing editor of *Forbes*. He suggested that Kodak fit the classic story form in 2004:

The crisis Kodak had falling sales and share prices and was faced with a change from traditional to digital photography.

The characters Kodak, as the hero, was an old dinosaur competing with Sony, Olympus, and others. Could it adapt quickly to changing technology?

Plot Kodak's past included the $1 Brownie camera in 1880, the bestselling Instamatic in 1970, and the first digital camera in 1975. But could it overcome this crisis, or would it fall like Polaroid did?

Resolution Kodak restructured from traditional film to a three-part imaging enterprise: consumer photography, commercial printing, and medical technology... and rides off into the sunset as the hero.

Storytelling fits Kodak's goal well: "... [to] expand the ways images touch people's daily lives." It uses multimedia to capture the emotions of consumers and professionals through its own story, and those of its employees and site visitors. Its own corporate history has all the makings of a good story.

You and your company also have good stories to tell. Tell them in an engaging way in the media to endear your intended audiences. Call on the internet community to tell their stories about your products, and to help forge your happy ending by co-creating products, web content, and more. That reminds us of the time when... but that is a story for another book.

Is Your About Us Page Boring?

The About Us page on your website is a great place to tell your story in an engaging way. You have one, but do you spend much time fashioning it into a great reputation builder? These pages by necessity end up being a holding place for all those bits of information frequently requested and legally required, yet they can be so much more when you write them to connect in a real way with the stakeholders you care about. We assume you have all the contact and other necessary information, presented in a user-friendly way—here we want to focus on the content and style of the About Us page.

As an example, consider the variety in About Us pages in the airline industry. You would think that the actual About Us page might include a brief company description along with a multitude of links (see the sidebar "Text on 'About Us' Page for Selected U.S. Airlines"). Not true. On one extreme is Continental Airlines, with absolutely no information about the company on its About Us page—just some ad links and news—and JetBlue, with only its Customer Bill of Rights (note JetBlue's use of voice: the topic is customers so why are all the pronouns "we" and "our"?). On the other extreme are United and Delta, each sporting a paragraph of factual route details. Southwest takes a middle ground by reprinting a story from its most recent *Spirit Magazine*. Also note the positioning—American is the largest, United is *one* of the largest, and Delta is the fastest growing.

> ## Text on "About Us" Page for Selected U.S. Airlines
>
> About Continental: "Work Hard. Fly Right." (with links to new ads); "From Chinatown to China's biggest town" (news story)
>
> About JetBlue: "JetBlue Airways exists to provide superior service in every aspect of our customer's air travel experience. In order to reaffirm this commitment, we set forth this Bill of Rights for our customers (click to learn more)"
>
> About United: "United Airlines operates more than 3,600 flights a day on United, United Express and Ted to more than 210 U.S. domestic and international destinations from its hubs in Los Angeles, San Francisco, Denver, Chicago and Washington, D.C. With key global air rights in the Asia-Pacific region, Europe and Latin America, United is one of the largest international carriers based in the United States. United is also a founding member of Star Alliance, which provides connections for our customers to 842 destinations in 142 countries worldwide."
>
> About Delta: "We're America's fastest growing international carrier with more than 60 new international routes added in the last year. We offer flights to 479 destinations in 105 countries on Delta, Delta Shuttle, the Delta Connection carriers, and our Worldwide Partners."
>
> About American: "As the largest airline in the world, we have a lot to offer our customers in the U.S. and around the globe. Look below for information on the routes and places to fly, employment opportunities, company press releases, and much more."
>
> About Southwest: "Colleen's Corner, As seen in this month's edition of 'Spirit Magazine'"

Where is the heartwarming company story on these airline About Us pages? If you check them out online, you'll find a patchwork of links, logos, and photos but no video or audio to touch the emotions. You might want to check your own About Us page to see if it uses engagement principles and tactics to help achieve your reputation goals. Go beyond the necessary facts, financials, and press releases to show the human face. As a starter, we provide the following guidelines to enliven your About Us pages:

- Tell your story in a clear and compelling way that engages readers. Do this by talking about who you are as people and why you are passionate about what you do (as well as what you've accomplished, of course). Avoid the simple cut and paste of company boilerplate.

- Use the page to build a relationship instead of simply presenting dry facts. Do this through writing as if to a person you like, and acting like you care about her.

- Use images, sound, and video to paint your story, as discussed in Chapter 7, as well as the other principles for creating high-quality, professional content.

- Tell the compelling, engaging story of your company.

- Be radically transparent. Give the readers an inside view by sharing your processes, struggles, and personality.

Online photo management company Snapfish has an About Us page that meets these principles better than most (Figure 8.2). It talks benefits, gives third-party testimonials, shows pictures of people, and features an employee (demonstrating to readers that the employees are passionate about their work). The page ends with something not usually seen: "Thanks to our 40 million users, from Elizabeth and the rest of the Snapfish family." Why not thank your customers in a personal way on your About Us page and show that you care?

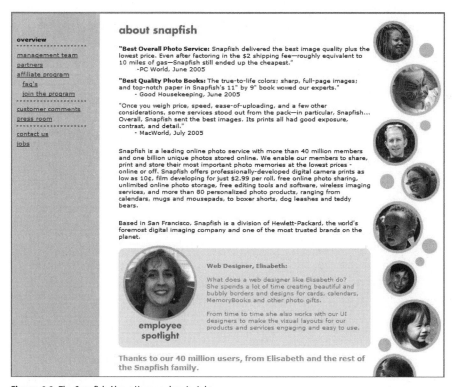

Figure 8.2 The Snapfish About Us page does it right.

Reputation-Enhancing E-mail and Other 1:1 Messaging

Just as white paper, website, and blog writing styles differ, e-mail, instant messaging, and text messaging have various writing protocols. Beyond style, you need to know which type of messaging to use for each situation. Adding to the complexity, these rules change depending on your relationship with the message recipient (the one who controls your reputation). Paralleling face-to-face and postal letter conversation, your message format and writing style are different with a friend, prospective customer, or your boss. Your reputation depends on learning these differences and putting them into practice. Speaking about these differences, literary education professor Eric Paulson notes that young people are well versed in using different writing for different audiences:

> " I think we often don't give kids enough credit with their control over language. They can text "IMHO" on their cell phones, write "my own opinion is" in a school essay, and read "it is my belief that your scar hurts when Lord Voldemort is near you" without getting discombobulated. "

In spite of the differences, there is one critical guideline that applies to all 1:1 messaging: if the recipient doesn't read your message, it won't help your reputation—and could hurt it. There are two important and controllable reasons that this could happen.

The first involves spam blockers at your recipient's internet service provider (ISP) or in his e-mail software. You'll read about these "reputation managers" in a few paragraphs. The second reason is that your message subject line, content, or even your e-mail return address may cause the entire message to be trashed. E-mail overload is a pressing problem for all of us. This means that e-mail must be designed in a way to capture the reader's attention or it won't be read—unless you are writing to your mom. Even your employees won't read all your messages.

Don't forget who controls the delete key. If your message or its particular format is not desired, it won't be read. Worse, it might be given a four-letter word that negatively affects your reputation: spam. Recognizing the growth in marketing message overload for consumers, Seth Godin coined the term "permission marketing." He encouraged advertisers to ask customers and prospects if they want to receive marketing communication before sending it to them. Eight years after Godin's book on the same topic, e-mail spam is an even bigger problem; however, most well-reputed marketers have adopted opt-in or unsubscribe features to give readers the choice of receiving their messages. We feel so strongly about this that we want to leave you with this thought:

Perceived spam = less trust and a lower reputation

Great E-Mail Can Make a Huge Reputation Difference

Every e-mail you send is an opportunity to build your reputation, or it can backfire and create poor perceptions of you and your firm, as previously mentioned. Your e-mail can be informal with friends and family because they already know and love you. You should be more professional and formal, and pay greater attention to the reputation you portray in your e-mail when writing to co-workers, employees, business partners, customers, and prospects. Ernest Hemingway said, "The most essential gift for a good writer is a built-in, shock-proof, shit detector." Use this "gift" to edit your own e-mail and other writing for the internet. Before we make specific content recommendations for these important recipients, there are some general tips for using e-mail to enhance your reputation—or avoid reputation-detracting traps:

- E-mail carries a quick response expectation with it. If you must take over 48 hours to respond, then explain this clearly on your website or wherever your e-mail address is available. It is important to manage recipient expectations: under-promise and over-deliver.

- Your message must be relevant for the recipient or it will reflect poorly on your reputation. The less relevant, the more it looks like spam.

- Before you write, think about the purpose for your e-mail and what you want the recipient to do in response. If you are clear about this, your e-mail will more likely read well and gain that response. Most business e-mail has one of these goals: performing a transaction (confirming orders, and more), providing customer service (building relationships), providing or requesting information, or making a call for action (attend this meeting; download this white paper). Of course, reputation building is always part of the purpose.

- Carefully walk the tightrope between corporate branding and recipient engagement. As we've said before, corporate spin doesn't play well online, and e-mail is no exception. You want to control your brand or personal reputation, but also be authentic and show your attention to the recipient's needs.

- Write e-mails well, using the principles in this chapter. Be sure to use spell and grammar checks, don't "shout" by using all capital letters or "whisper" with all lowercase, and so forth. Be careful not to bring all your instant messaging abbreviations into your more formal e-mail.

- Wait a few hours before you hit "send" if you are feeling any negative emotion at all when composing your response to that complaint or flame—or run it by a colleague for feedback on the e-mail's tone.

- Follow the U.S. CAN-SPAM Act regulations about maintaining a secure server, honoring unsubscribe claims, and more. See www.ftc.gov/spam for more information.

- Stop before you send along those jokes and other e-mails forwarded to you. Most people become annoyed with this junk and think less of you for sending.

- Think carefully before hitting Reply to All, when you really should only reply to the sender.

- Also, let recipients know if a reply is not needed. This will avoid all those "thanks" emails that just clutter inboxes.

Finally, automated e-mails are your friends and can enhance your reputation if used well. If you are going to be away from e-mail for a while, an automated "vacation" response will let senders know when you will attend to their needs, thus managing their expectations well. A word of caution: "vacation" e-mail auto-responders can irritate discussion group members and others who include you on a mass distribution mailing, so you might want to unsubscribe before using the vacation option. Website-generated automated e-mails include thank-you notes for opting-in, downloading white papers, registering, and more. By communicating immediately, site visitors will trust that your site is real and operational, and that you noted their actions—they are also reminded that the next e-mail from you is not spam because they asked for it.

Other automated e-mails that help your reputation include: a thank-you for ordering that includes product, price, and shipping details; notification that the product has shipped and when it will be received (usability studies have shown that including a tracking number will increase trust); and confirmation messages for any other transactional or customer service action. According to Jakob Nielson, principal of the Nielsen Norman Group:

> ❝ Email is one of a web site's most powerful tools for strengthening customer service and increasing users' confidence and trust in the site. Good email that respects users' time and quickly tells them what they need to know can do wonders for your customer service reputation. People don't really trust web sites, but when they get a confirmation message, it seems like something is actually happening. ❞

Nielson's usability research found that poorly designed e-mail erodes a company's credibility. On a scale from 1 to 7, with 7 being the most trustworthy, good design elements increased a company's trust ratings by two full points. Nielsen's subjects noted the following big concerns: lack of contact information, too much e-mail, and not getting to the point quickly enough. The next sections offer advice for reputation-building e-mail message design.

Your Return Address Is a Branding Tool

Your e-mail address is often the first thing recipients see when determining whether to delete or read. Is it meaningful and descriptive, or is it inappropriately humorous and bland? You've probably received students' resumes from e-mail address such as *VeryFancyPants@Yahoo.com* and *Hunk69@AOL.com.* Not good.

The best e-mail address is *yourname@yourcompany.com* (e.g., *John.Smith@Acme.com*) or *yourname@youruniversity.edu* because using your actual name in the address tells who you are and is the current business protocol. Using your own domain shows that your company has the resources and staying power to have its own domain name. Also good is *JohnSmithCEO@Acme.com* because it is more descriptive. Automated and bulk e-mails gain credibility when they have descriptive addresses as well: *ship-confirm@amazon.com* and *newsletter@companyname.com.*

Next best is *yourname@Verizon.com* because it gains credibility from a well-respected enterprise ISP. The least effective domain name for business mail is a consumer-oriented domain such as aol.com, msn.com, or hotmail.com, because they make you look like an internet beginner or spammer. In these cases, note that you are branding the ISP instead of your own firm. Of course, if you are applying for a new job or communicating socially, sending e-mail from these consumer domains is better.

Thought Byte: Which E-mail Address Is Best?

Which of these e-ticket confirmations, actually received, is the most engaging and descriptive?

- Member@p21.travelocity.com (Travelocity)
- pgtktg@bangkokairwaysna.com (Bangkok Airways)
- SouthwestAirlines@mail.southwest.com (Southwest Airlines)
- notify@aa.globalnotifications.com (American Airlines)
- itinerary@pcsoffice02.de (Lufthansa)
- travelercare@orbitz.com (Orbitz)
- confirmation@uasupport.com (United Airlines)
- travel@expedia.com (Expedia)

As you consider these, think about the value of making your company name and the e-mail purpose known at a quick glance. These airlines and agencies own their own domain names and can pick any *address@companyname.com*—how did they do?

Write a Great Subject Line

E-mail recipients first look at the subject line or the return address. The same principles for creating great headlines apply here. Engage the reader to entice her into the message content, and also be very descriptive of the e-mail purpose. If it is a short e-mail to colleagues about an upcoming meeting, use the subject line: "Staff Meeting Nov. 12 at 3 pm," or "Help: please check my computer for a virus." If you are writing to anyone outside of the company, use your brand name in the subject line. Kodak's monthly newsletter comes from Membership@smile.kodakgallery.com with a subject line, "August Exposure is here!" followed by the newsletter month and name.

Remove the "re: re: re:" ad infinitum, and check your subject lines for meaning. "Important information," "Checking in," and "costs" say nothing enticing to recipients.

The All-Important Message Content

Be brief and to the point.

Start with a greeting. If it is a formal e-mail, use "Dear Dr. Jones," and if informal you can use "Hi," or simply the name: "Jane, thanks for the pricing figures." Never use the traditional "Dear Sirs." Unless you are volleying quickly on a topic, we think you should always use the person's name as a greeting because most people like to see that personalization and attention to them.

For the body, open with the purpose ("I'll be in the office late on Tuesday" or "The new CAN-SPAM amendment means that we must change our security protocols"). Use a linear structure for any needed support, and end with a call for the desired response action ("please confirm that you can attend"). This opening, body, and call for action can be one sentence, such as "Lunch meeting changed to Wednesday—pls. bring the Smith file." End with a closing ("Warm regards," "Sincerely," "Cheers") and then type your name, even if you use a signature file (below).

Include an Appropriate Signature File

The signature file is one of your best reputation assets. It can promote your company or individual brand and provide contact information hundreds of times a week. It is quite standard to include a name, business title, company name, and full contact information (except your e-mail address because it is in the message header). You can also save space by omitting some contact information if it is easily accessible via the website link in the signature file. The .sig file can be so much more than your ID tag, however. Reputation savvy e-mailers include:

- Links to websites, blogs, or other reputation assets, such as Flickr photos.
- Calls to action with links, such as "contact us," "download now," or "subscribe to RSS feed."
- A statement about the brand, such as: "Amazon.com… and you're done!" Be careful that it is not too slick.
- Announcement of a new product or company news.

Many e-mailers use quotes in their signature files. These are good if they are relevant to the recipient because they reveal more about the writer, but they can easily backfire if you're presenting anything controversial. We especially like the quote created by Wiley development editor David Ziegler: "Just because the English language continues to change doesn't mean we have to help it along." This quote is his attempt to preserve the quality of the written language, and totally appropriate to append to e-mail to authors.

> **Defining Moment: Signature File**
>
> According to Wikipedia, "A signature block (often abbreviated as signature, sig block, sig file, .sig, dot sig, siggy, or just sig) is a block of text automatically appended at the bottom of an e-mail message, Usenet article, or forum post. This has the effect of "signing off" the message." Signature files are usually text only because many e-mail programs block images.

Most people have several signature files, and rotate them for different audiences. You might want one file for internal use, one for external, another for posting in blogs, and one for each forum you use. Recall that this is a huge reputation opportunity and the more closely relevant to the reader, the better. According to Judith Kallos of Net-Manners.com, "keep in mind that the perception your signature file gives will lend to the perception of who you are, what you believe in, whether you follow the rules, and if you know how to use technology—or not."

Finally, do your best to avoid the lengthy signature files full of legal liability notices, virus-scanning methods, and multiple contact methods. These are not brand building and are easy for the reader to skip. One exception is for e-mail newsletters. These need a longer .sig file for their administration, including things such as how to unsubscribe or change account information, the company's postal mailing address (a CAN-SPAM requirement), privacy policy, the usual contact information, and more.

Your Reputation Counts with Spam Filters

In 2004, it became public that internet service provider AOL improved its e-mail spam filters and began blocking nearly 80% of all mail to AOL account holders. This irritated legitimate senders, who sometimes ended up in the junk folder. In 2007, users report receiving more spam than in the past, and both ISPs and e-mail users have refined their blocking methods. The Pew Internet & the American Life Project found that 71% of e-mail users have ISPs that use spam filters, and 41% use their own filters to block spam.

According to e-mail marketer Return Path, an e-mail sender's reputation is the sole cause of e-mail filtering in 83% of the cases—not the message content. Different ISPs use varying reputation data points when filtering, so Return Path's Sender Score Reputation Manager uses 60 different variables to compile an e-mail reputation score. Some of these are volume of e-mail sent, filtering rates, unknown user rates, security practices, identity stability, blacklist counts, and unsubscribe functionality (see www.senderscore.com for details and explanations). Other reputation managers evaluate the sender's past behavior and its ability to receive e-mail.

Your precious e-mail to prospects and customers may be blocked, even if it is sent to an opt-in address (see the sidebar "E-Mail Blacklists"). To keep this from happening, learn more about e-mail reputation filtering by reading one of the popular books on e-mail marketing or by checking with the Direct Marketing Association (www.the-dma.org).

E-Mail Blacklists

Blacklists are lists of e-mail and IP addresses from known spammers. They are used by ISPs to block spam. Fortunately, you can check to see if your address is on any of the lists by running a check online (and get it removed from the list if it is). For example, mxtoolbox.com offers a free online test that "will check a mail server IP address against 147 DNS based email blacklists. (Commonly called Realtime blacklist, DNSBL or RBL)." Another service, Delivery Monitor (www.deliverymonitor.com), will track your outgoing mail to see if and where it is blocked. Note that there are other things that can stop your mail, such as a bad MX file—this file specifies which mail servers handle mail for your domain.

Using Instant and Text Messaging

Unlike e-mail, instant messaging (IM) offers immediate, quick communication with people who are online simultaneously. This real-time communication is not just for teens—35% of employees use IM at work, according to the American Management Association's 2006 Workplace E-Mail, Instant Messaging & Blog Survey. Employees use IM to communicate with colleagues, partners, and clients. It is a good medium for locating a person or to get a quick answer about a meeting or project, among other things (see the sidebar "How Businesspeople Use Instant Messaging").

If you use IM, include your screen name in signature files and on your business cards to let stakeholders know that they can reach you instantly. Also, follow the same rules you use for e-mail. Specifically, pick a professional screen name, write clearly and succinctly, and check your spelling and grammar. Also, IM participants expect quick responses, so be careful about multitasking—you want to give your full attention to that client who needs you right now. Finally, be sure to change your online status so that others know when you leave your desk or are unavailable for response.

IM can help your reputation because you are more available with answers for the people you want to impress: for instance, you can improve customer service using IM to answer client queries from the office, from the airport with your PDA, or anywhere else. This kind of service builds relationships because of the real-time collaboration and informal nature of IM—it is easy to be radically transparent in IM messages. For more complex questions or for especially needy clients, however, this kind of customer service might take too much time. Sometimes, a simple phone call is more efficient and effective. Or you can try a live chat function on your website.

In contrast, IM can wreak havoc on your reputation. You can easily be seduced by its chatty and seemingly untraceable nature to reveal unbecoming information. The

American Management Association study found employee use of IM to include sending jokes, gossip, rumors and disparaging remarks (24% of respondents admitting to the practice); confidential company, employee, and client information (12%); and sexual, romantic, and pornographic chat (10%). Be as careful of what you say in IM as in e-mail because any IM conversation participant can copy and paste the entire stream into a Microsoft Word document and share with others. We encourage you to be radically transparent, but not to the point of ruining your good name while just having fun IMing colleagues. We'd hate to see you end up in court for a sexual harassment suit based on that joke you told via IM.

How Businesspeople Use Instant Messaging

According to AOL and the Opinion Research Corporation's Third Annual Instant Messaging Survey, the top uses of IM at work include:

- Communicate with colleagues (58%)
- Get a quick answer on a business matter (49%)
- Communicate with clients or customers (28%)
- Exchange files (25%)
- Send and receive information while on a conference call (24%)
- Send URLs to colleagues (23%)
- Organize in-person meetings (22%)
- Use a chat feature for work-related conferences (19%)
- Organize conference calls (15%)
- Avoid a potentially difficult in-person conversation with a colleague (12%)

About half of the nearly 230 million U.S. cell phone owners have used their phones to send or receive text messages, according to internet consultancy Sterling Market Intelligence. "Text messaging, or texting, is the common term for the sending of 'short' (160 characters or fewer) text messages, using the Short Message Service (SMS), from mobile phones," according to Wikipedia.

Text message use is primarily social, among friends and family. Some businesses have been successful in getting consumers to send messages—such as the *American Idol* reality television show, with its call for audience members to text a vote for their favorite idol each week. Others have experimented with promotional use of text messaging, but most of the outstanding B2C examples occur in countries outside of the United States, where many more cell phone users enjoy text messaging.

If you use text messaging to consumers or other stakeholders, follow the same rules outlined for e-mail and instant messaging. Because your cell phone number becomes your address, you don't have to worry about fashioning a reputation-building address, but you do want to adhere strictly to permission marketing principles. If e-mail spam will get you a lower reputation, cell phone spam will kill your reputation.

Become an Online Multimedia Star

You now have all the tools in your multimedia content palette for painting a great reputation online. You'll note that Chapter 8 was not as visually engaging as was Chapter 7, which discussed images, video, and sound—words alone are not enough to engage your audiences and create your desired reputation (although we hope you read Chapter 7 anyway). Online, you'll exhibit your thought leadership on websites and blogs—both yours and those belonging to others in similar fields. Your brilliance will show up in your e-mail and other text communication, and in white papers, social network profiles (e.g., LinkedIn), online forums, special interest groups (e.g., Google Groups), wikis, audio and video podcasts, on video- and picture-sharing sites (e.g., YouTube and Photobucket), and even in virtual worlds (e.g., Second Life)—in short, your insightful multimedia content is appropriate for all social media platforms. The next chapters will show you how to use blogs, social networking, and more for enhancing your good name.

The Power of Blogs

The blogosphere is a vibrant collective of voices discussing your brand and helping to define your reputation. Building and launching a blog can add a lot of value to you and your business but is not something that should be done halfheartedly. The software you select, the style of blog you use, and the way you engage your readers all play an important role in determining your success or failure in the blogosphere. Understanding what your stakeholders expect from you and how to reach them with an authentic, radically transparent voice will ensure your blog is a positive reflection on your reputation.

Chapter Contents

The Daddy of Blogging

On August 13, 2007, Go Daddy CEO Bob Parsons used his personal blog (BobParsons.com) to discuss the possibility the company would not air a television commercial during the 2008 Super Bowl. Considering the domain registration and hosting company had built its 4.3 million active customer base in part due to the sexy TV ads, the suggestion was one that caught the attention of Go Daddy's customers and the media. Parsons himself acknowledged the tremendous benefit the company had received from its previous Super Bowl ads posting, "[The 2007] Super Bowl was also good for the company. Our market share climbed to 38% right after the game and is still inching up." Still, Parsons explained the previous hurdles Go Daddy faced in getting its controversial ads approved by the television network and suggested that the estimated $10 million needed to create and air the commercial might be used on alternative opportunities available to the company.

Traditionally, such an announcement from a company of Go Daddy's large size would have been difficult to disseminate to stakeholders. A press release would be overkill for something that was more contemplation than firm decision. Likewise, a press conference wouldn't likely draw much attention—especially with the Super Bowl nearly six months from airing. However, Parsons' blog post entitled "The 2008 Super Bowl, Why Go Daddy might sit this one out" (see Figure 9.1) was the perfect platform for him to float a trial balloon, open up a dialogue with customers, and reach the news media—perfect because Bob Parsons is among the elite CEO bloggers who take the time to regularly post thoughts, opinions, and company news to a web log. Says Parsons, "When customers read my blog, they know that I write it and it's not a sanitized piece of marketing literature." By making the Super Bowl announcement on his blog—which is consistently ranked as one of the most popular blogs in the world by Technorati—Go Daddy's founder and chief ensured his message reached the right audiences.

Within hours of his blog post, Go Daddy's customers were leaving comments in reply to Parsons—something that the CEO blogger has a knack of encouraging. "I know the type of articles our customers like to see," says Parsons. "I don't write about stuff our customers consider to be a yawn." The opinions of those leaving comments were split down the middle. Some Go Daddy customers felt the company needed to continue with the Super Bowl commercials because they were part of the company's branding. Others left comments in support of Parsons' decision, agreeing that the company should explore other advertising options. Parsons embraces readers' comments on his blog. "It's opened up what many customers feel is a direct relationship with me," explains Parsons.

The following is visible within the figure:

BOB PARSONS
CEO & Founder of GoDaddy.com®

| Hot Points Blog | Go Daddy LIVE Podcast! | About Bob | Bob In The News | What Would Bob Do? | Bob's 16 Rules |

2007 | 2006 | 2005 | 2004

Monday, August 13, 2007

The 2008 Super Bowl. Why Go Daddy might sit this one out.

It's that time of year again. Time to start thinking about advertising in the 2008 Super Bowl. Here are the facts:

Go Daddy is the industry leader — by far.
Go Daddy now has more than 4.3 million active customers, with over 23 million domain names under management.

Go Daddy's market share of new ICANN domain names being registered averages about 39% and occasionally – depending on the day – sometimes creeps as high as 50%. To put this into perspective, our closest competitor has fewer than 8 million domains under management and an average daily market share of new ICANN registrations of less than 9%.

There's no doubt Go Daddy's low prices, wide range of domain enabling products – all of which are developed at Go Daddy – and our Industry Best customer support—certainly have made a big difference. Our overall offering is unmatched by any of our competitors – hence their insignificant market shares.

The Super Bowl has played a key role in our success.
As good as our overall offering is, the simple fact is customers need to know we exist before they will do business with us. This is where the Super Bowl and Go Daddy's edgy advertising have made a big difference.

2005 Super Bowl.
Go Daddy advertised for the first time in the 2005 Super Bowl. Our market share of new registrations jumped from 16% before the Big Game to 25% after the game.

QuickSearch
[Search]

Syndicate This Blog

XML **RSS 2.0 feed**
XML **Go Daddy LIVE**

What People Are Saying...

I love your new Amanda Beard commercial! —Gena on Oct 29 2007

The new commercial has a "classy" touch. I personally like it, though I wouldn't mind if it were any hotter. —John W. Furst on Oct 29 2007

I love your ads, I specially like how you play "sexual tensions" in an easy way. —Francisco on Oct 28 2007

Figure 9.1 Go Daddy CEO Bob Parsons' blog

Reaching Go Daddy's customers is enough reason for Parsons to post his thoughts using a blogging platform. However, Parsons knows that his blog is also a great way to get his message out to the news media, "My blog is so well followed, anytime I write anything, if there's a message I want to get out, it's picked up immediately, all over the world." That's exactly what happened with Parson's Super Bowl post. Within 24 hours of its publication, the news that Go Daddy might not make another Super Bowl ad spread to online news sites ClickZ and AdRants, and made its way into the mainstream media via *The Arizona Republic* newspaper.

Bob Parsons' blogging efforts exemplify a radically transparent CEO. By sharing his thoughts and business strategies with the stakeholders of his company—customers, employees, and the media—Parsons understands that blogging provides an open and honest connection. "It makes it worth their time. People are not going to visit my blog if it's nothing but marketing hype." This kind of radical transparency results in a reputation of trust for Parsons and Go Daddy—desired audiences anticipate and respond to his valued words.

While Parsons says that blogging is "a lot of work," he also freely admits that it "translates into a lot of benefits" for Go Daddy. Aside from the company's Super Bowl ads, Bob Parsons' blog and online radio show help the company reach many new customers: The company manages 23 million domain names and enjoys a market share that averages between 39% and 50% of all domain names registered. In fact, Parsons often finds that the more radical he is in his blog posts the more it seems to help Go Daddy's business. Parsons says of his blog, "The more controversial it is—even if I write about something that is negative—business goes up."

Blogging is a vital component of any online reputation management initiative. Not only does a blog help grow the reputation of a company or individual, but it's one of few channels that allows direct communication between you and those who have a say in the perception of your brand. Additional benefits include a chance to provide optimized web content for Google spiders and faster access to the media—remember that 51% of journalists read blogs. These benefits are just some of the reasons you should consider a blog as part of your efforts to become radically transparent. However, simply publishing a blog and expecting it to transform your reputation is akin to Pontiac building a new car and expecting it to sell like hot cakes without any effort on its part. As Parsons explains, "You have to make it known that you have a blog. If it doesn't get read, it doesn't matter what you're writing."

Over the course of this chapter you'll learn which type of blog is best for you and how to ensure your blogging efforts result in a positive online reputation.

Further Reading on Blogging

Throughout this chapter you'll learn how you can use a blog to build and manage your online reputation. While you'll gain insight on the benefits of blogging, you might still have questions about why you or your company should blog and how to handle all of the technical requirements of setting one up. If this sounds like you, we recommend two books. Robert Scoble and Shel Israel's *Naked Conversations* is a great book for those who want to fully understand how blogs are affecting businesses and marketing messages. Debbie Weil's aptly titled *The Corporate Blogging Book* is another great read, especially suited to companies that need step-by-step instruction in setting up and maintaining a corporate blog.

Building Personal and Corporate Brands with Blogs

There are many reasons that you or your company should use a blog as part of your branding strategy. Perhaps the most compelling is that, along with the proliferation of blogs, the number of people reading blogs has also grown. Remember that 57 million Americans are already reading blogs on a regular basis, and you'll realize that it won't be long before blogs become one of the largest and most important channels of current online information.

Used for brand building, a blog is a powerful platform that can connect you with all of your stakeholders and engage them in a conversation about your industry, your products, or your expertise. In *The Corporate Blogging Book*, Debbie Weil explains, "As a marketing strategy, blogs are often more effective than traditional web sites." In fact, blogs are at the heart of any radically transparent effort. They're easy to launch—much easier than a typical website—and their quick "journal entry" style formatting make them perfect for holding casual conversations with those who have a stake in your reputation. "Blogs are a quick, easy way to communicate and make a connection with your customers and the media," agrees Weil.

Blogs are the perfect outlet for achieving your goals. This is true whether you're a professional hoping to enhance your personal reputation or a company seeking to better connect with your customers. The fundamentals of radically transparent blogging are the same for both personal and corporate identities, but the benefits are slightly different—although there is a lot of overlap. For example, while Parsons' blog builds his personal reputation, the corporate Go Daddy reputation also benefits. The next sections describe personal and corporate blogging benefits.

Blogging Benefits for Personal Brands

Ask bloggers what they gain from their blog posting and you'll likely hear enthusiasm for engaging and interacting with their readers in a way that positively affects their reputations. In fact, most successful blogs have one thing in common: the blogger is able to connect with his audience in ways not realized by many other media. As Darren Rowse, blogging expert and owner of ProBlogger.net. says, "One of the reasons that many are finding blogs to be a useful form of communication is that they have a real ability to build trust between bloggers and their audience." Building an audience and generating trust with your blog readers will help enhance your personal reputation because you'll be perceived as a credible, authentic, and trustworthy expert. As mentioned in Chapter 3, a strong personal reputation online will open many career and revenue-generating doors.

Establish Yourself as Credible

Simply owning a blog isn't quite enough to build your reputation and establish yourself as an expert in your chosen field. After all, if your blog is only used to discuss your child's latest school play or the last vacation you took, your audience will likely be confined to friends and family—who already know what a great person you are. Instead, you should look at your personal blog as your "professional reputation" blog and look for ways to use it as a platform to demonstrate your thought leadership and credibility in your line of work.

This might require a second blog, separate from your personal ramblings, but it's worth the effort to keep things focused on your area of professional expertise if you want to develop a stellar reputation that will keep you marketable in your field. Rowse has found this to be true with his blogging at ProBlogger: "It leads to opportunities to sell myself as an expert on my topics. This has ranged from opportunities to speak at conferences, to writing books, to selling consulting time, to being quoted in others books, to media opportunities."

This doesn't mean that you should avoid all personal references in your professional blog. We've already mentioned that customers and other stakeholders trust people who are authentic online. As mentioned in Chapter 3, even the highly professional Robert Scoble is radically transparent with comments such as, "I didn't get to the Under the Wire conference. Sigh. I slept in and missed my plane." This admission makes readers believe that the rest of what he says must be honest and transparent, too.

Network with Others

If you've ever watched two motorcyclists pass each other on opposite sides of the road, you'll see an instant camaraderie between them. Despite the increased risk of a crash by removing one hand from the handlebars, that doesn't stop them from offering a wave to each other. Motorcyclists bond over their love of bikes. At motorcycle gatherings, they help and trust on another more because they are like-minded (recall that we trust people like us). The same is true of bloggers—you'll quickly discover that maintaining a blog earns you an instant membership to the blogosphere.

By keeping your blog focused on your area of professional expertise, you'll likely find that you attract readers with similar interests and skills. They'll leave comments, link to your posts, and even share their expertise with you—all in the name of blogging. As a blogger, you'll build respect among your peers and experience a growing business network—probably faster than you could with a service such as LinkedIn. In fact, it's not uncommon to find that even your counterparts at your biggest business rival will become more approachable if you both have blogs.

The Blog Is Your New Resume

When sites such as Tripod.com first offered free web pages, it was common to find some individuals using the space to host their resumes. Even to this day, many professionals buy a domain name that matches their personal name and point it at their online resume. You'll find that a professional blog takes the place of your online resume. Potential employers may have already received your resume via e-mail or a career site such as Monster.com, but what they want now is to find any skeletons in your closet. If instead they find your blog they'll realize that you're web savvy, articulate, and radically transparent—especially since you've read this book and now use your blog to display your expertise and knowledge of your industry.

Blogging Benefits for Corporations and Brands

"Corporate blogging done right should not feel like a marketing experience. It should come across as the inside story, the pulse, the personality of your company," suggests Debbie Weil. Your corporate or brand blog should first and foremost satisfy the needs of your stakeholders. By doing so, it will naturally bring you the benefits your business ultimately desires such as increased name recognition, better search listings, or higher company revenue. There are many ways that a corporate blog can benefit your business reputation—the following are worth highlighting.

Informal Company Communication

As Bob Parsons' blog demonstrates, some announcements need to reach your stakeholders quickly yet informally. A company blog removes a lot of the red tape and corporate spin that often surrounds a press release or advertisement. You've already learned from Seth Godin that your customers are desperate for a "purple cow" and they'll certainly get one if you provide a blog offering clear and honest dialogue with them. As Weil suggests, "Blogs are a new way to close the gap between you and your customers."

Collecting Customer Feedback

In case you thought that a corporate blog meant you'll have a one-way monologue with customers, think again! According to Weil, "Corporate blogging is a communication and marketing channel, but with a twist—it's two-way." In fact, blogging is one of the best ways to hold an online conversation with your customers and other stakeholders. By allowing comments on your blog—something we encourage you to do—you'll find that your blog readers are willing to share valuable insight on your products, services, and marketing messages. Refer to Dell's story in Chapter 2 for a great example of how to use online feedback for improving the company and customer relationships.

With this in mind, don't be alarmed the first time a customer leaves a negative comment about your business. Remember, that customer would likely have expressed her comment somewhere online, so it's better on your blog where you can react and respond. In his *Corporate Weblog Manifesto*, Robert Scoble warns that you should be prepared for both the positive and negative feedback on your blog: "Don't try to write a corporate weblog unless you can answer all questions—good and bad—professionally, quickly, and nicely." A negative comment is an opportunity to show your professionalism and radical transparency via a great response.

Value for Your Customers

When you launch a company blog, you shouldn't focus purely on "what's in it for us." Recall that online you must walk the tough line between user control and managing corporate and brand messaging. If you give additional value for your customers you'll also increase their positive opinion of your brand. This indirect, often intangible, benefit won't be readily apparent during the initial stages, but your blogging initiative will likely separate you from your competition and demonstrate to your customers just how much you care about them.

For this reason it's important to put your best foot forward and avoid a half-hearted attempt to blog. A blog that starts off with a bang but then fizzles out after just a few posts will leave your customers feeling that your transparent efforts were a head fake—an attempt to win their trust without any intention of adding any value to the conversation. You should avoid this at all costs. In fact, you could learn from Go Daddy's Parsons, who treats his blog with the same level of quality as any other company offering. "I look at the blog just as I look at any other product," says Parsons. ■

The Secret Blogging Benefit

While there are a lot of readily apparent benefits to having a corporate blog, there's also one that's rarely discussed. If your company blogs in an authentic and transparent way, you'll be less likely to have your reputation attacked by other bloggers. There have been no studies to measure this assertion, but generally bloggers appear more apt to attack a company that doesn't have a blog or engage the blogosphere (not a member of the "club"). Companies that do blog find that they're less likely to be accused of having poor customer service and of not listening to customers, or that they are full of corporate spin.

Choosing Your Blog Writing Style

There are many different writing styles you can use when publishing your blog. In fact, there's really no wrong style of blog, except for the "flog" (see the sidebar "Defining Moment: Flog"). As long as your blog is transparent and well written, and serves the needs of the reader, the actual style of blog you use doesn't matter much. Most important is to decide on your blog writing style at the outset and stick to it. A blog that starts off being open and engaging will lose a lot of credibility if it gets quiet during a company crisis. Likewise, if your personal blog switches from regularly discussing industry events to including detailed reports of recent trips with your cat to the vet, you'll lose a lot of momentum.

The key to any successful blog is not so much determined by which style you use—all can be effective—but by picking the one that best suits you or your business and sticking with it. The following are some typical blog styles that work very well.

> **Defining Moment: Flog**
>
> A flog is a fake blog that is often created by a public relations or marketing team with the goal of passing as a normal blog. Flogs are labeled "fake" because they often have an ulterior motive—such as launching a new product—and are rarely written with an authentic voice. Recall what we said about corporate spin's effect on social media users.

The Individual Expert Blog

The individual expert blog is best suited for professionals looking to build their own personal brands. Typically the blog communicates the views and activities of a single individual and the blog posts are not the official writing of any company—although the company may benefit indirectly from the blogger's efforts. The expert blog is a great opportunity for you to establish yourself as an expert in your chosen field and build status among your peers. Additionally, an expert blog will likely stay with you throughout your career, even when you change companies, and may even help you land your next job or client.

Before starting an individual expert blog, it's important to check with your employer to see if there are any guidelines or restrictions on employee blogs. Many examples exist of employees that revealed too many corporate secrets in their blogs and were consequently "dooced."

Examples of expert blogs include Robert Scoble (scobleizer.com), Guy Kawasaki (blog.guykawasaki.com), and Michelle Malkin (michellemalkin.com).

> **Defining Moment: Dooced**
>
> *Dooced* is an internet neologism that means "to lose one's job as a result of something one wrote on the internet," according to Wikipedia. Its origin can be traced to Heather B. Armstrong, who was reportedly the first blogger fired from her job at a start-up for her satirical posts about her employer.

The Company Executive Blog

The company executive blog is perhaps one of the most effective blog styles. Typically written by the CEO or some other high-ranking company executive, the blog is a great way for your company to add a human touch to its corporate communications. Most company stakeholders will assume your CEO is out of reach and not available for comment, so this style of blog will win their trust and respect—as it did for Parsons of Go Daddy.

There's no hard and fast rule regarding how often your CEO should add blog posts, but she should at least be consistent in her frequency. And of course, more frequent posting increases stakeholder engagement. It is fine for CEOs to write while traveling and e-mail the post to a blog administrator for posting, but it is vital that the CEO not use a ghostwriter. If word gets around that your CEO doesn't write her own blog posts, the blog will lose all credibility—as could your CEO.

Why We Don't Recommend Blog Ghostwriters

In an attempt to join the blogosphere and connect with your stakeholders, you may be tempted to employ a ghostwriter—someone who writes blog posts for you and publishes them using your name. This is the antithesis of being radically transparent.

While it's permissible to publish anonymous blog posts (that don't display the author's name), using a ghostwriter is deceptive and will run the risk that one day your ruse will be discovered. If you don't have the time to post to your blog on a regular basis—even once a month is frequent enough—our advice is to consider an alternative to the company executive blog format.

Blogging isn't right for every CEO. Your CEO may not have much of a personality or may feel too restricted by Securities and Exchange Commission (SEC) or industry regulations to write anything of substance. The key thing with any CEO blog is to ensure that your CEO wants to blog, is passionate about connecting with stakeholders, and is dynamic enough to attract readers. In fact, if your CEO isn't able to engage his audience, that could be worse than not having a blog at all. As Bob Parsons warns, "For a CEO, if you write a blog and it has nothing to do with your business and it gets read, you're far and away better than a blog that has everything to do with your business but nobody is looking at it."

Examples of company executive blogs include Sun Microsystems' Jonathan Schwartz (blogs.sun.com/jonathan; Figure 9.2), GM's Bob Lutz (fastlane.gmblogs.com), and Go Daddy's Bob Parsons (bobparsons.com).

Figure 9.2 Sun CEO Jonathan Schwartz's blog

The Company Team Blog

Although the company executive blog is a great way to connect customers with your CEO, sometimes the best blog posts come from your employees. The company team blog is a collaborative blog style that draws on the thoughts and musings of different employees, such as Kodak's *A Thousand Words* and *A Thousand Nerds* blogs (Chapter 7). Readers are typically much more trusting of the comments coming from the rank and file employees—probably because many CEOs tend to speak in sound bites or corporate rhetoric. With this style of blog, you can draw on the most appropriate employee for the theme of the blog post, while also taking advantage of the simple economics of who actually has the time to write a post.

For your company team blog to work, it must be as open and transparent as possible. While this doesn't mean allowing your employees to publish blog posts without any procedure or accountability, it does mean enabling your employees to use their natural voice and connect freely with readers (we'll cover corporate blogging guidelines later in the chapter). When you allow your employees to hold conversations with your stakeholders in this manner, you'll be able to connect with them in a way not possible with press releases or advertising campaigns. The company team blog is a great way to add a human face to your corporate entity.

Great examples of company team blogs include The Official Google Blog (googleblog.blogspot.com), Southwest Airlines' "Nuts About Southwest" (blogsouthwest.com; Figure 9.3), and Direct2Dell (direct2dell.com).

Figure 9.3 Nuts About Southwest blog

The Company Update Blog

The goal of the company update blog is to offer timely, accurate information on the status of your company and its products. Although the company update blog may not be as exciting and engaging as its corporate blogging counterparts, it can still provide a lot of value to your stakeholders. Typically, the blog is used as a platform for keeping your customers (and journalists) updated on new product rollouts, service outages, and other known company issues. It's unlikely that this style of blog will win you more customers, but it might just save you from losing some.

The company update blog doesn't rely on a regular posting schedule—you simply update as needed. You should use the same honest, conversational tone as with other blog types. Likewise, you will benefit by listening and responding to comments left by your readers—especially if there's an unexpected product delay or service glitch.

Many companies provide a company update blog, including Google's Blogger (status.blogger.com), Skype's Heartbeat (heartbeat.skype.com), and DreamHost (dreamhoststatus.com).

The Company Crisis Blog

While the company update blog is designed to be available 24/7, providing continuous updates to customers, the company crisis blog is only used in emergencies. If your company is not quite ready to launch a full-time blog, you may wish to at least consider building a crisis blog. This style of blog is designed, built, and ready to be published at a moment's notice and is only used in times of a company emergency—such as product recalls or company scandals. While the other blog styles are designed to build trust and transparency, the crisis blog is used only when your company faces adversity.

If you decide to build a crisis blog, it's vital that you create it before you need it and rehearse its deployment. Understand who will post to the blog, how you'll respond to critics, and how the blog will integrate with your other crisis communications channels. Although the blog will initially operate in "stealth" mode—either password protected or available only on the company intranet—once publicly deployed, it should be open, honest, and transparent.

There are many anecdotal reports of companies using crisis-only blogs. Unfortunately, many companies are guarded when it comes to discussing them—hoping the blog will look like an authentic response, rather than a canned response. In light of this, it's virtually impossible to find a company that will admit to having a crisis blog under wraps.

The Internal Company Blog

The last blog style indirectly helps your public reputation building by boosting your company's internal marketing and communication efforts. Internal company blogs are a great choice if you're not quite ready to commit to a public company blog but want to test the waters or establish which public voice might best suit your business. The internal blog is a great way to engage some of your most important stakeholders and get them all on the same reputation page—your employees. It is hosted on your company intranet, which is a lot more secure than hosting publicly and simply using a password.

Many companies "publish" their blog internally first—allowing them to fine-tune the format—before making it available to the general public. In fact, you'll notice that many company blogs launch to the public already populated with half a dozen posts or more. Quite often the blog has been active internally for some months, while the company decides who gets to blog and what they should say.

You may also decide that you want a blog specifically for the purpose of updating your employees—especially if you have employees located in multiple offices or in different time zones. You'll be among great company as many businesses have found that an internal company blog is a great way for management to keep employees in the loop. "A CEO's blog on the intranet can kill off water-cooler rumors about things like layoffs or address difficult issues facing the enterprise," says Nathan Rudyk, CEO of market2world in a *Business Edge* report. "It replaces town hall meetings."

Companies that use internal company blogs include Google, IBM, and McDonald's.

Selecting Your Blog Platform

Now that you've defined your blogging style, you need to decide how your blog will look and act in the blogosphere. Setting up a blog can be quick and simple, sometimes taking less than five minutes, or it can be a long, complex task. The ease or difficulty of the launch depends greatly on which blogging platform you select and where you decide to host your blog. There are many options from which to choose, so we'll walk you through the most common scenarios, starting with which blog software to use.

Choosing Your Blog Software

In order to set up and publish your blog, you'll need to select your blogging software of choice. The technology used to publish and maintain a blog is very similar to a traditional content management system. Effectively, the software handles the creative look of your blog, the different components used, and the creation of each blog post page. Once you have the blog software up and running, publishing new posts is a quick and painless process. One of your first and most important decisions involves choosing among the various blog software solutions. Why is it such an important decision? Simply, once you decide on a blog software solution, it is notoriously difficult to switch to a different one. Taking the time to carefully evaluate your options now could save you a lot of headaches in the future. Here's the *Radically Transparent* guide to the two most popular solutions: developer-hosted blogs and user-hosted blogs.

Developer-Hosted Blog Software

Developer-hosted blogs reside on the software provider's server and require no installation by you. Blogger.com, TypePad.com, and WordPress.com are all examples of developer-hosted blog solutions. The number one reason for selecting this option is that you don't have to worry about server configurations or having to manually update your blog software—it's all provided for you.

Blogger and WordPress.com are both completely free and will get you started blogging within a matter of minutes. You'll find them easy to use and you'll be among the many millions of bloggers who have chosen these two solutions for their blogs. Figure 9.4 shows the Blogger interface.

Both Blogger and WordPress.com offer great functionality, with options for comments, categories, and design customization. In contrast, they are not as sophisticated or adaptable as their cousins, user-hosted blogs. If you're an individual or small business that needs a simple option for launching a blog, you'll likely find the developer-hosted blog option is the best fit for you. However, most companies will find that they'll quickly outgrow the developer-hosted blog and will yearn for the greater functionality and customization offered by user-hosted solutions.

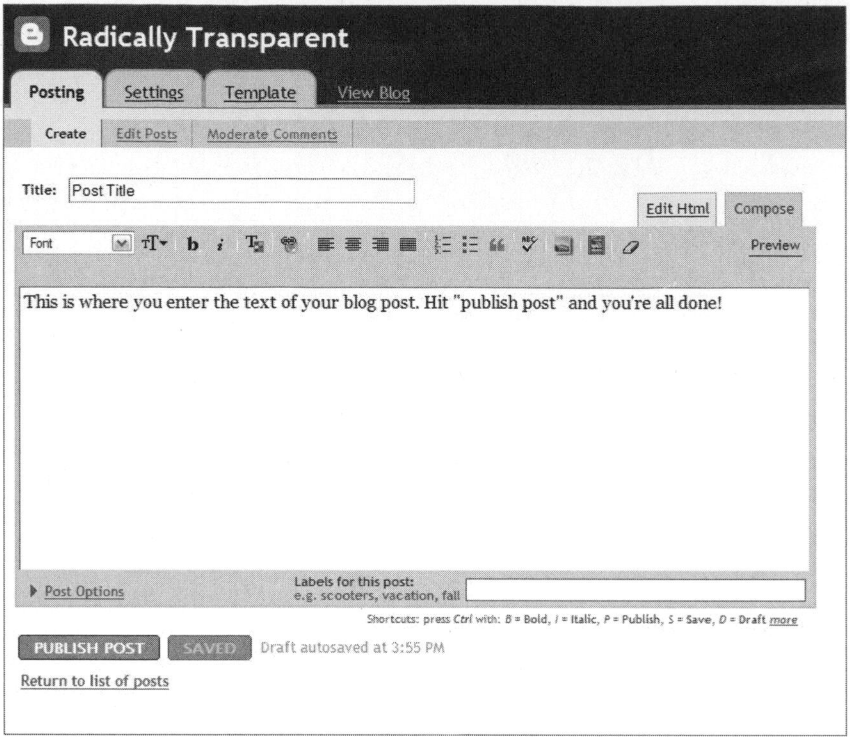

Figure 9.4 The Blogger publishing interface

User-Hosted Blog Software

User-hosted blogs take a little more work to build and deploy than developer-hosted blogs, but you'll be rewarded with a more flexible solution. Drupal.org, Movable-Type.org, and WordPress.org (not to be confused with WordPress.com) are among the most popular user-hosted blog solutions. The key difference with these types of blogs is that you upload and install the software on your own web server—something that requires a little knowledge of web programming, database management systems, and hosting configurations.

Drupal and WordPress are completely free and widely supported by the software creators and the community of bloggers who use them. WordPress is perhaps the most widely used and offers a good balance between being highly customizable and relatively easy to use.

The main advantage of user-hosted blog software is that you'll find a wider array of programming and design options—known as "plug-ins"—which will help you to customize your blog. User-hosted blogs tend to offer greater benefits for SEO, are more easily customized to fit the look of your company website, and give you the peace of mind that all of the files are stored on your own servers.

> ### Defining Moment: Plug-ins
>
> Plug-ins are computer programs that you can add to your blog to increase its functionality. Drupal, Movable Type, and WordPress each have a wide selection of third-party plug-ins that allow you to customize the look and usability of your blog. For example, one plug-in automatically imports your photos from your Flickr account to your blog.

Choosing Your Blog Location

As with the physical location of your business, the web location of your blog is an important decision. The domain name, or URL as it is often called, lets your stakeholders and the search engines know where on the Web to find your blog. You should give careful consideration to the location of your blog because once you've launched it you can lose a lot of brand equity by moving it to a new domain name.]

Locate It at Your Blog Host

Certainly the easiest and least expensive, often free, option is to use a developer-hosted blog. Services such as Blogger, TypePad, and WordPress.com will provide you with a blog URL free of charge. Typically this means that your blog URL will be a subdomain and will look something like *yourblog.wordpress.com*.

This might seem like the best choice because you'll get to use your name, but although you'll get the SEO benefits of a credible subdomain, you may come to regret this decision in the long term. Not only do you lose the opportunity to build a unique brand for your blog, but should you ever decide to switch blog software, you'll have to find a new URL for your site. Anytime you move the URL of your blog, you risk losing reputation points as well as both visitors and spiders as they struggle to associate the new URL location with your blog.

This is a great option for "individual expert" blogs as it involves no additional fees for custom domain registration.

Locate It at Your Company Site

A popular option for any company-related blog is to find a home for it at your existing website. This is a great option if you decide on a user-hosted blog solution as you'll need to upload the software to a server anyway—so it may as well be the same one you use to host your main company site. Locating your blog at your company website will also allow you to keep your blog tied to your main company brand.

If you decide to locate your blog on your company site, you'll likely select either a subdomain or subdirectory. With a subdomain your blog URL will look something like *blog.yourcompany.com*. Selecting the subdirectory option will result in a URL along the lines of *yourcompany.com/blog*. Select a subdomain if you want to have a blog that Google will consider separately from your main website, while still benefiting from your company's reputation. A subdirectory is the way to go if you want your main site to benefit from the additional web pages the blog will provide to the search engines.

This is a great option for any of the "company style" blogs.

Locate It at a Separate Domain Name

If you want to give your blog a brand of its own, consider purchasing a unique domain name for it. Individuals can use their own name, such as BobParsons.com. Companies can use a name that ties into their main brand, such as BlogSouthWest.com. Or you can try something more creative: Direct2Dell.com.

While you won't get the SEO benefits that come from locating your blog on your main company website, you'll find that a separate domain name has other benefits. Perhaps the biggest is that other bloggers will be more apt to discuss and link to your blog. Free from the fear that they might appear to be endorsing your company, you'll find that even your peers will feel more comfortable linking to your blog post if it's not located within your main website. This helps to increase the popularity of your blog, which is great news if you want your blog to show up on the first page of Google's search results.

A separate domain name for your blog is a great choice for "company executive" or "company team" blogs. It's also a good option for "individual expert" blogs.

Essential Blog Elements

Now that you've decided on your blogging style, platform, and location, you're probably itching to launch your blog to the world. Before you hit "publish" on your first post, you should know that your blog is likely missing some vital components. Just as many new cars need some additional upgrades to make them more appealing—sunroof, satellite radio, heated seats, and so forth—your blog could use some add-ons and fine-tuning.

Great content and a transparent voice are vital for the success of any blog, but there are some things you can do to ensure your blog is super-charged and ready to bolster your online reputation.

	Developer-Hosted (Wordpress.com or Blogspot.com)	User-Hosted (Wordpress.org or Drupal.org)	Blog Host Domain Name (yourname.wordpress.com)	Company Domain Name (blog.company.com or company.com/blog)	Separate Domain Name (companyblog.com)
Individual Expert Blog	★	★	★		★
Company Executive Blog		★		★	★
Company Team Blog		★		★	★
Company Update Blog		★		★	
Company Crisis Blog		★		★	
Internal Company Blog		★		★	

Figure 9.5 The Radically Transparent Blog Selection Matrix (Overview of the following sections)

Make It Google Friendly

In Chapter 6 you learned valuable skills for optimizing web content for Google. Unfortunately, most blogging software isn't too search engine "friendly" out of the box. With a little fine-tuning, most blogs can become a great source of fresh, optimized web content for Google's spider. Here are the most important SEO enhancements to make:

Carefully select your blog's name. The name of your blog—and its URL—can help with your Google ranking. To help your branding, use your full name (or company name) and an industry-related keyword. *Mike Smith's Real Estate Blog* will help your Google reputation better than *Mike's Blog*.

Use keyword-rich page file names. Check to make sure your blog uses the title of your blog post as the naming convention for post pages. Many blogs will use a default format for each blog post URL that looks similar to this: *yourblog.com/post-1234*. WordPress, for example, lets you change this to a more Google-friendly format such as *yourblog.com/the-title-of-the-blog-post*.

Use unique TITLE tags. You already know the importance of keyword-rich TITLE tags on each of your web pages. Unfortunately, many blogging platforms haven't learned that lesson yet. Still, many allow you to make changes to the design template or use a plug-in that will ensure each blog page has a unique TITLE tag. The easiest option is to simply instruct your blog software to use the same headline of the blog post article as the TITLE tag for the page.

Avoid duplicate blog content. Whenever Google's spider discovers two or more pages with the same text, it tends to pick only one page and discard the others from its index. The last thing you want is Google deciding which page should be used in the index and which should be ignored. Unfortunately, most blogs are full of duplicate content. When you publish a blog post, that exact post is often found on the home page, the post page, a category page, and in the archives. There could be as many as half a dozen duplications for each post you publish. Look for a plug-in that helps manage duplicate content issues or prevent Google from indexing the duplicate pages by using your site's robots.txt text file (visit google.com/support/webmasters/ or robotstxt.org/wc/robots.html for more details on configuring your blog's robots.txt file).

Make It Sticky

When it comes to making your blog "sticky" or "giving it legs," most blogging solutions fail to make the grade. To reach your stakeholders and create a positive perception of your brand, your blog should encourage repeat visits and be easy to share with the masses. Here are three crucial design elements your blog should have at launch:

Subscribe by RSS. Most blog designs include a text link or graphic that allows readers to subscribe to the site's RSS feed. Unfortunately, not all blogs make this link as prominent as possible. The link to your RSS feed should be one of the first things readers see when they visit your blog. Readers will likely return to your blog if they subscribe to your RSS feed and receive automatic updates. Services such as Google's FeedBurner.com provide a lot of tools for promoting and enhancing your blog's RSS feed. Use the standard graphic ![RSS icon] that indicates a link to a blog's RSS feed.

Subscribe by e-mail. While RSS is the most popular format for receiving blog updates, many of your readers will prefer something a little more traditional. Allow your readers to receive updates in their inbox, if desired. FeedBurner and FeedBlitz.com both offer an e-mail option.

Share using social bookmarking links. One of the most effective ways to publicize your blog is to use social bookmarking links. Each of your blog posts should include links that allow readers to save a bookmark to del.icio.us, Digg.com, or their favorite social bookmarking site—often sharing them with their friends in the process. By encouraging the sharing of your blog posts, you'll likely attract new readers who trust the opinion of their friends.

Encourage Comments

If you're breaking out in a cold sweat at the thought of allowing readers' comments on your new blog, relax. While you may have concerns that comments can expose you to attacks on your reputation, you need to see the bigger picture. Right now your stakeholders—customers, investors, employees, journalists, and so forth—are discussing and critiquing your brand online and offline. Allowing comments on your blog doesn't encourage discussion that wouldn't have normally occurred. Instead, it merely allows you the opportunity to hear those comments and respond to them on your terms—on your blog.

Blog comments are a fantastic way to engage those who influence your brand. Your reputation is in their hands, and by listening to their feedback and suggestions, you'll gain valuable insight. Later in this chapter, we'll discuss how to listen and respond to readers' comments. In the meantime, here are some tactics for getting the most out of your blog comments:

Moderate the comments. Most blog solutions give you the ability to pre-screen comments before they're published to your blog. We don't suggest you delete anything negative—that's not radically transparent—but you can screen for abusive language, off-topic rants, or competitor sabotage.

Filter for spam. Once your blog starts to gain traction and popularity, you'll likely attract the blog comment spammers. Install a plug-in that monitors and deletes spam comments, and you'll have fewer headaches. For WordPress users, *Akismet* is a preinstalled plug-in you can use to automatically filter out spam comments.

Create a comment policy. One way to help ensure comments are on topic and not abusive is to create a comment policy. Published on your blog, it should instruct readers on what will and what won't be tolerated in your comments. For example, you might prohibit multiple links to third-party websites—a great way to prevent your competitors from using your comment section to promote their own business.

> ### Thought Byte: What's in Your Comment Policy?
>
> What will you allow readers to post to your blog posts' comment section? Launching a corporate blog without a comment policy will likely encourage a free-for-all on your very first blog post. Take the time now to create a list of what you will and won't allow readers to say in their comments. Abusive language, personal attacks, and off-topic links are all things you might wish to consider prohibiting. Likewise, you may wish to disallow anonymous comments—which will encourage transparency from those leaving comments. It may seem counterintuitive, but posting explicit guidelines makes you more of a transparent blogger because your readers will know precisely the rules of engagement for your blog.

Explain Who You Are

When you first launch your blog, don't assume that every visitor will know who you are, what your company does, or the purpose of the blog. Just as in real life, you only have a few seconds to make a great first impression. Your blog should display a prominent link to an "About Us" page (for companies) or "About Me" page (for individuals). This page is your chance to explain the purpose of the blog and tell the story of why it exists. Figure 9.6 shows the About page for Edelman blogger Steve Rubel (steverubel.typepad.com/about.html).

If the blog is written by your CEO, or it's your personal blog, consider including a brief business bio highlighting career accomplishments and expertise. A smiling photo is also a great icebreaker and allows the reader to visually connect with you (see Chapter 7 for more on creating reputation-enhancing head shots). Similarly, if the blog is a company team blog or designed to provide updates, explain that to readers. Let them know who's contributing, what they'll discuss, and how often the blog will be updated.

Your About page is your opportunity to make a connection with your blog's readers. Making a connection will increase the chances they'll return to your blog and tell others about it as well. If you need a refresher on creating an About page, refer to Chapter 8.

Incorporate Other Media

An effective way to make your blog more engaging is to use a variety of media. Your blog is a great place to show off your multimedia palette (see Chapter 7) and provide more than just static text to visitors.

Many of the user-hosted blog solutions offer plug-ins that allow you to incorporate images, video, and sound into your blog. You don't have to be the size of Kodak to include podcasts, photos, or candid video interviews on your blog. Adding other media formats to your blog will help you create a buzz by allowing readers to share content in the format of their choice.

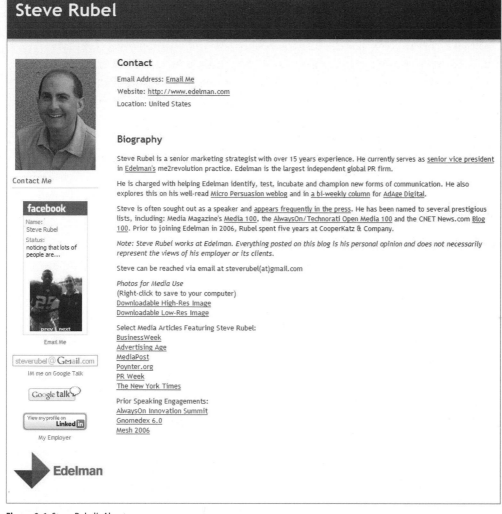

Figure 9.6 Steve Rubel's About page

Creating Blogging Guidelines

There's one last step to consider before you launch your blog, allow your CEO to post, or give WordPress accounts to your employees. Even though your blogging plans include being radically transparent, each blog author will have a different definition of what is and isn't acceptable to publish. For this reason, it is critical to take the time to define what can and cannot be published on your blog, and what guidelines need to be followed in order to preserve your reputation.

For individuals, this is more of an exercise to help you pin down what you'll write about and how you'll interact with other bloggers. For corporations, setting guidelines and policies is a crucial step to ensure that everyone is on the same page and understands how their blogging actions can affect the company's reputation. While this might seem like an obvious action item, close to 70% of all companies don't have any employee blogging guidelines in place (according to Edelman's "The Rise and Effective Management of Employee Bloggers" report). Crafting guidelines for your blog is an important step, and we've taken the pain out of it by creating a template for you.

Radically Transparent Blogging Guidelines

As a radically transparent blogger, your reputation will benefit from being honest and authentic in your communication. This may not come naturally, especially if your company is accustomed to a more formal channel of communication. You'll find a lot of benefit in crafting guidelines for your blog. We took Forrester Research's *Sample Blogger Code of Ethics* and WOMMA's (Word of Mouth Marketing Association) *10 Principles for Ethical Contact by Marketers* and blended them to create the Radically Transparent Blogging Guidelines. You can use these principles verbatim for your own blogging guidelines or customize them to fit your needs.

1. **Always be honest and tell the truth**—even if this might cause a negative impact on your reputation. While you may want to cover up a scandal, ProBlogger's Darren Rowse warns that bloggers have "a habit of uncovering such instances and the blogosphere can be a very unforgiving place when such an instance is found out." Likewise, don't ever ask someone else to lie for you.

2. **Clearly explain your intentions, who you work for, and who you are.** "Being transparent is very important, especially to your site visitors. Clearly state the intent of your blog [and] who is blogging," suggests Kodak's Denise A. Stinardo.

3. **Make sure your writing is accurate, high quality, and spell checked.** As you learned in Chapter 8, the quality of your writing will enhance or detract from your reputation.

4. **Be honest about any mistakes you make and correct them promptly.** While you may be tempted to defend your actions or plead mitigating circumstances, you'll find that the blogosphere will ultimately expect an apology from you. You'll have more chance of preventing a "blogstorm" if you quickly take responsibility for being wrong.

5. **Never delete a blog post.** Once you click "publish," your blog post will be archived elsewhere anyway. If you make a mistake or change your position on a topic, it's more transparent to preserve the original post and use notations to show what has changed. However tempting it may be, deleting a post will likely

raise suspicion and hurt your reputation. "Break the trust of readers and you harm your chances of a future relationship with them and can ruin your reputation," explains Rowse.

6. **Don't delete comments left by readers.** Just because you don't agree with a reader's comment, that's not a good reason for deleting it. Only delete comments that are abusive, that are spam, or that violate your published comments policy.

7. **Respond to e-mails and blog comments.** Although it may be difficult to reply to all feedback on your blog, try to respond to e-mails and comments that are relevant or that require your input.

8. **Respect the opinions of others, even when disagreeing.** While it is your blog, and you do have the loudest voice, you should not talk down to your readers or attack those who leave a dissenting comment.

9. **Link to original sources of information.** It might seem counterintuitive, but always link to the originating source of information. Your readers will be more trusting that you're sharing *all* information with them by demonstrating you're not afraid to point them to another website.

10. **Always disclose conflicts of interests or business relationships.** Although you may believe that disclosure will devalue your blog posts, Darren Rowse assures that you'll see more benefits by being transparent in your relationships: "Disclose your interests and you'll find that quite the opposite can happen—you'll build trust further and become an even more respected figure."

> ### Defining Moment: Blogstorm
>
> According to Wikipedia, a blogstorm is when "a large amount of activity, information and opinion erupts around a particular subject or controversy in the blogosphere."

Involving PR and Legal Departments

As you prepare for the launch of your corporate blog, there's a good chance you'll receive increased interest from your PR and legal teams. Both have your best interests at heart and have likely become accustomed to being involved in your company's PR and marketing campaigns. Your newly formed radically transparent ego will probably scream at you: "Do not listen to anything they have to say." After all, how can you possibly create an open and authentic dialogue with your blog's readers if your PR and legal teams have to okay everything you say? Your readers will wholeheartedly support that notion because they're tired of receiving filtered communication from you.

Don't fret: there is a solution that will allow your transparent voice while keeping your PR and legal teams happy. Their input during the creation and implementation of your blog will ensure that you stay on message and avoid any potential legal trouble. Their advice will improve your corporate blogging guidelines and help identify topics that shouldn't be discussed—such as future company earnings. This is especially important for publicly traded companies because the SEC watches blogs closely for any release of material information to investors. As Go Daddy's Parsons points out, "I have a little more latitude than a CEO of a public company." If you get it right prelaunch, you shouldn't have troubles later on.

Once your site launches, it's important to navigate the blogosphere without the filtering and dilution of these two departments. Keep them on stand-by in case a crisis occurs, and give them instant notification of all new blogs posts. However, unless you're using your blog to respond to a crisis or legal issue, that's where their involvement should end. Your blog should be the one place that stakeholders can receive unfiltered communication from you. As Robert Scoble advises, "Don't get corporate lawyers and PR professionals to cleanse your speech. We can tell, believe me." In addition, too much involvement by these teams will hinder your opportunity to be the first to discuss topics with your stakeholders. Scoble adds "You'll be too slow. If you're the last one to post, the joke is on you!"

> ## Thought Byte: Assign a Blog Manager
>
> Who is ultimately responsible for the content in your corporate or team blog? You may wish to assign a person to act as the manager or editor of your blog. This person is responsible for ensuring posts are published correctly and that your comment policy isn't being abused, and for alerting your PR and legal teams to any potential issues. They can also help manage large groups of bloggers so they don't step on one another's toes by writing about the same topic.

Five Rules for Radically Transparent Bloggers

Now you're finally ready to launch your blog. You'll likely have feelings of excitement and anxiety on the day that your blog is finally published for all to see. Some describe the feeling as being similar to a first date—will you make a good impression, will she like you, and did you remember to brush your teeth? For you it may feel more like watching your child start her first day at school—will the other kids like her, did you pack enough for lunch, and will she get good grades? Pick your own analogy.

While many noncorporate blogs grow their audience and reputation based on a raunchy-style, exclusive news scoops, or controversial opinions, your radically transparent blog is different. The success of your blog will be determined by a number of factors, including the blog platform used, how well the site is structured, and the blogging style you chose. But the most important key to constructing a blog that enhances your reputation and assists in building your brand is the transparency and authenticity of the content you publish. Just like your child's first years in school—or your first few romantic dates—you'll establish your own rules for success. To help you start off on the right foot toward a reputation-building blog, keep the following five rules in mind.

1. Your Blog Voice Represents Your Brand

With the casual conversation style and ease of publishing, you may find yourself tempted to use your blog as an excuse to let your hair down and live a little. While we want to encourage you to be transparent and authentic in your blog posting—after all, that's what stakeholders are longing for—that doesn't mean you can afford to be reckless. Remember that your stakeholders will form brand perceptions and use your blog to measure your reputation. A cavalier attitude and a few off-the-cuff remarks might seem witty and endearing, but it is easy to inadvertently cross the line between being transparent and harming your brand.

Every post, comment response, and single remark made on your blog is a reflection of you and your company. Be conversational and open in your blog posting, but realize that you will still be held accountable for what you put in writing. Following your own blogging guidelines will help you and your employees to stay on topic and avoid creating controversy. Even Go Daddy's outspoken Bob Parsons realizes that there is a line between being authentic and hurting the company's brand: "I will say pretty much what's on my mind, within reason," says Parsons.

2. Be First to Break the News

In 2007, Dell faced a potential media crisis when news reports revealed that its laptop computers were bursting into flames. Instead of waiting to respond to any resulting media attack, Dell's Lionel Menchaca took the bold step of posting video of a Dell machine in flames on the Direct2Dell blog. While he took a lot of initial heat from Dell's own legal counsel, Menchaca understood that this type of incident would quickly spread through the blogosphere, so Dell would be wise to play host to any comments or questions about the incident. By being one of the first blogs to post a video of the incident, Menchaca realized that he wouldn't be able to stop the conversation, but he could at least attempt to minimize its impact. "This is what blogs are about. Everything has changed. We have to be transparent and honest. People are talking about this, they're posting these images, [and] we can't ignore it. We have to deal with it directly," said Menchaca at the time of the incident.

When bad news breaks, you may be tempted to stick your head in the sand and try to weather the ensuing media storm. While it may seem counterintuitive, there's a lot of respect and accolades to be gained from embracing negative news. As Robert Scoble explains, "It's all about building long-term trust. The trick to building trust is to show up! If people are saying things about your product and you don't answer them, that distrust builds." Obviously, you don't have to use your blog to purely respond to negative incidents; you can also link your readers to the positive stories that involve your company. "If people are saying good things about your product, why not help Google find those pages as well?" suggests Scoble.

Ultimately, your blog can play the role of being the first place your stakeholders turn to whenever they need to hear from you. If your blog is willing to discuss the negative news, along with the positive, you'll gain a reputation for authenticity. With this type of radically transparent communication, your stakeholders will be less likely to let their perceptions of your brand be influenced by the comments of others.

3. It's Better to Give than Receive

One of the hardest lessons for a new blogger to learn is that blog success often hinges on your willingness to acknowledge your peers. In fact, if you want to dramatically increase the chances that your blog will be well read and respected, you should discuss your competitors and even link to them. Before you choke on that last sentence, consider this: ignoring your competitors does not make them go away. The media, your customers, and your employees are all aware of your competitors' actions—and their impact on your business. You don't have to sing your competition's praises, but by at least acknowledging their existence—perhaps comparing your products to theirs— you'll continue to build trust with your blog's audience.

A giving attitude also means the willingness to give your readers as much information as possible. Many corporate bloggers become paranoid that information sharing will give the competition too much insight into their business. There's no need to worry. Your competitors are probably already smart enough to figure out what's going on inside your company walls, anyway, so why lose out on being open and transparent with your important stakeholders?

Likewise, individuals tend to hold back on the knowledge and expertise they share on their blog for fear of losing their competitive edge. Don't hold back. As Darren Rowse explains, "It is a new paradigm for many new bloggers to get their heads around and takes some time to get used to but in my experience being a generous blogger has some real payoffs." The more freely you share your expertise, the more respected and popular your blog will become.

4. Engage Your Readers

Hopefully you've taken our advice and set up your blog to publish comments from your readers. Well done! It takes a lot of courage and a radical departure from conventional business practices to provide a channel for your stakeholders to communicate openly with you. The next step is to encourage your readers to actually leave comments, knowing that you're ready and willing to listen to their feedback. As Kodak's Denise Stinardo suggests, "Make your readers feel as though they are directly interacting with your company through comments. You want to have a direct conversation with people who matter—your customers and influencers." Refer to Chapter 4 and the engagement tactics sprinkled throughout this book.

How you decide to respond to comments depends on several factors. If the site is a corporate team blog or company update blog, you may assign an individual to monitor comments and respond accordingly. If you're a CEO or professional, and you are the only one blogging, readers will expect you to respond personally to comments. They'll also understand that you're probably too busy to respond to every comment posted, and will cut you some slack. Still, you may want to have your assistant (or blog manager) monitor comments and bring to your attention any that need a direct response.

It is important to be consistent in your responses to the comments left by your readers. If you decide to respond to all blog comments, and then fall silent during a crisis, you'll lose your credibility. Likewise, don't attempt to respond to a comment—especially a negative one—without first collecting all of the facts. "If you don't have the answer, at least acknowledge you see the problem and will respond as soon as you have an answer," says Jeremiah Owyang, who shares web strategy advice at his blog *Web-Strategist.com*. Robert Scoble concurs, suggesting that "Not having the answers is human. But, get them and exceed expectations. If you say you'll know by tomorrow afternoon, make sure you know in the morning." In part 3, you'll learn more about responding to negative criticism.

Of course, not every comment will be negative. Your blog is a place for your stakeholders to communicate with you directly. Their ranks will more likely include dedicated employees, passionate customers, or committed investors, than determined detractors. By reading their comments and engaging them in conversation, you'll learn a lot of valuable information about what they want from your company and what they're willing to do to help in return.

5. It's All or Nothing

Your blog's success will depend on your willingness to allocate the time and resources to its continual development. Success can be measured using the metrics outlined on the following pages, but note that blogs rarely become an overnight hit. In fact, unless you happen to be a celebrity or Fortune 500 company, it may take many months before you see any noticeable benefit from your blogging efforts. During the initial launch stage, it's important to remain focused on your goal—to build your brand while being radically transparent—and remain committed for the long term.

Your blog is a valuable tool in your online reputation campaign. Consistency, authenticity, and transparency all play their part in building a blog that engages your stakeholders and provides a channel to communicate with those who influence your reputation. Once you launch your blog and start the conversation, it will be very difficult to turn back without creating a negative perception on your brand. As Paul Gillan writes in *The New Influencers*, "Once you start, there's no going back. If you launch and then discontinue your blog, the media will wonder what's wrong at the company and your competitors will ridicule you." It is similar to the shame of having to close one of your retail stores or branch offices. You blog needs to be nurtured, and to offer the company point of view at all times—no matter how tough things get or what crisis your company goes through. Your commitment will pay off handsomely with better access to stakeholders, faster responses to crises, and greater access to the media.

Measuring Your Blog's Success

One of the most difficult challenges of any new blog is measuring the success of your efforts. Many companies struggle trying to place a return on investment for the hard work that goes into building and maintaining a blog, but it can be done. Here are some different ways that you can measure the success of your blog.

Number of Visitors

You don't need to add expensive web analytics to your blog in order to track how many visitors it receives each day. Google Analytics (www.google.com/analytics; Figure 9.7) is a completely free solution that offers a wide range of web visitor statistics and reports. While your blog may not ever achieve the same visitor numbers as your company site, you should still measure its growth and the number of repeat visits.

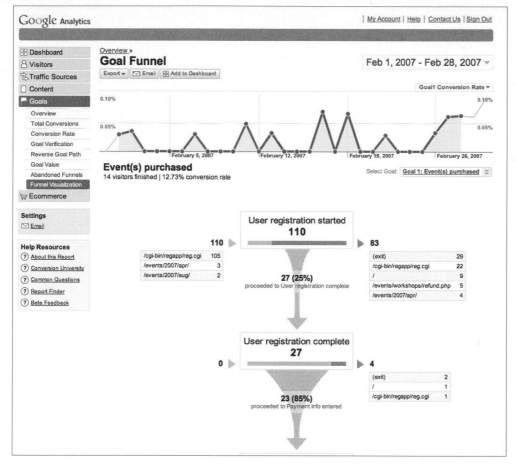

Figure 9.7 Google Analytics

Number of Blog Citations

Type in the URL of your blog at Technorati and it will return a list of all blogs that have linked to it. Check that number regularly to track your blog's popularity in the blogosphere. See Figure 9.8 for the blog reactions to BobParsons.com.

Number of Links

Yahoo! Site Explorer (siteexplorer.search.yahoo.com) is a great tool for checking the number of all web links pointing to your blog—not just those links coming from other blogs. The more links that point to your blog, the more successful it is, and the more likely it will be to rank well in search engines.

Figure 9.8 Technorati blog reactions

Number of RSS Subscribers

We've already mentioned FeedBurner and the extra functionality it brings to your blog's RSS feed. FeedBurner will also allow you to keep track of the number of people who have subscribed to your RSS feed and its upward (or downward) subscription trend.

Number of Blog Comments

It's not always about the number of people who read your blog, but how many engage with it. You may not have the customer numbers that Dell or Go Daddy enjoy, but you can still measure the success of your site by how often your readers leave a comment.

Number of Media Mentions

With so many journalists reading blogs while looking for story ideas, you should be able to at least make a tenuous link between your blog and an inquiry from a journalist. In addition, it's quite common for the media to simply pull a quote from your blog—resulting in a story about your business that your PR team didn't have to initiate.

Number of Sales

One of the hardest metrics to compile is the effect your blog has on the revenue of your business. If you have a link to your retail website, you can use click-through and conversion rates. If you use customer relationship management (CRM) software, such as that offered by Salesforce.com, you can track white paper downloads and follow this lead through the sales funnel. You could promote coupons or special offers, only available via your blog, and then keep track of their success. You could also ask your customers how they heard about you or why they did business with you—perhaps some will mention your blog. Tracking how much new business you receive as a direct result of your blog is often very difficult. As Go Daddy's Bob Parsons admits, "It's your gut feel, it's very difficult to quantify."

Tips for Growing a New Blog

We asked ProBlogger's Darren Rowse to share his top tips for growing the audience of any new blog:

Write Useful Content Write posts that will enhance your reader's life in some way.

Be Distinct Find a way to stand out from the crowd and develop a unique voice, style, and content.

Network It's very important to interact with other blogs, forums, and websites in your field of interest. This can generate a reputation, incoming links, and direct traffic to your blog.

Love Your Readers Some bloggers fall into the trap of always looking for new readers and yet don't look after the ones they already have. Pay them attention, answer their questions, and involve them in your blog.

Alternatives to Publishing a Blog

Building a successful blog takes a lot of time and consistent effort. Without this commitment, a newly started blog can fizzle out very quickly and end up doing more harm than good to your reputation. With this in mind, you may decide that you can't commit to your own blog at this time. If you're an individual or small company, it may be especially hard for you to find the resources needed to build your own blog.

While there is plenty of evidence to support starting a blog, you shouldn't feel compelled to launch one. You may decide that you can better serve your stakeholders with other initiatives such as e-mails, viral videos, or online public relations. Blogging is not for everyone and we'll be the first to tell you that you shouldn't start a blog just because it's trendy to do so. Many great companies have built fantastic reputations without any apparent endorsement of blogging; computer manufacturer Apple is one of them. Likewise, many individuals have built phenomenal reputations without the help of a blog; Chick-fil-A founder Truett Cathy built his impeccable reputation without a computer, let alone a blog.

Although a blog is a great way to grow your reputation and directly influence online conversations, you might instead try some of these alternative ways to embrace the blogosphere in an indirect manner.

Guest Blogs

A great option is to find a blog that serves your industry and is already well established, and offer to write guest blog posts for them.

A guest post on someone else's blog doesn't bring the same branding benefits that come from publishing your own blog, but if you consistently provide guest posts, you can still build your reputation. Here's what to look for when finding a blog to host your guest posts:

- Does the blog focus on your industry or area of expertise? It's important that your voice reaches your target audience.

- Does the blog have a great reputation? You guest post will associate your reputation with that of the blog's. Fully research the blog to make sure it is consistent with your branding goals.

- Will the blog help promote your brand? You'll likely provide your guest posts for free, in return for the extra publicity. Make sure you get the most out of the arrangement by asking that your post include your name, your personal or company bio, and a link back to your website. But be careful that your posts don't seem to be self-promotional—include only these items and a few words of simple content.

Individual Employee Blogs

Many companies benefit from the blogging efforts of their passionate employees. Robert Scoble's blog (Scobleizer.com) helped Microsoft's reputation greatly while he worked for the company. Likewise, CooperKatz & Company, Inc., enjoyed many benefits from the blogging efforts of PR guru Steve Rubel (MicroPersuasion.com). The individual blogs of your employees can provide a great opportunity to place a personal face on your corporate image, but the benefits do come with some risks.

One of the most important challenges to any company that embraces employee blogging is deciding what employees can and cannot say about your company. Left unchecked, your employees could accidentally let slip details of a new product launch, or might ignorantly bad-mouth a competitor. Understanding the risks, Forrester Research drafted a *Corporate Blog Policy*, which you may wish to consider adapting for use by your company's employees (refer also to IBM Guidelines in Chapter 3):

- Make it clear that the views expressed in the blog are yours alone and do not necessarily represent the views of your employer.

- Respect the company's confidentiality and proprietary information.

- Ask your manager if you have any questions about what is appropriate to include in your blog.

- Be respectful to the company, employees, customers, partners, and competitors.

- Understand and comply when the company asks that topics not be discussed for confidentiality or legal compliance reasons.

- Ensure that your blogging activity does not interfere with your work commitments.

Another risk you'll face is that your employees may not work for you in the future. Robert Scoble left Microsoft to join PodTech.net, and Steve Rubel resigned from CooperKatz to join rival Edelman. With this in mind, it's important to understand that your employees will likely build their own brands, along with yours—especially if they've also read this book. Still, you shouldn't overlook the immense benefits that come from having employee bloggers also enhance your reputation. As Jeremiah Owyang explains, "When it comes to trust, prospects and customers may trust employee bloggers that don't have the corporate logo on their blog."

Sponsor Blogs

Although not quite as effective as publishing your own blogging content—or letting employees do it for you—there are some benefits to be gained from sponsoring or advertising on industry-related blogs. Much in the same way you might research a guest blog partner, you can often find blogs that are willing to accept advertising from you.

In Chapter 5, we explored the methods for finding the influential bloggers in your industry. You can use the same techniques to research and select blogs that might make worthwhile advertising partners. Alternatively, you could work directly with a network of blogs such as those owned by b5media (b5media.com) or you could even tap into an advertising network that specializes in placing your ads on high-quality blogs. Federated Media Publishing (federatedmedia.net) is one such network that will help you place your ads on popular blogs such as BoingBoing.net, GigaOM.com, TechCrunch.com, and Dooce.com.

The difficulty with blog advertising is finding a solution that will adequately associate your reputation with that of the blog in question. Simply having your banner ad alongside the half dozen others displayed on TechCrunch won't necessarily help you piggyback the popular tech blog's reputation. When looking for blog advertising partners, keep in mind any opportunities that will help grow your brand reputation. The 2004 launch of auto-industry blog Jalopnik.com is a great example of synergy between blogger and advertiser. Car manufacturer Audi signed on as the exclusive launch sponsor and had their brand, logos, and imagery integrated with the design of the blog. They received the reputation boost without the effort needed to launch their own blog.

The Power of Blogs

Blogs are one of the most powerful tools for achieving your company, brand, or individual reputation goals. By their very nature they encourage radical transparency from their authors. If you make the commitment, you'll find blogs offer the potential for huge rewards. You'll establish clearer communication with your customers, and you'll provide both mainstream and new media with your spin-free message. Even if you decide not to start your own blog, your reputation will still rise and fall with the sentiment of the blogosphere—something you'll learn more about in Part 3. A blog will complement your other marketing channels, including social media networking—which is what we'll look at next.

Social Networking

Social networking provides an opportunity for your stakeholders to connect with one another and discuss your reputation. Creating your own social network, or building a profile at one of the many existing social networks, allows you to join the conversation. By understanding the different types of social networking platforms—and the best way to engage them—you can lay a foundation that builds a positive reputation for you or your business.

10

Chapter Contents

Aquafina Avoids Getting into Hot Water

The U.S. bottled water market is worth more than $15 billion and the average American consumes more than 50 gallons of bottled water each year. In our quest to find a healthier alternative to plain, simple tap water, we consumers embrace the potential health benefits of drinking water that originates from crystal-clear mountain streams or filtered by ancient volcanic rocks. Indeed, visit the beverage aisle of any grocery story and you'll find exotic brands such as *FIJI*, *Evian*, and *Iceland Pure Spring Water* beckoning you to taste their own version of the elixir of life. With dozens of "mineral," "spring," and "mountain" water options to choose from, how can one line of bottled tap water become the most popular brand on the shelf?

PepsiCo's Aquafina brand has managed to capture a solid share of the bottled water market and has built a loyal following. No doubt a big part of Aquafina's success is PepsiCo's fantastic marketing efforts which, along with TV, print, and online advertising, include using the social networking service MySpace (Figure 10.1). With its profile at myspace.com/aquafina, PepsiCo realized it could build brand loyalty long before consumers ever reached the retail beverage display stands. Instead of simply using MySpace to display its advertising, PepsiCo built a community with a passion for, and a deep emotional involvement with, the Aquafina brand.

With contests that challenge users to create a new music video for the Beastie Boys and interactive games—where players quench the thirst of smiling individuals—Aquafina focuses on creating a fun, hip brand that in turn results in higher retail sales. Aquafina has built a MySpace community of more than 11,500 friends, has attracted close to 500 comments, and has established itself as a trendy brand in bottled water.

In fact, Aquafina's brand image is so strong, that even when news broke in July 2007 that it was nothing more than purified tap water from a New York municipal water supply, this barely affected its reputation. Social networking allowed Aquafina to build a foundation of consumer engagement with its target demographic of 18- to 34-year-olds. Interactive games, cool contests, and its willingness to forgo blatant advertising ensured Aquafina built strong relationships with consumers. Its MySpace profile may not have single-handedly saved the day, but Aquafina faced less online criticism when confronting such a negative situation.

The Social Network Effect in Google

Whenever you build a social networking profile, you're creating web content that is highly focused on your personal or company brand. In Chapter 6, you learned that social networking profiles can be optimized to show up on the first page of Google for any keyword search for your brand. Keep that advice in mind as you build your social networking profiles and you can follow Aquafina's example: its MySpace profile is consistently on the first page of Google for the search term "Aquafina."

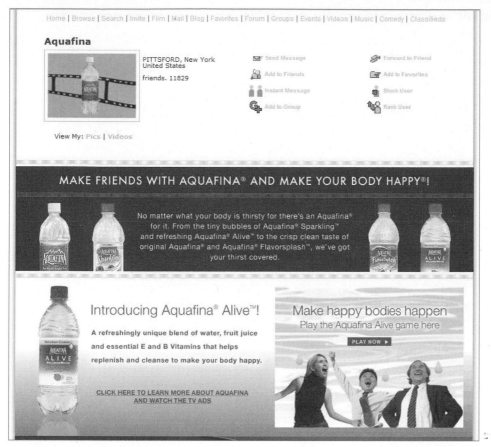

Figure 10.1 Aquafina's MySpace profile page

The Importance of Social Networks

Globally, there are more than 200 million people using social networking sites each month—with 67 million Americans turning to MySpace as their network of choice. Unlike other forms of social media, social networks rely heavily on community participation. Videos are fun to watch, blogs are interesting to read, and search engines are useful for finding new information; but social networks allow you to build deep emotional ties to the people in your network. As you've already learned from *The Cluetrain Manifesto,* "The Net connects people to each other, and impassions and empowers through those connections."

Social networks are also an important part of any reputation management or brand building effort, as experienced by Aquafina. Wherever communities are formed, the opportunity for conversations about your brand exists. Whether it's a Facebook group to discuss the quality of service received from your company, a question on Yahoo! Answers to determine if your products are reliable (or not), or a reference request on LinkedIn by a potential employer, there's no escaping the role social networks play in shaping the perception of your brand.

Over the course of this chapter, you'll learn the different types of social networking platforms, the keys to ensuring that your social networking activities are successful, and some alternatives strategies for leveraging social networks. Social media luminary Dave Winer called 2007 "the year of the social network," and with our help, you'll learn how to use social networks to build your brand and strengthen your reputation.

Understand the Social Networking User Types

In the report "Never Ending Friending" (compiled by MySpace, Carat, and Isobar), social networking (SN) users can be categorized into five different groups. Understanding the different types of SN users will provide you with an opportunity to better tailor your social networking participation.

The Pros

- Size of SN universe: 19%

- Demographics: Mix of males/females ages 14–17 and females 19–24 (average age 21)

- Life stage: 64% single, 32% married or living together, 63% student

- SN tenure: long (1–2 years of use), elaborate and creative profiles, with 40% using SN for 2 years or more

- Social networking is: *an essential part of life*

The Connectors

- Size of SN universe: 18%

- Demographics: Older: females 25–34, males 18–34 (generally not teens) (average age: 24)

- Life stage: 53% single; 43% married or living together; 41% student; 12% professional

- Social networking tenure: Short (6 months–1 year; 55% less than 1 year)

- Social networking is: *all about other people*

The See and Be Seens

- Size of SN universe: 14%

- Demographics: females 19–34, males 25–34

- Life stage: 24% professional/executive; 41% student; 51% single; 43% married or living together

- Social networking tenure: Long (1–2 years)

- Social networking is: *all about appearances*

Understand the Social Networking User Types *(continued)*

The Explorers

- Size of SN universe: 24%

- Demographics: 25–34 males and females

- Life stage: 24% executive/professional; 35% students; 55% married or living together; 42% single

- Social networking tenure: Shortest: 64% less than 1 year

- Social networking is: *one part of my busy life*

The Rookies

- Size of SN universe: 25%

- Demographics: Males and females 19–34

- Life stage: 50% single, 45% married or living together, 41% student

- Social networking tenure: Short (6 months–1 year)

- Social networking is: *something new I'm checking out*

The Five Pillars of Social Networking

In early 2006, the idea of using social networks to build your brand hardly registered in marketing surveys or published studies. Social networks were merely a place for individuals to connect with their inner circle, discuss products, and meet new friends online. Companies had just started to take note of the power contained within an online environment that fostered relationships and allowed people to discuss everything from which car to buy to their favorite brand of laundry detergent. Companies knew how to eavesdrop in online discussion forums, but they hadn't yet figured out how to enter the conversation successfully.

That same year, internet marketer Ben Wills wrote the eye-opening article "The Five Pillars of Social Media Marketing" and carefully outlined the five basic types of social networks. Wills was one of the first "social media marketers" to identify the different types of social networks and explain to businesses how they could enter the conversation and build relationships with stakeholders. For the first time, companies realized they could use social networks as part of their marketing and branding efforts. By mid-2007, LEWIS PR reported 33% of firms planned to implement a social networking initiative and that by 2008, 70% of firms would add social networks to their marketing efforts.

> **Thought Byte: Is Social Networking for You?**
>
> With social networks predominantly made up of web-savvy individuals, it's just not a viable option for some industries—how many farmers have you seen on Facebook recently?
>
> Before getting involved with any social network, take the time to carefully research whether your stakeholders can be reached, influenced, and engaged via this medium. If not, then maybe you'd be best served by implementing an online PR campaign or starting a blog.

With nearly two thirds of consumers stating social media content has informed their buying decisions, it's no wonder that such a high number of companies are planning to add social networks to their marketing mix. It's therefore natural to look at how social networks can help your efforts to become radically transparent and build your online brand. We've taken Wills's advice and carefully adapted it to fit your goals of building a positive online reputation. Let's take a look at the enhanced "The Five Pillars of Social Networking."

1. Social Networking Profiles

The bedrock of a social networking profile is the presentation of key information about you or your brand. This is your best chance to claim your online identity and begin crafting a positive reputation. Your social networking profile will likely include a description of your company or your personal bio. There are opportunities to add images, video, and a whole host of interactive multimedia content. Most social networking profiles allow, and encourage, the building of a network of friends. It is this "friending" that allows you to build your reputation among your stakeholders by creating a following of brand advocates.

> **Defining Moment: Friending**
>
> Friending is used to describe the action of adding someone to your list of friends on a social networking site. For social networks such as Facebook and MySpace, connecting with your friends is an important component of building your social network profile.

Example Networks

Some examples are:

- Facebook.com
- LinkedIn.com

- Naymz.com
- ZoomInfo.com

In Action

In his quest to secure the Democratic nomination for the 2008 Presidential Election, Senator Barack Obama has carefully leveraged social networks to build a loyal following of supporters. Visit his Facebook profile and you'll discover a smorgasbord of reputation-building channels. Not only has Obama shared personal information—such as his love of basketball, Miles Davis, and Moby Dick—but he's also enabled his profile with many multimedia plug-ins. More than 140,000 followers of Obama's Facebook profile can browse over 300 photos, watch videos from his rallies, and interact with other campaign supporters. More than 15,000 comments have been left for Obama and, judging by proclamations such as "keep going strong" and "the people support you," it seems Facebook is helping the presidential hopeful build a positive reputation.

And, in case you had any doubt that Barack Obama is using his Facebook profile to influence his reputation (see Figure 10.2), you need only take a look at his stated Election 2008 position. It reads "President"—you can't get much more persuasive than that!

Figure 10.2 Barack Obama's Facebook profile

Best Application

Social networking profiles offer the best opportunity for individuals looking to build a positive reputation. Whether you are looking to promote your personal expertise—maybe you too wish to be President one day—or you want to help highlight your fledgling company, social networking profiles are a great way to connect with your stakeholders. For example, Jason Calacanis, CEO of start-up search engine Mahalo.com, has a LinkedIn profile.

There are many different social networking profile websites for individuals. You should certainly build your profile at a popular network because you'll reach more people that way, but you should also consider building a profile on more than one network. Doing so will give your brand a wider reach—both in terms of audience size and demographics.

Best Advice

Despite an eMedia survey suggesting 31% of social networking users falsify their profile information, we don't suggest you do the same. Neil Patel, owner of the personal branding blog QuickSprout.com, says, "Be honest and upfront in your profile. It's better not to place something in your profile than to tell white lies." Likewise, care should be taken when deciding which friends to add to your network and which interest groups you join. Brian Solis, principal of FutureWorks, cautions at his BrianSolis.com blog: "Whether you know it or not, your profile, your feed, the groups you belong to, the events you attend, and the friends you share say everything about you." Something to consider before joining the "Legalize Cannabis" Facebook group.

Your social networking profile should be an honest reflection of your brand. As Ben Wills suggests, your profile "is your declaration of your value, who you are, and where you can be found." At the same time, you should follow Barack Obama's lead and create a profile that reflects positively on your brand and initiates a great first impression. Wills points out that "your social networking profile is one of the few online identities that you, as a provider, define and declare."

2. Social Bookmarking and Voting

Social bookmarking sites allow individuals to keep track of their favorite web content. Unlike browser-based bookmarks—such as your "favorites" in Internet Explorer—social bookmarks are designed to be shared with people who have similar interests. Social voting works much the same way but varies in that your favorite web content is voted upon by others in the same social network. The more votes your suggestions receive; the more prominently the web page in question will be displayed to others browsing the network.

For the radically transparent, social bookmarking and voting provide an opportunity for your brand's fans to help spread word of how great you are. The more often your web content is bookmarked or voted for, the more likely your reputation will precede you.

As Ben Wills explains, social bookmarking is the online equivalent of your "customer wearing your company's logo proudly."

Example Networks

Some examples are:

- Del.icio.us
- Stumbleupon.com
- Digg.com
- Reddit.com

In Action

When Apple CEO Steve Jobs announced the much-rumored launch of the iPhone, one of the first images of the new device appeared on the photo-sharing site Flickr. Within minutes of its upload, the image was submitted to the social voting site Digg.com (See Figure 10.3) by web designer Jeremy Flint and quickly gained enough votes to deem itself worthy of being displayed on the Digg.com home page.

In just a few short hours, the photo had received thousands of votes—eventually earning more than 24,000 "diggs" and hundreds of comments. As a result, the photo achieved close to 150,000 page views and over 2,000 web links, and was mentioned by dozens of bloggers. Apple's iPhone launch was a huge social media success. Meanwhile, Jeremy Flint earned a following of 142 other Digg users and a reputation as an expert on all things Apple.

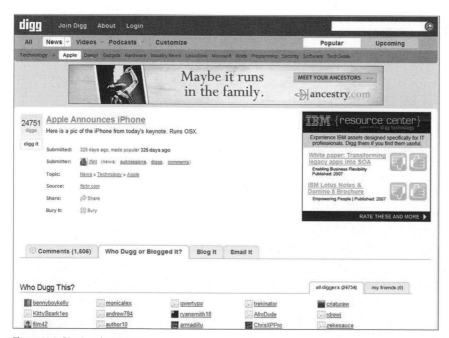

Figure 10.3 Digg.com homepage

Best Application

Opportunities exist for both individuals and companies. Individuals can use social bookmarking sites to demonstrate that they have their finger on the pulse of their fields of expertise. Whenever you add a bookmark to your Del.icio.us network or submit a web page for voting at Digg.com, you're given the opportunity to prove your value to the community. By consistently sharing quality web resources, you'll quickly gain the reputation of being an expert in that field: a thought leader. For example, establish yourself as an expert in uncovering news on intellectual property law and you'll soon build up a following of "friends" who'll seek you out whenever they have a question on that subject.

For businesses, the reputation management opportunities occur at the beginning of the social bookmarking transaction. Your goal is to be the company that provides the valuable web content individuals are looking to bookmark. Your online press releases, blog posts, and viral videos are all excellent fodder for those interested in your industry. Adding graphical buttons to your web content will help social bookmarkers share your content and your branding message with their peers (as shown in Chapter 8).

Best Advice

There's a common theme that you'll notice throughout this entire book—honesty really is the best policy. Many reputations have been shattered at the foot of social bookmarking sites, as individuals and companies attempt to game the system.

For individuals, it can become tempting to build multiple profiles with the intent of artificially inflating the number of votes your submitted web content receives. Meanwhile, many companies have been caught trying to buy votes from users of Digg, in an attempt to "stuff the ballot." While these shortcuts may appear tempting, using them will run the risk that you'll be discovered, criticized by the community, and publicly embarrassed. With your brand already subject to the critical eye of your stakeholders, the last thing you want to do is create a situation that can put it in harm's way.

3. Social Conversations

Social conversations represent a two-way conversation in a social networking environment. Although not quite real time—such as phone conversations or instant messaging—social conversations are still your best opportunity to engage your stakeholders and address them directly. As Ben Wills explains, "social conversations allow your stakeholders to create their own declarations or questions, and afford you the opportunity to respond."

Social conversations can take place in a variety of different formats. Internet forums and message boards are classic examples of social conversations—someone starts a message thread and others join in, adding their thoughts and observations to the thread. A little less structured are Usenet (now hosted at Google Groups) and other similar newsgroups. Here, conversations are often decentralized—typically using e-mail—and are usually focused on niche topics. Lastly, a new type of social conversation has emerged that uses a question and answer format. With these sites, individuals post questions on a wide variety of topics and subject-matter experts provide the answers.

Example Networks

Some examples are:

- iVillage.com
- Groups.Google.com
- Giganews.com
- Answers.Yahoo.com

In Action

When Yahoo! Answers launched in December 2005, it was intended to compete with the rival service offered by Google Answers. Both services provided a Q&A format—ask a question and real people will answer—but they differed in their execution.

Google Answers relied on a limited number of experts that Google itself carefully screened. Yahoo! took a different approach and trusted in the "wisdom of crowds." Anyone could answer a question, but the community helped decide which answer was the best. With its community structure, Yahoo! Answers flourished while Google's offering failed (and eventually shut down).

SEO expert Matt McGee (smallbusinesssem.com) is one of the many Yahoo! Answers users who have built a brand around answering the questions of others (See Figure 10.4). McGee regularly answers questions about internet marketing—earning the "best answer" vote 38% of the time—and has built a solid reputation as an expert in his field. McGee is enthusiastic in his endorsement of the service as a reputation builder: "Yahoo! Answers is a great way to share your knowledge with people who are looking for it—a direct connection with potential customers."

Figure 10.4 Yahoo! Answers

Best Application

Social conversations are an excellent way to hold a conversation with those that have a say in the perception of your brand. You should start by joining a social conversation site that's targeted to your area of expertise. Adding your thoughts to a hot topic or answering the questions left by others is a fantastic way to build your credibility and bring people to your website. McGee reports, "I spend about 1–2 hours a week answering SEO and marketing questions, and that small investment of time never fails to bring more traffic to my [website]."

For businesses, social conversations are your opportunity to answer the questions posed by your customers, employees, and investors. These key stakeholders are likely to use an online forum to seek information about your reliability, or use Yahoo! Answers to ask whether your company is a good fit for their needs. Listen to these conversations—you'll learn more on how to "listen" in Part 3—and look for opportunities to engage your stakeholders. Additionally, you can build a great reputation with potential new customers by selflessly helping them with their questions. Provide accurate, unbiased advice and you may win their respect and earn the opportunity to discuss your own products or services.

Best Advice

As with any social networking effort, you'll reap huge rewards by being transparent in your actions. Obviously lying in a social conversation is just as bad as lying in a real-world conversation, but transparency also involves being up front in your intentions and identity.

For companies, it's vital that you join the conversation as a clear representative of your firm. While it may be tempting to create a fake profile—perhaps even pretending to be a satisfied customer—if discovered, the damage to your company's reputation will be greater than any benefit you achieved from your deceit. Make it clear that you're there on behalf of your business, be unfiltered in your discussions with others, and make yourself open to all feedback—good or bad. Doing so will earn you a lot of respect and will more likely ensure that you are given a fair hearing in a time of crisis—as experienced by Aquafina.

Individuals should follow many of the same suggestions. In addition, avoid using funny nicknames or cute avatars (you'll learn more about this in Chapter 11). While these might seem like a good idea at the time, it will make it a lot harder to associate your great advice with your personal reputation. Neil Patel advises, "Make sure your user profile is your name and there's an image of yourself."

4. Social Communities

Social communities are the backbone of any social network. While many individuals join social networks so they can create their profile and connect with friends, their long-term engagement is usually facilitated by their involvement with different social communities. These social communities bring together those who share a common interest and provide a platform for them to discuss their passions, fears, likes, and dislikes. Likewise, companies are using social communities to share business interests and connect with partners, investors, and employees.

While social communities can exist at many different types of social networks—PepsiCo built Aquafina's on MySpace—you're not confined to building yours on an existing platform. The key is to build a community that gathers around a common topic or theme, and that community can exist as part of one of the mega-social networks or on your own custom-built social network.

Example Networks

Some examples are:

- MySpace.com
- Facebook.com
- Bebo.com
- Ning.com

In Action

While the athletic apparel maker Nike maintains a number of popular MySpace communities—including myspace.com/nikesoccer and myspace.com/nikewomen—their success is overshadowed by the custom social communities the company has built. Tapping into the passionate followers of different sports, Nike has branded many communities, including basketball (nikebasketball.com), football (nikefootball.com), and their biggest hit: Nike+ (nike.com/nikeplus).

Nike+ is a joint effort with Apple's iPod that allows runners to listen to music while measuring how many calories they've burned and the distance they've ran (See Figure 10.5). Members of the Nike+ social community can share data and songs with their friends, arrange running meetups, and create exercise challenges. Not only does Nike+ help the company to interact with its customers and build brand loyalty, but it's also helping Nike to win new customers. In September 2007, Trevor Edwards, Nike's vice president of global brand management, told *BusinessWeek* that 40% of Nike+ users become new customers for the company.

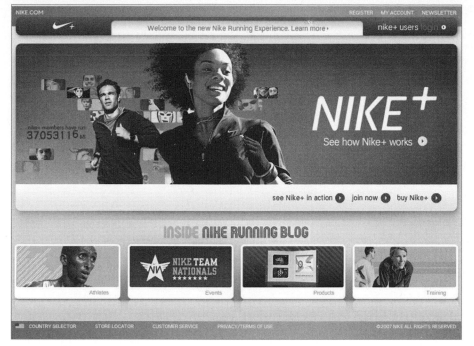

Figure 10.5 Nike+

Best Application

The benefits of social communities are certainly tipped in favor of company reputation building. Most social networks provide opportunities to either create a social community around a company profile—Aquafina's MySpace profile, for example—or let a company start a social community for individuals to join, such as the "Barack Obama for President" Facebook group. Using existing social networks is a great option for companies that don't have the resources to custom build their own social community. As Neil Patel puts it, "Why build something when it already exists?" If your brand is comparable in size to Nike, you should consider building your own social community. Services such as Ning.com make it easy to build and customize your own social network.

Individuals can still use social communities to build their reputation; you just need to be a little more creative. Are you an expert on California real estate? Create a Facebook group for others that share your interest. Can't find a MySpace profile for a popular piece of software? Create the "unofficial" community and brand yourself as the software's "guru."

Best Advice

The toughest lesson to learn about social communities is that you can't force yourself on your stakeholders. While you may create the official MySpace profile for your company, your customers may prefer the unofficial version because it's less stuffy and more fun. As Wills suggests, "Present yourself to them, but do so respectfully. As much as it's an opportunity for them to tell you what they love and hate about your product, it's also their choice whether to do so or not." In addition, any blatant attempt to promote your products will likely kill your community before it even gains attention. Patel recommends you "focus more on your brand than your products or services" and advises building a community "that is useful and makes people want to return and keep connected with you."

Social communities don't come with a money-back guarantee of success. Just because you build it doesn't mean they will come (sorry, Kevin Costner). Don't think about how you'll grow your social community—that's the wrong attitude. Instead, think about how you'll present your community to your stakeholders; they'll decide how they want to grow it.

> ### Thought Byte: Which Social Community Is the Best Fit for You?
>
> Although MySpace and Facebook are the most popular social networks, that doesn't necessarily mean they're the best place for you to build your social community. Consider the demographic make-up of a social network before making your selection and maybe even ask your stakeholders which one they prefer. As Neil Patel suggests, "The best social network is the one that the majority of the people in your industry are using."

5. Social Events

You'd expect companies such as Google, Microsoft, and Apple to have a strong online following. Search, software, and gadgets are prime candidates for social networking communities, but that doesn't stop all three companies from also arranging conferences, meetings, and other real-world gatherings. Like them, you'll find that meeting your stakeholders in person allows you to add a human element that's impossible to do in an online-only environment. Looking your stakeholders in the eye and shaking their hands, can add warmth to your brand and better protect your reputation in times of crisis. As Ben Wills puts it, "Nothing beats face-to-face."

With this in mind, some social networks have flourished by connecting an online enthusiast to an offline environment. These social event sites inform likeminded individuals of real-world meetings and conferences—allowing them to connect with one another before, during, and after the event.

Example Networks

Some examples are:

- Meetup.com
- Upcoming.org
- Eventful.com

In Action

The launch of Halo 3 was one of the most anticipated ever in the history of video games. For months, fans of the first-person shooter series had posted rumors on blogs, discussed screenshots in forums, and planned their strategy for getting first in line for the game's launch on September 25, 2007. The buzz surrounding the game was huge and Halo 3 was single-handedly expected to ensure the continued success of Microsoft's Xbox console. Even financial guru Jim Cramer predicted a huge financial win for all companies involved in the game's launch.

With success all but guaranteed, Halo 3 could have simply ridden the positive hype that had circulated on the Web for many months. Yet Microsoft knew that where two or more enthusiasts meet, the passion and excitement for a product increases. Thus, the company invited dozens of fans, bloggers, and journalists to a prelaunch party at their California offices using social event site Upcoming (See Figure 10.6) as well as their own private invitation site (iammasterchief.com).

With food, cocktails, and the chance to play the game before it went on sale, Microsoft ensured attendees would continue spreading the buzz once the game launched. Did this extra effort help Halo 3 to become a success? Attendees' photos and blog posts helped first day sales top $170 million and the game earned more in its first 24 hours than the blockbuster movie *Spiderman 3*.

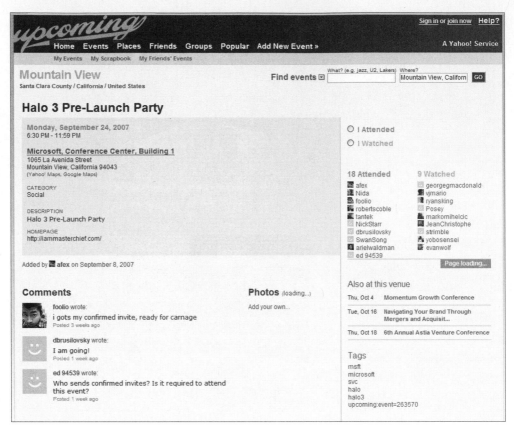

Figure 10.6 Halo 3 prelaunch party on Upcoming

Best Application

Organizing conferences and events using one of the many online social event sites makes it easier to send out invites, keep track of who's attending, and interact with stakeholders. By providing a platform for attendees to connect online, you also increase the chances your event will be well attended and a big success.

For individuals, social event sites such as Meetup.com allow you to get an idea of who is attending and let you plan your networking accordingly. If you know that you'd like to chat with an industry journalist, you can plan ahead, knowing that they'll be in attendance. Meetup also allows you to meet people online with similar interests, and take the conversation to offline venues—meeting them in real life.

Companies that integrate social event sites with their planning will benefit by eavesdropping on attendees prior to the event. Sites such as Upcoming.org let users comment on the event and ask questions ahead of time. This is a great opportunity for you to learn their expectations and make any last-minute programming changes you feel will make the event more successful.

Best Advice

Social events work best when you understand the opportunity to connect with others and share similar passions. Whether you're a company hosting the event, or an individual attending, it's important to have a "giving" mind-set. While you may want to get as much out of the event as possible, you'll help your reputation more by freely sharing your knowledge and helping others.

Alternatives to Social Networking Participation

Just like the other forms of social media, you might find that none of the five types of social networking appeals to you or fits your goals. You might want to consider these alternative options:

- Build a widget or plug-in for one of the popular social networks. Popular movie rental company Netflix provides a branded widget that lets Facebook users share which movies they plan on renting next.

- Build a group within a community. Many of the social networks allow users to join groups targeted to their interests. Stumbleupon.com has a group for fans of the video game Halo (halo.group.stumbleupon.com).

- Sponsor or advertise on a social network. Many of the online social networks allow you to run advertising to promote your brand. You can also find many sponsorship opportunities. You could sponsor a MySpace profile for your company, sponsor a cool Facebook application, or sponsor a major conference in your industry.

For individuals this means looking for opportunities to connect with other attendees and helping them with their needs or solving a problem they have. You may not be one of the official speakers, but offering advice to a fellow attendee over lunch is a great way to build your reputation.

Companies should look at these events as an opportunity to give back to their constituents. While free wine and food will go a long way toward building brand loyalty, it's your transparency and open dialogue that will impress the people you've invited. CEOs should mingle with attendees, listen to their customers' concerns, and tap into the wealth of market research each event offers. It's your chance to listen in on the conversations that would normally take place on Facebook groups or blog comments.

Achieving Reputation Success with Social Networks

Whether you decide to implement just one of the pillars of social networking—or all five—there are four keys to your success.

First, be transparent in your motives. Make it clear why you're there, what it is you want from your stakeholders, but more importantly, what you plan on giving them in return. Any attempts to manipulate them will likely result in your social networking activities being exposed as a sham and your reputation damaged.

Second, let your stakeholders connect with your brand. Of course you want social network users to love your products, but first they need to embrace your brand (refer to Chapter 4 for more on engagement). Aquafina doesn't maintain a MySpace profile so they can use it as a channel to directly sell more bottled water. Instead, they provide cool games and enticing contests, which in turn build a positive brand sentiment in the minds of their network of "friends." This puts Aquafina "top of mind" when consumers next visit the grocery store.

Third, be proactive in growing your network. Simply creating your profile or community won't automatically help with your reputation. If you create a LinkedIn profile, you'll not only need to make it appealing to potential customers or employers, but you'll need to build your network of business connections. You can't expect your social networking profile to be a roaring success if you're not sharing it with others.

Last, realize that every action you take reflects on your reputation. If your company launches a contest on MySpace, but then cancels, the community will likely turn on you. Likewise, posting abusive rants on your Facebook profile will come back to haunt you if a recruiter discovers it.

The five pillars of social networking provide a great opportunity to tap into a dynamic conversation that reflects the discussions that would normally take place in offline environments. Your entry into those conversations should mimic your attempts to join a conversation at a cocktail party. Be graceful, don't be pushy, don't talk only about yourself, and most of all, be engaging.

Your Online Activities: You Are What You Do

Your actions have a huge impact on your reputation. We've already discussed your character and values, and now we'll explore how some of your actions affect your reputation. Stakeholders review your books at Amazon, your products at Epinions, and your online retail store performance at Shopzilla—the more positive the reviews, the better your reputation. On eBay, positive feedback will yield higher prices for your goods. In Second Life and other virtual worlds, you can build a fantastic reputation that will cross over to your first life—it may be time to play the game along with 11 million other avatars.

11

Chapter Contents

Working With Strangers
The Online Trust Market
Understanding Reputation Management Engines
Quick Clicks That Can Harm Your Reputation
Becoming Well Respected in Virtual Worlds
You Have the Tools—Now What?

Working With Strangers

How do companies find competent and well-respected consultants in the global talent pool? One way is to use an online marketplace for freelance talent. When entrepreneur Chris Riche needed a software development team for his new web-based business, he began his journey to find a good marketplace using Google. His first search returned Elance.com and oDesk.com as sponsored links. Riche knew of Elance and had used Guru.com successfully in the past, so decided to employ these three marketplaces for his vendor quest (Figure 11.1).

> ### Defining Moment: Online Marketplace
>
> According to *PC Magazine*, an online marketplace is a "business-to-business Web site for a particular industry. It provides a meeting ground for buyers and sellers in a specific field, and rather than being advertising based, may charge a transaction fee for each purchase. Also known as a vertical portal, or 'vortal.'" Marketplaces are places to purchase either products or professional services. Online marketplaces, such as eBay, exist in consumer markets as well.

Figure 11.1 Guru.com marketplace for freelance talent

It was important to use several marketplaces because each varied greatly in vendor membership database breadth, specialty depth, website functionality, and contract terms. For example, Elance appeared to have more software developers than the others, while Guru appeared to have a broader range of supplier expertise, and oDesk allowed hiring companies to observe vendors working on the contracted project via webcam. At the same time, the top suppliers in each marketplace seemed to be different companies. oDesk's webcam capability seemed appealing initially, but also raised doubts about potential impact on the client/vendor relationship. Riche decided to use all three marketplaces. Together, they provided a wide range of suppliers, good supplier descriptions and feedback on the site, and relatively easy processes to manage prospective suppliers through the bid process.

To help set expectations and minimize the chance for miscommunication, Riche developed an 80-page document specifying the requirements for his complex, open source, data-driven website. He posted a summary of this on all three marketplaces, along with questions for vendors to answer. Here's what followed:

1. Riche received 60 responses to his project posting, with about 30 coming from Elance. Surprisingly, some vendors sent generic boilerplate answers and didn't respond to Riche's specific questions, which was telling in itself. He immediately dropped these suppliers from the list—Riche reasoned that if they were not going to take the time to send a tailored response in trying to get a client, how well would they act when the work commences?

2. Next, Riche evaluated the quality of vendor responses, their skills in software development, and their ability to communicate in the English language—important for collaborating on the project. After additional probing via e-mails it became clear that while the salesperson for the firm had very good English-speaking and sales skills, the post-sale client management and communication skills would likely be a real challenge. Depending on their other responses, this risk ruled additional firms out.

3. In preparation for a more detailed discussion of the project, once a nondisclosure agreement was signed, Riche provided the full requirements document to the remaining suppliers. Riche then interviewed them on the telephone. By listening to the questions they asked, Riche was able to get a good idea of how well they really understood the project and what was going to be necessary to successfully deliver on it. Also, it was important to see exactly who would be on the project team and, given the high turnover it appeared some of the firms had, whether or not they might remain with the company long enough to complete the job. For example, the high turnover among some teams operating in India filtered them out in this stage.

Throughout this process, Riche read the marketplace reviews for each vendor (posted by hiring companies at the completion of each previous contract). As part of that process Riche queried vendors about anomalies. For example, why were some ratings clearly poor: "this team sucked," or "they delivered the job late"? It was important to understand whether these comments were due to the supplier or the client. If there were no reviews, why not? If the vendor's profile showed many completed projects but a relatively low number of feedbacks, did this indicate a cultural reluctance among hiring companies to criticize vendors? If there were no completed projects, was this a new association of developers and what did the feedback look like on the prior projects?

To help manage all the information and filtering down of prospective suppliers, Riche created a Microsoft Excel spreadsheet to evaluate each based on his criteria. During the process Riche learned to read recommendations carefully because there was much hidden meaning. At a macro level, the overall level of recommendations varied by marketplace—one had very high recommendations for most vendors, while another contained a much broader range of ratings. At a micro level, some vendors received very high scores in their ratings, but the words associated with each appeared to tell a different story: "This is a very capable developer with good skills, but they had a different vision so I decided to get a new team." Did this mean that the vendor neither listens nor takes direction from the client?

Satisfied with his short list of suppliers, Riche called the references on his vendor short list, hired a development company in a country that wasn't even on his radar at the start of the process, and began working with "strangers" halfway around the world. As of this writing, the project is partially completed and going well.

The Online Trust Market

The internet is a network of strangers. You quickly and easily trust people like yourself whom you've never met in person—but only when the stakes are low. Online discussion helps to shape your own opinions about brands, companies, and other people via blogs, forums, chat rooms, and network profiles. Book and music recommendations from strangers influence you to purchase a low-cost book or CD. However, buyers take a much closer look at customer recommendations online when the price is higher and the vendor unknown, such as experienced by Chris Riche. Can the recommenders be trusted? We also scrutinize reviews more heavily when buying anything through an online auction from unknown sellers. In these cases internet ratings and recommendations from strangers provide an important trust filter for screening out potential vendors, hotels, retailers, individual sellers, and more.

An old Japanese proverb states, "When the character of a man is not clear, look at his friends." This is the thinking behind internet rating and recommendation systems that evaluate the strangers with whom you want to do business.

This chapter is about your activities online and offline, and how they affect your perceived credibility online. First we'll discuss how to get great online ratings and recommendations from others. For example, if Chris Riche's development team delivers as contracted, it might result in a good recommendation from Chris on the marketplace website. Conversely, if an online retailer falls in customer service, such as Dell's Hell discussed in Chapter 2, it will get slammed in online reviews. Next, we'll explore some of the errors you can make offline and online that can dent your reputation—things such as hitting "reply to all" on an e-mail. Finally, we'll talk about virtual worlds and other online games where your online activities can definitely make or break your "in-world" reputation and spill over to the terrestrial world as well.

Understanding Reputation Management Engines

We've already noted that Google is more than a dominant search engine; it's the world's most trusted reputation engine (Chapter 6). This is because incoming links to a website is one of the key algorithm components Google uses to compute site value. When tens of thousands of websites direct their users to a recommended site, this indicates a high level of trust. We've also discussed automated reputation engine filtering of e-mail into spam folders (Chapter 8). At this point we turn to reputation management engines used by Amazon, eBay, and others, for aggregating customer satisfaction and dissatisfaction ratings and written recommendations. According to Gary Wolf, *Wired* magazine reporter:

> **"** …news is filtered by reputation-based systems like Slashdot's, and conclusions about our professional status or competence are influenced by Google's page-rank algorithms. All these systems rely on automated processes that aggregate minor human actions into public judgments that are nearly impossible to appeal. **"**

In general, the best way to improve your reputation ratings when selling something is to perform as promised and to provide good customer service during the process. Chris Riche advises, "Managing expectations and ensuring good ongoing communications are important for the vendor—especially when dealing with clients from other countries, cultures, and time zones. Spend more time up front making sure the expectations for the job are clear and it will pay off when it is client feedback time."

It also helps to gather as many recommendations as you can. Customer trust is higher when the number of raters in a recommendation engine is large, such as the Google ranking system and the huge number of eBay raters for frequent sellers. That is, an online retailer with a 4.5-star average rating by 300 raters beats a 5-star rating from 2 raters every time. Naturally, users rely less on recommendation engines when dealing with a well-respected brand name company, product, or individual. However, when this same well-respected company begins business in a new market (especially in another country), the recommendation engines become more important again.

Reputation engine users always wonder if the ratings were artificially inflated by owners or deflated by disgruntled employees. In fact, there is a parallel market for eBay feedback ratings, with people buying and selling feedback, that is neither controlled nor sanctioned by eBay. In the following sections, we'll expand on this, briefly describe several of the more popular websites using recommendation engines, and then offer advice about building your reputation within those systems.

> **Defining Moment: Reputation Management Engine**
>
> According to usability expert Jakob Nielsen, "A reputation management [engine] is an independent service that keeps track of the rated quality, credibility, or some other desirable metric for each element in a set. The things being rated will typically be websites, companies, products, or people…" Individuals who use or purchase the thing rate it based on their satisfaction or dissatisfaction. Often there is a point or star system that might appear online as an average rating from all users. As well, users can often write text explaining their rating: these are called recommendations.

Acing Online Auction Grades

Your online and offline auction performance record can make or break your reputation, whether you operate in business-to-business (B2B), business-to-consumer (B2C), or consumer-to-consumer (C2C) marketplaces. Buyers expect quick responses to their e-mail queries and professional transaction and merchandise delivery. These offline customer service and handling tasks, when added to accurate product descriptions, are the basis of customer post-auction satisfaction or dissatisfaction. If you want high ratings, you'd better perform offline as advertised online.

The C2C market online is riskier for buyers because they have to pay for the merchandise after only seeing a product description and image, unlike newspaper classified advertising, which usually includes a face-to-face transaction. Thus, the power rests with sellers online. Reputation management engines mitigate the risk for buyers and equalize the power because if buyers are unhappy, they can complain to a few hundred thousand potential customers via the platform's rating system.

Several studies have found that highly rated eBay sellers are more likely to sell their merchandise and to receive price premiums for products. Conversely, sellers with negative feedback have been found to have more unsuccessful auctions and lower transaction prices. In one study of 861 eBay auctions for golf clubs, researcher Jeffrey Livingston found that sellers had a 3.4% higher probability of selling their clubs and received 5% higher prices when they improved their feedback scores from zero to 25 points. Thus, a good reputation translates to sales success on eBay. See Figures 11.2 and 11.3 for the eBay feedback system and an example of a highly rated "Power Seller."

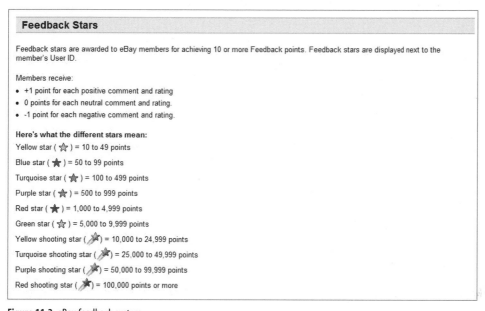

Figure 11.2 eBay feedback system

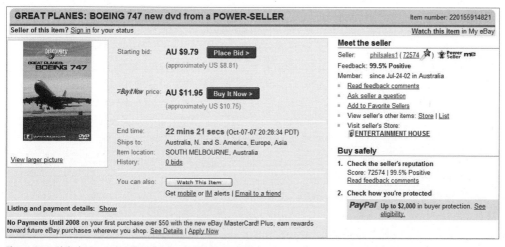

Figure 11.3 Philsales1, an eBay Shooting Purple Star Power Seller

How do you earn good feedback at eBay and in other auctions? As you've already learned: perform as promised. Beyond that, you can suggest that satisfied buyers take a minute to leave seller feedback (see the sidebar "How to Encourage Positive Feedback from eBay Buyers"). If someone does leave unwarranted negative feedback, you can reply to the buyer or leave a public follow-up comment with your side of the story. You can also dispute the rating and remove it with the mutual consent of buyer and seller, or ask for mediation to resolve the problem. Finally, research has shown a high correlation between seller and buyer mutual feedback, so if you give your buyers good feedback, they will likely reciprocate.

A final warning is in order. eBay and other auction sites are ripe with credibility scams. Academic researchers Jennifer Brown and John Morgan found an entire market for feedback itself at eBay, with an average value of at least $0.61 per feedback point (compiled with over 5,000 feedback market transactions). Searching for "positive feedback" at eBay, they found sellers offering an eBook along with one positive feedback point for $0.01. After the researchers purchased the eBook via PayPal, they received a three-page PDF file, representing the product sold, so this was a legal transaction. The book text included the following:

> " Look on eBay for items that cost next to nothing. You can find the eBay search feature to find items which cost anywhere from $0.01 to $1.00. Try this… Now bid on 100 items. If you want to speed things up a bit, try and find auctions with the "Buy It Now" option. If the seller offers PayPal as a form of payment, go right away and pay for the item… If you do this with a hundred different sellers you should be able to get your feedback score up to 100 in just a few days. "

eBay does not allow feedback point transactions; however, it seems that they can't stop this huge market, thinly veiled as legitimate, because reputation brings price premiums and increased sales. However, because both sellers and buyers perceive the reputation system to work well and are generally unaware of these scams, eBay ratings remain credible, according to researchers Paul Resnick and Richard Zeckhauser.

How to Encourage Positive Feedback from eBay Buyers

The basics for positive feedback include accurate product listing headlines and descriptions, and fast product delivery (some people suggest that buyers expect shipping within two days of payment). Beyond that, it is important to communicate with buyers. Send an e-mail when you have shipped the item, including a tracking number. It might help to be personal: "Thank you for the order. I shipped the product today on my way home from work and hope you will enjoy it as much as I did."

Become a Highly Recommended Online Retailer

Online retailers know that delivery and customer service are key to getting good recommendations from customers. It is more difficult online because many factors creating trust at brick-and-mortar retail stores disappear when the transaction is online (see the sidebar "The Offline Retailer Trust Advantage"). Nonetheless, several online retailers have closed the gap by developing credible brand names, such as Amazon and Expedia, and others have successfully brought their well-known offline retail brands to the internet (e.g., Target and Best Buy).

Recommendation engines help buyers select among products at Amazon, Buy.com, and other general retailers. This engagement strategy gives retailers valuable insight about how consumers feel about the products they have purchased. Their reputation becomes more positive by allowing radically transparent product reviews right on their websites (as opposed to reviews of the retailer itself). Both retailer and customer waltz happily into the sunset.

The picture is less sweet for Amazon's partners and other sellers represented on the site. If you are a used bookseller, for example, you gain credibility by association with Amazon, but you must also earn your own positive store reviews to be selected by buyers among a list of other sellers of similar items (unlike Amazon, which does not display customer satisfaction ratings for its own performance). It also helps to gather lots of ratings, because high numbers of positive ratings make a difference, as we've already said.

The Offline Retailer Trust Advantage

There are seven key factors that generate buyer trust with traditional brick-and-mortar retailers, according to academic researchers Paul Resnick and Richard Zeckhauser:

- Buyers can inspect the merchandise quality in person.

- Buyers tend to have frequent interactions with the same retailer in their neighborhoods.

- Local retailers have well-known reputations in a market area.

- Retailer reputations occur in the context of a community, and this gives them incentives to maintain that trust.

- Reputations are built over many years and result in well-known brand names.

- New products sold by well-known retailers benefit by association.

- Significant physical structures indicate credibility, such as a fancy store on New York's Fifth Avenue.

Third-Party Review Sites

Online retailers gain credibility by managing their reviews at third-party sites as well. For example, Shopzilla's BizRate (www.bizrate.com) rates more than 99,000 merchants, based on thousands of customer satisfaction surveys conducted after purchase at each store's website. Buyers can read reviews at BizRate's site and also compare prices (Figure 11.4). We encourage retailers to take advantage of third-party customer research as a way to engage and listen, as well as to enhance reputation by promoting positive customer satisfaction scores on their own website. Obviously, a third-party review carries more credibility with your customers than does self-administered customer satisfaction research.

Figure 11.4 BizRate reviews more than 99,000 merchants.

Other third-party recommendation sites include consumer reviews at TripAdvisor.com (hotel and travel industry) and Epinions.com (every product imaginable), and professional recommendations at CNET.com (technology reviews). The latter is a pioneer with its video product reviews, so you will definitely want to send new products to their staff for review.

We recommend watching your reviews closely at these third-party sites. You can gain valuable information by listening to dissatisfied customers, as we've said many times. You can engage them in conversation and use the information to improve your business. If your reviews are consistently stellar, by all means refer to them on your website and enhance your online reputation. If they are not stellar, the radically transparent retailer, hotel, manufacturer, or other seller will not bury the legitimate comments but address them in open discussion forums—as did Dell (Chapter 2).

Also, don't forget to check for YourCompanyNameSucks.com sites, especially if you are a large company. Many former employees and upset customers have started sites like these to air their views. More about this in Part 3.

A word of caution: Don't be tempted to stack the reviews for your book or product with glowing words from friends—unless they are being genuinely honest. If you are discovered, this tactic will backfire and hurt your reputation. If clients tell you how much they like your products, however, do ask them to post this online in an appropriate place, or seek their permission to add their comments to your own website. Conversely, if you find your product reviews filled with flames from enemies or disgruntled former employees, contact the website to discuss possibilities for removing the revenge reviews. See Chapter 14 for more information on when and how to repair problems like this.

Become a Highly Rated Reviewer

Epinions and Amazon are double reputation managers because individuals review products, and then other people rate the reviewers. We spoke in Chapter 3 about Amazon's most highly rated reviewer, Harriet Klausner, who has posted over 14,000 book reviews at Amazon.com and received publicity in *Time* magazine, *Wired*, and OpinionJournal.com. We aren't suggesting that you read that many books, but it is a good idea to post candid reviews for many books in your area of expertise. If you want to develop a thought leadership reputation, this will help. Take care with the reviews and you will gather positive ratings for providing the community with value, and you can use your ratings on your own website—along with copies of your reviews and a bookshelf of recommendations in your area.

Epinions hosts millions of unmoderated reviews on every type of product (Figure 11.5). The site offers monetary incentives for creating content that customers value. If you want to build your reputation by becoming a strong Epinions reviewer, you'll have an opportunity to create a reviewer biography page and become a trusted expert by the community. Beware of violating the Epinions user agreement, though—you'll get a "ticket" as a flag that you are no longer a trusted reviewer. For instance, reviewers get tickets for intellectual property infringements or offensive language.

Figure 11.5 Epinions review by customeright, a five-star reviewer

Quick Clicks That Can Harm Your Reputation

There are a few things you might do at your computer that can definitely hurt your reputation if you are not careful. First is a reminder that your web browser caches your recent website viewing, so you want to be careful what sites you visit at work. Your employer or colleagues can easily and accidentally get into your browser cache. For example, they might be with you at your computer and reach out to type in a website address and get stopped when their "www.mo" instantly brings up www.monster.com—you posted your resume there yesterday. Of course, more serious snoopers might check out your browser history feature.

Second, don't forget that your e-mail outbox has a great record of all the personal e-mails you sent from work, unless you delete them and then empty the deleted e-mail folder. Even then, many companies archive outgoing e-mail on their servers, so it is better to avoid sending compromising personal e-mail from your work e-mail account. E-mail is so ubiquitous that it is easy to forget that e-mail recipients might also forget to dump their deleted files. Portland, Oregon, Police Chief Derrick Fox-worth learned this the hard way when he was demoted to precinct commander after 58 romantic e-mails to Angela Oswalt surfaced. He was her supervisor when the romance began and when he ended it five years later, she threatened a lawsuit and made all the e-mail public—excerpts are still available for all the world to read from a 2006 story on the *Portland Tribune* website.

> ### Thought Byte: Browser and E-mail Review
>
> What damaging e-mail rests in your deleted and sent e-mail folders? Maybe it is time to clean out the files before someone else finds reputation-detracting content—and to stop sending anything that could hurt you via your office e-mail account. Have you been to any questionable websites on your office computer, even accidentally? If so, clean the cache in Internet Explorer 7 by clicking on Tools and "delete browsing history." Once there, you can remove cookies, website history, and more. Firefox and other browsers offer similar options.

Finally, double-check your e-mail recipients before hitting Send. We've all had the misfortune of replying to entire distribution lists when we meant to reply to the individual sender. Usually this results in harmless inbox junk, but it can be much worse for your and your company's reputation. Consider the case of Spirit Airlines CEO Ben Baldanza, who received a heartfelt customer e-mail complaint: "…On multiple occasions, we observed your employees talking rudely to customers and just in general, exhibiting extremely poor customer service skills…" Baldanza accidentally hit Reply to All from his Blackberry when he meant to respond to internal staff and the disgruntled customer received this:

> " Please respond, Pasquale, but we owe him nothing as far as I'm concerned. Let him tell the world how bad we are. He's never flown us before anyway and will be back when we save him a penny. "

This incident was the subject of many blogs, and was subsequently written about in an Orlando, Florida, newspaper and now in this book. Baldanza is not the first to make this kind of simple error, but there is no evidence that he's tried to repair this reputation problem. We'll have to send him a copy of this book.

Becoming Well Respected in Virtual Worlds

Why discuss game playing in a book on reputation management? Online gaming has become big business, with players such as IBM, Cisco, Starwood Hotels & Resorts, Johnson & Johnson, Pontiac (Chapter 4), and many entrepreneurs using games for education, training, commerce, health care, and brand building. The growth in online gaming is phenomenal. It has been called "the fastest growing consumer-spending segment in the U.S. and Europe/Middle East/Africa regions" by professional services firm PricewaterhouseCoopers. Research firm Gartner Group predicts that 80% of active online users will join a virtual world by 2010 (an estimated 50 million to 60 million people). If you are in that 80%, these games will affect your online reputation and bleed into off-world brand images.

Games are unique spaces online because others can easily judge your appearance and behavior through your avatar clothing, spontaneous conversation, nonverbal communication, and other social interaction—even if your online persona is a peacock. According to Dale Carnegie, author of *How to Win Friends and Influence People*:

> **66** There are four ways, and only four ways, in which we have contact with the world. We are evaluated and classified by these four contacts: What we do, how we look, what we say, and how we say it. **99**

Unlike most other web destinations, in online games all of these things matter. And when other players know your true identity, it spills to your offline reputation.

Choose Your Game Wisely

There are many types of online games with social interaction, from two-player chess to massively multiplayer online games (MMOGs)—sporting thousands of players moving about as avatars at the same time (see the sidebar "Defining Moment: Virtual Worlds and Other Online Role-Playing Games"). Some games have storylines or plots with players accomplishing goals and increasing skills and power, and others are completely nonstructured with players designing the action. These all have two things in common: first, they are being used for a variety of business goals, and second, social interactions and online discussion among players can affect reputations.

Virtual worlds, or metaverses, are unique because players create their own experiences in casual spaces. This offers businesses much opportunity and flexibility, and is why we think that the current growth explosion will continue. Virtual worlds have even attracted politicians—California Representative George Miller started a virtual House of Representatives in Second Life, and others have found it a good place to connect with voters.

Defining Moment: Virtual Worlds and Other Online Role-Playing Games

Online games come in many varieties. For this discussion, we include role-playing games where more than one player logs in at the same time and engages with the content created by the game author or by other participants. All use player avatars—a graphical representation of the player in a virtual space. Here is how the field sorts out (definitions in quotes from Wikipedia):

- A role-playing game (RPG) "is a game in which the participants assume the roles of fictional characters and collaboratively create or follow stories. Participants determine the actions of their characters based on their characterization, and the actions succeed or fail according to a formal system of rules and guidelines. Within the rules, players can improvise freely; their choices shape the direction and outcome of the games." RPGs usually have predetermined settings and tasks to accomplish, such as the well-known Dungeons and Dragons game, and often a game master will create setting criteria for each play.

- A massively multiplayer online role-playing game (MMORPG), a subcategory of MMOGs, "is a genre of online role-playing video games (RPGs) in which a large number of players interact with one another in a virtual world...which continues to exist and evolve while the player is away from the game." MMORPGs were estimated to have 15 million global players that generated over $1 billion in USD revenues in 2006. World of Warcraft may be the most popular MMORPG, with 8 million monthly subscribers worldwide. Like Dungeons and Dragons, players can increase their power and skills through successful task accomplishment and interaction with others—avatar selection, social roles, and interactions during game play are important features in this genre.

- Metaverses, commonly called "virtual worlds," are "fully immersive 3D virtual spaces. These are environments where humans interact (as avatars) with each other (socially and economically) and with software agents in a cyber space, that uses the metaphor of the real world, but without its physical limitations" (such as human avatars who can teleport or fly). Metaverses are a particular type of MMORPG where there is no game master or predesigned plot and the players invent the world and most of its rules (except for software code limitations). Second Life may be the most well-known metaverse.

There are a number of virtual worlds, such as the popular Second Life, RuneScape, and World of Warcraft. Others appeal to niche demographics. For example, children care for virtual pets at Webkinz.com and can chat with penguin avatars in Club Penguin. Teens hang out at Habbo.com, and create dorm rooms and rock their wardrobes in Zwinktopia (Zwinky.com).

As of this writing, Google is rumored to be exploring the idea of turning its Google Earth into a virtual world called MyWorld. All eyes are on Google because it already owns SketchUp for 3-D modeling and Google Maps. If Google brings a social networking property into MyWorld, this might become the definitive virtual world for business networking and commerce.

Which virtual world is best for your reputation needs? It takes money and a lot of time to do it right, so choose wisely. Second Life (SL) has a huge population and a steep learning curve, and doesn't currently scale well for hosting large in-world events (over 70 avatars in one place taxes the software, so you'll have to purchase many adjoining properties to host large events). Other worlds are more user-friendly but may not have the player/target market match for your business needs. Source credibility is also important, so evaluate the reputation of the games before taking the plunge. For example, SL has a reputation of cybersex and has been in the news for pornography, so that could stain corporate residents (not that this has bothered IBM and others). Another consideration is that virtual worlds may be a bubble about to burst, bringing consolidations soon—you want to be with the survivor so you won't have a new learning curve and subsequently change all your marketing communication materials.

Virtual worlds offer a great reputation-building venue that will be an important part of your online networking future, if Gartner growth projections are right. Because SL is the most well known and been in existence long enough to have established reputation-enhancing practices, we'll use it as a brief example.

Creating a Great Second Life Reputation

Second Life has nearly 11 million residents, with over 400,000 logging in during a seven-day period (SL statistics in September 2007). Millions of U.S. dollars are traded monthly between residents and nearly 50,000 in-world business owners. Pontiac holds many special events in-world, promoting them on company websites. The Royal Liverpool Philharmonic Orchestra gave a live performance in SL in 2007, and Ray Giordano landed a job via a SL virtual job fair hosted by advertising and communications recruiting firm TMP Worldwide. Is SL a game or is it a way to network, do business, and build your reputation? For some, SL is a reputation-enhancing vehicle that crosses over to their first life (offline, real life). But you have to know how to play the game for this to happen.

Your Second Life reputation depends on many things:

- The way you look, communicate, and behave in-world
- Your avatar name and profile pages
- Your in-world property
- The ratings you receive from third-party rating services

However, the ultimate goal is to cross-fertilize your first and second life reputations to increase trust and credibility for your first-world name and business or to sell more product in-world (capitalizing on your first-world reputation). There is a lot more to SL, but we'll focus briefly on these reputation-building aspects in this discussion. For more in-depth information, we recommend *Designing Your Second Life* by Rebecca Tapley or *Second Life: A Guide to Your Virtual World* by Brian A. White.

Your avatar selection In SL you can have any persona you want. Your avatar can be a human of the same or opposite sex, or an animal. An important feature of all role-playing games is that the player identifies with the avatar he creates. Players create fantasy characters that excite them, and this is what keeps them engaged in the game. More importantly, if you pick an avatar persona that matches your desired reputation and thought leadership goals, you will be consistent when you interact with others—an important characteristic for building trust. So, be a cat if you want to be wise, strong, and gentle, or a rock star if you want to be rich, successful, and powerful.

How you look Just as in real life, how you look makes a good or bad first impression (Figure 11.6). It doesn't matter as much what form you take as it does how you dress your avatar—for example, if you use standard-issue SL clothing or hair, you'll look inexperienced and second class. Instead, fly to a cool in-world merchant and purchase duds and hairdos that exude the reputation you want. You will also look inexperienced if you walk and stand in-world using standard-issue poses. Instead, purchase special animations that make you look more real and give you a full repertoire of subtle and interesting body movement—you can even buy gestures that come with sound. Finally, you can hire other avatars to complete your look, such as the banker who hired a couple of bodyguard type avatars to walk behind him.

Figure 11.6 Looking hot in Second Life

Your avatar name and profile These features may be the most important for your reputation-building crossover efforts. SL has a series of standard last names to choose among unless you want to buy and pay annually for a vanity last name—a good idea for reputation building. Otherwise, residents can create first names consisting of 2–31 characters (you can't ever change your name, once selected, so choose wisely). You can use a first name that includes your brand or real name, and this will create great reputation crossover and make it easy for residents to find you via in-world search—but of course, you'll need to behave well in-world or hurt your offline brand reputation. Intellectual property is taken seriously in SL, so it is not likely that an unrelated avatar will use your brand or company name.

Your profile page is akin to a mini-website, with images and a written description about you (Figure 11.7). It also includes your "picks" as links to your favorite SL locations, such as places you like that are consistent with your thought leadership area (if you are a stock broker, list in-world financial institutions). It is better to list your company properties in the classified ad portion of your profile because these appear in SL's worldwide search function. One important feature of the profile pages is a "1st Life" page, where you can reveal who you really are. There are other tricks for publicizing your brand in your profile pages, so we urge you to get more information about this important feature. It is very important to create a profile page, because avatars walking around with blank profiles definitely appear inexperienced.

Figure 11.7 Second Life profile pages reveal first life information.

How you communicate When you meet another avatar in-world, you can use a chat window to type her name (visible above the avatar) and a few words, such as "How are you today?" You can also talk with your real voice using Skype, but others may not want to talk back out loud because a real voice coming from an avatar reveals its gender and age. Further, there are private in-world instant messages (IM) and offline e-mail, and public main chat channels, so learn which to use for professional communication. Finally, if you are giving a presentation at an SL event, how you communicate becomes much more important. Think about making a grand entrance by emerging from a fireball and using interesting and engaging communication tactics. Otherwise the avatar audience may fall asleep. The bottom line about reputation-building communication is to be careful what you say and to know who is listening or who is awaiting an IM or chat response from you.

How to network You can join groups of avatars who share your interests or business goals. This provides an instant reputation because your title in groups appears above your avatar name, defining your persona. "…many designers and business people in SL use Groups to make announcements to customers, affiliates, and other interested parties—you can send a single IM to everybody belonging to a group," according to author Rebecca Tapley. You can also script doors into a building to only allow group members to enter. You can ask avatars to be your "friends" after you feel comfortable with them and ask their permission (because this allows you to track one another's whereabouts and is considered quite forward if asked prematurely). Calling cards are an important SL feature that serve as first-world business cards. They include your name and a shortcut to your full profile, so offer them to avatars you want to know better.

How you behave in-world Be sure to follow Second Life's "big six" community behavioral guidelines on intolerance, harassment, assault, disclosure, indecency, and disturbing the peace—or pay a big reputation price. Beyond that, the best thing is to start slowly and observe how others move and act. You are bound to physically bump into other avatars when you first start learning to control your avatar, but a simple IM apology will take care of it. Apply common courtesies you use in your first world, and you will probably be fine—for example, it is okay for your avatar to fall asleep during a lecture, but not if this is a potential first-world client presenting. If you bring employees into a corporate SL experience, be sure you create a code of conduct for them as well. It is easy to hide behind an avatar and the fantasy and act in ways that might hurt your offline reputation.

Your in-world property You can buy property in-world using "Linden dollars" from SL owners, Linden Labs, but only if you have upgraded from a free basic to a paid premium account. A premium account is also necessary to buy more Linden dollars with real-world cash, and you'll need more cash to buy or build reputation-enhancing property. SL residents prefer premium account holders because this means that Linden Labs has first-life account information, thus increasing legitimacy, accountability, and credibility. The word on the Second Life street is that all the troublemakers are basic account holders—the second-class citizens. So upgrade your account, buy an island for a couple thousand US dollars (and $295 a month in maintenance fees), and increase your in-world reputation. Of course, then you have to buy the materials to make buildings and other things. Don't worry—you can start smaller by purchasing business property from another resident.

SL resident and merchant ratings Recognizing the need for better avatar and in-world merchant ratings than it could provide, Linden Labs now refers SL residents to third-party rating services. Real Reputations (www.slrealreps.com) uses public reputation profiles, feedback, and trust networks to compile public profiles on rated residents. RatePoint, TrustNet, Ban Link, Sloog.org, and Slicr all compete to be the most-used reputation destination for SL residents. The field is likely to change quickly, so we refer you to these sites to see which end up being the definitive SL reputation services.

Second and first life crossover While privacy and fantasy are key in SL, it is perfectly acceptable to reveal your true name and affiliation when asked. As previously mentioned, your avatar name, profile, group memberships, and SL property can all bring your great offline reputation to create instant in-world credibility. Conversely, you can bring a great SL reputation into your first-life business. One way is to include your avatar name on your business card. You can also create IM, e-mail, and Skype accounts using your avatar name for consistency and transparency. This will encourage SL residents to seek you in the first world, and also entice real-life clients to find you in SL. If you invest the time and money to create an SL or other virtual world presence, use both worlds to build your reputation.

Does this sound like a lot of work? It is. If the growth projections are accurate, getting on the learning curve now will be akin to starting a website in 1994. You'll have prime property and a thriving reputation. And if this sounds too much like real work, don't forget that you can have a fully anonymous personal avatar to live out the fantasies that your professional avatar can't.

You Have the Tools—Now What?

Are you overwhelmed? In Part 2 of this book we've shown you how to use blogs and social networking to create a great reputation. We've discussed search engine optimization, RSS feeds, and public relations for buzz building about you, your brands, and your company. We've provided lots of tips for using multimedia building blocks to engage your important stakeholders in a radically transparent manner, and to craft the story about you that will help to achieve your every career and reputation dream. And now, you have to also become a star reviewer in your area of thought leadership and build an avatar to enter Second Life. And you still can't even keep up with your e-mail—although we hope they've improved with our advice.

Prepare to embark on Part 3, where we'll show you how to put this all together. You'll start with a look at the shape of your current reputation online, and then figure out whether you need to build or repair it. Finally, we'll part ways by giving you a plan to get started, one step at a time. Take a breath and turn the page.

Monitoring, Repairing, and Planning your Online Reputation

III

Even with your best efforts to build and manage a positive online reputation, you are still exposed to the critique of your stakeholders. Taking the time to monitor conversations about you will ensure that you are alerted the moment your reputation comes into question. Joining the conversation will give you an opportunity to tell your side of the story and repair any damage to your good name.

These chapters answer the why, what, where, when, and how of monitoring and repairing your reputation.

The Importance of Reputation Monitoring

Now that you've built a stellar online reputation, it's time to make sure it doesn't come under fire. Monitoring the Web will ensure you're alerted the moment your reputation faces critique. In order to get the most out of your online reputation monitoring you'll need to know why it is important, what keywords to monitor, where to watch, and when to take action.

12

GlaxoSmithKline Monitors for Adverse Reactions

Few industries are subject to as much public scrutiny as the pharmaceutical industry. Although drug companies invest billions of dollars in scientific research, bring breakthrough medications to market, and help patients overcome devastating illnesses, the industry continues to face reputation attacks. Animal testing, drug recalls, and high prescription costs are just a few of the many reputation challenges drug companies must overcome on a regular basis. With 78% of consumers considering a drug company's reputation when selecting drug treatments (according to a PricewaterhouseCoopers study), it's no surprise that many pharmaceutical companies keep a close eye on what is being said about them.

Britain's GlaxoSmithKline (GSK) is one drug company that pays close attention to the chatter surrounding its brand. The second-largest pharmaceutical company in the world—earning a profit of £7.8 billion in 2006—GSK has a lot at stake when it comes to guarding its reputation. Like most drug companies, GSK is continually under the microscope. Concerns over its involvement with animal laboratory testing, lawsuits involving its biggest drug brands Paxil and Avandia, and a $3.1 billion IRS settlement in 2006—the largest in history—are just some of the reputation challenges facing GSK in recent years. It is not an easy task to manage the reputation of a multibillion dollar company operating in one of the most tightly regulated industries in the world. Yet, GSK is ahead of the pack when it comes to monitoring and managing its public perception.

GSK has invested billions in programs and initiatives that are designed to show the drug firm as a conscientious corporate citizen. With its HIV vaccine research in more than 25 developing nations, its "GSK for You" prescription assistance programs (Figure 12.1), and many other sponsorships and charitable activities, GSK donated more than $600 million in charitable giving in 2006 alone. In addition, GSK's own grassroots outreach campaign—using sales representatives to evangelize the company—provides the firm with a positive public image.

All of these efforts have helped the company to counter instances of negative publicity—especially those that surface on the internet. Conduct a search for "GlaxoSmithKline" on Google, and you'll fail to find a single web page—among the first 20 listings—attacking the pharmaceutical giant. Conduct the same search at Technorati and you're more likely to find a positive blog post than you are a negative one. Still, GSK doesn't assume that its traditional corporate communications will always be effective in countering any negative attacks on its reputation. The company knows that a single seed of discontent can quickly grow into a full-fledged reputation crisis. As Michael Pucci, GlaxoSmithKline's vice president of external advocacy, explains, "You've got to be aware of what your critics are saying."

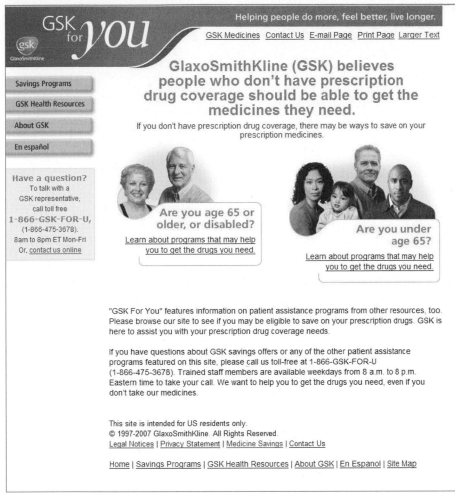

Figure 12.1 GlaxoSmithKline's "GSK for You" website

Avoiding Surprises

Being "aware" of what's being said about your reputation online is a vital component of any effort to produce positive results while becoming radically transparent. The lessons you learned in Part 2 of this book will help you to build a great foundation, but even the most solid reputation can be shattered by the murmurings of an unhappy stakeholder. In Part 3, you'll learn how to monitor your brand on the internet, how to react to an online crisis, and how to repair your reputation should you suffer a crisis. In this chapter, you'll learn why monitoring is vital to your reputation management efforts. In Chapter 13, you'll become familiar with the different tools available to monitor your online reputation. In Chapter 14, you'll discover strategies and tactics for repairing any damage to your reputation. And in the final chapter, you'll piece everything together using our seven-step action plan.

The internet is a "growing source of information," says Pucci, which is why GSK keeps a watchful eye on what's said about the company. The pharmaceutical mega-firm knows that by monitoring the conversations involving its brand, it can stay one step ahead of any pending reputation crisis. "The purpose is not to be taken by surprise," says Pucci. By monitoring your own reputation, you won't be taken by surprise either.

Why You Should Monitor

Despite 95% of chief executives believing corporate reputation plays an important role in achieving their business objectives, only 19% have a formal system in place to measure their company's reputation (according to a survey by PR firm Burson-Marsteller). And, as you learned in Chapter 1, only 20% of corporations have a formal process for monitoring blogs posts that mention their company. What appears to be a mere business oversight is actually an act of reputation *hara-kiri* when you consider recent research from John Tschohl, president of the Service Quality Institute in Minneapolis (www.customer-service.com). According to Tschohl, a recipient of good customer service will tell only five other acquaintances on average. Yet, a recipient of bad service will tell ten people—maybe even hundreds if he's a blogger or a member of a social network. Ask Dell about the damage a single computer owner can do to a company reputation. Speak to JetBlue about the devastating damage a brand can suffer when it strands hundreds of passengers without explanation. Listening for stakeholder discussions on blogs, social networks, and other social media may not prevent a reputation crisis from occurring, but the earlier you learn of stakeholder grumblings, the faster you can react.

This lesson was learned by computer manufacturer Lenovo. The Chinese-owned company closely tracks any online mention of its company name or its most popular product line: ThinkPad. In September 2006, as part of its web monitoring efforts, Lenovo tracked a report that a laptop computer had burst into flames at Los Angeles International Airport (LAX). The following report was posted in a forum at SomethingAwful.com.

> " So we're waiting for a flight in the United lounge at LAX. The flight next to ours was heading to London and in the middle of final boarding when suddenly this guy comes running the wrong way up the jetway, pushing other boarding passengers out of the way, he quickly drops his laptop on the floor and the thing immediately flares up like a giant firework for about 15 seconds, then catches fire. "

From additional reports and photos, the laptop was identified by forum members as a Lenovo ThinkPad. Once this identification was made, it quickly came to the attention of Lenovo's Vice President of Marketing David Churbuck. "Within four hours of the incident it hits my radar," reveals Churbuck. Realizing that time was of the essence, Churbuck had a team of Lenovo scientists on an airplane to LAX within an hour, with orders to examine the laptop that had caught fire and replicate the incident. In the meantime, Churbuck and his marketing team continued to monitor the online conversation. Churbuck tells us he "tracked that initial SomethingAwful post which then extended to the LA Times, which then hit the blogs and went like wild-fire over 3 days." Fortunately for Lenovo, this early awareness allowed it to quickly confirm the issue came from a Sony-supplied battery and promptly issue a recall—Sony later went on to recall millions of laptop batteries.

Mainstream Journalists Monitor Your Reputation Too!

Outside of a sex scandal, a corporate crisis is the next best thing for a newspaper or television network. Any time mainstream media can report on the downfall of a company—even if it's only a single flaming laptop—they're going to sell newspapers or attract viewers. If your brand is widely known, you should expect that mainstream reporters are going to monitor the Web for anything newsworthy about you. But don't think you'll fly under the radar just because your company is not a household name. Journalists still monitor general industry news and, if they find a particularly juicy piece of gossip or scandal about your brand, might report on your dire straits.

The lesson here is that you need to know exactly what's being said about your reputation online. If you follow our advice and suggestions, you'll likely hear about it before the *LA Times*. Even a single-hour head start on discovering a scandal is better than hearing it first from a journalist on the other end your telephone.

Early notice of events that affect your reputation, either positively or negatively, is one of the many reasons that you should monitor your reputation. You've worked hard to build your brand—maybe even spending millions of dollars in the process—and a single unanswered incident can quickly unravel your hard work. As Churbuck suggests, "Things can escalate negatively, very rapidly. An individual consumer, a random John Smith, can do an immense amount of impact on our reputation in a matter of days."

What You Should Monitor

Before you start any reputation-monitoring campaign, it's important to take the time to identify which brands and identities could come under fire. Your company name, your product brands, and your own personal reputation are a given—you certainly want to know any time these are mentioned on the internet. However, effective reputation monitoring requires you to also keep a watchful eye on your competitors and trends in your industry. As internet marketing firm RedBoots's Nan Dawkins recommends, "To be proactive, you need to monitor a broader range of topics, issues, even events the organization is linked with publicly." To ensure you're not blindsided by a reputation crisis, here are the five areas we recommend you monitor closely:

- Your own brands
- Your marketing campaigns
- Industry trends
- Your competitors
- Your known weaknesses

Your Own Brands

As GSK understands, there are many touch points for stakeholders to interact with your brands—ranging from consumers to media, doctors, and regulatory agencies. The drug firm is constantly subject to review, criticism, and also praise. In fact, GSK is a prime example of a company that has multiple brands to monitor.

Company Name

GSK has multiple versions of its company name to track. GlaxoSmithKline, Glaxo, and GSK are just the tip of the iceberg for the company. As a result of multiple mergers, the company also has legacy brands to worry about such as Glaxo Wellcome and SmithKline Beecham—each of which has its own historical brand lines.

Compiling a list of all the iterations of your company name will help you understand what you should track on a regular basis. Even if you're lucky enough to have just one or two variations on your company name to worry about, add them to the list of company brands to monitor.

Products and Services

How many product brands or service marks does your company have? GSK has hundreds of prescription brands—including Advair, Wellbutrin, and Imitrex—as well as dozens of well-known over-the-counter products—such as Aquafresh, Nicorette, and Tums. With so many product names, GSK would spend hours monitoring its reputation and leave little time for the research needed to create groundbreaking medicine. So how can GSK, and you, determine which products should be monitored?

If you have just a handful products or just a couple of services, you'd be wise to add all of these brands to your tracking list. However, if you're like GSK, with hundreds of products to monitor, we recommend that you play close attention to those that matter most to your business. These are those products or services that contribute a significant share to your revenues, as well as any that are predisposed to comment by stakeholders—GSK's antidepressant Paxil is constantly discussed by patients and the media. How you determine which make your list, and which don't, is up to you. However, we suggest paying close attention to those that are more closely tied to your brand—Lenovo is mostly concerned about "ThinkPad" mentions.

Tracking Trademark and Copyright Infringement

Monitoring your online reputation also means watching for trademark and copyright infringement. Not only should you watch for conversations that involve your brands, but you should also keep a lookout for their unlawful use. While trademark and copyright laws don't prevent others from using your brand names, they do afford you protection should another company try to use your trademark name for their products or to copy your sales material.

If you want to outsource your copyright infringement monitoring, Copyscape.com offers automated services starting at $4.95 per month.

Executives and Spokespeople

Jean-Pierre Garnier is rarely out of the public eye. GSK's chief executive has the ability to garner attention on controversial topics such as animal rights testing and has even faced a shareholder challenge of his compensation package— which was consequently overcome. "I'm no shrinking violet," says Garnier in an interview with *The Guardian* newspaper. "Being a chief executive is not a popularity contest—sometimes you have to go against the grain." Your CEO may not be quite as vocal as Garnier—or GoDaddy's Bob Parsons—but you can be sure that at some point, his comments will spark a discussion that affects your reputation. However, while your CEO is often subject to the brightest reputation spotlight, there's often plenty of room for others to gain their fair share of examination.

Anyone that speaks on behalf of your brand should be added to your list of keywords to monitor. For GSK, Michael Pucci is often the public spokesperson for the company. Likewise for your company, you may have key individuals who speak at conferences or participate in media interviews. Those who have the potential to stick their feet firmly in their mouths should be added to your list. If the only reputation you need worry about is your own—as with Senator Barack Obama—add your name to the list and hope you never provide a sound bite worthy of criticism. Of course, as Hillary Clinton discovered, even a trusted fundraiser can also cause reputation havoc.

> ### Thought Byte: Some Stakeholders Can't Spell
>
> Pay attention to common variations and misspellings of your brand names. GlaxoSmithKline is often spelled as three individual words ("Glaxo Smith Kline") and Michael Pucci also goes by "Mike." You can guess how many times *Jean-Pierre Garnier* is misspelled by bloggers and consumers.
>
> What are common misspellings of your brands? Add these to your monitoring efforts.

Your Marketing Campaigns

Potential disasters or corporate crises are not the only activities needing reputation monitoring. Your marketing efforts are designed to share good news about your brand and ignite passion in your stakeholders. To be sure they achieve their goals, you need to track these as well!

"There's a lot of opportunity for positive comment," advises Will Critchlow, director of Distilled, a reputation-monitoring company in the United Kingdom. Positive comments are definitely going to happen—especially if you use our suggestions in Part 2. If you're proactive in guiding the conversation, you'll generate many opportunities to track the positive sentiment surrounding your brand.

When Lenovo decided to create the "Lenovo Tapes" (Figure 12.2)—a spoof video that showed ThinkPads with holographic projectors and jet thrusters—it decided to plant a link to the videos using the comments section of a single blog. The company then waited for mention of the video to start reaching their reputation radar. "We did a lot of care to track that stuff," says Churbuck. "We wanted to see if we could track the spread." Track it they did. And within 72 hours, Lenovo had tracked the campaign from a single innocuous comment to dozens of news sites and blogs.

Industry Trends

Sometimes conversations take place that affect your reputation without ever actually mentioning your company, products, or executives. Trends in your industry can reveal areas of opportunity, or potential disasters, long before your brand is specifically mentioned. Proposed legislation by the Food and Drug Administration (FDA) may not explicitly mention Glaxo, but if it has any impact on the company's drug research, product launches, or patents, you can bet the company wants to know about it.

THE LENOVO TAPES

Note: The following website contains footage of alleged tests taking place at a Lenovo research facility. The producer of this site has no opinion pertaining to the authenticity of the media.

Welcome to The Lenovo Tapes.

Earlier this year some very interesting tapes were handed to me from a long standing acquaintance of mine. The tapes originated at a Lenovo (the Chinese company that recently took over IBM Thinkpad) research facility and appear to feature test footage. When my acquaintance watched the tapes back, he found some footage that he just had to get it out into the public domain. I've watched the material myself and I've got to agree with him – it's pretty amazing stuff.

The Tapes

There are nine tapes in total, featuring hours of footage - most of which consists of an empty room with not much going on. I've sifted through most of the film and pulled off some of the most interesting sections I have found. Assuming Lenovo haven't freaked and threatened to sue me, I'll post some more soon.

Lenovo

I've read just about the entire Lenovo site and although they state that they are a global leader in the PC market who develops, manufactures and markets cutting-edge, reliable, high-quality PC products, blah, blah, blah… the tests that appear to have been recorded here are taking things to a whole new level. Do Lenovo intend to release this technology on the market or are these concept laptops to show what they can do? I've done some internet research of my own and found some interesting stuff, have a look at my links page.

To protect his identity, my acquaintance asked me not to mention where the test facility is or disclose any information about the company he works for, so please don't track me down and ask me, OK?

Figure 12.2 The "Lenovo Tapes" website

You should monitor any keywords that relate to your industry. Dawkins suggests, "If you are an SUV manufacturer you obviously need to pay attention to conversations that are building around SUVs, energy consumption, climate change, etc." Knowing what's being discussed in your industry not only helps you prepare for problems that could impact on your reputation but also sheds light on positive trends that you can leverage for your benefit. "When the niche you are working in is being talked about, that's when potential customers are open to hearing about your side of the story," says Critchlow.

Thought Byte: What Trends Affect Your Reputation?

What industry trends might affect your reputation? While you hope never to find yourself embroiled in a heated industry topic, thinking ahead now will allow you to learn if your company is ever mentioned.

Your Competitors

Prescription drug manufacturing is a competitive industry. Pharmaceutical companies are in a constant race to research, test, and release new blockbuster drugs. GSK finds itself chasing the tail of Pfizer—the world's largest drug company—while fending off challenges from rivals Novartis, AstraZeneca, and Merck & Co. Understanding each competitor's strength, weaknesses, and reputation challenges helps GSK better position its brand in the marketplace.

Whether you have a single competitor, or dozens, adding their brands to your monitoring efforts will bring big rewards. Every time your competitors are mentioned on a blog, or discussed in a forum, there typically follows valuable information that can assist your reputation-management campaign. Coca-Cola would have a hard time tracking the reputation of every brand of bottled water, but you can bet they closely followed the reaction to news that rival PepsiCo's Aquafina was simple tap water. Coca-Cola's own Dasani brand also uses tap water from local municipal water supplies.

Your Known Weaknesses

You won't always have advance warning of a reputation crisis. Lenovo's laptops had never caught fire in an airport before, so keeping an eye on media mentions for "laptop fires in airport" did not occur to David Churbuck and his team. However, knowing in advance that a laptop battery could catch fire—something that happened to Dell just three months prior to Lenovo's plane incident—was enough to put the company on notice to keep a lookout for the potential issue.

Your brand has a weakness. If this is a shock to you, we apologize for being the bearer of bad news. However, it's better that you acknowledge your failings now than wait to have them pointed out to you by one of your stakeholders—or the *LA Times*. Your weakness could be your customer service or the quality of your products, or it could be a CEO who likes to "go against the grain." Whatever your weakness, add it to the list of things to monitor on a regular basis.

> ### Thought Byte: What Are Your Weaknesses?
>
> Make a note of any potential brand weaknesses. If your customer service is a work in progress, tracking media mentions that include your brand and "customer service" would be worthwhile. "Sucks," "boycott," "recall," "worst," and "evil" are just some of the many qualifiers that could be included in an online conversation that includes your brand.

Where You Should Monitor

There are two trains of thought when it comes to monitoring your online reputation. Lenovo's Churbuck likes to "cast the net wide," believing "you can't write anyone off as insignificant." Alternatively, you can focus on the "centers of influence," choosing to concentrate your monitoring efforts on the "people like me" locations. There are advantages and disadvantages to each approach, so let's review each strategy in more detail.

Casting a Wide Net

Deciding to monitor a wide range of activity is the easiest strategy to set up, but it is often the hardest to filter and make sense of what's discovered. Taking this approach is a great option if you're not sure where your stakeholders hang out on the Web. Instead of spending hours tracking down the forums related to your industry or carefully analyzing which bloggers tend to discuss your area of operation, you set up a perimeter fence—a cyber trip wire, complete with bells that ring whenever a stakeholder approaches your reputation territory. If anyone mentions your company name, products, or biggest rival, you'll know about it.

Likewise, for those of you with little time, the wide net approach is a great way to experiment with just how vulnerable your reputation is. If you find that your brand is hardly ever discussed online, you have a safety net that gives you peace of mind should a rare reputation attack happen. However, if you find that your wide net is quickly full with online conversations and feedback, you can then decide to take a more targeted approach to your monitoring efforts.

The wide net approach may suit you well. You'll be able to track mainstream media, bloggers, forums, and most other social media. In the next chapter, you'll learn there are plenty of tools available to help you cast a wide monitoring net and see what you haul in. Conversely, you may find that the ease of setup that comes from the wide net approach is offset by having to filter irrelevant noise and false positives. Churbuck admits that of the brand mentions that are caught in his net, "half of them we just dismiss." In fact, Churbuck tells us that of the "400 blog mentions of ThinkPad or Lenovo per day," more than half are false positives—including sales literature, spam, and what he calls "accidental mentions."

Finding the Centers of Influence

A little more effort—but potentially less work in the long run—is to take the time to identify and monitor the centers of influence for your brand. As you learned in Chapter 1, your stakeholders tend to hang out together online in special-interest groups, social networks, and blogs. Savvy travelers will likely participate in discussions at TripAdvisor.com.

Computer aficionados might share their thoughts on the forums at CNET. Similarly, car fanatics might interact within the blog comments on Jalopnik.com or Autoblog.com. Your centers of influence will be unique to your brand. Your stakeholders may swarm around message boards but stay away from blogs. Alternatively, you may find them hanging out on social networks. Understanding your stakeholders' preferred gathering point will help you better refine and target your monitoring efforts.

Industry Blogs

Most of you will have influential bloggers that regularly discuss your industry and exert their influence on the perception of your brand. In Chapter 5, you learned how to locate bloggers that focus on your area of expertise. That same list you built for your public relations campaign can be used to seed your list of blogs to monitor on a regular basis. If these blogs mention your brand, your CEO, or an emerging trend in your industry, you need to know about it. Even with a broader approach to monitoring, Churbuck admits that Lenovo pays "a lot of attention to who blogs about us on a regular basis and who has audience."

Vertical Communities

In Chapter 10, you learned about the different social networks (e.g., LinkedIn), and in particular social communities, (e.g., MySpace). But which communities should you monitor on a regular basis? As you heard from Neil Patel, "The best social network is the one that the majority of the people in your industry use." While MySpace and Facebook are likely to be on your list of social networks to monitor, there are many specialized networks targeting specific niches. We call these networks "vertical communities."

Vertical communities are social networks hyper-focused on your industry. We already mentioned TripAdvisor many times throughout this book, and it is a great example of a community formed around a niche topic: travel. As social networks continue to grow in popularity, so do the popularity of vertical communities. Finding the vertical communities that are most likely to discuss your brand will help you better target your reputation-monitoring strategy.

Employee Hangouts

If you want to get a good idea of where your stakeholders hang out on the internet, ask them! Okay, so your customers might be a little freaked-out if you ask them where you can find them lurking on a Friday night, but they're not your only stakeholders. Your employees—especially those passionate about your brand—will often frequent online discussions that relate to their careers. Ask your employees where they go to discuss your company, which networks they use for their industry information, and which blogs they read on a regular basis. Uncovering the favorite web destinations of your employees will likely reveal the same haunts used by your customers, investors, and journalists.

Your Business Location

If you think your reputation monitoring begins on the internet, you're already one step behind. The conversations you discover on the Web typically started with some kind of memorable experience with your brand. Understand where your stakeholders first interact with your brand, and you'll have a better chance of intercepting their grumblings, before they start up their computer.

If you have a storefront or real-world premises, begin your reputation monitoring at every stakeholder touch point. It could be a survey you ask a customer to complete, a clearly displayed toll-free number for feedback or complaints, or a simple "How was your experience with us today?" question from a manager. If you don't have face-to-face interaction, an online survey, e-mail follow-up, or instant "live" chat box are just as effective.

The key is to monitor your customer's satisfaction with your brand as soon as possible. The old adage "An ounce of prevention is worth a pound of cure" applies here.

A Blended Approach

If you're struggling to decide which monitoring strategy will best suit your circumstances, we have good news for you: you can do both. In fact, you may find that your reputation-monitoring plan starts off with a wide net and then quickly narrows focus as you determine your centers of influence. Additionally, even if your strategy involves paying attention to just a couple of bloggers or forums, you may cast a wide net just in case your own "Jeff Jarvis" blogs about your business.

A blended approach to reputation monitoring is a great balance between keeping a close eye on a voracious industry blogger while still maintaining enough peripheral vision to avoid being sideswiped. The tactics we present in Chapter 13 will help you achieve this blended approach to your reputation monitoring.

When You Should Monitor

When is the best time to start monitoring your reputation? Now! That might sound somewhat flippant, but we really do want to stress how important it is for you to start monitoring your reputation right this minute. Even while you've been reading this book, conversations have taken place that mention you or your business. The sooner you set up your monitoring initiative, the sooner you'll discover your reputation strengths, weaknesses, opportunities, and threats. There's also the opportunity to create a benchmark of where you reputation is today (see the sidebar "Benchmarking Your Online Reputation"). How is your brand perceived, how often are you getting your message across to bloggers, and how many results on Google are positive versus negative?

Benchmarking Your Online Reputation

Before you begin monitoring your reputation, it's important to understand your starting point. Depending on what channels you decide to monitor, you'll learn a lot about your reputation-building progress by keeping track of your accomplishments. You might use spreadsheet software to record some of the following data points as benchmarks for comparison with future success:

Customer surveys If you're not already surveying your customers, you should consider doing so. Understanding your customers' satisfaction with you or your business will help you better identify areas of weakness and give you ideas for potential issues to monitor. If you know ahead of time that your customers rate you "poor" for customer service, you can monitor for any mention of poor customer service across the Web.

Ratings and reviews If you're a consumer electronics company, benchmark the reviews and rankings on sites such as Amazon.com or Epinions. If you sell products on eBay, what's your current seller/buyer rating?

Social media relevance How many bloggers have linked to your website? Technorati will show you that number. How many times has your business been mentioned on Digg.com? Search for it at the social bookmarking site and you'll discover that number. In Chapter 10 you decided to participate in particular social networking sites. Measure the number of friends in your network or the number of people who have already joined your group.

Google reputation You've already identified your main keywords to monitor: company name, products, executives, and so forth. Search for each of these keywords in Google's web search and take a close look at the top 10 results for each. How many talk positively about you? How many would you rather weren't displayed due to their negativity? Put these numbers into a spreadsheet and update your progress frequently.

Other data analysis In the next chapter you'll learn how to mine your website analytics software to discover trends in website traffic. You'll also learn about sentiment analysis and how you can keep track of how positively or negatively your brand is perceived. You should add these data points to your benchmark report too!

Need more ideas? In Chapter 9 we looked at "Measuring Your Blog's Success" and provided different measurements to track. Many of these can also be used for your benchmarking.

Not only should you benchmark your reputation as soon as possible, but you should also set a schedule for how often you monitor. Deciding to monitor your reputation "whenever you can" is akin to getting your oil changed "now and then"—it sounds good until the engine blows up on you. A damaged car engine is expensive to repair, but a damaged reputation can be even more costly. So, how often should you monitor your reputation? David Churbuck says Lenovo needs to monitor their reputation "almost in real time."

How You Should Monitor

Before you faint at the level of work needed to maintain that ideal, don't panic! In the next chapter we're going to show you how to automate a lot of your reputation monitoring. And in case you really don't have the time or resources to monitor your reputation yourself, you'll also learn about some low-cost monitoring tools, as well as the more expensive, professionally managed services.

Monitoring Your Online Reputation

Now that you understand the importance of monitoring your online reputation, it's time to decide on your approach. Many free and inexpensive tools make it possible to set up a monitoring system without breaking your budget. If you prefer to automate your monitoring efforts, there are some solutions that offer to do the heavy-lifting for you—while still keeping you in full control. Alternatively, if you'd rather your reputation-monitoring campaign be handled by experts, you can outsource the task to a professional monitoring firm.

13

Chapter Contents
Do-It-Yourself Reputation Monitoring
Making Sense of the Data
Automating Your Reputation Monitoring
Knowing When to Take Action

Do-It-Yourself Reputation Monitoring

Many free or inexpensive tools are readily available to assist with your reputation monitoring. Although there are some professional services for outsourcing this task—as you'll discover later in this chapter—it's definitely worth the effort to give DIY monitoring a try. By setting up your own monitoring campaign, you'll learn firsthand where your stakeholders are hanging out. In addition, no one understands your brand like you do. Even the best reputation-monitoring company might overlook a blog post you would find important, or ignore the comment of a forum user whom you happen to know is one of your best customers. Even if you ultimately find it too much work to do yourself, you'll at least have a better understanding of what needs to be monitored, if you give it a try.

Three Essential DIY Monitoring Tools

How you decide to monitor your reputation is entirely up to you. Some companies get by with a daily visit to the most important blogs or a quick scan of industry news each morning. However, you'll likely find it far more useful to set up an automated system that will monitor the Web for you and let you know if it finds something that matches your monitored keywords—such as your company name. Automated monitoring comes in many shapes and sizes, but you'll find these three tools essential: an RSS reader, e-mail updates, and tracking software.

RSS Reader

Throughout this book, you've read about the pervasiveness of RSS feeds in social media. The fact is, RSS and social media go hand-in-hand and just about every social media site is accompanied by an RSS feed. Keeping all of these RSS feeds in a central place is the job of an RSS reader, or "aggregator." An RSS reader manages all of your subscribed RSS feeds and lets you sort and filter the delivered content, based on your specific needs. Google Reader is one of the best RSS readers—and the market leader. Google Reader (google.com/reader, Figure 13.1) is available for free and lets you do the following:

Create folders to manage different RSS feeds.   All feeds related to your company name are automatically added to the appropriate folder or you could separate RSS feeds by type of content—blogs, mainstream media, social bookmarks, and so forth.

Sort your RSS feeds by date updated.   This allows you to keep track of how a conversation spreads to different sites.

Highlight new items while archiving older ones.   You'll know about the most recently updated RSS feeds, but can also search through the old ones too!

Share RSS feeds.   You can create your own RSS feed and share items with others on your team. You can also e-mail a new RSS item to someone else at your company—perhaps your PR team.

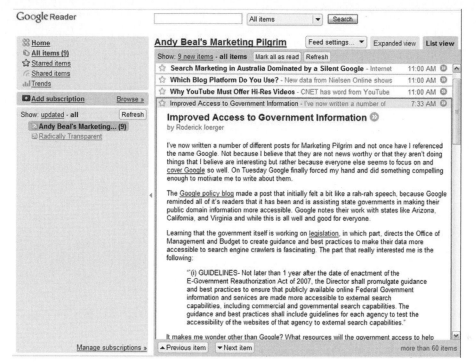

Figure 13.1 Google Reader

An RSS reader will be the single most important tool in your DIY monitoring toolbox. Most of what you track can be done using RSS feeds and a good RSS reader.

Alternative RSS Readers

If you don't like Google Reader, you'll find many other options available. Also worth using are Blog-lines.com and NewsGator.com. You can also set up a customized browser start page—complete with your RSS feeds—using services such as Netvibes.com.

E-mail Updates

In addition to RSS feeds, some of your monitoring will be done via e-mail updates. Although not quite as efficient as RSS—you could end up managing multiple e-mails to your inbox—e-mail updates are important because not all websites provide an RSS feed. For example, you may wish to monitor an important industry newsletter for trends or the possible mention of your company. It's likely the newsletter is only accessible by visiting a particular website or subscribing to an e-mail version. In these instances, you'll need to create specific rules and folders in Microsoft Outlook, or your e-mail software of choice, so that you can keep track of these important e-mails.

What if e-mail is the only option available to you? What if you just don't want to learn how to use an RSS reader? That's okay. While an e-mail-only approach won't quite give you the same monitoring options as RSS, it's better that you monitor using e-mail than not at all.

Convert Any RSS Feed to E-mail

If you're sure you don't want to deal with an RSS reader, FeedBlitz.com offers a service that will convert any RSS feed into e-mail. Simply provide FeedBlitz with the URL of the RSS feed you wish to monitor and it will send any updates to you via e-mail, instant messenger, or even Twitter!

Tracking Software

There are some websites that just don't make it easy for you to track them. Business profile sites such as the Better Business Bureau, consumer complaint sites such as RipOffReport.com, and even your competitors' own websites lack an RSS feed or e-mail update. How do you keep track of these? For tracking the "untrackable," you can turn to specialized—but easy-to-use—software designed to monitor changes in web content.

Search Google for "monitor web pages" and you'll find a slew of tools that offer web content tracking software. Our favorite is Copernic Tracker (Copernic.com, Figure 13.2), which, for a onetime fee of around fifty dollars, lets you keep track of changes to just about any web content. Here are some suggestions of what can be tracked using Copernic Tracker:

- Specific forum threads that mention your business
- Business profiles on sites such as the Better Business Bureau
- Your competitors' websites, especially their company news page
- Just about any web content that doesn't offer an RSS feed or e-mail subscription

Twelve Channels for DIY Reputation Monitoring

The channels you decide to monitor will be determined by your goals and your industry. If you operate in a very tech-savvy field—such as Lenovo—you may find that you need to pay greater attention to blogs and forums. Others might find the need to monitor specific communities that focus on their industry—such as Cafepharma.com for

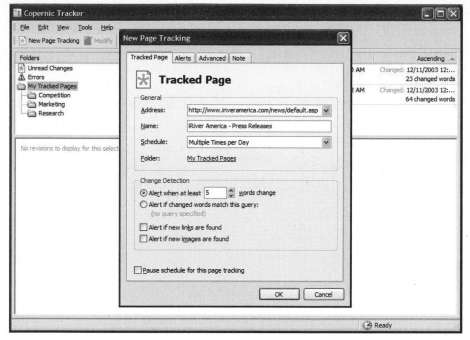

Figure 13.2 Copernic Tracker

pharmaceutical sales professionals. As you discover which channels are more likely to include conversations about your reputation, you'll hone your listening skills. In the meantime, we've compiled a list of 12 conversation channels to consider:

- Your own content channels
- Social media and blogs
- Google's network
- Industry news
- Stakeholder conversations
- Social communities
- Social bookmarking sites
- Multimedia content
- Forums and message boards
- Customer reviews
- Brand profiles
- Web analytics

The first four channels provide a "wide net" approach to your reputation monitoring. Those of you looking to also find your "centers of influence" should include all channels.

Your Own Content Channels

Before attempting to track the millions of blogs that make up the blogosphere or diving into the thousands of forum threads that discuss your industry, your first task is to ensure you're monitoring your own company channels. Whether stakeholders have a complaint or a compliment, they'll likely register it at an official company channel first. This means that you absolutely need to have a system in place to keep track of comments left on your own blogs, threads added to your own product forum, and statements made on any company maintained social community. Likewise, track feedback that comes via your customer service toll-free number or e-mail, and log any complaints or suggestions made by your employees.

Tracking customer feedback on the internet is a difficult task. You can save yourself a lot of work by identifying customer issues or employee concerns before they hit the Web.

Social Media and Blogs

The majority of your DIY reputation monitoring will occur via the use of a broad-sweeping social media search engine. Throughout this book, you've heard a lot about Technorati. Now it's time to put the leading social media search engine to good use. Technorati doesn't just track the 110+ million blogs that float around the blogosphere—it also indexes video content and mainstream media articles. It's Technorati's ability to make a wide sweep of your online reputation that secures Lenovo's vote as the most important channel in its DIY monitoring toolbox. "Our primary daily tool is Google Reader with RSS on Technorati," says Lenovo's David Churbuck.

Technorati offers a number of search options, so it's important to tailor your initial search correctly—otherwise you could miss an important comment about your brand. Here's how best to set up Technorati to track your reputation:

1. Conduct a search at Technorati for one of your previously identified brand keywords.

2. Select your chosen level of "authority." This is a useful filter for monitoring purposes. If your brand is mentioned many times a day, such as "GSK," you may wish to refine your search to look for content that has "a lot of authority," meaning the blog or news site is very popular. However, as you know, even a new blog can start a cascade of negative reporting, so we advise selecting "any authority" as your search preference. To select this option, go to the Blog Search Settings box, which is located in the upper right of the search results screen, and make a selection from the With Authority pull-down menu.

3. By now you should have a Technorati search results page that looks something like the one shown in Figure 13.3. This represents everything Technorati has found on the Web that matches your chosen keyword search.

4. Your last step is to click the Subscribe link—located just above the right hand of the search results—and add this search as a custom RSS feed to your RSS reader of choice. Now whenever Technorati discovers new content—blog post, video, news article—that matches your search criteria, you'll receive an update in your RSS reader.

If you set up searches in this way for all of your identified brands, you'll create a monitoring system that will track roughly 80% of all possible mentions of your reputation. However, Technorati does have some holes in its net, which is why the next channel is also important.

Figure 13.3 Technorati search for "GSK"

Google's Network

Google is important to your reputation-monitoring campaign, not just because it's the world's largest search engine, but because it's the world's largest reputation engine. Perhaps the most important reason for adding Google to your reputation channel lineup is that you need to be aware of all relevant web content that makes its way into its search index. If there's a positive review about your business, you need to know about it, but if a negative blog post makes its way into the first ten results for your brand, it's even more important to be alerted immediately.

While software such as WebTrends's WebPosition (WebTrends.com) offers the ability to monitor Google search results for multiple keywords automatically, it's not an officially sanctioned Google product. Instead, Google offers its own Google Alerts service (Google.com/alerts) to help you monitor your reputation across Google's network using e-mail alerts. Google Alerts is a reputation lifesaver with the option to monitor your keywords across the following channels:

Web Content that appears in Google's main search engine index.

News Items that appear in the 4,500 news sources of Google News

Blogs Blog posts that are discovered by Google Blog Search

Video Videos discovered by Google's comprehensive video search engine

Groups Posts and threads across Google Groups, including its Usenet archive

Comprehensive All of the above channels

While you can set up custom RSS feeds for all of these channels (except Web), Google Alerts actually works very well using e-mail. Enter your brand keyword and then select from one of three alert frequency options: Once a Day, Once a Week, or As It Happens. Whenever Google finds a match, you'll receive an e-mail complete with a summary of the discovered web content, along with a link to the original source.

Google Alerts allows you to customize multiple keyword alerts, each with the channel and frequency of your choice (see Figure 13.4).

We recommend selecting Comprehensive and As It Happens to ensure the fastest and widest monitoring option, but you could be creative in your customization. Here are some ideas for customizing your alerts:

• Receive a once-a-week summary of your competitor's blog mentions.

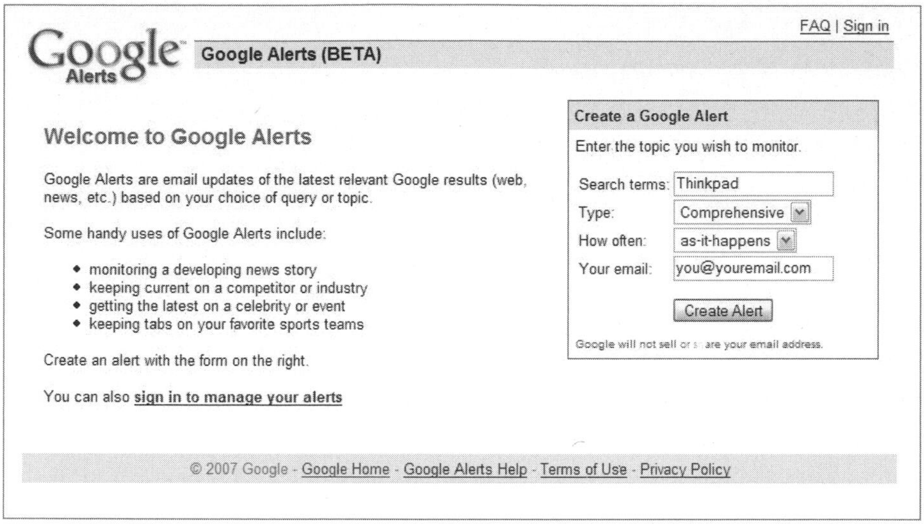

Figure 13.4 Google Alerts

- Get a daily recap of news specific to your industry.
- Set up comprehensive alerts for your brand name and the word "sucks" and get notified the moment you're mentioned this way in a Google Group.

Between Technorati and Google Alerts, you can build a DIY monitoring campaign that would rival even the most sophisticated professional tools—saving you a lot of money in the process.

Refining Your Search Queries

As you start monitoring your reputation, you may find that your chosen keywords are not specific enough. Maybe you share a name with a famous football player and don't care to get updates on their career, or perhaps your company shares the name of a famous fruit (Apple) and would prefer not get alerts on the state of the fruit industry. There a few things you can do to refine your search queries:

- If you're tracking keywords with multiple words, place them in quotation marks to tell Google, Technorati, and so forth, that you want to see *only* results that match exactly the entered text. For example, use "Glaxo prescription benefits" (with the quotes included).

- Google and many other monitoring tools also allow you to include "negative match" keywords by appending your query with a minus sign and the word to ignore. For example "Joe Montana -football" (no quotes needed) would be a good idea if your CEO's name happens to be Joe Montana and you want to filter any results about the former football player.

Industry News

Predetermining all keywords that you wish to monitor can be a tough task. Unless you happen to own a crystal ball, it is hard to think of all the future trends that might affect your industry. With this in mind, monitoring general industry-related news can help you look for opportunities to promote your brand, or to make provision for protecting it from a looming industry crisis.

Moreover.com is one of the largest providers of industry-specific RSS news feeds, and you can browse a list of industries it covers at Moreover.com/rss. You can track additional industry-related news by subscribing to one of the many topic-focused RSS feeds found at Yahoo! News (news.yahoo.com/rss) or Topix.com (topix.com/dir).

Keep an eye open for "meme" tracking sites that cater to your industry. These aggregators of industry news often provide RSS feeds to allow you to keep up-to-date on industry-specific blog posts or news articles. Examples include Techmeme.com (Figure 13.5) for technology-related news and Memeorandum.com for political news.

Figure 13.5 Techmeme.com

Stakeholder Conversations

It is difficult to track conversations that happen outside the confines of a blog post or forum. As Lenovo's Churbuck admits, "The hard thing for us is tracking comments… those are not easily detected." Whether a single comment on a blog or a conversation at one of the many social conversations sites (see Chapter 10), it's a difficult but important part of your DIY monitoring campaign.

If you already know the blogs most likely to discuss your brand—maybe there's a post about you published already—you can look to see if they offer an RSS feed to just their post comments. If they do, subscribe to this feed and you'll be able to monitor post comments for mention of your brand. If you can't locate an RSS feed for a blog's comments, services such as Co.mments.com will track comments for you and give you an RSS feed subscription.

If you want to track the spread of a conversation from one blog to another, BlogPulse.com's Conversation Tracker (Blogpulse.com/conversation, Figure 13.6) will let you enter the URL of a blog post and add a keyword—such as "ThinkPad." This allows you to use the resulting RSS feed to remotely track other blogs that link to the original blog and discuss that keyword.

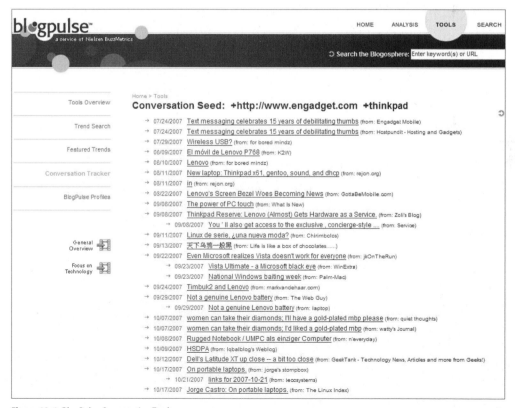

Figure 13.6 BlogPulse Conversation Tracker

Lastly, many conversation sites offer an RSS feed that allows you to track discussions specific to your brand. For example, Yahoo! Answers will provide an RSS feed that tracks any question (or answer) that includes your brand name—simply enter the keyword in the search box and subscribe to the resulting feed.

Social Communities

While you have a good chance that either Technorati or Google Alerts will bring to your attention any mention of your brand on a social network such as MySpace, you shouldn't rely on it. While some social community search engines exist—IceRocket.com offers a MySpace-specific search index—they are few and far between.

Once you've identified the social communities your stakeholders tend to frequent, your best bet is to look for any RSS feed provided by the community, or use a tool such as Copernic Tracker to monitor for mentions of your brand.

Social Bookmarking Sites

If your reputation comes under fire, you can bet that others will start bookmarking the blog posts or forum threads that discuss your downfall. Likewise, if you create a positive viral marketing campaign—such as the Lenovo Tapes—your reputation will receive a big boost from stakeholders sharing the content with their friends and peers.

You have two options for monitoring mention of your brand across the dozens of social bookmarking websites. First, and most arduous, is to visit each individual site, enter your keyword, and subscribe to the resulting RSS feed. The second, and more convenient, option is to let a service such as Keotag.com (Figure 13.7) do the heavy lifting for you. With Keotag, you simply enter the keyword you wish to track and the service then presents you with matching bookmarks from 18 different sites, including Digg, del.icio.us, and Reddit. As an added convenience, Keotag provides the RSS feed for each option too, making it easy to subscribe without having to visit each social bookmarking site individually.

Multimedia Content

Images, video, and other multimedia content will be your toughest monitoring challenge. Unlike the HTML standard—used by most web pages—multimedia appears in many formats and standards, making it hard for the search engines to index and for you to monitor. Fortunately, there are still some ways to set your multimedia monitoring on autopilot.

Figure 13.7 Keotag Search for "Lenovo"

When it comes to tracking web videos, Google leads the pack with its Google Video service (video.google.com, Figure 13.8). Originally designed to keep track of videos uploaded specifically to Google, the video search engine now indexes video from multiple video sources. While you can use Google Alerts to keep track of videos discovered by Google, the service is also one of the few that Google offers with an RSS feed for results. Enter the keyword you wish to track and look for the subdued "RSS" link at the top right of the screen. Subscribe to this feed and you'll receive updates any time Google Video finds a match.

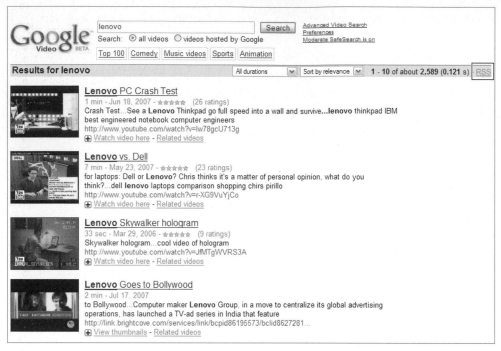

Figure 13.8 Google Video search for "Lenovo"

For image monitoring, we suggest paying close attention to Flickr.com. The service is a leader in image hosting and if your CEO is snapped exiting a strip club, the photo will likely be posted on Flickr. Should you want to cast your net wider, you'll find the general search engines fail to provide RSS feeds for their image search indexes. However, Pixsy.com offers a comprehensive image search index; the site will let you sort images by most recent and provide an RSS feed so you can monitor for new image results. Also refer to Chapter 7 for other photo-posting sites that might contain relevant images.

Forums and Message Boards

The structure used by most forums and message boards is not conducive to reputation monitoring. A forum thread can be started on any topic and each thread can have dozens—even hundreds—of replies. When you multiply this by the number of forums for your industry, you can see why your reputation can so easily be damaged by a forum without you ever discovering the conversation.

To track forum conversations, we recommend a two-pronged approach. First, conduct your research from Chapter 10 to determine the most influential forums for your brand. Depending on their size, you may select two to five of these forums to monitor closely for conversations about your reputation. If your targeted forums offer

RSS feeds, consider yourself blessed because most forums don't—if not, look for e-mail alerts or simply use Copernic Tracker to track changes to forum threads.

The second tactic is to use a service such as BoardTracker.com (Figure 13.9) to set up custom search results for your monitored keywords. BoardTracker monitors more than 32,000 message boards and forums, so it's definitely worth taking a few minutes to set up custom searches for your most important brand keywords and subscribing to the resulting RSS feed.

Figure 13.9 BoardTracker search for "Glaxo"

Customer Reviews

Your industry no doubt has its identifiable sources for reviews and opinions. E-commerce sites are often rated at Epinions, computers are reviewed by CNET, and the latest prescription drugs are discussed at WebMD. Even if you're a manufacturer or distributor—meaning you deal with other businesses, not consumers—there's still likely an online location to rate and review your company.

Monitoring your online reputation also includes watching the places your stakeholders convene to share opinions and ratings for products and services in your industry. You may be lucky and discover just one or two popular web destinations—*many* travel reviews happen at TripAdvisor—or you may find reviews are spread over multiple sites. The key is to determine the online locations that exert the most influence on your reputation and track them closely. With the majority of review sites not designed to offer updates, you'll likely need to use tracking software to keep up to date with any changes to the reviews of your company.

Brand Profiles

As you've learned throughout this book, there are many websites that keep a profile on you or your business. LinkedIn, Naymz, Facebook, and many others allow you to control what is said about you. However, many online profiles provide you with little or no control over what is said about your brand. With this in mind, it's important to keep a close eye on sites that could influence a customer's buying decision or a journalist's perception.

Public profiles can take many shapes and formats. Your brand could be summarized on a broad profile site such as ZoomInfo.com. Additionally, your niche might be covered by a specialized profile site. For example, physicians are rated at HealthGrades.com. If your brand is very well known, you might even find your company, founder, or spokesperson profiled on Wikipedia. Identify the sites that are most likely to influence your stakeholders—maybe the ones that are on the first page of Google for your name—and add them to your DIY monitoring efforts.

> ### Thought Byte: Check Your Own Background
>
> Did you know that just about anyone can conduct a background check on you for less than ten dollars? Do you know what would come up in any resulting report? Individuals should check what's displayed on any background report, correcting any errors, and companies should check what's shown on a background report for their CEO, investors, and so forth. Intelius.com is one of many services that offer background checks.

Web Analytics

It is easy to overlook the last channel when compiling your own monitoring campaign. While keeping track of your reputation across the Web is important, sometimes you can find clues by monitoring the traffic coming to your website. Free web analytics tools are becoming more commonplace—with Google Analytics leading the way—so there's no excuse for not monitoring your website data.

You web analytics package can provide an early reputation alert, sometimes highlighting trends before they show up via one of your other monitored channels.

While there are many reports you can analyze, web analytics expert and author of *Web Analytics: An Hour a Day* Avinash Kaushik suggests focusing on three main areas:

What search terms are being used to bring visitors from Google? Kaushik advises, "If you're suddenly getting a lot of traffic for your brand name plus 'sucks,' that's something to think about."

Look for swarms of traffic from a single source. "Look for traffic that is showing up from Technorati, or from Digg, or these kinds of aggregators. Individual blogs may not show up, but these kinds of sites will," suggests Kaushik.

Watch for changes to the top entry pages. Kaushik says that changes to the top entry pages may be "an indicator that something is going on." If you see a sudden change in the most popular entry page to your site, then it could indicate a new conversation about one of your products or services. If most visitors enter your website via your home page, a jump in web traffic leading directly to one of your product pages could signal a new conversation.

Making Sense of the Data

A challenge of setting up your own reputation-monitoring campaign is figuring out what to do with all the data you collect. Although you might simply read each RSS or e-mail alert and respond accordingly, this approach leaves a lot of valuable data on the table. Filtering the "signal" from the "noise" will help you target the web content that truly affects your reputation. Likewise, keeping track of developing stories will ensure that you don't overlook a single blog post. And, lastly, what's the overall sentiment of the conversations? Are you improving your reputation, or is it in a tailspin? Drilling down into the data will make sure your monitoring efforts truly help you grow and manage your online reputation.

Appoint a Reputation Manager

Have you decided who's going to be responsible for reading each of the alerts that arrive in your inbox or fill up your RSS reader? When you find a conversation about your brand, which department should be sent the details? Is it a function of marketing, PR, or the web development team? Will you have a single person monitor your reputation, or will you assign a team to monitor the data? Taking the time now to answer these questions will help ensure that when your company is mentioned on a blog, a process is in place to ensure that the correct action is taken.

For Lenovo, David Churbuck considers reputation monitoring to be an "extension of the PR team." Churbuck uses a small team to monitor Lenovo's reputation throughout the day, with the responsibility of taking action resting squarely on his shoulders.

Drilling Down on Conversations

As you'll learn in Chapter 14, not every forum discussion or MySpace comment needs a response. For GlaxoSmithKline, there are numerous mentions of their brands, and a response to each would require a team with dozens of eyeballs. Instead of responding to everything, Mike Pucci and his team look for the continuation of a conversation or some sign that the conversation is starting to spread. Pucci says, "Anything more than 15 mentions and it starts to become significant." That's when Pucci starts "looking under the covers at the situation."

When you first discover a conversation about your brand, that's when you should flag or tag the conversation. The action you take will depend on the potential impact on your reputation. Here are some suggestions for drilling down on discovered conversations.

- Does the conversation platform offer an RSS feed? For example, if you discover a blog post that mentioned the quality of your customer service, you may want to subscribe to the blog's RSS feed (plus the comment feed, if offered) and watch specifically for the continuation of the conversation.

- Start tracking the spread of the conversation. We've already mentioned Blog-Pulse and Co.mments.com, but you can also use Technorati to watch for signs that other blogs are joining the conversation. Simply enter the URL of the discovered page into the Technorati search box and it will show you a list of all blogs that link to it.

- Use Copernic to monitor the page for changes. The conversation starter might return to the site to update her original blog post or forum thread. These updates may not make it into the site's RSS feed. Copernic will allow you to monitor for any changes to the page.

- Look for new phrases or statements to add to your monitoring efforts. "Dell Hell" didn't become a popular sentiment of discontent until Jeff Jarvis used it on his site. Did a blogger just accuse you of "warranty deceit"? Add that to the list of keywords you're monitoring and make sure it's not spreading to other stake-holders or members of the media.

"Tracking the overall conversation topics, tone, and even growth of specific communities, can help you address inaccuracies or rumors early in the game and help you guide your communication strategy," suggests Redboots's Nan Dawkins.

Sentiment Analysis

For Dell's Lionel Menchaca, understanding the company's reputation means "looking at sentiment beyond anecdotal evidence." As Dell's online reputation watchdog, Menchaca carefully analyzes the company's perceived reputation, in particular whether it is considered positive or negative. Of the blog posts, comments, and conversations tracked by Menchaca, "48% were negative at the high point" in 2006, with that number "down to 28%" in 2007—a dramatic drop. With this kind of sentiment tracking, Dell is able to go beyond the simple observation of conversations about its brand and understand how well it is doing in identifying and shifting the tonality of the conversations.

So how exactly do you keep track of whether conversations are positive or negative? Well, you can use one of the many professional monitoring services you'll read about later in this chapter, but you can also implement your own simple sentiment analysis tracking. Take a look at Figure 13.10 and you'll see a suggestion for a simple sentiment analysis spreadsheet. We recommend you add this to the benchmarking suggestions we presented in Chapter 12.

Sentiment Analysis						
	Positive Count	Negative Count	Total Per Channel	Positive Last Month	Negative Last Month	Total Per Channel
Own Channels	20	8	28	16	12	28
Blogs	55	19	74	43	25	68
Google's Network	37	11	48	40	8	48
Blog Comments	112	38	150	56	22	78
Del.icio.us bookmarks	16	2	18	13	5	18
Flickr Images	6	1	7	3	9	12
Forum Mentions	19	7	26	12	18	30
Amazon Reviews	3	1	4	0	2	2
						0
Total for Month	268	87	355	183	101	284
Sentiment Percentage	75%	25%		65%	35%	

Figure 13.10 Sentiment analysis spreadsheet

When you create your own sentiment analysis spreadsheet, include the channels that you've decided to monitor. Each month, create a new sheet and update the numbers. By archiving the data, you'll be able to track changes and trends in your online reputation. Here's a final tip. If you're not sure how to determine if a conversation should be labeled positive or negative, simply ask yourself whether you would want to show the conversation to your biggest customer. If the answer is "yes," mark it as positive—if "no," it's more than likely a check for the negative column.

Automating Your Reputation Monitoring

Even if you're overwhelmed at the thought of setting up your own reputation-monitoring tools and digging through the data, it's still very much worth the effort. Taking the time to create custom alerts and conducting your own sentiment analysis has a way of ensuring that you're fully engaged with your stakeholders—and highlights just how vulnerable your online reputation is. Still, you may decide that you'd rather find a way to put your reputation-monitoring efforts on "auto-pilot" or hand the task to a provider that's already built sophisticated monitoring and reporting tools. If this sounds like you, then the remainder of this chapter is dedicated to you. Over the next few pages, you'll learn about some low-cost solutions that remove much of the elbow grease involved. If that still sounds like too much work, skip to "Managed Reputation-Monitoring Services" and you'll discover where you can find professional monitoring companies to do all of your reputation monitoring chores for you.

Automated Monitoring with Manual Analysis

If you're content to collect the data and analyze the sentiment but just don't want to set up all of the different RSS and e-mail alerts, we totally understand. Setting up your own reputation monitoring, while highly beneficial, is also extremely laborious and not everyone has the time needed. Fortunately, realizing this, a few companies offer services that attempt to automate a vast amount of the monitoring work, leaving you to focus on the output rather than the setup. Of the many tools that offer an automated approach to reputation monitoring, you may wish to consider the following.

ACS's Serph

There are few free reputation-monitoring tools that offer an intuitive interface and cast a net wide enough to monitor most conversations on the Web. ACS's Serph (Serph.com, Figure 13.11) is not only easy to use, but also monitors sites such as Technorati, Google, and Flickr. Best of all, you won't pay a penny to use it. Of course, with such a low price tag, Serph is pretty lean when it comes to customization and filtering options. For example, while you can conduct as many searches as you wish, there's no central management system for keeping track of results. Still, Serph is a great tool for those who don't have time to set up individual feeds and offers features such as:

- You can add a list of website URLs you don't want to see included in Serph's results (such as your own company blog).
- There is a unique RSS feed for each keyword search.
- Serph's web interface lets you see where the results came from (e.g., Technorati or Google).
- Serph offers a list of suggested keywords to consider based on your current search.

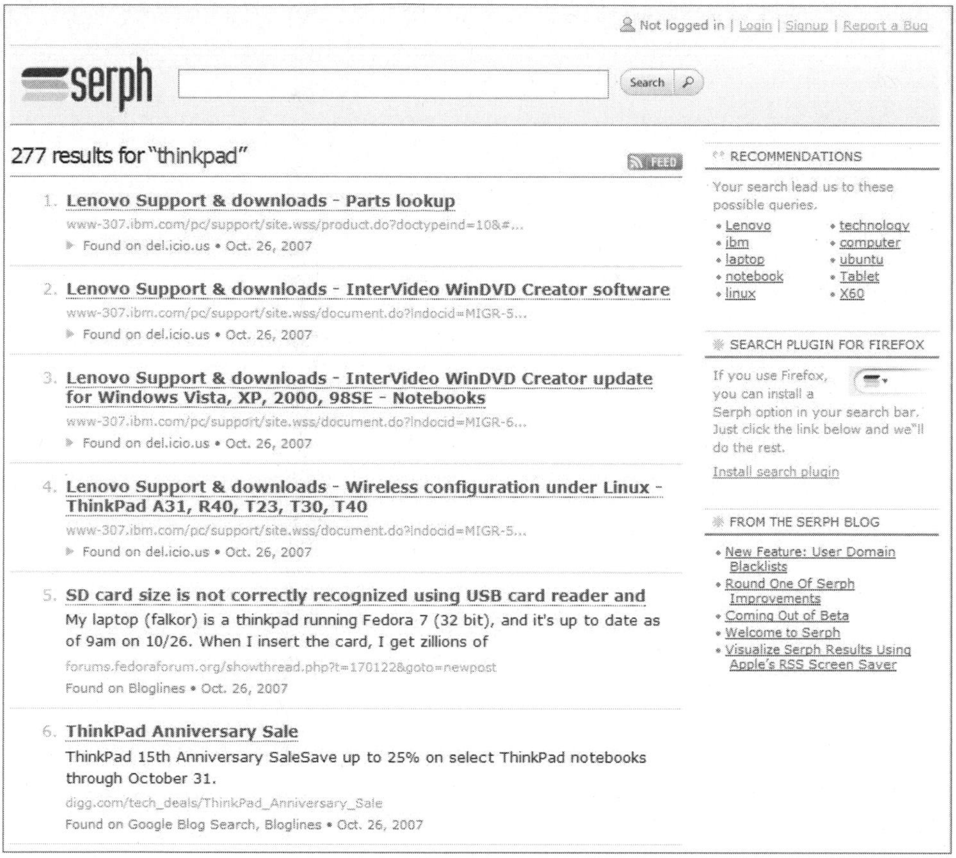

Figure 13.11 Serph search for "ThinkPad"

Distilled's Reputation Monitor

Distilled's Reputation Monitor (www.Distilled.co.uk, Figure 13.12) is a great option if you need an automated monitoring solution but would still like to be able to fine-tune some of the settings. While not free—pricing starts at around $10 a month—you'll likely find that the convenience of not having to set up multiple RSS feeds manually far outweighs the cost of the service. With Distilled, there's very little to set up, you don't need to worry about telling it which sites to monitor, and its own search engine is comprehensive enough to cast a wide net for you. In addition, Distilled's solution offers the following features:

- You can filter out results from your own web properties.
- You can add negative match keywords to filter content that's not about you (e.g., Joe Montana).

- Discovered items are marked on a scale of 1 to 5—1 being least likely to be about you and 5 being most likely.

- You can view discovered items using a detailed web interface or have them sent to you via a single RSS feed.

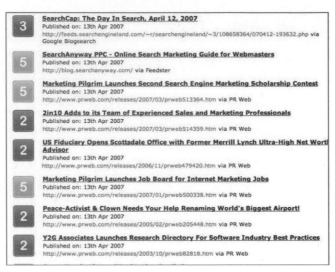

Figure 13.12 Distilled's Reputation Monitor

The World Bank's BuzzMonitor

When the World Bank decided it needed to monitor social media conversations, aggregate the data, and share it with others, it couldn't find a solution that met its needs. So it built one. Best of all, the World Bank has provided BuzzMonitor as a gift to the Web—there's no charge to use it! BuzzMonitor (buzzm.worldbank.org, Figure 13.13) is a monitoring solution that you install on your own web server. While this makes the initial setup and configuration a task for your web development team, it does allow you to use a feature-rich, fully customizable monitoring tool. Once installed, BuzzMonitor will track blogs, podcasts, videos, and photos. There are many features offered by BuzzMonitor, including:

- If BuzzMonitor discovers the same blog post via Technorati, Google, or some other search engine, it filters the duplications for you.

- BuzzMonitor will show you the Technorati and Alexa.com authority rank for each discovered item—helping you understand the popularity of the originating source.

- You can add your own tags, comments, or bookmarks for each discovered item.

- Various graphing options let you quickly visualize trends.

- You can customize RSS feeds for each keyword search or tag.

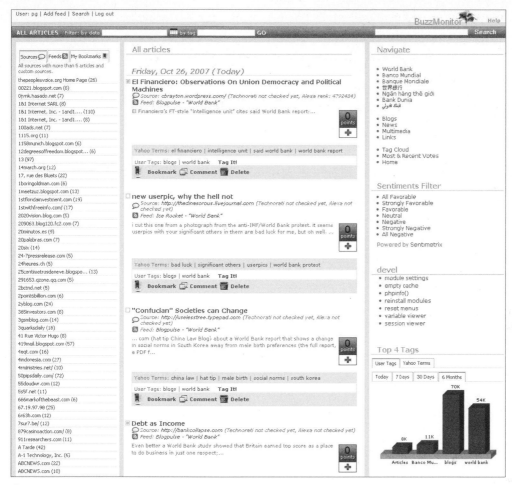

Figure 13.13 BuzzMonitor

Many reputation tools are available to help automate all or part of your monitoring efforts. We recommend making a list of the features that are important to you and estimating how much time you'd save by having access to a tool that automates the monitoring process for you. With this information in hand, you can test-drive monitoring services to see which one best fits your needs and budget. If you're lucky enough to have a line item in your budget for managed reputation monitoring—services that handle all of the setup, monitoring, and sentiment analysis—then read on.

Managed Reputation-Monitoring Services

If you decide to outsource your entire reputation monitoring and management efforts, you'll find a host of specialist companies waiting to help you. In fact, at our last count more than 80 different vendors around the world offered some kind of professionally managed reputation-monitoring services. The biggest attraction to using one of the many vendors is that the entire process is handled by a company that knows exactly how to locate your stakeholders, what conversations to monitor, and how to present the data so that you can keep track of your online reputation.

With so many companies to choose from, where exactly should you start your search for a provider that "gets" what your needs are? Social Target (SocialTarget.com) surveyed more than 30 reputation-monitoring companies and compiled a detailed report, "Guide to Social Media Analysis." In the 77-page report, Social Target provides in-depth vendor profiles, which include an overview of each company's service, pricing structure, and contact information.

While Social Target's guide isn't cheap—you'll pay $495 to get your hands on it—it more than justifies its price tag by saving you weeks of research and comparison. In the guide you'll find summarized information on the main providers in the field—including BuzzLogic, Converseon, Factiva, and Nielsen BuzzMetrics—as well as the opportunity to review some of the lesser-known monitoring companies. Figure 13.14 shows an extract of the profile for Converseon.

Although Social Target's report is an excellent resource, it doesn't offer any advice on which company is the best, nor does it offer tips for selecting a reputation-monitoring provider. While we can't tell you which company is the best option for you, because you have unique needs, we can help you with your vendor selection. Here are ten questions you should ask a vendor before placing your valuable reputation in their hands.

1. **What services do you provide?** Does the provider offer only monitoring services or will it also help you engage social media and manage your reputation?

2. **In what format are reports provided?** Are reports simply e-mailed to you, or does the company offer a web-based dashboard? Will the company customize the reports to match your business objectives?

3. **How much does your service cost?** In particular, ask the company if its fee includes unlimited users or is on a per-seat basis. If you have multiple team members, costs can quickly add up if you have to pay extra for each of them to have access to reports. Also ask if they offer a free trial or demonstration before you hire them.

4. **What sources do you monitor?** Some companies only track traditional media mentions and blog posts. Others include monitoring of images, videos, and social networks. Some providers will also monitor your customer service e-mails and support tickets. You should also ask how they filter duplicate news items and false positives.

5. **What type of analysis do you provide?** Will the company only provide reports on keyword mentions or does it provide full sentiment analysis?

Converseon

www.converseon.com

Social media monitoring and analysis combined with search marketing and social media marketing

1140 Broadway, Suite 501
New York, NY 10001
USA
+1 212-213-4297 ext 301

Other locations
Coeur d'Alene, ID

Converseon combines social media analysis with multidisciplinary capabilities in a communications-focused social media marketing agency. The company's Conversation Mining service typically supports their social media marketing services. Analysis emphasizes human insight and is delivered through reports, presentations and a client dashboard. Converseon also offers search-engine marketing services, including search-engine reputation analysis.

Converseon's engagements follow a detailed lifecycle that considers business, creative, technical, educational and policy requirements. Conversation Mining is an early step in a systematic plan to influence online conversations for clients.

Software–assisted human analysis
Converseon collects its own data and uses automated systems for preliminary analysis, including limited text analytics. The company emphasizes the benefits of human analysis in its finished research.

Traditional and new online techniques
Converseon's staff is drawn from a variety of marketing specialties, including advertising, PR, interactive, direct response, search and web analytics. The company views social media as an interdisciplinary field that benefits from a flexible approach.

- **Web analytics and Conversation Mining**
  Converseon correlates social media analysis with web analytics results. Analysis of traffic from social media sites, traffic quality and engagement metrics.

- **Hybrid influencer analysis**
  Influencer analysis combines link analysis with an

☑ Monitoring
☑ Research
☑ Consulting
☑ Dashboard
☑ Agency
☐ Software

Highlights
- Focus on research
- Social media marketing
- Human analysis

Founded	2001
SMA since	2004
Employees	10/25
Revenue from SMA	25%
White label	No
Traditional media	Yes

Contact
Rob Key
robkey@converseon.com

Geography
North America, Europe

Languages
English, French, German, Russian, Chinese, Korean, Spanish

Company bloggers
Constantin Basturea,
blog.basturea.com
Paull Young,
youngie.prblogs.com

converseon>>

Figure 13.14 Converseon vendor profile by Social Target

6. **How do you analyze the data you collect?** Does the provider rely heavily on human analysis or do they have automated software solutions? Humans are prone to error, and will limit the scale of the campaign—there's only so much they can track. Meanwhile a heavy reliance on software could mean that subtle nuances or colloquialisms are missed.

7. **Which countries and languages do you monitor?** If you only conduct business in the United States or English-speaking markets, you'll find a wider selection of

providers available to you. If you have stakeholders in China or need tracking in Spanish, you should make sure the provider can accommodate these needs.

8. **Which companies have you worked with?** Like any vendor selection process, it's important to speak to existing customers and make sure they are happy. For example, BuzzLogic will tell you that Lenovo is one of its clients.

9. **Will you work with my other agencies?** If you outsource your corporate communications to a PR firm, will your vendor of choice work closely with them and share resources?

10. **What type of client support do you offer?** Some service providers offer limited web-based support, while others offer experienced account managers. Decide what level of support you'll need from any selected vendor.

The Benefits of Outsourcing Your Reputation Monitoring

Although professional monitoring services often come with a hefty price tag—expect to pay upwards of $10,000 per month for some companies—there are many good reasons for outsourcing your reputation monitoring. We asked Social Target's principal Nathan Gilliatt to explain the main benefits of using an external company:

There's no learning curve. "Outsourcing lets you start immediately, without the learning curve and potential hiring required to build your own capability."

You have access to skilled professionals. "You can't hire the level of experience that specialist firms already have on staff."

You can mix and match vendors. "You may want to work with more than one vendor to take advantage of their different strengths. This is particularly relevant in the international context, but it also applies to the different services available and how you might choose to apply them."

Knowing When to Take Action

Whether you decide to set up a DIY monitoring campaign, implement one of the many automated tools, or outsource the entire job function to a professional monitoring firm, there will come a time when you'll need to take action on what you uncover. If you're lucky, you'll be blessed with many happy stakeholders, and your monitoring efforts will reveal nothing but praise and admiration for your brand. If you live in the real world, you'll more likely discover that even the most respected reputations— JetBlue, Dell, Matt Mullenweg—are subject to the errant rant of a single blogger, the critical probe of a journalist, or the collective complaints of forum users.

Even with the strategies you learned in Part 2 of this book, it's almost inevitable that your monitoring efforts will at some point discover an attack on your reputation. It may be a legitimate complaint—JetBlue customers really were stranded for hours—or it might be a misunderstanding—such as Matt Mullenweg's search spam incident. Just as damaging, a false rumor could arise—perhaps something your competitor started—and without action could become a dark cloud of doubt hanging over your otherwise stellar reputation. Your reputation-monitoring efforts will ensure you're alerted to all online conversations—good or bad—but when you discover an attack on your reputation, it's important to take rapid, appropriate action. In the following chapter, you'll learn the best way to respond to a reputation attack and repair any resulting damage.

Repairing Your Online Reputation

Despite your best efforts to build a positive repu-tation, there will be occasions when your brand faces an attack from a blog, forum, or social network. It's inevitable, and it's often difficult to predict or prevent a reputation attack. But you can quickly show your stakeholders that you're listening to them and learning from their criti-cism. This chapter shows you how to identify a reputation attack, when you should engage your attackers, and what steps you should take to repair your damaged reputation.

14

Chapter Contents

Apple's Reputation Sours

When Apple launched the much anticipated iPhone on June 29, 2007, the product was a success by any standard. After months of waiting for the electronics company's first foray into cell phones, consumers lined the streets outside Apple stores—each eager to be one of the first to buy an iPhone. Loyal Apple customers and new converts helped the company sell 270,000 iPhones in the first two days of availability. With the most popular model selling for $599, Apple expected to add hundreds of millions of dollars to its bottom line and saw its stock price climb from $129 per share in June to $144 at the beginning of September. Apple's reputation as a company that produced high-quality, innovative products that attract loyal customers was firmly cemented. The company was on a roll, and there was seemingly nothing that could derail the iPhone juggernaut—except perhaps Apple itself.

On September 5—less than two months after the iPhone launch—Apple's CEO Steve Jobs made the unexpected announcement that it was cutting the iPhone's price tag from $599 to $399. The move came as the company attempted to align the iPhone's price with a new line of the company's flagship iPod music player, while also making the cell phone more attractively priced for the holiday shopping season. Steve Jobs justified the move by saying:

> **❝ It's very clear we have a breakthrough product on our hands, but it's also clear that many can afford it, some can't. We'd like to make it affordable to even more folks going into this holiday season. ❞**

The news sent shockwaves throughout Apple's stakeholder communities. The media speculated whether Apple's iPhone sales were slowing while investors were spooked by the severity of the price drop—causing the stock price to fall 5% by the end of that day. Meanwhile, customers—Apple evangelists willing to stand in line to be among the early adopters—felt they had been cheated into overpaying for their iPhone. Journalists peppered the company with questions, bloggers discussed whether customers had been deceived, and forums were buzzing with critical comments. Steve Jobs himself "received hundreds of emails from iPhone customers" who were upset about Apple dropping the price. Apple's previously flawless reputation was bruised, and the company needed to move quickly to avoid leaving a sour taste in the mouths of its stakeholders.

Steve Jobs Quickly Repairs the Damage

While some companies may have ridden out the storm of criticism or stood firm in their decision, Steve Jobs understood that continued stakeholder passion is an intrinsic part of Apple's success. Within 24 hours of his price-drop announcement, the CEO posted an open letter on Apple.com announcing a $100 store credit to all customers who had previously purchased the iPhone. The letter explained the company's reasoning for the sudden drop in price, but also acknowledged that the company had failed to take care if its loyal customers. The final paragraphs of Steve Jobs's letter read:

> " …even though we are making the right decision to lower the price of iPhone, and even though the technology road is bumpy, we need to do a better job taking care of our early iPhone customers as we aggressively go after new ones with a lower price. Our early customers trusted us, and we must live up to that trust with our actions in moments like these.
>
> Therefore, we have decided to offer every iPhone customer who purchased an iPhone from either Apple or AT&T, and who is not receiving a rebate or any other consideration, a $100 store credit towards the purchase of any product at an Apple Retail Store or the Apple Online Store. Details are still being worked out and will be posted on Apple's website next week. Stay tuned.
>
> We want to do the right thing for our valued iPhone customers. We apologize for disappointing some of you, and we are doing our best to live up to your high expectations of Apple.
>
> —Steve Jobs, Apple CEO "

This token of goodwill helped Apple avoid what could have been a catastrophic reputation crisis. The company's response was swift, reasonable, sincere, apologetic, and authentically delivered by Steve Jobs himself. Most importantly, Apple's griping customers positively received the compromise and quickly went back to evangelizing the company's products.

By listening to its stakeholders and responding quickly, Apple went on to realize a 67% profit rise in its fiscal fourth quarter, a stock price high of $189, and total iPhone sales of 1.4 million by the end of October. It wouldn't be the last misstep the company would make with its iPhone in 2007, but Apple had learned the valuable lesson of listening to its stakeholders' complaints and reacting quickly to protect its valuable reputation.

Why a Reputation Attack Is Inevitable

Apple's iPhone misstep is a great example of just how quickly a crisis can escalate on the Web. Even though the company boasts one of the world's most respected brands, Apple simply didn't anticipate the widespread backlash it would face from the iPhone price reductions. While it may appear that the company had tripped up for the first time in its 30-year existence, it simply faced its first major revolt of the social media–enabled era. Apple's iPhone fiasco occurred during the increasing adoption of blogs, social networks, and other social media as a platform for sharing complaints. Customers had complained about Apple's products, services, and policies before, only now the amplification of social media ensured Steve Jobs, and a few million others online, heard the message loud and clear.

As you've discovered throughout this book, there are many opportunities for your stakeholders to share their views about your reputation. If you ruin a traveler's vacation plans, she'll seek revenge by seeding message boards with negative comments, complaints on review sites, or telling friends in her social network. Likewise, if enough laptop owners suffer at the hands of your poor customer service, they'll support a blogger ready to pick up the flag and lead the attack against your reputation. Or, it could be a simple case of a customer frustrated at not being able to get an official response from your company, so he instead decides to post a complaint on RipOffReport.com in an attempt to get your attention.

Figure 14.1 shows the JetBlueHostage.com blog that appeared shortly after JetBlue stranded its passengers in February 2007.

> ### Thought Byte: Do You Have a Service Recovery Plan?
>
> Many reputation attacks can be avoided by simply ensuring that you have a plan in place to respond to customer complaints before they reach for their computers. Customer service strategist John Tschohl suggests that JetBlue could have avoided a PR nightmare if it had taken faster action. "No one at Jet-Blue made an empowered decision to get those passengers off those planes," Tschohl says. "And when the airline offered passengers a free ticket, at an average price I would put at about $200, it was too cheap in its compensation, particularly for passengers who had endured 11 hours on its planes."
>
> Tschohl recommends companies put in place a service recovery plan for immediately responding to customer complaints. "When a customer approaches you with a problem, you must act quickly, take responsibility, make an empowered decision, and offer some form of compensation," Tschohl says. "When you do that, you will have a customer who will be loyal for life."

THURSDAY, FEBRUARY 15, 2007

Daily Sally Blog: Jet Blue Boo-Boo

http://dailysally.blogspot.com/2007/02/jet-blue-boo-boo.html

Jet Blue Boo-Boo

"Well, it's good to be free from there. Especially when the windows were iced over, you're kind of like in a sound-proofed coffin." Carolyn Faucher, JetBlue passenger stranded 8 hours

I've never trusted Jet Blue. I can't explain why exactly. It just seems a brash, inexperienced upstart compared to the big airline companies.

Apparently I'm not totally wrong.

Who lets 100+ people sit in an airplane on the tarmac for 8-10 straight hours? No matter the weather conditions, at the three-hour mark it's time to unload the plane and review options.

But instead, after 11 hours of no food, overflowing toilets, fetid air and justifiably distressed passengers, Jet Blue finally unloaded stranded passengers because ... wait for it ... the crew's flight time had "expired."

You'd think Jet Blue would have done the math before it reached that point. Think about it. They know when the crew's time will expire. They know how long the flight takes once in the air. Why wait until the crew's time has actually expired?

I don't know about you, but if my pilot's been sitting in a stuffy, overheated, under-ventilated plane with no food or toilet facilities for more than three hours--forget 8 or 10--I don't want him to fly me anywhere.

SEARCH JBH.COM

[Google Custom Search]
[Search]

IMPORTANT SHORTCUTS

ALL THINGS RUTH
ALL OFFICIAL JETBLUE CORRESPONDENCE
JETBLUE EMPLOYEES SPEAK

IMPORTANT LINKS

Charlie Becker
My Favorite travel partner and forever Valentine.

We Should Not be the only Ones
This is the project of one of passengers on #351 with me. It is an important movement, much like the Passenger Bill Of Rights. Please support.

JetBlue Press Room
I HIGHLY recommend checking back here regularly.

YOUR JETBLUE HOSTAGE COMMUNITY

My Name is Genevieve McCaw and I was a passenger on JetBlue #351 on Valentines day along with my boyfriend Charlie. We were en route

Figure 14.1 JetBlueHostage.com

Whatever the complaint (whether justified or not), your reputation will at some time or another attack in one channel or another because the Web empowers your stakeholders to take action whenever they feel that you or your brand has not lived up to its reputation. It's so easy for stakeholders to do today. As social media consultant Tamar Weinberg suggests, "Today, we're in a world—a network—where you can make one slip and you could really tumble down." With the advice you've learned from this book, you already understand the importance of using the internet to build a positive reputation. However, as you monitor the Web for mentions of your brand, at some point you'll discover a stakeholder backlash that completely blindsides you. How do you identify a reputation attack? When and how should you respond? And how do you clean up the mess and restore your reputation to its former glory? Throughout this chapter, you'll receive the answers to those questions and learn strategies you can use when your reputation comes under fire.

First Steps When Your Reputation Is Attacked

When you first discover an attack on your online reputation, it can be an unnerving event. It can feel like a kick in the ribs to see someone attack your good name. Now is the time to take a deep breath and acknowledge that if a company with as great a reputation as Apple can come under fire, so can you. In fact, with a solid reputation-monitoring campaign in place, you can guarantee that you'll discover a negative blog post, comment, or forum thread about your brand. The key is not to hit the panic button, but instead set up a strategic plan that outlines how you'll react to a negative incident.

Plan Now for a Reputation Attack

As you read through this chapter, you'll learn tactics for putting together a response in the event of an online reputation crisis. Use these tactics to create your own process for reacting to a reputation attack. You'll find it easier to react when you have a predetermined plan in place, instead of scrambling to put one together at the time of the attack. It is common for companies to have offline PR crisis plans in place, and if you are one of them, simply integrate these online tactics.

Check Your Facts

When you first discover what appears to be an attack on your reputation, it can be easy to dive right in and try to quickly resolve the situation. You may be tempted to immediately concede to the critic's demands—a new laptop perhaps—or you might even decide to ignore him and hope he goes away. While your response could include either of these choices, and more, it's important to first take the time to assess the situation before planning your course of action. Failure to do so could result in your reaction being overkill and create a precedent that will come back to haunt you. Just as likely, you could end up making the situation worse.

Rob Key, CEO of reputation management company Converseon, recommends an initial assessment before joining any conversation that involves your reputation. Key suggests looking at whether detractors "have a legitimate reason for being upset" and "how damaging might the information be" before deciding whether to engage them. If a blogger claims to have received a dud product from you, try to verify the validity of his claim—is it actually one of your products? Likewise, check as many of the facts as possible before taking any action. A customer who purchased a five-year-old Pontiac car and then complained about a leaking radiator is not as action-worthy as one who made the same complaint after driving a brand-new car off the dealer's showroom floor.

As you'll discover throughout this chapter, you'll have plenty of options for engaging an unhappy stakeholder, but don't dive into the conversation without first doing a preliminary check of the facts.

Defining Moment: Detractor

A detractor is anyone who has something negative to say about your reputation. Later in this chapter you'll learn more about the different detractor types.

Seek Trusted Advice

Although time is often of the essence when dealing with a reputation crisis, there's always time to seek advice from your trusted advisors. Just as it pays to get additional insight before firing off a heated e-mail response, so too it helps to discuss strategies before replying to a forum thread or leaving a comment on a blog.

You may already have a board of advisors, management team, trusted friend, or even a PR firm that you can tap for advice. If you don't already have any of these advisors in place, then now is the time to get them in place—don't wait until your reputation is under attack. Find someone who knows your industry, who is levelheaded, and who has dealt with similar situations.

The key is to have an individual or group with whom you can share details of the reputation attack and get input on how best to respond.

Check the Potential Damage

One of the most important early steps you should take when discovering a reputation attack is to determine the level of threat to your brand. While it's true that any online criticism can quickly escalate into a full-blown communications crisis, not everything you discover will warrant immediate action on your part. Of the hundreds of weekly discussions about Lenovo, the company carefully analyzes the chatter about its brands and engages just a handful of detractors. Here are some tactics for gauging the potential threat to your reputation.

Conversation Size

How you determine the voracity of a conversation involving your brand will vary depending on its venue. A single negative comment left on a blog post about your company might merit further observation, but not necessarily a reply from you. As Rob Key asks, "If somebody is saying something in a non-influential venue, do you want to jump in on something like that?"

Conversely, a multipage forum thread that discusses your company's poor customer service would likely warrant your full attention and participation. The number of comments on a blog, replies in a forum thread, or members of a Facebook group: these are all metrics you can use to determine if the conversation is large enough to warrant your participation.

Conversation Spread

Another important measurement is the pervasiveness of the discovered reputation attack. If you're monitoring your reputation in near real time, you'll likely discover a negative attack close to its inception. Even though the initial blog post, video, or image might not appear to have reached a large audience, it can quickly spread among other blogs and social media. Use the tactics you learned in Chapter 13 to monitor the conversation to see if it grows outside of the initial channel. If you see the conversation spreading to blogs and other social media, you may need to take action and engage the conversation in order to protect your reputation.

Thought Byte: Will It Show Up on Google?

In Chapter 6 you learned how to ensure that your web content is displayed on the first page of Google for a keyword search related to your brand. When you discover a negative attack on your reputation, assess the content to determine if it appears to be search engine optimized. Does it have your brand in the title, page name, and throughout the content? If the answer is yes, you may need to take action simply to prevent it from showing up in Google. Later in this chapter, you'll learn the tactics to use should a negative attack make it into your Google reputation.

Conversation Influence

It's one thing to learn of a negative attack on your reputation, but not all detractors have the same level of influence. In Chapter 5, you learned how to determine the most influential bloggers for your online PR campaign. Those same tactics are useful here for determining whether your detractor is influential in your industry. The same analysis can be done for most social media platforms: check the number of links to the site, check the size of its audience, and check the chances that the site will make it to the radar of mainstream media journalists.

These are the early steps, and later we'll look at the specifics of responding to attacks, whether or not those attacks are legitimate. But first, you have to understand your detractors.

Understanding Your Detractors

Before responding to any attack on your reputation, it's important to understand as much as you can about your attacker. Not all detractors are created equal, and they don't all share the same motivation for bringing your good reputation into question. Taking the time to understand if the complaint is coming from a professional griper, a loyal customer, or even a competitor masquerading as a client will provide valuable insight and help shape how best to respond.

In just about every incident, you should review the detractor's previous complaints. Not only will this tell you if he makes a habit of complaining online—perhaps he knows that the squeaky wheel gets the grease—but you'll also be able to determine if there's a course of action that appeared to appease him the last time he complained about a company. Even if you're not able to determine much about the detractors, you'll likely find they fall into one of the following five types.

The Virgin Detractor

A virgin detractor is someone who has never used the internet as a medium for complaining about a company, or at least has never before used the Web to challenge your good reputation. His reason for complaining is likely due to poorly conceived expectations about your products or services. It could also be that he simply fell through the cracks of your normal great customer service follow-up—and feels he is being ignored. Whatever his motivation, the virgin detractor will likely respond well to a personalized response from you—such as a simple apologetic e-mail.

The Platinum Detractor

You might think that a platinum detractor gets her name from her hard-hitting attack on your reputation, but that's not what she's about. While her critique may well be harsh—and she may use multiple channels to voice her chagrin—she earns her platinum designation because up until this point, she's been one of your most loyal and valuable customers. Apple's early iPhone buyers would likely fall into this category. Platinum detractors often require a "white glove" approach as they are not only authentic in their complaint because they've earned the right to know what to expect from your business, but they represent potential lost revenue if they decide never to buy from—or recommend—you again.

The Determined Detractor

There is long-honored internet advice for the detractors who appear determined to make your life miserable and continually attack your reputation: "Don't feed the trolls." If you a face a determined detractor, you'll discover she requires careful consideration before making any decision to engage her. Conspiracy theorists, serial complainers, and former employees with a grudge all fall into the category of determined detractor.

You'll likely never satisfy your determined detractors, so for the most part you'll simply accept that they exist and go about your normal business—you can't please everyone. However, monitor your determined detractors to ensure they're not spreading their unjustified rants with others. If your detractor is going to "multiple different venues and spreading the same misinformation," that would be a reason to engage her, says Key. We'll discuss how to address inaccurate information later in this chapter.

The Undermining Detractor

Unfortunately, not every detractor is exactly what she claims to be. Some of your detractors will likely be your competitors, doing their best to undermine your reputation. Equally unfortunate is that it's very difficult to be 100% positive that you've uncovered an undermining detractor. She'll likely hide behind an anonymous profile, leave comments on blogs that are hard to verify, and report problems in forums without providing specifics. Fionn Downhill of search engine marketing firm Elixir Systems explains: "A very high percentage are competitors [attacking] because they can… We had one client where we traced 90% of what was going on to one IP address that belonged to a competitor."

Engaging an undermining detractor takes some finesse. Generally, their complaints will lack an audience as they'll be too vague to be seen as credible—your other stakeholders will call them out for you. However, should you suspect that a reputation attack is coming from a competitor, one of the most effective solutions is to offer an e-mail address or telephone number they can use to speak to you personally. Without a real complaint, they'll lose their voice and scurry off into the web wilderness, like rats in a flashlight beam.

The Professional Detractor

No, you don't have to worry about hired reputation hit men who accept envelopes of cash in return for an attack on your good name. A professional detractor is someone who earns a living from reviewing, critiquing, and evaluating products and services for your industry. It could be a blogger, a newspaper journalist, consumer advocate, or a podcaster. The key is that he is typically well respected, has a large audience, and can make or break your reputation with a tap of his keyboard.

Although this may sound somewhat unnerving, it's his professionalism that will help you when it comes time to engage him. He doesn't have a personal vendetta, he's not a competitor, and he tends to have a realistic expectation that not every company is 100% perfect. If he writes a scathing review, you can typically contact him and offer your side of the story—which he'll likely publish.

Figure 14.2 shows the website for the Utility Consumers' Action Network (UCAN). This consumer advocacy group website—for public utility companies in San Diego, California—is one example of where you might find a professional detractor.

Responding to a Legitimate Attack

Even though you'll discover many conversations that don't warrant your participation, at some point an attack on your reputation will meet two important qualifications. First, the attack is a legitimate critique and the detractor deserves a response from you. Second, the attack has a growing audience and left unattended will likely result in measurable damage to your reputation. Either one of these factors could be enough to engage your detractor, but whenever both are at work, it's time to roll up your sleeves, find your radically transparent voice, and respond to your critics. Take five steps when responding to a legitimate attack on your reputation:

1. Make a response from the top.
2. Admit mistakes and apologize.
3. Host the conversation.
4. Seek resolution.
5. Change from a detractor to an evangelist.

Figure 14.2 UCAN.org

Step 1: Make a Response from the Top

When you decide to respond to a detractor, the response should come from a senior, transparent, and humble voice. While you may have a public relations team available to counsel you on crisis communication, they should remain in the background and not be used to deliver any message on behalf of you or your company. Any attempt to respond using your PR team, legal department, or the designated customer service scapegoat will be met with disdain by your stakeholders.

You could follow Apple's example and have your CEO deliver the response directly, or you could assign the responsibility to another senior executive in your company. The title of the person delivering the message is not that important. What is important is that you create the perception that the issue is important enough to you to warrant a response from someone senior. "When you are getting into really influential venues, having someone speaking from authority is really important," says Rob Key. "It demonstrates that level of transparency and authenticity that social media demands."

Step 2: Admit Mistakes and Apologize

Okay, so you've decided the response should come from someone in authority—yourself, or someone preferably at the C-level—but what should you say? This is not the time to beat around the bush, make excuses, or try to defer any kind of responsibility. Remember, you're facing a legitimate attack on your reputation. You've screwed up and your stakeholders want to hear why they should continue to trust you and support your brand. Being radically transparent means eating humble pie and asking for forgiveness. "If there is a problem, admit it," says Dell's Lionel Menchaca.

Be open, be honest, and most of all take the time to explain how this crisis could possibly have occurred, what you're doing to rectify the situation, and the steps you are taking to prevent a repeat incident. Menchaca advises telling your stakeholders, "Here's what we know about it, here's what we are going to do." Taking this approach will very much help to defuse the crisis and give you an opportunity engage your detractors. "Most people are just happy to have someone talk to them and not treat them like a moron," says Lenovo's Churbuck.

Step 3: Host the Conversation

When Apple faced the contempt of its customers, the conversation spread far and wide. Complaints appeared on forums, in blog posts, and in the content of hundreds of e-mails to Apple's customer service. Responding to each complaint individually would have been akin to trying to put out wildfires one bucket of water at a time—the conversation would have continued to spread in the meantime. Instead, Apple took the approach of hosting the conversation. It decided on the venue for response, and it chose the safe harbor of its own company website.

When responding to a crisis, think twice before engaging a detractor on her own turf. "We're not going to work an issue in the comment section of their blog," explains Churbuck—who prefers to hold the conversation on neutral or company-owned channels. Engaging a critic on his own blog, forum, or social network tips the balance in his favor. Your detractor might take his time approving your blog comment, may edit the content of your forum reply, or might simply refuse to publish your response altogether. For these reasons, you should look for ways to quickly move the conversation to a more favorable arena where you have the ability to exert at least some control. Here are some suggestions for hosting the conversation:

Offer your toll-free number, cell phone, or e-mail address. Do this publicly and show your detractor and observing stakeholders that you're willing to discuss the matter with them directly.

Publish a response on your own blog or website. This worked well for Apple, and Dell has even taken the step of creating websites to discuss particular issues—such as its battery recall site (dellbatteryprogram.com). Moving the conversation to your own website will allow your stakeholders to interact with you while still giving you some control over the rules of engagement.

Find an influential conversation host. Offering yourself for an interview can be a powerful way to address a reputation attack, but needs to be done with care. If you're sure your loudest detractor is not a competitor, or someone determined to trash your good name, you can agree to an interview with her to address the issue at hand. If you have any doubts about whether you'd receive a "fair hearing"—or your detractor is using a platform that is not conducive to an interview, such as a forum—then consider reaching out to a journalists or bloggers who carry respect and authority in your industry, and offer to do the interview with them. Doing so will allow you to address your critics and answer concerns, knowing that it will be published on an unbiased website or blog.

Launch the crisis blog you've prepared. In Chapter 9 you explored the idea of building a blog that is only deployed in times of reputation crisis. If you don't already have a blog, and have instead built a crisis blog, consider whether the situation merits its launch.

There's No Such Thing as "Off the Record"

Whichever approach you take to respond to your detractors, assume that everything you say will make it into public record. Churbuck warns, "All communications are going to get blogged, [and] all phone calls will get taped." While you may get lucky—your detractor may keep your conversations private—many companies have seen their private e-mails and phone conversations published online. When you're trying to repair your reputation, the last thing you want is a threatening e-mail, cease and desist letter, or offers and suggestions as to how to rectify the matter being spun on their site as juicy bribes.

Step 4: Seek Resolution

Ultimately, your efforts should be focused on seeking a resolution that benefits both you and your detractor. You don't want to have your own personal "Jeff Jarvis," willing to spend the next 12 months looking for opportunities to comment on your products' unreliability. Instead, you want to avoid having your detractor's initial criticism leave a black mark on your reputation. As Lenovo's David Churbuck explains, "Any negative comment from an upset customer can represent a permanent scar in the search index, something which, if left unanswered, can linger."

How far should you go to seek a resolution with someone attacking your reputation? Here's a good rule of thumb: if you've already decided the detractor warrants a response from you, you should do whatever possible, within reason, to make him happy. Tamar Weinberg recommends, "It is more important than ever to go above and beyond what you'd typically expect of yourself because people really do appreciate it and that publicity can be great for you." RedBoots' Nan Dawkins agrees: "If you fix the problem successfully, you create an opportunity to generate positive word of mouth."

> ### Thought Byte: Now's the Time to Negotiate
>
> Have you considered whether the incident will leave a "permanent scar" in the search index for your brand? As part of your efforts to resolve your detractor's complaint, make sure your proposal is mutually beneficial. If you offer to replace a faulty laptop or offer compensation for flight delays, seek a concession from your detractor too. It's likely the original complaint found the attention of the blogosphere and other media venues. The more sites that linked to the original complaint, the more likely the post, comment, or forum thread will show up in a Google search for your brand.
>
> Later in this chapter, we'll show you how to try to remove a negative listing from your Google reputation, but it's far easier to simply ask your detractor to remove or update the offending post as part of any agreed resolution.

Step 5: Change From a Detractor to an Evangelist

As John Tschohl's research suggests, a recipient of good customer service will tell five other people, while a recipient of bad customer service will tell at least ten people. But what about a recipient of bad service with whom you later work and turn their experience into a positive one? Tschohl says that if you win back a detractor, they'll become a fierce evangelist—singing your praises to 20 others! Nan Dawkins saw this firsthand when Apple responded to complaints about its iPod. "They finally started paying attention to a couple of vocal detractors who were angry about their scratched screens," says Dawkins. "One of the detractors was quite vocal on forums about his satisfaction with [Apple's] response and how much he loved the product."

When customers complain about your products or services, it's mostly because they're passionate and feel let down by your actions—or lack thereof. Whenever you're able to turn a negative situation into a positive one, you should harness that experience to the benefit of your reputation. After Dell took the time to listen to Jeff Jarvis and implement some of his recommendations, he went from the company's biggest detractor to a key ally—eventually writing a glowing article about the company for *BusinessWeek*.

How *Not* to Respond to a Legitimate Complaint

Now that you've learned the radically transparent way of responding to an online reputation attack, it's time to take a quick look at responses that rarely work in your favor.

No Response There is only one situation where your decision not to respond at all is justified: if you know the complaint is completely unfounded—such as a competitor trying to cause trouble—and you've assessed the risk to your reputation and have decided that the impact will be low or nonexistent. Just about everything else will require a response from you or your company. As Lenovo's David Churbuck explains, "Some incidents, left unattended, will flare into something dramatic."

An Official Statement or Press Release After digesting the information in this book, you should already know that responding to an online attack on your reputation requires an authentic and transparent conversation with your stakeholders. The last thing you want to do is respond to a stakeholder using a one-way channel such as a press release. Rob Key warns against a response coming from anyone other than you. "Don't have a public relations agency do the outreach on your behalf," he says.

Using Fake Advocates If you happen to be Apple, you'll likely have a legion of loyal stakeholders ready to defend your good name—just try writing something negative about the company and you'll see this firsthand. Although a positive response from your advocates helps to quell any discontent, do not be tempted to create multiple fake profiles in an attempt to make it appear you have many supporters. Fake advocates are nearly always discovered, and when they are, you'll further hurt your reputation.

Using Your Attorney Unless you're suffering at the hands of continuous incorrect and defamatory attacks—which we'll cover later in this chapter—involving your legal counsel is not the way to resolve a reputation crisis. Sending a cease and desist letter will likely backfire. Not only will it not resolve the situation, but calling in the lawyers makes you appear heavy-handed—which will likely bring more supporters to your detractor's camp.

Responding to False Attacks

On May 16, 2007, popular consumer electronics blog Engadget.com posted details of an internal Apple memo that stated the company would have to delay the launch of the iPhone to October and its new Mac operating system to January 2008. Here's part of Engadget's post:

> **❝ This one doesn't bode well for Mac fans and the iPhone-hopeful: we have it on authority that as of today, the iPhone launch is being pushed back from June to... October (!), and Leopard is again seeing a delay, this time being pushed all the way back to January. ❞**

Within minutes of Engadget publishing its post, Apple's stock price dropped almost 3% as investors rushed to assess the ramifications of the product delays. What Engadget didn't know was that the memo was fake and did not originate from any officials at the company. Within half an hour of its original post, Engadget started to update its statement, confirming that it had received official word from Apple that there were in fact no product delays. Apple also took the step of informing its employees that the e-mail was not sanctioned by the company. In a follow-up memo, Apple stated:

> **❝ You may have received what appeared to be a Bullet*News from Apple. This communication is fake and did not come from Apple.**
>
> **Apple is on track to ship iPhone in late June and Mac OS X Leopard in October. ❞**

Apple was both unfortunate and fortunate that Engadget had been the first to publish the fake internal memo. Unfortunate, because Engadget is one of the most popular blogs in the world—with an audience powerful enough to affect Apple's stock price. Also unfortunate, because Engadget thrives on rumor and speculation, which meant it would publish the leaked memo without first checking the validity of the details with Apple. However, Apple was fortunate that Engadget had a loud enough voice that the electronics manufacturer was quickly alerted to the incorrect blog post. Also fortunate for Apple was that Engadget desired to maintain its credibility with its readers—and avoid legal action by Apple—and quickly updated its original post.

Once Engadget realized its mistake and published a correction, Apple's stock price recovered most of its value, as Figure 14.3 shows.

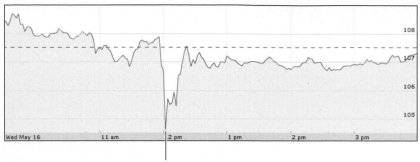

Time of Engadget.com's report on Apple delays

Figure 14.3 Apple's stock drop on May 16, 2007

Protecting Your Good Name

When you face an attack founded on incorrect information or motivated by the desire to defame your good name, always take swift action to prevent damage to your reputation. This is especially true if the attack runs the risk of spreading to influential blogs and news sites. "If a false rumor has a lot of velocity, you need to jump in," says Key.

A minor mistake by a blogger or mainstream journalist might only warrant a quick e-mail or comment with the correct information. When contacted, 94% of bloggers will remove, edit, or add correct information to any incorrect blog post, according to research by Technorati. However, there will be times when you face a determined detractor who is not motivated to remove an inaccurate statement or post. When that happens, consider the following steps:

Make personal contact. If an e-mail or comment doesn't result in the removal of an incorrect or defamatory attack, it's time to pick up the phone and call them directly. If the site in question doesn't publish a phone number, you can try looking up the site owner and phone number by examining the official WHOIS domain name registry. DomainTools.com offers such a service.

Send accurate information. When Apple discovered incorrect information posted on Engadget, it quickly sent the blog the correct information. Any time you discover incorrect information about your brand, sending the publisher evidence to the contrary is the best way to ensure they realize their mistake and amend their work.

Request a complete retraction and apology. There are two things you should seek from anyone who posts incorrect information. First, you want them to completely remove the offending information. While you may only succeed in getting the publisher to update the content with the correct information, it's better for you when the information disappears completely from the Web—remember, you don't want it to appear in Google. Second, just as you should apologize for any mistake you make, you should also ask for an apology from anyone who publishes inaccurate information that hurts your reputation. Always ask for a public apology—you may not get one, but a public apology is something you can point to should anyone bring up the matter again.

Reach out to influencers.   When Engadget published its post about Apple's rumored product delays, other bloggers started to repeat the story. If you find yourself in the same situation, make sure you get the correct information not only to the site that first published the incorrect information, but also to other influential stakeholders who have joined the conversation.

Take legal action.   There are very few times when you should involve your legal counsel in your reputation management campaign, but this is definitely one of them. If someone is publishing incorrect information and refuses to correct the mistake, your next step is to hand the information to your attorney and treat the incident the same way you would treat any libelous attack.

Cleaning Up the Mess

Now that you've taken steps to repair the damage to your reputation, your work is by no means complete. The Web has a photographic memory—you could even say a photocopier memory—with the potential for a single negative incident to replicate itself across many internet channels. Just because you've managed to make amends with your detractor or successfully removed incorrect information from a blog, that doesn't mean that it's not still being perpetuated by other social media channels. The last thing you want is for your reputation disaster to linger like a bad hangover. The following steps will help ensure there are no residual negative effects on your reputation.

Watch for the Spread

Even though Apple had quickly alerted Engadget to its mistake, the company didn't simply close the file and take an early lunch. Dozens of other bloggers had already linked to the Engadget blog post and now mainstream journalists and investors were knocking at Apple's door, seeking an explanation. While a definite inconvenience to the company—especially because it was not of its own doing—Apple engaged stakeholders across the Web and ensured anyone with influence was given the official company response. Popular technology news site CNET received such a response, publishing the following statement:

> " An Apple representative confirmed that there has been no change in the company's schedule for both Leopard and the iPhone. "The communication is a fake and did not come from Apple," the representative said. "

Once you've resolved any conflict with your detractors—or had them remove incorrect information—take the time to monitor the Web for continued discussion about the incident. You may wish to add new keywords to the list of those you monitor, even if it's only for a few days. Apple likely paid close attention to "iPhone delays" after the Engadget mistake and "iPhone store credit" after Steve Jobs's open letter to Apple's customers. In addition to monitoring topical keywords, you can use BlogPulse.com's Conversation Tracker or Technorati to make sure that news of a resolution is reaching your stakeholders or that incorrect information is no longer being spread.

Make Use of Your Supporters

When you're trying to clean up after a reputation attack, it can be hard to spread word of any resolution. Unfortunately, negative news spreads faster on the internet than the positive variety. People love a scandal and when your reputation comes under attack, blogs, forums, and social networks will buzz with the sound of gossip and discussion. Now that you've resolved the situation, you're going to find it an uphill task to get those same people to spend as much time and energy discussing the positive outcome—it's just not perceived to be as discussion-worthy.

With this in mind, you're going to need the help of your biggest supporters and sympathizers. If there are journalists, bloggers, forum moderators, or social networking groups that tend to favor your business, now's the time to bring them into your reputation repairing efforts. Send them details of the changes you made to your products, show them your detractor's follow-up post, and offer them interviews with executives at your company. If the negative news has spread to dozens of other blogs and forums, you will likely not get every one of them to follow up and close the loop on the incident. However, if you can get enough social media influencers discussing how you stepped in, apologized, and promised to make changes, then you'll have a good chance to add balance to the original discussion.

Watch for Urban Legends

If you've played the telephone game, you know just how easy it is for a message to lose its original meaning as it's passed on to others. Line up ten people, give the first person a sentence to repeat to those down the line, and by the time it reaches the last person, it has often wildly changed. The same can be said of social media—especially blogs. What might start off as a customer complaining that she spent 30 minutes waiting for her plane to take off can easily morph into a 30-hour delay with no food or water by the time the story has passed through a dozen bloggers.

Whether you've resolved a stakeholder complaint, or corrected false information, you should watch for inaccuracies in any reporting on the Web. SC Johnson, the manufacturer of Glade PlugIn brand air fresheners, has been subject to so many suggestions that its products randomly catch on fire it finally issued a statement in an attempt end the urban legend. Part of SC Johnson's official response reads:

> " ...SC Johnson recently learned that there have been postings on the Internet that have claimed that our products were involved in fires. It is important that you know that all of our PlugIns® products are safe and will not cause fires. We know this because PlugIns® products have been sold for more than 15 years and hundreds of millions of the products are being used safely.
>
> Because we are committed to selling safe products, SC Johnson thoroughly investigated these rumors. First, we confirmed that no one had contacted SC Johnson to tell us about these fires or to ask us to investigate them. Additionally, we had a leading fire investigation expert call the fire department representative who is identified in one of the Internet postings. That fireman indicated that he has no evidence that our products had caused any fire... "

Share Your Side of the Story

While it's always important to ensure that your detractors update, modify, or remove their original comments, it doesn't hurt to post an official response on your own website or corporate blog, too. You've already learned the importance of hosting the conversation, but that doesn't mean you'll always get the opportunity to resolve an incident by posting a CEO letter to your corporate website—as did Apple. There will be times when the conversation didn't take place on your own blog, or when a crisis was resolved over the telephone and not on a company message board. Still, you may wish to ensure that you leave an official response for Google, media, and future customers as a balance to what was said during a crisis. Whether it's a post on your own blog, an announcement in your press center, or even a link to the retraction posted by your detractor, consider how you can ensure your stakeholders are made aware that the crisis is not ongoing and that you did the right thing in response.

Repairing Your Google Reputation

There's a good reason why *Radically Transparent* includes an entire chapter on managing your reputation using search engine optimization (see Chapter 6): any significant reputation attack will likely make its way into Google. You should have already prepared a foundation of positive content for the search engines and applied the advice offered in the section "Five Steps to Being Radically Relevant for Google" in Chapter 6. The blogs, social networks, and profiles you built will act as a buffer against a negative attack on your reputation. However, despite your best efforts, there will still be occasions when an attack on your reputation will manifest itself among all of the positive content in a Google search. When that happens, you'll need to take the following steps to try to keep it off the first page of any search for your brand.

Assessing the Google Damage

When a detractor attacks your good name, his remarks might not immediately show up in a Google search for your brand. Google not only looks for corresponding information on a web page—in this case, mentions of your brand—but it also looks for how many other web pages link to the originating source. With this in mind, it can take a few days for a reputation attack to show up on Google.

If you haven't already signed up for Google Alerts and aren't using the service to receive notification of any new pages in Google's Web index, now's the time to do so. The moment the web page being used to attack your good name appears in Google, you need to know about it. Equally important, you should now make it a part of your daily routine to monitor the first 30 listings in Google for your brand name. Why the first 30 and not just the first 10? Your detractor's web page may not initially appear on the first page in Google (first 10 results) and may instead start off somewhere on the second or third page. While it remains off the first page, you have a good chance your stakeholders will never find it. However, you need to monitor its position to ensure it doesn't start creeping closer to that first page of results.

Some Google Results Don't Stick Around

Should you see your detractor's web page land in the first ten results of a Google search for your brand, don't immediately reach for a Kleenex. Google constantly updates its index, and its search results can fluctuate on a daily basis. One interesting phenomenon applies to blogs. When a blogger publishes a post, it typically appears on the blog's home page. The home page of any website—especially a blog—tends to have the highest credentials in the eyes of Google's algorithm. Therefore, any blog post that appears on a blog home page will naturally rank a little better in Google's search results.

However—and here's where it gets interesting—as a blogger adds more posts to her blog, the one attacking your reputation will slowly move down and eventually lose its position on the home page. Once this happens, the blog post loses the additional boost that Google gave it, which could be enough to see the post drop off the first page for a search for your brand. It may not always happen this way—especially if lots of other web pages link to the blog post—but sometimes negative results in Google simply disappear on their own.

Manual Removal by Your Detractor

As we mentioned earlier in this chapter, if you are able to come to a mutually agreeable resolution with your detractor, you should ask that the original attack be greatly edited and updated, or even removed. Even though you may have resolved the situation, Google doesn't know this and will still spider the content and add it to its index of search results.

If you're not able to get your detractor to remove the content completely, any of these compromises will help reduce the negative impact on your Google reputation:

Change the title of the blog posts, comment, or forum thread. Instead of saying "Apple is a deceiving company and I'll never buy from them again," ask your detractor to update the title to "Happy with Apple again, now they've offered a store credit."

Update the content of their complaint. What Google—and your stakeholders—will pay most attention to is the first few sentences on the web page. Unfortunately, when most detractors update their complaint, they do so by adding their words of satisfaction to the end of their original rant. Instead, ask your detractor to consider adding the positive wording to the top of their initial complaint.

Ask the detractor to remove your full name from the content. If the attack is against your personal name, or it is used as part of an attack on a company, ask the author to remove your name completely—or at least remove your last name. Google's search results for "Steve Jobs" will less likely show a complaint if the author changes the content to read "Steve J" instead of his full name.

Hide the page from Google. Adding a simple "noindex" tag in the web page code or the equivalent command in the site's Robot.txt file will allow your detractor to keep the page published, while barring Google from indexing the page.

Be Careful When Requesting Any Changes

Your best chance to get your detractor to remove or edit her complaint is during any resolution (Step 4). That is when she will be most open to making changes to her original comments. If this opportunity has passed you by, be careful about approaching a detractor with a removal request. If it has been months since the original complaint—and especially if you never resolved her issue—asking your detractor to remove her complaint could backfire on you. Fionn Downhill of Elixir Systems warns, "We stay away from trying to get something removed. It can have adverse effects where people feel you're trying to control what they say." That could lead them to author another complaint that you're now trying to bully them.

Pushing Down Negative Google Results

If a negative web page does appear in Google during a search on your brand, then it's time to step up your SEO efforts. Everything you read in Chapter 6 applies here, but there are some other tactics you can use to muscle out an unwanted page from Google's search results. It all boils down to a single statement offered by Page Zero Media's Andrew Goodman: "The only way you can trump negative publicity is with more positive publicity to crowd out those negatives." So, where is the positive content to push out the negative?

Your Web Properties

While you can build social profiles and issue press releases, Fionn Downhill recommends you focus your efforts on your web content channels: "Take control of the space with sites that you have complete control over." Not only will you maintain complete control over their content, but the sites you own will likely rank better—it's hard for Google to find web content that's more relevant than sites that are official corporate sites. Downhill says that your goal is to "surround the result with corporate controlled information that is positive."

Content for Purchase

If you're really facing a Google reputation nightmare and don't own enough websites to help spread positive content, you may need to buy some additional help. As you read in Chapter 6, companies such as PayPerPost.com, ReviewMe.com, and Sponsored-Reviews.com will put you in touch with bloggers willing to write a positive post about your company in exchange for a small fee.

Look for bloggers who are highly relevant to your industry and already have a strong presence in Google. Ask them to write about your positive achievements and most popular products as a balance to your detractor's negative comments. You're better off buying just a handful of reviews from blogs that have a good chance of displacing the negative content rather than buying dozens of reviews from poor-quality, irrelevant blogs.

Radical Transparency Extends to Blog Reviews

While using paid blog review services is a great way to push positive web content into Google's search results, don't sacrifice your authenticity and transparency in doing so. Ensure that any paid reviews include a clear disclaimer by the author that the review is a paid endorsement.

Look for Neutral Content

When you're trying to push down a negative blog post or forum thread, you don't necessarily need to displace it with something positive. Many opportunities exist in the "neutral" arena. Perhaps you share a name with someone in Hollywood, or you discover a company in another country that uses the same brand as you. Exercise a little SEO benevolence by pointing some links to their web pages and see their content creep up to the first page of Google results and push down the negative web page in the process. Sure, the web content isn't about your business, but it's better that a Google searcher find something unrelated to you than an attack on your reputation.

Look for Opportunities on Page Two

One of the best ways to identify web pages that you can optimize and push to the first page of Google results is to look at what's just outside the first ten listings—the web pages that Google ranks in positions 11 through 20 for a search on your brand. If you see your own content, or material from some of your business partners, you might be able to apply some fine-tuning or add a few links and give them enough of a boost to get them inside Google's top ten results.

When It Just Won't Budge

We would love to put your mind at ease and tell you that any negative Google result can be pushed down with some SEO brute force. Unfortunately, there will be instances when, no matter how hard you try, you simply cannot get rid of that negative web page entrenched at number one on Google's results page. We offer some final ideas to help with a negative Google result that you can't make vanish:

Address the negative result on your own site. If you're continually asked about the negative result in Google, it's better to be the one that starts the conversation. Use your own site to explain how you've addressed the criticism and what changes you've made.

Surround the negative result with positive results. If you find you can't fully remove a negative Google result, the next best thing is to surround it with as much positive content as possible. If a future customer or journalist sees that the negative content is an isolated incident, they'll likely be more understanding or think it is unimportant.

Change your name. A touch drastic, we admit, but it's certainly an option you can consider. For companies, a new name can not only signal that your business is making a fresh start and changing its past practices, but you'll also leave behind the negative Google result. Of course, you'll also leave behind your portfolio of positive recommendations and ratings online. This approach might seem tough for individuals, but even using your middle name or referring to yourself as "Steven" instead of "Steve" might be enough to distance yourself from your detractor. One warning, though: if your detractor is of the determined variety, there's nothing to stop them from attacking your new name and using your name change as "evidence" that you're disreputable.

Report them to Google. We confess, this is a long shot, but it's worth taking the time to review the negative website to see if it's violating any of Google's Webmaster Guidelines. "Hidden text," "duplicate content," and "doorway pages" are all violations that could see a website banned from Google's Web index. Search Google for "Google Webmaster Guidelines" to get a full list of prohibited items and the procedure for reporting any offending website.

> ### Thought Byte: Can You Take Legal Action to Remove It?
>
> There are a few instances when you can attempt legal action to have a negative item removed from a search engine's results. If the negative content is libelous or factually incorrect, you can try obtaining a court order—either requiring the publisher to delete it or the search engine to remove it from its index. Likewise, if the negative result infringes on your copyright or trademark, you can file an official request for removal with Google. A lot of web content is protected by "fair use" laws, but it might still be worth trying.

Preventing a Repeat Incident

Now that you've successfully resolved the concerns of your detractor, ensured the conversation is not spreading, and cleaned up your Google reputation, it's time to take action to prevent a repeat incident. As the saying goes, "Fool me once, shame on you; fool me twice, shame on me." Your stakeholders will be on the lookout for any repeat behavior, and they'll be less forgiving the second time around. With that in mind it's important to understand that your reputation is in a fragile state. You're effectively on probation until your stakeholders are confident that you've learned from the experience and seen the error of your ways. It's time to win back their trust.

Learn from Your Mistakes

In hindsight, Apple should have realized that a $200 price reduction, less than two months after launch, would leave a sour taste in the mouths of many iPhone customers. Still, hindsight is 20-20, and what really matters is that Apple learned a valuable lesson from its actions. The company now knows that if it launches a new product and then drastically reduces the pricing shortly thereafter, its customers are going to retaliate with a reputation attack. In fact, Apple's customers are now more likely to hesitate before buying any new Apple product—just in case the company pulls the same stunt again. What Apple needs to do now is to demonstrate that it has learned from the experience and will not reduce new product prices so quickly in future.

When you face an attack on your reputation, you have a good chance of repairing the damage and receiving a second chance by your stakeholders. However, you should absolutely put in place a system, procedure, safeguard—whatever it takes—to prevent the incident from happening again.

Make Stakeholders Aware of Changes

Now that you've put in place changes to your business practices, it's time to let your stakeholders know what to expect from you. JetBlue understood the importance of this when it quickly introduced its "Customer Bill of Rights," outlining the changes it had made to the way it treats passengers. Dell also realized that it needed to do a better job of explaining the changes it made to its customer service. The company achieved this with the launch of its blog and customer forum. Dell's Menchaca explains, "Show customers that you are closing the loop. That you are actually taking their feedback and doing something with it. That builds your credibility and there is no substitute for that."

PREVENTING A REPEAT INCIDENT

What If You Can't Make Changes?

While it's always beneficial to change anything that causes dissent among your stakeholders, the truth is there are some things you simply cannot change. Lenovo cannot change the fact that its largest shareholder happens to be the Chinese government—which leads to questions about whether its ThinkPads are used to spy on Americans—but it can change the public perception by ensuring it addresses these false rumors. "If fixing the problem isn't an option, or you are the target of an attack that won't stop no matter what you do, consider addressing it by telling your side of the story," recommends Nan Dawkins of RedBoots Consulting.

Include Stakeholders in Improvements

If you really want your stakeholders to buy into the idea that you're making improvements, then make them a part of the process. Remember, your stakeholders maintain partial ownership of your brand anyway and they're defining your reputation online, so bring them on board for some of the decision making and let them take some ownership of your improvements. Converseon's Rob Key says, "If they care enough to be talking about brands online, companies need to get together with consumers and co-develop and make them feel part of the brand."

Dell does this brilliantly when it allows its customers to share their new product ideas on IdeaStorm.com—which helped convince Dell to launch a Linux line of computers. "When people feel like they have a vested interest in a brand, they're going to become stronger advocates for you over time," explains Key.

Change Your Stakeholder Outreach

There's a good reason that Google includes bloggers as part of its public relations outreach. Sure, Google knows that bloggers are often very influential and can drive a conversation before anyone in mainstream media joins in, but that's not the only reason. If Google sends a blogger advance news of a story, or includes her in a conference call with a Google executive, that blogger will more likely say something positive about the company. Of course, it's not guaranteed that the blogger won't say something negative, but Google understands that by reaching out to bloggers, they'll hear the correct information firsthand, will be more likely to focus on the message Google wants to share, and will be less likely to bite the hand that feeds. Google increases its goodwill among bloggers, and in turn the bloggers are less likely to attack the company—why would they jeopardize their great relationship without good reason?

Three Little Words to Live By

There are three words that you should add to your reputation management lexicon: sincerity, transparency, and consistency. These three words will act as your reputation safety net and ensure that at all times you're acting in a manner that will protect your reputation from future attacks.

Sincerity If you're called out negatively for your past practices, simply saying "sorry" is not enough, unless you change the associated behavior. While you may appease one critic, many others will be standing by. And, should you continue to make the same mistakes, your critics will feel duped by your false apology and likely attack with greater fervor.

Transparency Once you've realized the error of your ways and decided to make a change for the better, you'll need to admit your mistakes and demonstrate why your critics should believe you have changed. Whether it's an open letter to your customers, an interview with your critics, or your own company blog post, it's important to be open and honest about your mistakes and future plans.

Consistency If you've made just one mistake, chances are you'll be able to make amends with your stakeholders. However, if your company has built a reputation of one mistake after another, it will take a lot more to convince your detractors that you have changed your spots. Your sincerity and transparency will buy you a reprieve and some breathing room, but it's your consistency in your future actions that will change the ongoing perception by your critics—and we don't mean consistent mistakes.

In Chapter 5 you looked at how to improve your PR outreach to better connect with bloggers. If you want to improve your chances of avoiding a future reputation nightmare, consider expanding your corporate communications to include influential bloggers, forum moderators, and social network owners. They'll be thrilled that you're talking with them and will more likely contact you directly—should they have a complaint—before they hit "publish" on their website. In short, treat social media journalists as well as you'd treat traditional journalists.

Bringing It All Together

Congratulations! You've successfully become radically transparent. If we could hand you a certificate as a reward for your hard work and willingness to engage your stakeholders, we certainly would. You've come a long way from Part 1 of this book—where you first learned about the importance of your online reputation, Part 2—where you learned how to use social media to build and manage your reputation, and Part 3— where you've built strategies for monitoring your reputation and repairing any damage to your brand. We can't give you a certificate—it would have gotten creased while trying to stuff it in this book anyway—but we can provide you with one last chapter that you'll hopefully find even more beneficial. In Chapter 15, we're going to share with you our seven-step action plan to build, manage, monitor, and repair your reputation. You'll find it ties everything you've already learned into a simple framework you can start implementing immediately. So let's go!

Seven-Step Action Plan

Reputation management requires new skills in this radically transparent world. To prepare for this, and to craft the kind of reputation online that will open any door, you need a reputation management and monitoring plan. The seven-step plan in this chapter asks you to do some deep introspection about your offline character and goals, then devise strategies and objectives for reaching your reputation dreams using online media. In the process, you'll set up monitoring tactics and a crisis management plan for long-term sustainability. Note that the worksheets in this chapter are available for download online (www.radicallytransparent.com/).

15

Chapter Contents

Positive Reputations Are Strategy Driven
Step 1: Identify Your Stakeholders
Step 2: Conduct a Reputation Audit
Step 3: Uncover Your Internal Reputation Assets and Liabilities
Step 4: Write Your Goals
Step 5: Craft a Strategy and Write Objectives
Step 6: Create an Implementation Plan
Step 7: Build a Plan to Sustain Your Reputation
Radically Transparent Reputation Management Is Now in Your Hands

Positive Reputations Are Strategy Driven

By now you are convinced that your company, brand, and personal reputations are important, and perhaps you even put some attention on reputation management offline. You watch your actions to be sure they project the integrity and character that is consistent with your values and the company culture. You might ask customers for testimonials to put on your website, and you deal sensitively with customer complaints. You might even have a PR crisis management plan. However, do you have a complete reputation management plan for building your reputation as well as for protecting it? Even if you have built a stellar offline reputation, you may not yet have a plan for extending it into the online environment—especially in light of the rapidly growing social media and high level of trust consumers have in each other (and not in your company spokesperson).

Not many chief executives have a formal system in place to measure their company's reputation, much less a full reputation management plan. Yet, most companies have business or marketing plans to guide them toward their goals. A strong reputation is impossible to obtain and keep without effort. Like JetBlue, you might fly high for a few years after start-up, but then the inevitable customer or employee complaint online will spoil your good name. According to communications firm Fleishman-Hillard:

> **"A strong reputation develops from disciplined focus. Achieving a stellar reputation is a strategy-driven and systematic process that builds, maintains, measures, and protects the company's reputation and allows it to achieve business goals, including creating shareholder value. "**

It is time to create an action plan for becoming radically transparent while monitoring and managing your reputation online. Before you start on the seven-step plan, however, you must decide which reputations are its focus: your company name, its product or service brand names, your executives or CEO, or yourself. Decide which among these have a reputation risk—that is, it will suffer a harmful impact with negative public opinion.

There is one final consideration before you begin. A good reputation management plan will integrate offline and online activities. The following plan begins with this holistic view of your stakeholders, reputation assets and liabilities, and reputation goals. It then focuses on reputation management strategies and tactics for implementation online. After completing this plan, we recommend integrating these with your offline reputation management strategies so that there is one clear set of mandates for both venues. There is a lot written about offline reputation management, little about online reputation management except for this book you are holding, and nothing about how to integrate the two. A holistic approach is critical because online and offline reputations easily flow between traditional and social media.

Step 1: Identify Your Stakeholders

Which individuals, communities, and organizations have a vested interest in your mission? Review Figure 3.3 (Chapter 3) for a typical CEO's primary and secondary stakeholders. Customers and employees will appear at the top of every organization's list. Now it is time to think about this more deeply—who will help the company achieve its goals if engaged in a dialogue about products and plans? Some of the many stakeholders we've mentioned in this book include:

Customers Include first-time customers (because they may need special communication for retention). Also include high-value or long-time customers because of their importance to the company (such as high-mileage frequent fliers if you are an airline company).

Online journalists Traditional and social media journalists and influential bloggers can have a huge influence on your reputation (see Chapters 5 and 12).

Industry opinion leaders These vary by industry, but commonly include industry analysts, traditional journalists, prominent bloggers, thought leaders, and CEOs of leading firms. Recent research shows that it is difficult to seed opinion leaders with new ideas that spread, but if your idea rides the tide of an emerging social trend, opinion leaders will be quick to create a buzz when given the right information.

Communities Online networks populated by professionals in your industry can have a huge impact on your reputation, such as LinkedIn if you are in human resources. The same can be said for vertical communities online, such as Epinions.com reviewers if you are a retailer. Also check the forums formed around your brand (such as Pontiac's Yahoo! forums).

Detractors As mentioned in Chapter 14, some of these represent a high threat to your reputation—such as disgruntled employees or competitors who might spread their complaints in the social media or start companysucks.com websites.

An individual's stakeholders are people who share their values in their personal lives, or who depend on the quality of their work in their professional lives. In Chapter 3 we suggested that you think of each role you play, and each stakeholder group that can affect your work in that role—for example, book reviewers affect an author's reputation and recruiting firms affect the job seeker.

To begin the action plan, list your important stakeholders, along with their roles in your reputation management objective in the worksheet below.

> **Thought Byte: Look Under Every Rock for Stakeholder Communities**
>
> Where can you find stakeholder communities? Every industry and profession has them, so look hard. See Chapter 12 for guidance on identifying stakeholder communities.
>
> FlyerTalk (www.flyertalk.com) has nearly 135,000 members who post their air travel problems and tips for readers. Scott O'Leary, managing director of Customer Experience at Continental Airlines, reportedly spends several hours each day reviewing this and other travel websites to identify customer complaints. He posted over 500 comments last year on FlyerTalk, answering questions and stopping rumors, according to *The Cincinnati Post*.

Action Plan Worksheet 1: Stakeholders

List important stakeholder groups below, such as high-value customers.

Important stakeholders	Importance to my reputation
1.	
2.	
3.	
4.	
5.	

Step 2: Conduct a Reputation Audit

What is your current reputation? Evaluate both offline and online sources to answer this question. Remember when we said in Chapter 1 that research is a key skill for reputation management? This is your chance to prove your online research skills! Once you know where you stand, you can identify the gaps between your current and desired positions as a basis for your reputation strategy online.

There are two ways to discover the opinions of people you want to impress: 1) ask them directly, or 2) collect data from their writing and actions that involve you, your company, or your brands. Recall that it is their perceptions that matter, not what *you* think they should think about you.

Ask Your Stakeholders What They Think About You

Survey research is a scientific way to uncover your reputation among customers, online communities (such as flyertalk.com members), and many other stakeholder groups. For example, companies often conduct image surveys to discover consumer perceptions of their brands. You can ask these folks to rate you, your company, or brand on a seven-point scale from untrustworthy to trustworthy or unreliable to reliable, for example. You could also ask some of your customers, partners, or colleagues this question: "Would you recommend me to a friend or colleague?" You might follow up a negative response with questions to discover the nature of dissatisfaction so you have actionable information. Real estate agents, attorneys, salespeople, and others often use this approach to gain referral business and learn about their reputations in the meantime.

As we mentioned in Chapter 12, if you have a storefront or real-world premises, you should collect information about your reputation at every stakeholder touch point. If you are not already measuring customer satisfaction levels, perhaps it is time—even for professionals with a small client base.

It will be more difficult to discover your reputation in some stakeholder groups via survey research, partially because they won't respond to your survey (e.g., journalists), and possibly because you might be uncomfortable surveying them or they may not feel free to give honest opinions (e.g., your employees or colleagues). Fortunately, many of these stakeholders leave mouse tracks online for your data points—as you'll see in the next section.

Discover Your Current Reputation Online

As we've mentioned several times, your stakeholders tend to hang out together online in particular special-interest groups, social networks, and blogs. Find these centers of influence and you'll collect rich data about your reputation. Remember, at this point you are only doing an audit to benchmark your current reputation. In Step 7 of this plan, you'll put some of these on a longer-term watch list for monitoring your reputation over time.

There are two parts to this online audit. The first is to see how many mentions you or your brand, company, website, or blog receive. This is a conservative estimate of the number of people who are aware of you. Second is to do a sentiment analysis to determine their attitudes about you—your reputation. See Figure 13.10 (Chapter 13) for instructions about how to build a spreadsheet to evaluate the positive or negative nature of the conversations and data you find in this audit. During this process, you will learn which online places are important for your reputation monitoring and management efforts.

Here are some of the places to look; however, your particular stakeholder cyber hangouts will vary considerably, so make your own list by reviewing the suggestions here and in previous chapters. Be sure to look at this from the two perspectives previously mentioned—the number of mentions and the sentiment of this content.

Feedback on your content As we mentioned in Chapter 13, you should measure the number and sentiment for e-mails and comments you receive from stakeholders on your own website, blog, or company-sponsored forum or other online community.

Ratings, recommendations, and reviews If you sell products online, then someone is rating you somewhere, and you need to track the average reviews, starting now. Retailer ratings exist on BizRate.com, Epinions.com, Amazon.com, and elsewhere. Authors will see their work reviewed at online booksellers. If you participate in eBay auctions, check your feedback score. Finally, if you make recommendations on some of these sites, check to see how others review the quality of your recommendations.

Google network reputation Search for keywords around your company, brands, executives, marketing campaigns, and more, to see how many relevant links appear in the search engine results pages—and how close you appear to the top of page one. Search all the Google channels: web, news, blogs, videos, and groups. Repeat this for the other two big engines (or other niche engines in your industry): Yahoo! and MSN/Live Search. What you find is a test of your SEO savvy.

Multimedia content If you post videos on YouTube or photos on Flickr, you'll want to check the number of times they were viewed and the number and sentiment of the comments.

Social relevance This is a measure of your mentions in the social media. Check the number of bloggers linked to your site (Technorati.com), the number of people who "dugg" your article (Digg.com), and the number of people in your social network (LinkedIn.com, MySpace.com, and so forth). You'll also want to see how many people bookmarked your web properties by searching del.icio.us and Reddit, or using Keotag.com (see Chapter 13).

Website popularity You are probably already measuring the traffic to your website, and if so, use this as a reputation benchmark number. You might also count the number of people who subscribe to your company newsletters, download your white papers and podcasts, and subscribe to the RSS feeds from your online pressroom. As well, using the protocol "link:www.yourwebsite.com" at Google.com will show you how many web pages link to yours.

Blog popularity Measure the number of visitors to your blog, links into your blog (Technorati.com and Yahoo! Site Explorer), number of RSS feed subscriptions, and number/sentiment for comments on your blog. Depending on the size of your blog, set a time period that makes sense—such as daily, weekly, or monthly.

Stakeholder conversations Look beyond the blogs and feedback on your website to the discussions in forums and other communities where your stakeholders discuss you or your products.

Industry news If you do not already work with a PR firm on media relations, search for your keywords or article headlines to see if the news media have quoted you or if there are stories important to your industry (via Google News). You can also try sites such as Topix.net that monitor news media and user-generated content and will return a list of stories and graph of your mentions for the previous year.

Personal and professional profiles If you want to evaluate a personal reputation (yours, the CEO, or executives), add ZoomInfo.com to your search because this site compiles profiles by combing the internet for information. Also check profiles important to your industry, such as HealthGrades.com (medical professionals) and RateMyProfessors.com (college faculty). Don't forget to check the background reports available online for less than ten dollars (such as PeopleSearch.com).

In Chapter 12 we suggested selecting either a wide net or focused approach to reputation monitoring, so review that prior to beginning your reputation audit benchmarking. We don't want you to give up when you see this long research project—remember they won't all apply to you unless you are fully engaged in social media or a large company, and it is better to start small than to do nothing. So, open a spreadsheet, create columns to document your findings as benchmarks for the rest of this plan, and get started with worksheets 2a and 2b.

Action Plan Worksheet 2a: Document Your Online Audit

Complete the worksheet to discover your level of awareness online, and then to determine if it is positive or negative. If the mention is neutral, leave the sentiment columns blank. Note that some of the items will not apply for the sentiment analysis.

Online Channel	Number of Mentions	Positive Sentiment	Negative Sentiment
Feedback on your content (company blog, website, forum, and so forth)			
Ratings, recommendations, and reviews			
Google network reputation			
Multimedia content			
Social relevance			
Website popularity			
Blog popularity			
Stakeholder conversations			
Industry news			
Personal and professional profiles			
Total Mentions			
Sentiment Percentage (see Chapter 12)			

Where Do You Stand?

Where do you stand in the river of online opinion? You've surveyed some of your stakeholders and you've completed the reputation audit in Worksheet 2a. What do the survey results, sentiment analysis of online discussion, social relevance, various popularity measures, and other measures reveal about your reputation? Answering this question requires objective analysis of the reputation audit. Write notes on this and get to the bottom line, as shown in Worksheet 2b.

If you are in Categories 1 to 4, congratulations! You are either in great shape or have a tremendous opportunity to make a good name for yourself online. It is easy to go from a blank slate or neutral sentiment to a positive one. Nothing is in your way. Conversely, if you are in Category 5, you'd better start some repair work right now (Chapter 14) and come back to the rest of the plan later.

Step 3: Uncover Your Internal Reputation Assets and Liabilities

Before moving to the next steps that will take you to that great reputation online, you should consider your own strengths and weaknesses. In this step, you'll evaluate your own company, brand, or individual online content and consider other factors affecting your reputation.

Your Online Content Channels

Now, you should evaluate your own online content as discussed in Chapters 7, 8, and 9. Consider any of the applicable areas that follow and then use Worksheet 3a to record your findings. You might not think it appropriate to use all of your content channels, but the ones you use should be high quality, radically transparent, and engaging. Be sure to take notes of the specific areas needing improvement.

Your own website Check your website for quality, accuracy, easy navigation, and up-to-date content. Is the writing clear, professional, and engaging? Is it all boring boiler-plate? Do you use great multimedia to tell your story? Look at everything, from your bio and head shot to your About Us page. Evaluate the voice you use in your writing and how well the site engages visitors. Do you have white papers showing your expertise available for download? Do you use testimonials that help build your reputation?

Your online pressroom Evaluate your pressroom for content currency and value to journalists in traditional and social media. Have you used the social media press release, as shown in Chapter 5? Are your releases Google friendly?

Your blog If you have a blog, evaluate it using the criteria in Chapter 9. Does it provide value, content currency, and original content, and does it display your professional expertise? Is it Google friendly? Does it encourage engagement by soliciting comments and by providing RSS subscriptions and other techniques to give it legs? Do you post often enough?

Search engine optimization Are you SEO savvy? Evaluate your online content channels for organic search engine optimization. Review Chapter 6 and note the strengths and weaknesses for reputation management in your organic search tactics. Specifically, does your content identify your brands, make sense to Google spiders, include radically relevant title tags and content, and have lots of relevant incoming links? If your website did not do well in the reputation audit in Step 2 of this plan, your SEO tactics may need boosting.

Radically transparent Are you honest and authentic in all of your online content channels? Do you go the extra step of being radically transparent, revealing internal processes and work in progress? Do you respond honestly and openly to feedback on your sites? Do you admit to your errors and take action to repair them, and then report back afterward?

Contributions to other sites Do you provide written comments, videos, and images for other websites, such as blogs, YouTube, and Flickr? If you do use multimedia, be sure that these show you in a positive light and that you use tagging and other means for stakeholders to locate and link to the images or video. If you think podcasts are appropriate for your stakeholders, do you tag them and make them available widely?

Outgoing e-mail Don't forget about your e-mail. Are you using your signature file to build a positive reputation? Do you follow the guidelines in Chapter 8 (for e-mail addresses, subject lines, content, and spam filter avoidance)?

Action Plan Worksheet 3a: Your Content Channel Analysis

Evaluate each of your online reputation assets on the seven-point scale that follows. Add any additional assets that apply to your situation.

Asset Reputation Detractor	Positive Reputation Ready						
	(Needs Work)				(Good to Go)		
Website currency, accuracy	1	2	3	4	5	6	7
Website writing and white papers							
Website multimedia use							
Website is engaging							
Online pressroom							
Blog displays professional expertise							
Blog engages visitors							
Blog uses RSS /has legs							
SEO for website and blog							
Radically transparent							
Multimedia content for other sites							
Tagging images, videos, podcasts							
Outgoing e-mail							

Your Identity

Before you move forward in this plan, you need a clear understanding of who you are and what you represent as a company or individual. This understanding will help you build a focused reputation online and make it easy to create policies for online content as well as to respond quickly to criticisms.

As we mentioned in Chapter 1, trust is a key component of any reputation. Your character, as evidenced by your integrity and actions, will trump any of your online words about what a great person you are. Stakeholders demand authenticity, credibility, honesty, quality products and services, quality workplace management, fiscal responsibility, and socially responsible activities. If you were trashed online in your audit, you might want to consider the underlying reasons. Are your messages confusing online readers or in conflict with your offline communication? If so, build a consistent communication campaign. Is there something in your offline behavior that is causing this reaction (such as poor customer service)? If so, consider improving your weak areas offline before embarking on a reputation building campaign online. Note any character weaknesses in Worksheet 3b.

Next, consider the external influences on your reputation, as mentioned in Chapter 1 (Figure 1.3). There may be things beyond your control, such as a negative perception of your industry (e.g., tobacco) or a positive perception of your CEO that has a halo effect on the entire company—brands, employees, and more (e.g., Richard Branson).

Beyond this, take stock of your special strengths and weaknesses that affect your reputation. If this plan is for a company or brands, what are your key criticisms and where do you excel? Review your mission, vision, and values for clues.

For CEOs, professionals, and other individuals, what are your unique skills and areas of expertise? What skeletons are in your closet that might cause a problem if you become more visible online?

Your Reputation Assets and Liabilities

It is important to document the reputation audit (Step 2) and the evaluation of your own content channels and strengths and weaknesses (Step 3) in some usable form before moving to the next plan steps. You might want to build a reputation scorecard to hold the key indicators for your reputation online. Or you can simply list your reputation assets and liabilities, noted from the previous analyses. We suggest that you keep track of everything you discovered in this external and internal audit, but you may want to focus on key issues at this point so you're spending your time on the most important things affecting your reputation. For this reason, we suggest you develop a priority order list of your key assets and liabilities in Worksheet 3b.

Action Plan Worksheet 3b: Your Reputation Assets and Liabilities

My professional skills/expertise/strengths (individuals):

_____

The brand/company key strengths:

_____

Individual/company character flaws that could affect reputation:

_____

External influences out of my control:

_____

Summary of the above and Worksheets 2a, 2b, and 3a

Key reputation assets

1.

2.

3.

4.

5.

Key liabilities

1.

2.

3.

4.

5.

Step 4: Write Your Goals

Now that you've done the hard introspection, it is time to decide what reputation you want online. This step is akin to product positioning—the company evaluates a current brand position based on customer perceptions, then decides what competitive position it desires in the marketplace. Once you know where you want to go, the road there will be clearer.

Your goals will depend on your specific situation, but here are some things to consider:

- Review your worksheet in Step 2. If you are a "blank slate," or had a "mostly neutral" reputation online, set a goal for building your desired positive reputation from the ground up. If you were perceived positively, make a goal to sustain this level or increase it. If you were fine but had a couple of negative items to bury, set a goal to show more positively online. If you were trashed, your goal is to turn this around.

- If your own online content channels in Worksheet 3a came up lacking, this is a good place to start. Set a goal of creating a reputation-ready website, blog, and so forth, that casts you in a positive light. If your reputation assets do not shout from the pages of your own online pages, create a goal to weave these into your content.

- If you have character flaws or reputation liabilities in your real life, make goals to fix these.

- Have a goal to better deflect online criticism.

- If this plan is for a CEO or professional, create a focused thought leadership niche.

- To remain marketable in your profession, create a strong online presence for recruiters.

- If you are an individual salesperson or other professional, increase your client base.

- Set a goal to become radically transparent online.

Now for a gut check: How much do you really want to reveal online? Throughout this book we've recommended a radically transparent approach. We've proven that authenticity and honesty breed trust. At the very least, you must respond honestly to criticism and be the first to disclose problems headed for the media. We encourage you to go further, however, and reveal as much of your internal processes and activities as legally possible. We want you to be the first one to admit to weaknesses in your system. Now is the time to really think about this and decide if your corporate culture is ready for this, or what needs to happen to make it ready.

If this plan is for an individual, think about the same items, but you have another question: how much are you comfortable illuminating online? People want to do business with those they like, and by posting stories and pictures about your social activities, you will be more personable. Do you want to put pictures of your family online? Photos of your last trip or sailing adventure? Do you want to write about that last marathon you ran in Boston? Think about this now and decide where to draw your own line.

> **Action Plan Worksheet 4: Your Reputation Goals**
>
> List your overall goals below. You might want to set short- and intermediate-term goals.
>
> 1.
>
> 2.
>
> 3.
>
> 4.

Step 5: Craft a Strategy and Write Objectives

The gaps between what you discovered in your audit and how you desire to be perceived are the springboard to strategy. Like most areas of this plan, your strategy and objectives should be tailored to fit your needs. One size does not fit all. If your reputation is unknown online, your strategies will get you on the radar. If you are already one of *Fortune* magazine's "America's Most Admired Companies," your strategies will help you stay there and manage online criticism.

In general, the strategies you select will involve content, stakeholder communication, social networking, SEO, and PR. The more quality content you have online, and the better you engage stakeholders in a radically transparent manner, the higher will be your reputation online. Here are strategies used by those enjoying stellar reputations:

- Spend at least 30 minutes per day on reputation monitoring.
- Make your own online content channels engaging and reputation enhancing.
- Add to your own online content channels (by creating corporate subdomains or co-branded pages, as discussed in Chapter 6).
- Broaden your reach online by posting multimedia content on other sites.
- Build a highly differentiated thought leadership niche online.
- Increase stakeholder dialogue on your site as well as others. Listen, learn, and make changes as appropriate.
- Increase your social relevance through more participation in social media.
- Muscle your own content into the top 10 search engines results at Google, MSN, and Yahoo! (review Chapter 6 for tactics).
- Create a bigger buzz online for your company, products, or services.
- Create a system for reputation monitoring online.
- Maintain a reputation monitoring crisis plan.

Next, write specific and quantifiable objectives for each of your strategies. Review the reputation audit in Step 2 for action opportunities. For example, you could write objectives for increasing the number of comments on your blog or for improving your social relevancy score. You might want to increase media mentions from your social media press releases or post more videos to other websites. Think about everything you've learned in this book, where you stand online, and how you want to be perceived, and then write objectives to get you there.

You'll need to select appropriate online media to carry out your strategies and write these objectives. These are your stakeholder cyber hangouts. Your online media selections are woven throughout this book. They include blogs, social networks (e.g., LinkedIn, MySpace), image-posting sites (e.g., YouTube, Flickr), review sites (e.g., TripAdvisor, BizRate, eBay), virtual worlds (Second Life), industry forums/bulletin boards (e.g., Google Groups), your own websites, and many more. Before you start, remember to follow the time-honored marketing communications mantra: craft the right messages and deliver them to the appropriate stakeholder audiences via highly targeted online and offline media.

Following is a specific example with 10 possible objectives:

Strategy: Build a highly differentiated thought leadership niche online.

Objectives for the next 12 months:

1. Add three white papers to the company site for visitor download.

2. Answer five questions a month at Yahoo! Answers.

3. Read and review one book a quarter in my field on Amazon.com.

4. Identify 20 important blogs in my industry and subscribe to the RSS feeds. Read them daily.

5. Display my expertise and add value to the social media by commenting on at least five blogs a month and editing a Wikipedia article.

6. Start a thought leadership blog and post two or three times a week.

7. Change my e-mail signature file to include a link to my blog and a sentence about my expertise.

8. Join LinkedIn and one other social network, building a profile that communicates my expertise.

9. Ask five clients for a testimonial that mentions my expertise area. Post on my website.

10. Solicit one podcast interview a month in my area of expertise for posting on an industry website.

Action Plan Worksheet 5: Your Strategies and Objectives

List each of your key reputation strategies, along with specific and measurable objectives for each. Don't panic: you don't have to accomplish them all this month. We recommend first creating a thorough wish list, and then sorting out priorities in Step 6 of the plan.

Strategy 1:

Measurable objectives:

(Repeat for each strategy)

Step 6: Create an Implementation Plan

Who will handle this reputation building, managing, and monitoring project? In previous chapters, we suggested that some things can be outsourced (e.g., SEO, new head shots) and others can't (such as writing a blog—except for employee or expert contributors). There are many companies offering reputation management services, but we think that you or your staff need to be in the trenches watching, listening, writing, engaging with stakeholders, and learning. Assuming that you agree with us, how can you tackle this puppy?

Given limited resources, there are two ways to approach this potentially huge project. First, you could pick the low-hanging fruit and accomplish these objectives in the first month—then go on to the more complex and time-consuming tasks in subsequent weeks. Second, you could prioritize your strategies and implement one per a week or month, depending on their complexity. Whichever you do, it is important to write an implementation plan as daily to-do items. Some of the things you might need to address before getting started include:

Digital tools, such as free download or paid software You might need Google Reader for RSS feeds, WordPress for content management software, Google Analytics for web traffic measurement/analytics software, or Copernic Tracker for tracking most web content changes (see Chapter 13 for more tool ideas). You might also need hardware, such as more web server space.

A policy and procedures manual for content management You will definitely need this if your employees post to the company site or blog, or if they maintain their own blogs. We also think it is a good idea to jot down a few guiding principles if you are a solo content author because it helps you focus on your desired voice and the thought leadership niche you want to establish.

Designated personnel for various strategies/objectives For example, who will write the blog, take the photos, upload videos to YouTube, or handle comments on your website? For instance, if you are a hotel manager, will you reply to TripAdvisor reviews? Who is capable of responding to social media crises? If you increase the engagement on your site, you'll need to staff for responding. It is time to decide who will manage this work.

An internal marketing plan You'll need to get your employees on board for your new radically transparent ways online. Do you want all employees to add particular items to their e-mail signature files? They'll need to learn about the social media and your new policies and strategies.

Action Plan Worksheet 6: Your Implementation Plan

1. List the software/tools you need to meet your key strategies.

2. Do you need a new policy and procedure manual or to adapt your current online procedures? Make notes here.

3. Which personnel will be responsible for each objective? List them here.

4. What plans do you need for internal marketing? Make notes here.

5. Get started (see Figure 15.1) and adapt to your situation. Set aside the time.

Sample Implementation Plan

How much time do you have for reputation management online? Figure 15.1 suggests priorities for your commitment to building, monitoring, and defending your reputation. They are necessarily generic, so please adapt for your plan. Start now, even if you have just an hour a week for this.

Online Reputation Management Priorities

First 2 Hours

 Create Google and Yahoo! alerts for your names and keywords.

 Complete step 1 of the plan: identify your stakeholders.

 Begin your reputation audit. Search key areas in step 2, such as the Google network, Technorati, review sites, and industry news (or profiles if you are an individual).

 Identify your crisis team and online media spokesperson.

 Handle any crises you find (this may take more than 2 hours).

Next 8 Hours

 Continue the reputation audit, including the sentiment analysis (worksheets 2a and 2b).

 Set up a basic reputation monitoring checklist (worksheet 7).

 Identify your online and offline stakeholders to prepare for an online crisis.

 Handle any crises you find (this may take more time).

Next 40 Hours

 Evaluate your own content channels (worksheet 3a). This may take more or less time depending on your content.

 Summarize your reputation assets and liabilities (worksheet 3b).

 Handle any reputation crises you find.

Next Steps

 Write your reputation management goals (worksheet 4).

 Identify your strategies and objectives that will move you toward your goals (worksheet 5).

 Decide what resources you need to get more deeply involved in the social media and to engage your stakeholders (worksheet 6).

 Fine tune your monitoring system and handle any crises you find.

 Start doing the writing, SEO, PR, and other work to meet your goals and objectives.

 Build a stealth crisis blog.

Figure 15.1 Online reputation monitoring priorities

Step 7: Build a Plan to Sustain Your Reputation

Repairing a soiled reputation is by far the most challenging stage of reputation management, say 66% of 950 global business executives in a survey of by PR firm Weber Shandwick (Figure 15.2). This is why many firms have crisis PR plans, but unfortunately, not many have woven social media tactics into their plans. For this step of your reputation management action plan, you will fix that by establishing an online monitoring system and an online crisis PR plan.

What is the Most Challenging Stage of Reputation Management?

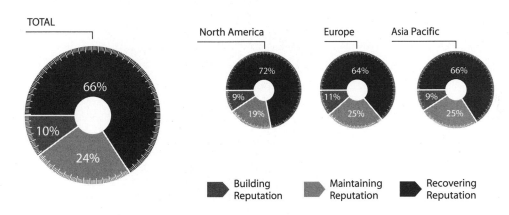

Figure 15.2 Reputation recovery is tough.

Establish an Online Monitoring System

This is the stuff of Chapters 12 and 13. You've already decided the subject of this plan (your company, executives, CEO, brands, yourself, and so forth), but now it is time to take a closer look at any associated items you might monitor. These include your marketing plans, industry, competitors, and known weaknesses. Next, you need to decide whether to cast a wide net or focus on specific centers of influence. Assuming the latter, you probably identified many of them in your reputation audit (Step 2).

Now, set up a monitoring system for all the channels that are a reputation risk, including your own online content. Some channels will push information to you after registering (e.g., Google alerts) or obtain special software (such as an RSS reader), and for some you'll pull the information by making a schedule of regular check ups (e.g., social bookmarking sites). To do this, review Chapter 13 and complete Worksheet 7a. Add any needed software to those you already listed in Worksheet 6. Note that in our suggested implementation plan we recommend adding monitoring to your reputation management efforts immediately. Don't wait until you are completely through the planning process to get started here.

Action Plan Worksheet 7a: Your Online Monitoring Checklist

First, list all the associated keywords needing monitoring (e.g., marketing plans, industry, competitors, and known weaknesses).

Second, complete the table that follows by replacing the generic channel with your specific center of influence. For example, for "Social Communities," list those specific communities you want to monitor that pertain to the subject of this plan (such as TripAdvisor.com).

Third, devise a priority list, automate as much as possible (see Chapter 13), and consider assigning employees to various channels if you have a lot to monitor. Don't outsource this, however, because only you know what is a crisis worthy of response, and what is not.

Channels for Reputation Monitoring	Your Specific Sites in This Channel
Your own content channels (both content and stakeholder feedback)	
Social media and blogs (using Technorati and RSS feeds)	
Google's network (web, news, videos, blogs, groups)	
Industry news	
Stakeholder conversations	
Social communities	
Social bookmarking sites (using Keotag or others)	
Multimedia content (Google, Flickr, or others)	
Forums and message boards	
Customer reviews	
Brand profiles	

Create a Crisis Plan

Don't forget that the purpose for tracking and analyzing your reputation is to act on what you find. This means both making internal changes after listening to stakeholder feedback and handling reputation attacks. As you learned in Chapter 14, reputation attacks are inevitable, and they are magnified through the social media online—you've seen plenty of examples of this throughout the book. Chapter 14 also suggested that you prepare in advance for an online crisis because they often bloom so quickly that you need to act immediately.

Your primary goal during any crisis is to protect your reputation. In general, if you communicate quickly, truthfully, and radically transparently—including necessary changes, apologies, and reparations—you'll be in good shape. As we said in Chapter 14, the three-word mantra is sincerity, transparency, and consistency. Tell it all, tell it honestly, and stick to your story.

So you can act brilliantly at a moment's notice, you should prepare the following items now, and integrate them into your existing offline crisis management plan (see Worksheet 7):

1. The crisis team   When an online crisis strikes, you need to know who will make the decisions and how to reach them, 24/7. It might be just you, but a company will have a team. At a minimum, the CEO, a PR executive, and the person closest to the problem area should be involved (e.g., for Apple's iPhone price reduction crisis it might have been the Brand Manager). Finally, include on a contact list others who might assist depending on the nature of the crisis: your attorney, technology security person, the PR personnel who will field media inquires, or any other backups your business dictates.

2. The online media spokesperson   Who is best person for responding to crises online? This point person will be a senior executive, close to the CEO (or the CEO herself), be adept at internet communication, and be able to respond quickly and sensitively in a number of online venues. This person may be a widely read company blogger, or someone who currently monitors your online reputation. As part of the crisis team, this person will craft a number of statements about the situation and disseminate them online, to media, and to all employees. A spokesperson for a small company might handle both online and offline channels, and a large company might have one spokesperson for each channel. The online media spokesperson will work alongside the company's traditional media spokesperson, as did Robert Scoble (former Microsoft online spokesperson and prominent blogger) and Bill Gates (Microsoft's traditional media spokesperson).

3. Your advisors   As suggested in Chapter 14, make a list of trusted advisors and contact information to use during a crisis. This might be your current advisory board, management team, a trusted friend, or even a PR firm.

4. Key offline stakeholders   Create a database of e-mail or IM addresses for your key internal stakeholders who might be contacted for information gathering or dissemination. These include executives, other employees, directors, and partners. Then add outside stakeholders who might be close to any crisis, such as journalists covering your industry and key financial analysts (for public companies).

5. Important online stakeholders   Build a list of the online venues that may be buzzing when you have a crisis, and that might be appropriate places to disseminate accurate information. This list will include blogs, social networks you inhabit (e.g., industry forums and more general networks), and widely viewed social media, such as Flickr and

YouTube (recall JetBlue's CEO posting an apology video on YouTube after the February 14 offline crisis). Your list of online contacts includes your industry's influential bloggers, social media authors or network owners, and traditional media journalists writing for the Web. It is also helpful to keep notes about the most recent conversations you've had with each of these people and whether they were sympathetic to your position.

6. Stealth crisis blog As mentioned in Chapters 9 and 14, you may want to create a blog now and rehearse its deployment. Know how this blog will link from your other online content and coordinate with other crisis communications channels. Put the blog on the company intranet, ready to go with the corporate graphic shell, legal notices, contact information, and all that can be done in advance. When the crisis hits, you'll simply need to move its location for public viewing after entering the agreed-upon information and company statements. If you do ever deploy this blog, be sure to send the URL to all stakeholders and online media. Also add a visible link to the blog on your home page and online pressroom pages, and have everyone in-house involved in crisis communication efforts place the URL in their e-mail signatures.

7. Online crisis response guidelines Finally, we suggest creating a list of guidelines for deciding if and when to respond to online crises, per our recommendations in Chapter 14 (see Figure 15.3 for an example). You might make these guidelines into a wallet sized, laminated card for your C-level executives and crisis team so they don't have to search their files when a crisis occurs, or post them prominently on your intranet.

Online Crisis Response Guidelines

1. Get the facts.
2. Decide whether or not the online attack deserves a response. Yes, if one or more of the below applies:

| Started by important detractors | Big conversation | Spreads widely | Influential online writers |

3. Gather the crisis team.
4. Seek counsel from trusted advisors.
5. Respond from the top (a senior, transparent, and humble voice).
6. Craft the right message:
    Admit mistakes and apologize.
    Be open and be honest.
    Explain how this occurred.
    Tell what you're doing to rectify the situation.
    Tell what steps you are taking to prevent a repeat incident.
    Don't volunteer too much, and don't talk off the record.
    Expect that every e-mail or web post you make will be widely disseminated.
7. Host the conversation on your web channels (deploy the stealth crisis blog).
8. After the dust has settled:
    Add new keywords to the list of those you monitor.
    Seek the help of your online supporters for promoting your reparations.
    Monitor more deeply in the first weeks/the first 30 listings in Google for your brand name.
    Learn from your mistakes by adding new procedures to prevent reoccurrence.
    Expand your corporate communications to influential bloggers, forum moderators, and social network owners.
    Add more positive content to the web.
9. Step up your SEO by following our *Five Steps to being Radically Relevant for Google* (chapter 6).

Figure 15.3 Online crisis response guidelines

Action Plan Worksheet 7: Your Plan for Online Crises

Create an Excel spreadsheet or Access database for the personnel in items 1 through 4 below. Post an up-to-date copy on the company intranet or in your network's shared directory for access by your crisis team and selected others (item 1 below).

1. Who is on your crisis team? List their names, titles, and all contact numbers (work, home, cell phone; IM, e-mail addresses).

2. Who is your online media spokesperson (and contact information)?

3. Who will be your advisors, for seeking counsel before reacting to a crisis? List them and their contact information.

4. Who are your key offline stakeholders needing information during a crisis (create an e-mail distribution list if none currently exists)?

5. Who are your important online stakeholders and information disseminating sites? List their contact information (both phone and e-mail).

6. Where is your stealth blog located? Who will add content and deploy it in a time of crisis (most likely your online media spokesperson)?

Action Plan Summary

This completes your plan to build, manage, and repair your reputation online. In summary:

Step 1: Identify your stakeholders. These are the individuals, communities, and organizations that have a vested interest in your mission and reputation online.

Step 2: Conduct a reputation audit. Survey your stakeholders and scour the internet to determine whether public opinion about you, your brands, or your company is positive, negative, or neutral.

Step 3: Uncover your internal reputation assets and liabilities. Evaluate your own company, brand, or individual online content channels; think about character strengths and flaws; and determine your special areas of expertise.

Step 4. Write your goals. Figure out what you can gain from reputation management online.

Step 5. Craft a strategy and write objectives. Find the gaps between your current and desired reputations online and create strategies and objectives to get there.

Step 6. Create an implementation plan. Decide what tools you need to accomplish your objectives, and begin the work.

Step 7. Build a plan to sustain your reputation. Put a reputation monitoring system in place online and create a crisis management plan.

Now you have a structure to adapt to your own situation and can begin the work of managing and monitoring your reputation online. A word of caution is in order—watch the internet, be nimble, and be ready for change at a moment's notice. You've seen plenty of examples of companies and individuals caught unaware online, and we don't want this to happen to you.

Radically Transparent Reputation Management Is Now in Your Hands

Throughout this book you've read that strong reputations help companies achieve their objectives, retain customers and employees, build partner and supplier relationships, protect them in times of crisis, and ultimately increase shareholder value. In fact, 95% of chief executives believe that corporate reputation plays an important role in achieving their business objectives, according to a survey by public relations firm Burson-Marsteller, and 63% of a company's market value is attributable to reputation, according to PR firm Weber Shandwick. Brands live and die on their reputations for delivering as promised.

Trust is a critical factor for individual reputations as seen through numerous examples in this book. Individual reputations are especially important for CEOs, politicians, professionals, salespeople, graduating students, and just about anyone who has a client-based business or might be looking for another job someday.

Reputation is something earned over time, based on your character, words, and actions. It is hard to build and easy to lose. The social media will monitor and discuss your words and actions, so we hope that we've convinced you to take action right now.

A search for "reputation management" in Google in November 2007 yielded 54.8 million results pages, with the number increasing daily. This book has many fewer pages of distilled information, and we hope that what you've gained will make your reputation soar in the future. But we advise you to keep reading and learning because internet best practices are a moving target.

There's a conversation going on about you online right this minute. It's time to join that discussion and become radically transparent. We are your biggest supporters in this effort!

Index

Note to the Reader: Throughout this index **boldfaced** page numbers indicate primary discussions of a topic. *Italicized* page numbers indicate illustrations.

Nike+ community, 242, *243*
Ning.com, 128
"Nuts About Southwest", 204, *204*

O

Obama, Barack, 44, 73, *150*, 235, *235*, 277
objectives in action plans, **358–360**
Odden, Lee, 91, **95–96**, 104, 106
"off the record" communications, **328**
Official Google Blog, 204
official statements in attack responses, **330**
offline stakeholders in crisis plans, 365
O'Leary, Scott, 348
one-to-one marketing, **64–65**
1:1 messaging
    e-mail. *See* e-mail
    instant and text messaging, **189–191**
online activities, 249
    auctions, **254–257**, *255*
    reputation damage, **260–261**
    reputation management, **253–254**
    retailing, **257–258**
    reviewing, **259–260**, *260*
    third-party review sites, **258–259**, *258*
    trust markets, **252–253**
    virtual worlds, **262–268**, *265–266*
    working with strangers, **250–252**, *250*
online books, writing, **171–172**
online content, **48–51**
    channel evaluation, **353–354**
    tags for, 163
online conversations, monitoring, 17
online journalists as stakeholders, 347
online marketplace, 250
online media spokespersons in crisis plans, 365
online monitoring systems, **363–364**
online photo libraries, **147–148**
online photo management sites, 151
online pressrooms, **83–84**
    blog posts, **86–87**
    community relations, **88**
    contact information, **89**
    evaluating, 353
    management and corporate bios, **88**
    navigating, **86**
    need for, **84–85**, *85*
    news, **86**
    rich media files, **87**
    RSS feeds, **88–89**
    testimonials, **87**

online stakeholders in crisis plans, **365–366**
opinion leaders as stakeholders, 347
organic search engine results, 111
Oswalt, Angela, 261
outgoing e-mail evaluation, 354
outsourcing monitoring, **312**
Owyang, Jeremiah, 221, 227

P

page file names, **212**
Page Zero Media, 113
PageRank scoring system, 33, 121
Parker, Doug, 42
Parsons, Bob, **194–196**, **200**, 202, 218–219, 225
participation inequality, 175
Patel, Neil, 236, 241, 244, 282
Paul, Joshua, 146
Paul, Ron, 44, *150*
Paulson, Eric, 182
pay-per-click (PPC), **112–113**
PayPerPost.com, 106, 139, 338
PDA contact lists, 49
Pearson, Bob, **24–25**
peer acknowledge on blogs, **220–221**
Pennsylvania Railroad, 90
people power, **6–8**, 7
People's Choice Podcast Awards, 162
PeopleSearch.com, 351
PepsiCo, 230, *231*
permission marketing, **182–183**
personal brands, 39
    blogs for, **196–198**
    CEOs, **42**
    flip side, **57–59**
    goals effects, **47–48**
    individuals, **51–56**, *52*, *57*
    online content and contacts, **48–51**
    politicians, **43–44**
    professionals, **44–45**
    radical transparency, **59–60**
    reputation, **41**
    salespersons, **45–46**, *46*
    super stars, **40**, *40*
    upward mobility, **47**
personal contacts for false attacks, 332
personal profiles, auditing, 351
personality
    in individual branding, 53
    in text, 174, 176
Peters, Tom, **44–45**
Pew Internet & the American Life Project, 101, **154–156**, *154*, 160–161, 188
Photobucket photo management site, 151

photos
    digital cameras for, **147**
    head shots, **148–149**, *149–150*
    for individuals, **134–135**
    online management sites, **151**
    online photo libraries, **147–148**
    and reputation, **147**
    SEO for, **162–164**
    in social media, **150–152**, *152*
Photoshop for Right-Brainers: The Art of Photo Manipulation (Ward), 146
Picasa software, 151
Piper Jaffray & Co., 110
Pixsy.com, 300
plans
    action. *See* action plans
    crisis, **364–367**, *366*
    reputation repair, 320
    service recovery, 318
PlateWire.com, 48
platinum detractors, **324**
plots in storytelling, 178
plug-ins, **208–209**, 247
PlugIn air fresheners, **334–335**
Podcasting for Dummies (Morris and Terra), 146
podcasts, **161–162**
    promoting, **164**
    SEO for, **162–164**
Pohlmann, Ken, 171
policies for blog comments, **213–214**
politicians, **43–44**, 148–150, *150*, 159
Pontiac, **62–64**, *63*, 69–70, 110, 115, *116–117*
Pownce.com, 239
PR. *See* public relations (PR)
PR Newswire, 90
press kits, 84
press releases, **90–91**
    for attack responses, **330**
    branding in, **97**
    distribution, **99–100**, *100*
    Google for, **96**
    limitations, **100–101**
    links in, **99**
    search engines for, **96–97**
    social media releases, **91–95**, *93*
    stock ticker symbols in, **98**
    titles in, **98**
    wording in, **97**
pressrooms. *See* online pressrooms
PricewaterhouseCoopers study, 15, 262, 272
ProBlogger, 198
product monitoring, **276–277**
professional memberships for individuals, **137**
professionalism, writing for, **172–173**
professionals, **44–45**
    detractors, **325**, *326*
    profile auditing, 351